# Matrix
## Meditations

# Matrix
## Meditations

### A 16-Week Program
### for Developing
### the Mind-Heart Connection

## Victor Daniels and Kooch N. Daniels

Destiny Books
Rochester, Vermont • Toronto, Canada

Destiny Books
One Park Street
Rochester, Vermont 05767
www.DestinyBooks.com

Destiny Books is a division of Inner Traditions International

Images on page 65 courtesy of Eleanor Criswell; photographs by Pamela Robertson
Image on page 158 courtesy of artist Jodi Carr.
Image on page 286 courtesy of Tara Daniels.
Photographs on pages 43 and 166 by Kooch N. Daniels.
All other photographs by Victor Daniels.

*Note to the reader:* This book is intended as an informational guide. The approaches and techniques described herein are meant to supplement, and not to be a substitute for, professional medical or psychological care or treatment.

**Library of Congress Cataloging-in-Publication Data**
Daniels, Victor, 1941–
  Matrix meditations : a 16-week program for developing the mind-heart connection / Victor Daniels and Kooch N. Daniels.
     p. cm.
  Includes bibliographical references and index.
  Summary: "65 dynamic meditation techniques for manifesting your desires and multiplying the power of your mind"—Provided by publisher.
  ISBN 978-1-59477-291-7
  1. Mind and body. 2. Centering (Psychology). 3. Body-mind centering. 4. Meditation. 5. Peace of mind. I. Daniels, Kooch. II. Title.
  BF161D25 2009
  158.1'2—dc22

                                                                                    2009007578

Printed and bound in the United States by Lake Book Manufacturing

10  9  8  7  6  5  4  3  2  1

Text design and layout by Virginia Scott Bowman
This book was typeset in Garamond Premiere Pro with Agenda as the display typeface.

*For Tara and Lila, and the teachers*
*who have illuminated our paths.*

*What is it to work with love? It is to weave the*
*cloth with threads drawn from your heart, even as*
*if your beloved were to wear that cloth.*

KAHLIL GIBRAN

In dedicating this book to our daughters, we hope to atone for
having taught them, as they grew up, no more than fragments of
what we knew about meditation. They did not ask for more and
we did not insist. We hope that they—and you—will find this
work useful in both savoring the joys and weathering the storms
of life. We have tried, as Gibran suggested, to weave the cloth of
its pages with threads drawn from our hearts.

# Contents

## PART TWO: CELLS OF THE MATRIX

# Acknowledgments

WE ARE DEEPLY APPRECIATIVE to the many who have contributed to the creation of this book in some way. We cannot overstate our debt to our inspiring teachers Harish Johari, Jakusho Kwong-roshi, and Sri Mata Amritanandamayi for inviting us to drink from their transcendent fountains of wisdom. We are extremely fortunate to have been guided in their meditation techniques and to have attended their informational and soul-enriching satsangs.

Also, we owe much to colleagues and professors Gordon Tappan, Eleanor Criswell, Laurence J. Horowitz, Diana Divecha, Robert K. Hall, Carl Mitchell, and Harold H. Kelley. In addition, we have been influenced by many more, whose workshops, seminars, lectures, and in some cases just days or evenings of conversation we have attended throughout the years. These include Mahayogi Pilot Baba; Eknath Easwaran; Tarthang Tulku, Rinpoche; Chogyam Trungpa, Rinpoche; Ram Dass; Swami Niranjanananda Saraswati; Dalai Lama Tenzing Gyatso; Swami Chinmayananda; Pieter Weltevrede; Fritz Perls; Carl Rogers; Rollo May; Erich Fromm; John Argue; Alta Kelly; and others. And as you will soon see, there is a vast multitude of other enlightened souls whose wisdom has been transmitted through time and space by the written word, and has found its way onto our paths and into these pages. We are also grateful for that which we have learned from sources that cannot be revealed.

We wish to thank our amazing literary agent, Bob Silverstein of Quicksilver Books, who stayed with our project from its stumbling beginnings. Not least among his priceless suggestions was the inclusion of the nature photographs. We are indebted to both our daughters for their support and inspiration. We give appreciation to our daughter Lila who critiqued and did an invaluable preliminary editing of the entire manuscript, and our daughter Tara who did the same with significant parts of it. We are grateful to F. Scott Chilcott, M.D., for reviewing the Health and Healing cells. We acknowledge with gratitude all our friends and family whose words of encouragement cannot be understated.

We feel blessed to be connected with Inner Traditions. It has been a mind-expanding pleasure to work with the individuals there whose insightful creative processes have advanced this project. In particular, we could not have asked for a better project editor than Anne Dillon, who both oversaw the editing and contributed many good words, copyeditor Margaret Jones, who was remarkable both for her attention to detail and the depth of her knowledge, and author liason Erica Robinson who was helpful in many different ways.

# Directory of Meditations

TO HELP YOU FIND specific meditations and awareness practices easily, we have classified them into four groups. Although there is not that much in the human psyche that is only this or that, for the purposes of this work each of these groups refers only to its dominant process. Many of the mindfulness meditations, for instance, include some measure of concentration, and vice versa. Likewise, most of the adventures in awareness and the contemplative meditations contain both of these elements to some degree, each within a slightly different context.

## MINDFULNESS MEDITATIONS

| Page | Cell Number | Title |
|------|-------------|-------|
| 60 | 0 | Feeling Your Breath |
| 63 | 1 | Finding Your Center |
| 67 | 2 | Relaxing Point by Point |
| 86 | 6 | The Yogic Seal |
| 90 | 7 | Just Noticing |
| 123 | 15 | Replaying Your Day |
| 185 | 28 | An Internal Frame of Reference |
| 190 | 29 | Frame by Frame |
| 211 | 33 | Total Attention |
| 221 | 35 | Imaging and Calming |
| 365 | 64 | Illuminating Your Own Path |

## CONCENTRATIVE MEDITATIONS

## ADVENTURES IN AWARENESS

## CONTEMPLATIVE MEDITATIONS

## INTRODUCTION

·····················

# Inner Awakening

*The outward freedom that we shall attain will only be in exact proportion to the inward freedom to which we have grown at a given moment.*

MAHATMA GANDHI

THROUGHOUT HISTORY, PROPHETS, SAINTS, and sages have helped people cross the great river within, from insecurity and suffering to love, serenity, and joy. If we discover how to truly look into ourselves, these transcendent teachers said, we can find grace and beauty within and around us. Then we can help others do the same. This beautiful dream of finding our own enlightenment and helping others find theirs has been a driving force for many great souls.

Cultivating a clear mind and a warm heart, as part of the path to realizing that dream, is an ancient ideal. A healthy blend of intellect and feeling is more useful than either one alone. Following the path of the heart has been compared to listening to a message that can be understood only on an intuitive level. Revered by many as a sacred path, it can degenerate when common sense, reason, and attentive awareness are ignored. On the other hand, following a path of the mind that ignores the heart's voice often leads to equally grave mistakes. The balanced approach that you will find in this book leads to a sense of wholeness and empowerment that integrates both sides of your being: the mindful and logical side, and the feeling and intuitive side.

Meant for people in every walk of life, from any religious background or none, *Matrix Meditations* offers a systematic, tested series of processes that can lead you toward greater composure, self-mastery, and enjoyment of life. Our cellular map of conscious existence, the Matrix of Consciousness, helps strengthen inner resources that lead to outer fulfillment through multiple, proven methods. Putting it into regular practice will inspire a heartfelt journey through previously unexplored potentials and possibilities.

Eastern and Western ideas have influenced each other since ancient days. These pages offer a carefully crafted integration of methods and insights from East and West. In Asia, meditation is a very old practice. Until about fifty years ago, deep contemplation was the only kind of meditation that most people in Europe and America had heard of. Now Eastern techniques for clearing and focusing your mind are becoming widely known. The blend of these methods with Western philosophy and psychology offered here creates a rich montage of methods that dance in dynamic interplay. Some meditations in these pages may feel austere, like Japanese calligraphy in a few brush strokes of black and white. Others may feel brightly colored and sensuous, like Gauguin's tropical paintings, in which the people, plants, and aromas of the tropics almost leap out from the canvas.

A unique framework for reflection on life's questions, problems, and possibilities, the Matrix will help you tap into your inner sage and find more harmony and adventure, too—even in a troubled world. Its goal is to teach you how to become inwardly more perceptive and outwardly the captain of your own destiny. As you become more adept at listening to your inner voice, you'll find it easier to choose consciously and wisely. This book will guide you through a carefully structured, step-by-step program for training your own attention and educating your own emotions. You will also receive gentle guidance in reflecting deeply on each of the many sides of the multifaceted gem that is your life.

The dynamic meditation program presented in the Matrix of Consciousness is self-paced. You can move through it as slowly or as quickly as you like. We have deemed it "dynamic" because you can continuously integrate its methods into the life you are leading now. To obtain its benefits, you don't have to retreat from the world, sit in a mountain cave, or follow a guru. (On the other hand, if you want to sit in a cave or follow a guru, that's just fine, too.)

From start to finish, this is a book for both thinking and doing. Every cell includes insights to stimulate your mind and inform your emotions, and a description of how to actually perform a specific practice. Certain cells build on skills presented in earlier ones, while others stand on their own. There are four kinds of practices:

*Mindfulness meditation* involves noticing what's going on inside or outside yourself. It sharpens your awareness of whatever is occurring in your mind, emotions, body, and environment.

*Concentrative meditation* shows you how to focus and control your attention more effectively. It develops your ability to pay attention and to keep your attention where you want it.

*Adventures in awareness* offer ways of taking what you learn in meditation into your daily life, along with intriguing explorations that can only be done as you move through your world.

*Contemplative meditation* helps you examine how you are handling various aspects of your life, using methods that are more penetrating than our usual forms of thinking.

Some of these practices may change your life or inspire you to set out on a great adventure. Still others may allow you to find tiny but beautiful mini-adventures that open doors to a transcendent realm of the spirit, in which everyday events become special and the ordinary becomes extraordinary.

This book offers an unusual entryway to a deep consideration of your relationship to the world. Mind and world are intimately connected. As Plutarch, the historian of ancient Greece, put it, "What we achieve inwardly will change outer reality." The Matrix of Consciousness shows you how to set out on a personal meditative journey that can inspire the dreamer within you and help you realize your dreams. Your own mind has the alchemical power to turn the mundane into gold.

Abraham Lincoln once remarked, "Books serve to show a man that those original thoughts of his aren't very new at all." In that spirit, we acknowledge that some of the reflections included here can be traced all the way back to the I Ching, written by Fu Xi and King Wen before the founding of the Zhou Dynasty in 1066 BCE,[1] and to the even older Vedas of India. From those and other ancient beginnings, we've drawn on insights and methods from around the world to provide effective tools for inner work. We've also added some new methods of our own, to offer you proven tools that can multiply the power of your mind.

This book can be an ongoing resource. You can turn to it to help you get through difficult situations or to make the most of the moment. You may find that the Matrix of Consciousness and its dynamic meditations become steadfast friends that help you navigate through both the calm and turbulent waters of the river of life. Forces of light and darkness, of sunshine and shadow, can become harmonious allies in accelerating the evolution and liberation of your soul's true spirit.

# The Matrix of Consciousness

THIS MATRIX INCLUDES SIXTY-FIVE "cells." Each one includes reflections followed by a meditation. If practiced in the systematic fashion laid out here, the Matrix consists of four practices to be done each week, over a course of sixteen weeks. Of course, you may also use it as a resource to dip into as need be, to help you with the dilemmas and opportunities you meet along life's path. But don't stress about staying on the weekly schedule—you can pace yourself in a way that fits your needs and inclinations, lingering over certain meditations for a longer time, or moving through others at a quicker pace.

## THE MATRIX OF CONSCIOUSNESS

| Week | Mind | Body | Emotions | Action |
|------|------|------|----------|--------|
| | Cell 0: Breath | | | |
| **1** | 1 Balance | 2 Relaxation | 3 Inner Peace | 4 Patience |
| **2** | 5 Flexibility | 6 Renewal | 7 Contentment | 8 Focus |
| **3** | 9 Contact | 10 Stress | 11 Visualization | 12 Choice |
| **4** | 13 Faith | 14 Security | 15 Integrity | 16 Karma |

| Week | Mind | Body | Emotions | Action |
|---|---|---|---|---|
| 5 | 17 Adventure | 18 Health | 19 Envy | 20 Courage |
| 6 | 21 Sound and Silence | 22 Sensation | 23 Self-acceptance | 24 Shadow |
| 7 | 25 Desire | 26 Listening | 27 Loss | 28 Judgment |
| 8 | 29 Presence | 30 Respect | 31 Limits | 32 Communication |
| 9 | 33 Wholeness | 34 Freedom | 35 Worry | 36 Anger |
| 10 | 37 Attachment | 38 Attitude | 39 Trust | 40 Difficulties |
| 11 | 41 Ego | 42 Healing | 43 Joy | 44 Success |
| 12 | 45 Transformation | 46 Hang-ups | 47 Love | 48 Defensiveness |
| 13 | 49 Conflict | 50 Strength | 51 Confusion | 52 Kindness |
| 14 | 53 Moderation | 54 Intuition | 55 Forgiveness | 56 Tolerance |
| 15 | 57 Purpose | 58 Creativity | 59 Gratitude | 60 Apology |
| 16 | 61 Beauty | 62 Celebration | 63 Generosity | 64 Unity |

# PART ONE
· · · · · · · ·
# WINGS
# TO
# SOAR

# 1

...

# Starting Points

## From Obstacles
## to Opportunities

*There are only two ways to live your life.*
*One is as though nothing is a miracle.*
*The other is as though everything is a miracle.*

ALBERT EINSTEIN

**LONG AGO IN ATHENS,** and on sun-splashed islands set like jewels in the blue Aegean, the ancient Greek philosophers asked some of the same questions people ask today—questions like *How can I enjoy a rich, full life and find happiness and peace of mind?* Most of the philosophers agreed that gaining wisdom, or *sophia,* was part of the answer.

But Pythagoras, well known in mathematics, pointed out that claiming to be wise can get us into trouble. We too easily end up committed to what we think we know, whether we're really right or not. We can, however, *seek and appreciate* wisdom without falling into that trap. And so he coined the word *philosophia* for "love of wisdom" and the "quest for understanding."

Socrates held that admitting to ourselves how little we truly know is a necessary starting point in that quest. More recently, Mark Twain quipped, "It ain't what you don't know that gets you into trouble. It's what you know for sure that just ain't so."

Trying to act wisely is an adventure that can last a lifetime. Of course, you need to know what wisdom is *not,* so you can tell when others are trying to sell you a mistaken view of it. You need to know what wisdom *is,* so you can recognize it when you stumble onto it.

The contemporary spiritual teacher and author of the 1971 bestseller *Be Here Now,* Ram Dass, comments: "Wisdom involves . . . the emptying and quieting of the mind, the application of the heart, and the alchemy of reason and feeling. In the wisdom mode we're . . . standing back and viewing the whole, discovering what matters and what does not, weighing the meaning and depth of things."[1] This book and its practices help develop qualities of mind and heart that can help you make these distinctions.

You can tell from any day's nightly news broadcast that the present state of the human psyche is something less than a stampede toward enlightenment. To cope with life's challenges, a vast array of sermons, therapies, and self-help workshops, books, and videos have appeared. In assessing many of them, we can remember H. L. Mencken's observation that "for every complicated problem there is an answer that is short, simple, and wrong." Taken together, the latest trendy offering can sometimes feel like a giant jigsaw puzzle with essential pieces missing. If crucial pieces are missing, or if some pieces are in the wrong place, the puzzle doesn't quite work.

Perhaps you are reading this now because you're actively trying to find some of those missing pieces and hoping to make your life lighter and brighter. Can the waters that flow from the fountain of your own consciousness be transformed from muddy to clear and healing? Is it possible to experience your soul? One or more of these questions may be lurking beneath the surface of your consciousness.

Perhaps when you face obstacles you tend to get stuck and would love to be able to handle such situations more efficiently. Or you might too often get in your own way and make things needlessly hard for yourself— and you'd like to stop doing that, and stop creating unnecessary stress.

But maybe none of this describes you. You might be a tower of strength, yet even so, find yourself asking questions like *How can I manage my business better?* or *I've done well materially but am hungry for something more,* or even *How can I find more happiness in my everyday family life and get off the "same old, same old" treadmill?*

Looking for good advice to help answer such questions is nothing new. It has been two-and-a-half millennia since Buddha, Confucius, Lao-tzu, Mahavira, and the philosophers of ancient Greece lived and taught about the nature of consciousness. Jesus left his body almost two thousand years ago, and Muhammad five hundred years later. The Vedas and the I Ching and much of the Hebrew scriptures are even older than most of those sources. With all of that insight at our fingertips, you might imagine that by now the kingdom of heaven would be blossoming in everyone's hearts.

You might think that we'd have become a world of loving people, working together to eliminate war and poverty.

Instead, all around us we see and hear people motivated by desires rooted in deprivation and insufficiency. The most obvious are hunger, thirst, and lack of shelter and essential health care—the basic survival needs. Many other people are driven by interpersonal needs. The worries you hear most often may include:

+ "Will my relationship turn out well?"
+ "Will I find love?"
+ "My kids are having some rough problems. Will they be okay?"
+ "How can I better handle my boss and the power struggles at work?"
+ "I'm sinking under a mountain of debt. Will my finances be alright?"

In addition, most people have concerns about education, work, and success. Perhaps every time you apply for a raise or promotion, your evaluations say something like, "Not ready yet." Or you might have an insecure position in a shaky company, but see no better alternative in what looks like a desert of forbidding possibilities. Sigmund Freud called concerns like these the "common misery of mankind."

He also noted that many of us are caught in the grip of "neurotic suffering" caused by the unfortunate results of past experiences. Here, several young people describe their dilemmas:

**Max:** "When I was a child, in my mother's eyes, my only purpose was to meet her needs. Our unwritten agreement said, 'I give up my aliveness, my will, and my freedom, and that way I can be safe.' The only way to gain her approval was to pretend I didn't have any feelings, until at last I believed it myself."

**Natalie:** "Every drug was my salvation, and every episode of sexual exploitation a way to fill my emptiness. After my tenth overdose in four years, one of my few friends held a mirror in front of my face and said, 'Look at yourself!' In the mirror I saw my life of self-deception plastered on my face like makeup."

**Ellen:** "I lived in denial to keep a relationship built on lies. When I spoke of my hopes and dreams, my husband laughed in my face. I wanted to scream so he would feel my pain. But it was financially safe to stay married despite my ugly, unhappy life. One day I decided that suicide

was the only answer, and that I'd have to take my children with me. I
quickly realized that sane people did not think that way and that our
marriage had to end."

**LeRoy:** "My father used to call me 'a little piece of shit.' He told me
I could never do anything right—and then he'd show me the right
way so he could look great. I still feel like I do everything wrong,
and still play the role of victim. Finally I'm seeing that by letting
people use me as a doormat, I'm making myself powerless and harming myself."

**Jennifer:** "Every woman I know is in some sort of conflict regarding her
body. From the time I was a little girl I was told that I 'look wrong'
and needed to 'fix' myself."

Although these situations are extreme, to some extent many people suffer
from similar issues. Wounds from the past that are buried in deep crevasses
of consciousness often become traffic signals that affect which avenues of life
you choose or shun. Says psychoanalyst Robert Langan: "The hurts of the
past recur in present suffering. We shy from the suffering we know so well,
yet we shy as well from risking change. Present ills, at least, are familiar. To
compensate, we may try to puff ourselves up, to drag others down, or to deny
anything is wrong."[2]

A characteristic sign of our times is the insatiable market for cosmetic
surgery. Often this is a sign that self-acceptance and inner contentment are
minimal. And that's just at the individual level. In our culture, the prospect of
enlightenment is still just a far-off dot at the end of the tunnel.

But since millionaires commit suicide, and sultry movie stars who have
had total surgical makeovers die of drug ODs, "having it all" is obviously
no guarantee of feeling good about yourself. Nor, as His Holiness the
Fourteenth Dalai Lama, Tenzin Gyatso, notes, does the technological development of society make any inherent contribution to our personal development or lasting happiness: "What is almost always missing is a corresponding
inner development."[3]

The most ancient of Chinese books, the I Ching, addresses inner development through this metaphor: "If a well is being lined with stone, it cannot be used while the work is going on. But the work is not in vain; the
result is that the water stays clear. In life also there are times when a man
must put himself in order. . . . By enhancing his powers and abilities through
inner development, he can accomplish all the more later on."[4] Of course such

change does not come easily. It takes time and effort—but may prove worthwhile a hundred times over.

Whatever your life has been until now, at this point who you become and what you do is up to you. Your untapped powers are greater than you imagine. Since decision making about your life starts in the mind, the more you learn to perceive its movements and fathom its depths, the more you can use it effectively.

Life holds joys as well as hardships, opportunities as well as obstacles—even if sometimes it's hard to tell when an opportunity is hiding behind an obstacle. But often, even pain and hardship can tell us what we need to do to open doorways to new possibilities.

With the help of a spiritual guide, teacher, therapist, or wise friend, you may come close to perceiving the whole potential of your own consciousness. But many people lack such a guide. In these pages we have tried to put the puzzle pieces from history's great thinkers in their right places. The wisdom of all the great spiritual, philosophical, therapeutic, and scientific traditions of the world can contribute to our understanding. They are all available for us to draw on as the need arises. It's not disloyal to your particular religion or tradition to consider the thoughts of great teachers from outside it as well as from within it. Doing so opens up new possibilities, by offering tools that can help you hear the guidance of your inner voice of wisdom.

When you step into the world that this book offers you, what you may experience may be no less than the beginning of a new mythic journey. You'll be intentionally participating in the evolution of your consciousness. The Matrix is intended as a compass to guide you through your days, and a lantern to guide you through your nights.

But perhaps you are skeptical: The obstacles in your path may be too hard. Circumstances may seem too difficult. Can these pages truly offer you the tools to find your way through them? Let's take a look.

# 2

# Your Personal Renaissance

## Dreams Can Come True

*Nowhere, either with more quiet or more freedom from trouble, does a man retire than into his own soul.*

MARCUS AURELIUS

**THE REMARKABLE PERIOD CALLED** the Renaissance emerged from a backdrop of plagues, cultural decay, and a thousand years of repressive rule by medieval kings and priests. "Within the span of a single generation, Leonardo, Michelangelo, and Raphael produced their masterworks, Columbus discovered the New World, Luther rebelled against the Catholic Church and began the Reformation, and Copernicus . . . commenced the Scientific Revolution," writes Richard Tarnas in *The Passion of the Western Mind*.[1] First in Italy and then throughout Europe, men and women threw off the chains of rigid traditions, began to exercise their freedom in ways that had been largely forgotten for a thousand years, and developed potentials that had long been discouraged. The energy of the time was expansive, energetic, and creative.

In parallel fashion, when things feel humdrum in your own life, you can break out of timeworn patterns of thinking and acting and undergo your own personal renaissance. While some people pursue the ancient search for an illusory fountain of youth, contemporary maps can guide us to psychological and spiritual rebirth and renewal.

Where? Part of the answer lies in the fact that most of us use only a fraction of our mental capacity. Perhaps you have wondered what that really means.

Does it mean that someone with an IQ of ninety can become an Albert Einstein? Not quite. Rather, it means that you can learn to stop using your mental and emotional energy in ways that sabotage your ability to think clearly, feel appropriately, and act effectively. Many of us are shackled by habits that make us mentally feeble, even while our bodies are still strong and healthy. Letting go of these habits makes that energy available for constructive purposes.

Have you ever had the experience of "losing your way" inside your own mind? If not, you're most unusual. If so, you have lots of company. We all get lost in our minds at least occasionally, even when we need to keep our attention present and focused. If you're like most people, your ability to recognize what your mind is doing is sometimes turned off when you need it most.

In response to that reality, a few farseeing souls have developed methods of mental training that help people step outside their own minds long enough to gain greater mental and emotional control. These methods offer a path of inner freedom that makes it possible to perceive what your mind is doing. That makes it easier to stop replaying the same old mental movies and rerunning the same unproductive emotional patterns. As you become adept at using the spotlight of focused awareness, at any given moment you can choose to continue, change, or transform what you are doing.

From our experiences in guiding students through mental disciplines that increase awareness, and from our own inner explorations, we have also created new methods that complement and extend those we've gathered from diverse thinkers and traditions. As you'll discover, the clarity that comes from effective meditation and awareness practices can illuminate your entire life. Here, several people describe how using the methods found in the Matrix of Consciousness has helped them:

**Kate:** "I developed a new kind of relationship with my family. A key insight that came to me is that my children are not my possessions. I stopped trying to make them act as I wished. They need both guidance and to choose their own directions. I've quit doing many things that are not essential and have begun to slow down and take more time with my husband and children. As a result, our lives are richer, fuller, and happier, with far less conflict and dissatisfaction.

**Fernando:** "My father's drug habit and his use of money our family needed for necessities was a central issue as I grew up. I was letting my rage about those matters control my life. I felt negative about everything. Watching my own mind in action showed me that my anger, not my father, was my real problem. Finally I talked to my father about my grievances at length, and started transforming my anger into compassion and forgiveness."

**Naomi:** "I began to see that all the years when I'd been blaming my parents for my problems, actually it was my bad choices in the present that led to my self-destructive actions. Letting go of blaming them freed me to make healthy choices myself."

**Allen:** "The meditation and awareness practices opened my senses. I see and hear more. I listen, love, and appreciate life more. I've begun to consciously stop myself before behaving blindly and automatically. I think about the likely outcomes of whatever I want to do before acting in ways that might bring results I don't want."

Your own quest is probably different from any of those. You might wish to accomplish one or more of the following:

+ Handle stressful situations more effectively
+ Step out of consuming whirlpools of thought and let go of old hang-ups
+ Expand and sharpen your direct awareness of events so that you perceive what happens with greater clarity
+ Make fewer "mistakes"
+ Feel good more often, using your emotions to inform, motivate, and delight
+ Appreciate yourself and your life, and criticize yourself less
+ Discover dimensions of your undiscovered self that you didn't realize existed, and open doors to new possibilities
+ Form heart connections with family and friends that are more truthful, unconditional, and enriching
+ Find greater beauty and enjoyment in each moment

This book is not just for people who are consciously following a meditative path. It offers something of great value to all kinds of people in diverse situations who are just trying to make it from day to day.

**Question:** Can the Matrix of Consciousness and its dynamic meditations really do all that?

**Answer:** It depends. Just reading and "looking in from the outside" will be of some help. To develop the skills explained here and enjoy their benefits, however, you have to actually go on the journey by trying them out and using them.

If you already have your life running on all cylinders, that's great! In that case, you can use this book to enhance your existence rather than fix problems. But why do most of us so often do the opposite? Why is it so easy to become confused and let ourselves get conned, scammed, or pushed around—or act in other self-defeating ways?

On our way through life, we've all become stuck in at least a few old ways of thinking and acting. Some of these are still useful. Some of them once were helpful but are now obsolete. Some of these ways of thinking and acting were drummed into us as children. Since some of these habits formerly helped us handle tough circumstances, we keep on repeating them even though we left those circumstances long ago. Still other old patterns of thinking help us keep painful feelings out of our awareness. The Matrix of Consciousness shines a spotlight on behavior that may have served you in the past but no longer does, and illuminates a path to changing it.

Certain kinds of mental habits are especially troublesome. One group of them involves getting caught in mental vortexes. When your head is filled with a chaotic maelstrom of whirling thoughts and mental pictures (and usually the emotions and physical reactions that go with them), you have less attention available to notice what's going on inside you and around you in any given moment. But by developing more responsive, moment-by-moment awareness, you can more easily terminate those negative mental habits, broaden your range of choices, and literally increase your inner freedom.

Some mental vortexes are harder to escape than others. The trickiest are interwoven with complexes or hang-ups. These are stuck-together patterns of thoughts, emotions, physiological responses, and actions that developed in response to traumatic or threatening situations in your past. Although these are harder to leave behind than ordinary, garden-variety mental vortexes (such as one's worry about an upcoming event), it is usually possible to do so—or at least to radically reduce how often they occur.

For the most part, meditation brings gradual change. But consistent effort bears fruit, like an athlete's daily practice sessions. If you sometimes slide back into unhelpful habits, that's normal. Since you've been accumulating them for a lifetime, they're hard to change overnight. But when you actively replace old habits with healthier new ones that are incompatible with the old ones, you simply won't be able to respond with your old counterproductive patterns anymore.

If you're skeptical about this, and are convinced that old dogs can't learn new tricks, look at recent findings in neuroscience. Research has shown that new neural cells keep on forming throughout a person's lifetime, and existing cells continuously form new synapses that make it possible to change old patterns and mental habits. Thus, the more you use a capacity, the more vigorously your brain creates new nerve cells related to it.

The methods taught here will help you perceive obsolete patterns as they arise or before they arise. Then you can stop yourself right then and there and do something else instead. For instance, Victor recalls: "I used to talk on and on, repeating the same point in several different ways. People tuned me out. Now when I notice that I'm starting to repeat myself, I interrupt myself with a phrase like, 'That's all. I've said it.' Then I fall silent."

As paradoxical as it sounds, the dynamic meditations contained in this book can help you become both more thoughtful and more spontaneous when each is appropriate. Before long you will be apt to find that you solve and resolve problems more quickly. You will probably lose less time doing things you don't really have to do. And you're likely to get better at remembering things you can't afford to leave undone. You'll get better at anticipating disruptive and destructive effects of what you do and will probably find it easier to back away from negative impulses.

Don't imagine that this is a solo journey. At times you may need emotional support, or information from others who are more experienced at something you need to know more about, or who know how to do it more effectively. At times even experienced people need knowledge or expertise they don't have. The most successful doers and leaders don't pretend to know what they don't know. Rather, they seek out the resources they need.

In that spirit, we recognize that no book can be everything to everyone. We are not swamis or Zen masters, and we don't claim to have all the answers. What we have done is write the most useful book we can for ordinary people living ordinary lives. Our methods and perspectives won't solve every problem or open all doors of opportunity—and there are some things that meditation is not. For the most part, it's not a quick and easy fix for major emotional problems. Some difficult issues or circumstances require another person's perspective, or methods that are outside the meditative repertoire. When that occurs, competent counseling, or advice from a trusted friend who has special expertise, can be of great value.

On the other hand, meditation and awareness practices can take you places where ordinary consciousness seldom goes. Deep reflection can open the gates of truth in a soulful way. As a starting point, remember the old adage, "You can make a hell out of heaven or a heaven out of hell." The Matrix of Consciousness helps you make the wiser choice.

# 3

# Portals to Your Inner World

## Entering the Matrix

*Trust that which gives you meaning*
*and accept it as your guide.*

CARL GUSTAV JUNG

EACH MEDITATION OR CELL of the Matrix is a like a doorway—a portal that leads to something you can think about and turn over in your mind, and also to a specific practice or activity.

In these cells, you will undertake a fascinating journey that will help you delve into the depths of your unconscious mind in ways that enrich your daily life. You'll travel through doorways of understanding that will open up new perspectives and possibilities. Some of them will help you answer questions about yourself and inspire you to address perplexing questions about how you might improve your world.

Among these cells are at least a few that are likely to lead you into inner chambers of your mind that you have never consciously gone into before. Exploration of these little-known sides of yourself may surprise you. You may find passions or potentials that were punished or discouraged earlier in your life. Or you may come across forgotten aptitudes that were at odds with what people around you accepted. These dimensions of yourself might even be deep and soulful sources of aliveness, but in some way they've been papered over by the demands of the people and institutions around you and the habitual patterns of your life. Whatever you don't like about yourself may become something you can accept in a nonjudgmental way, or find a way to change. You may develop greater appreciation for things you like about yourself. And you'll learn to do at least a few things—or maybe even many—that you've never done before.

There are several different ways you can use this book. You can undertake the journey to your true self via the pathways of this inner labyrinth by stepping through any of the following portals.

**Portal 1:** Follow it as a structured program, i.e., step by step (highly recommended for greatest results). Read the text that goes with one cell of the matrix almost every day. Immediately after reading, take a few minutes to do the meditation or adventure in awareness that is described in the cell. This approach is likely to bring you the greatest rewards—but it also requires commitment and discipline. We have structured this program for reading four cells per week. We figure that if you're like most people, you'll sometimes miss a day.

**Portal 2:** Follow it as a formal course in attentive meditation. If your central interest is meditation, we suggest you read chapters 4 through 8, and then follow the sequential order of the cells listed in the mindfulness meditations and concentrative meditations sections of the Directory of Meditations, beginning with cell 0 and ending with cell 45. However, if you're an experienced meditator, you may prefer a different order.

**Portal 3:** Jump right in. Open the book randomly to any page. Thumb back to the first page of that particular cell and start to read. Or thumb forward to the first page of the next cell and start to read. Let synchronicity be your guide in telling you which cell to work with. Use this method anytime you please. And do any of the meditations that pique your interest.

**Portal 4:** Follow the arrow of your interest or concern. Look at the table of contents found on pages vii–x and find any item or method that describes a dilemma or issue that you are facing, or a subject that you are drawn to. Turn to the indicated page and read the text for that cell.

**Portal 5:** Read this like you would any other book. Start at the beginning and read straight through to the end. To gain the full benefit, however, you will want to go back afterward and actually do each of the meditations and activities.

**Portal 6:** Pursue the active path—i.e., adventures in awareness. Perhaps at this point in life, you're just not inclined to sit quietly in introspection for fifteen minutes—or even five or ten. If that's the case, you can choose a meditation from the category of adventures in awareness. Choose one each day, or even each week, that you'd like to focus on and integrate it into your daily life, at your own pace.

**Portal 7:** Use the Matrix as an oracle. Let the message of a cell, or even several cells at once, open up new perspectives on a situation you are facing. Use what you read as a starting point for finding the guidance or answer(s) you've been looking for. (See chapter 9 for more details.)

**Portal 8:** Use the Matrix as a game. Players take turns using one of the methods mentioned above in portals 1 or 2 or 5 to go to any of the sixty-five cells. The player reads the text, or part of it, aloud and comments on how he relates to it. Then the other players each have a chance to say something about how the passage would apply to himself or herself.

You can return to any cell in the Matrix again and again. Each can be visited at many levels of varying depth. You may choose to move through the Matrix systematically, or carefully pick your way through, choosing each step. Or you may plunge into its depths and allow a longer period for each cell and its practice. However you use it, we hope you will find this book to be a valued friend that you will consult again and again whenever you wish, or when challenges arise.

At this point you may want to skip ahead to chapters 8 and 9, which describe several ways to use the Matrix, or turn the page to find out how the Matrix works, and why.

# 4

...

# An Incredible Lens

## Your Mind

*In meditation you pay attention to dimensions of yourself
which are seldom known—your own deepest, innermost
levels. Meditation involves a kind of inner attention that is
quiet, concentrated, and at the same time relaxed.*

SWAMI RAMA

**HAVE YOU EVER HAD** an eye examination? If so, you may recall sitting in a
dark room looking at an eye chart through frames into which the optometrist inserted a variety of lenses. Again and again, the optometrist probably
asked, "Do you see more clearly with lens *A*—or (switching to a different
lens) with lens *B*? With some lenses, the letters on the chart were clear and
sharp, while others were fuzzy or distorted. Finally you ended up with the
lenses through which you could see most clearly.

The meditations contained in this book do something similar, but in a different way. They help you train your powers of attention so that you become
aware of things you're doing that you hadn't previously noticed. It's as if you
are finding and using new lenses that help you perceive what both you and
others are doing more clearly. This includes lenses that increase your awareness
of your own thinking process, rather than being completely identified with
your thoughts—which for most people is a very common state of mind.

Actually, when perceiving both yourself and your world, you are almost
always looking through one lens or another. These filters are created by your
own temperament, physiology, physical abilities and limitations, past learning,
and whatever motive is driving you at a given moment. As a result, several people may see the same object or event, or hear the same story, quite differently.
A mailbox by the side of the road some distance ahead may be perceived by

four people riding in the same car as a child who might dart onto the road, a policeman, a garbage can, or—by the passenger with acute vision—a mailbox.

The same principle applies to more complex events. A situation may be seen by one person as a chance to make a profit, by a second as an opportunity to learn, by a third as a means to get revenge against an enemy, and by a fourth as a chance to help someone in need.

Developing the ability to perceive the events of your life through several different lenses, instead of being locked into just one way of responding, can help you make better choices. Meditation is an important tool that you can use to develop this capacity.

For a metaphorical preview of what happens during meditation, you might try this right now:

## LIKE FISH IN A RIVER

Imagine that you are sitting beside a clear river that's very deep. As you look down into it you see a school of minnows swimming among the underwater plants near the shore. As you peer further, you see several larger silvery shapes holding their position as they face upstream against the current. In the dark depths beneath them an even larger shape slowly moves away until it becomes invisible in midstream. At the very bottom of the river, a shadowy figure rises from the bottom, moves a few feet, and settles down again. You can tell from its form that it is a bottom-feeding catfish.

Next, imagine that your mind is a river just like the one you've been watching. Imagine that each thought that comes through your mind is like a fish. First notice the surface thoughts flitting back and forth. Then be alert to see what deeper thoughts, and feelings, perhaps, appear. Continue, and see whether any thoughts or feelings that seldom cross your mind in daily life rise up out of the hidden recesses of your consciousness. If so, are any of them important enough to need more attention than you've been giving them? Examine your thoughts and your mind introspectively for about five minutes (or longer if you wish).

In daily life, some of the big, important fish that lurk in the depths may escape your notice because your mind is usually occupied with the schools of little fish near the surface. The dynamic Matrix meditations in this book will help you look more deeply into the ever-changing currents of the river of your life.

One day as I was meditating, I stopped for a moment to jot down a thought in the pocket notebook that I usually carry. A friend walked up. "What are you doing?" she asked.

"Writing down an idea I had while I was meditating."

"Do you *think* while you're meditating?"

"Yes," I said, "but the thoughts sort of 'float' in a large pool of awareness, rather than being the main event in my mind."

Alan Watts captured this experience by saying that meditation is "the art of suspending verbal and symbolic thinking for a time, somewhat as a courteous audience will stop talking when a concert is about to begin." It's a good metaphor. In our higher quest, we rediscover a dimension of mind that we all knew as young children, but which for many adults is almost eclipsed by a constant flow of thoughts and conditioned emotional responses. When we meditate, we move into a state of mind that involves thinking less, as we become more mindful of both internal and external events. Thoughts become fewer, more visible, and more significant, with a more piercing view of inner truths. With practice, you can learn to reduce the amount of mental activity that goes into useless and unsatisfying thoughts, and to increase the amount that goes into direct awareness and useful thoughts.

Meditation does not, however, aim at bringing our usual thinking process to a complete standstill, a practice called *nirvikalpa samadhi* by yogis. It does quiet your mind and open up more mental space for truly important concerns to emerge. You will probably find that your mind becomes less distracted and clearer—like a machine that has been cleaned and oiled. You might also find that during meditation you recall things you've forgotten that really need to be done. And you will probably realize that some things you intended to do actually don't have to be done, or can be done more efficiently.

"Fishing" in these deep waters is a result of "witnessing the spontaneous free flow of the mind without interfering, censoring, guiding, or manipulating in any way," says cultural and ethnobotanist Wolf Dieter-Storl.[1] A fascinating paradox is that as you meditate, less becomes more.

If you can systematically spend just fifteen minutes a day meditating, you can realize some, or all, of the following:

> You will obtain greater awareness—through regular practice you will hone your ability to notice what's occurring both inside you and around you, and gain greater control over your attention.

You will deepen your communication with yourself. This opens the door to acting in ways that help you move more quickly, resolutely, and effectively toward what you want in life.

You will gain more aliveness. Through the reflective dimension of your inner journey, you may start finding it easier to lead a more sacred life that's aligned with the depths of your being. And you just may find that you enjoy life more.

Meditation is sometimes described as transcending ordinary states of consciousness. You have already had plenty of experience moving from one state of consciousness to another. Doubtless you've had moments when your awareness felt spacious and wonderful, such as when you've experienced joy at seeing a beautiful landscape. And you have probably had other moments when your consciousness felt dark and constricted, like being in a windowless room filled with thick smoke or fog. Sometimes such contrasting states mirror life's ups and downs, and sometimes they come unpredictably.

You probably already act in ways that you hope will change your state of consciousness. If you feel agitated, you might take a walk to calm down. If you are groggy, you might have a cup of coffee or tea to perk up. If you feel tense and anxious, depressed, or alienated from the world, you might get a prescription or have a drink at the neighborhood bar.

In this book you will find methods to alter your consciousness in intentional, controlled ways that do not depend on outside resources. To give you a sense of where meditation can take you in just a few weeks if you devote some time to it every day, here are a few brief entries from journals kept by some of our students:

+ "I found this method very soothing in the morning. It was a great transition into waking up and getting ready for the day. My mind and body both felt so peaceful."
+ "By the end of my meditation, I felt very composed and calm. Ending my day with this deep breathing practice was a great way to clear my mind."
+ "Through my practice I'm noticing the habitual chaos of my thoughts. I'm also discovering the calm that lies behind them and gradually fine-tuning my concentration. The power of the breath rules out distractions."

- ✦ "The methods help me develop a longer attention span, attain greater emotional stability, understand others' feelings more deeply, and release myself from the constraints I place on my own happiness."
- ✦ "Meditation changes my relationship to my emotions more than the emotions themselves. It lets me see mood fluctuations moment to moment, so that I can navigate around them."
- ✦ "My mind grew clear and my body melted into the firm ground. The only sound I heard was my breathing. The outside world did not exist. I reached a state of inner and outer stillness. In that short time I felt a sense of great calm and peace."
- ✦ "My thoughts were serene and pleasant. I am so thankful to have learned these various types of meditation. I will continue to pass on these techniques to my family and friends."

## CHOOSING A FORM OF MEDITATION THAT FITS YOU

The effects of contemplative meditations are multiplied as you learn to use your attention more effectively. "Happy combinations of the different forms of meditation," says Indian mystic and spiritual master Meher Baba, "facilitate rapid progress because they secure a harmonized and balanced mind. The right combinations are those forms of practice that [remove] the special obstacles with which [you are] faced at the moment."[2]

We don't prescribe the same method for everyone. The dynamic meditation approach outlined in this book is not a one-size-fits-all approach. On the one hand, it offers a structured, disciplined method. On the other, it can be customized with your own minor adjustments to make it a more effective fit to your unique habits and lifestyle. We've found that when different options are described clearly, most people have some sense of what they need most in a given moment—but not always. So we suggest that you will find value both in following your inner voice and in working through the meditation program from start to finish to increase your range of options. In the process, you will discover what works best for you—like a guitarist who plays better music after she has learned the chords and fingering.

Now we'll take a closer look at the attentive processes of concentration and mindfulness. If you'd like to understand how they produce the effects they do, continue on to chapter 5.

# 5

# Attention

## Fine-tuning Your Awareness

*Attention is like a searchlight; when its beam is spread over a
vast area, its power to focus on a particular
object becomes weak, but focused on one thing
at a time, it becomes powerful.*

PARAMAHANSA YOGANANDA

THE SUCCESS OF THE legendary detective Sherlock Holmes was due in large part to his extraordinary perceptiveness. Where others saw nothing unusual, he noticed tiny but important clues that gave him a remarkable ability to solve mysteries. That same quality of attentiveness can be developed, and it can prove just as valuable in helping you find clues to what makes a successful life.

Such awareness includes noticing details of ordinary behavior, other people's as well as your own. You've probably known at least a few people who typically seemed to be totally present. You felt like they truly listened to you and saw you, without being distracted by anyone or anything else. And you probably felt good about being heard and seen without that person's agenda intruding. By contrast, most of us, as we listen, are continually distracted by our own thoughts and feelings. We filter another person's messages through the lenses of our own reactions. As a result, often we're not quite all there with each other. The psychological approach called phenomenology is based on this fact. Its focus is on learning how to get as close as we can to hearing and understanding another person's reality *as it is for them*.

Something similar happens with our own thoughts. We start to think about something, then find ourselves distracted by worries about tomorrow or memories of yesterday—or fifteen years ago. In this case, we're not quite all there with ourselves.

27

Like Sherlock Holmes, as you learn to recognize and guide what you are doing with your attention, you become better able to perceive what's going on inside you and around you. That gives you more power to choose what you do, and to affect how others respond to you, making it easier for you to create harmony in your life. You do this by detailing one part of your mind to notice what the rest of your mind, emotions, and body are doing.

In yogic writings, this internal observer is often called the "Witness." When you tune in to your inner Witness, try to observe elements of your experience that sometimes escape your attention. Notice thoughts that slip through your mind like ghosts, almost unseen. Be attuned to feelings and sensations that would ordinarily have remained below the threshold of your consciousness. Instead of letting your mind drift on winds of fretful and forgetful wanderings, you can harness its power with the reins of focused attention. Psychologist and philosopher William James declared, "The faculty of voluntarily bringing back a wandering attention . . . is the very root of judgment, character, and will."[1]

## YOUR MIND FUNCTIONS
## WITHIN A CIRCLE OF ATTENTION

Modern psychologists and ancient sages alike have verified these facts: The mind has a limited capacity for attention. The attention you give to selected items is less available for noticing other items. Focusing your attention in certain directions increases your satisfaction, happiness, and peace of mind, while focusing it in certain other directions causes unnecessary and avoidable pain and suffering. Developing your ability to notice what your mind is doing increases your freedom to focus your mind in ways that are helpful rather than harmful to both yourself and others.

Psychological research shows that people can respond to and remember only a limited number of items at a time, even though we have a huge capacity to remember past events. Imagine for a moment that an empty circle represents your total capacity for attention. Next, suppose that half of your circle of attention is taken up by worrying about how an important meeting tomorrow will go, or how "that important someone" will respond to you. Draw a line down the middle of the circle and darken one side. That half of your mind is occupied.

This leaves only half of your attention available to notice other items or to think about other matters. In a sense, you're a half-wit, since you have only half your wits about you to deal with what you are doing now. This can occur, for instance, when a student has severe test anxiety. Some of his attention is taken up with worry about how he's going to do on the exam, and as a result he has less attention available to focus on thinking and writing. Fear of failure becomes a self-fulfilling prophecy. Something similar can happen in a job interview, during a business presentation, or on a first date.

Think of a job such as air-traffic controller, which requires a high degree of sustained, focused attention. The controller has to notice every blip on the radar screen. A few moments of daydreaming could lead to a plane crash.

But perhaps you are thinking, *That doesn't apply to me. I can keep my attention perfectly focused if I want to.*

Really? As an experiment, stop reading for just one minute and try this:

## JUST ONE MINUTE

Look at a clock or a watch that has a second hand. Your task is to keep your attention from wandering for sixty seconds.

*No problem!* you are perhaps telling yourself.

Well, let's find out. During the next minute, each time you notice that your mind has wandered off and you are thinking about anything else at all, count that incident. Then bring your attention back to your clock or watch. Try it now.

How many times did your attention wander?

You probably counted at least four or five instances of mental wandering. That's during just one minute. We think we're in charge of what our minds are doing, but in reality they're out of control much of the time. You're about to change that.

## ONE-POINTED AND
## MANY-POINTED ATTENTION

A calligraphy student was writing the words *The First Principle*. He wrote them again and again. Each time his teacher pointed out some flaw. The student's mind was divided between writing the letters, concern about whether he was doing them well enough, and worry about what the teacher would think. Finally, the teacher, sensing the student's self-conscious discomfort, left the room for a few moments.

*Ah, now's my chance!* thought the student. In the teacher's absence, he wrote the three words one more time. The teacher returned: "Perfect!"

While the teacher was present, the student's attention was many-pointed, darting back and forth among diverse thoughts and anxieties. With the teacher gone, he could focus completely on the task. His attention became one-pointed. Similarly, an expert musician, when "in the zone," will be focused on nothing but performing. Each time she notices that her mind has drifted off and the singing or playing has gone on autopilot, she'll bring her attention back, which allows her to put more skill, depth, and feeling into the session.

This ability to guide your attention to where you want it to go is invaluable. It can help you think, talk about, or do what you truly prefer to do, instead of what someone else, a magazine ad, or a TV commercial wants you to do. As you get better at recognizing when your attention gets hooked, you develop the freedom to unhook. Then you can respond in a flexible way that fits your present needs and wishes.

In doing that, you are developing your ability to maintain one-pointed attention: to focus on just one thing at a time. In our everyday consciousness, our attention is forever darting around among competing thoughts, sensations, emotions, and perceptions—often in a distracted and chaotic fashion. Sometimes you may even feel like you're caught in a mental vortex of thoughts that you can't escape. You might feel like your mind is spinning out of control. Perhaps it is! For the most part, each new meditation in the first half of the Matrix of Consciousness requires just a little more attention and leaves you with just a little less distracted mental energy. When you reach the last step, it's likely that you won't be able to meditate and be distracted at the same time. You will be completely present in the moment.

## CONCENTRATION AND MINDFULNESS WORK TOGETHER

You can't always change an old habit just by programming yourself to act differently. Sometimes you have to discover the details of what you are doing that interferes with changing. Only when you can clearly perceive what you're already doing can you choose to do something else.

Meditation opens an empty space in your mind where there are fewer distractions than usual. This makes it easier to notice old patterns and release them. A meditative voyage of inner discovery can sometimes lead to unexpected realizations that bring dramatic changes almost overnight.

Like everyone, you have at least two distinct kinds of awareness. The first is a broad sensitivity to whatever you happen to notice. The second is a sharper focus on what you're attending to at a given moment. Such *bare attention*[2] includes two elements. One is an ability to concentrate—to focus your attention where you want it. The second is your ability to notice whatever is going on right now, both within and without. For example, as you watch a sunset, your mind may be filled with so many thoughts that you barely see it. But if you've developed a capacity for bare attention, you will first notice that you are not quite in the moment, and then let go of thinking about other things long enough to enjoy the blazing light in the sky as the sun sinks into the horizon. How delicious!

*Concentration* means placing or keeping your attention where you want it. It is sometimes misunderstood to mean "pushing things you don't want to think about out of your mind," which in itself is difficult, as shown by the instruction, "Don't think about watermelons." If you are trying to not think about something, you are still thinking about it. Actually, in concentration you focus your attention on an item, process, or subject. When you notice that your attention has wandered elsewhere, you gently pick it up and bring it back to where you want it.

Swami Vivekananda, one of the first to bring Eastern meditative practices to the West, defines concentration as a state that exists when you focus your mind on one object, either inside you or outside you, and keep it there. This need not mean that no other thoughts come through your mind. Rather, when they enter, you notice them, and then let them go while you retain your focus on the single object of your concentration. An ability to center your mind in this way leads to a great increase in mental control. Your mind becomes steady and almost unshakable, no longer darting here and there in response to internal or external stimuli.[3]

"In concentration," says Yogic Master Swami Rama, "the goal is not to make the mind empty, but rather to quiet the mind by giving it a single focus. . . . This is in contrast to a scattered, distracted state of mind. Concentration means an alert, yet relaxed, focus of attention, and if you are relaxed and comfortable, this kind of concentration should not be difficult. When you cannot concentrate, it means your ability to choose to direct the flow of your mind has been impaired."[4]

Indian yogi and guru Paramahansa Yogananda adds, "By the power of concentration, man can use the untold power of the mind to accomplish that which he desires."

*Mindfulness* means noticing where your attention is and what it's doing from moment to moment. You can be mindful of your thoughts, feelings, sensations, perceptions, or overt actions. We could say that you are mindful of events in your environment, or that you are mindful of yourself perceiving those events. You notice what you are doing, as you do it. Then you can move your attention back to what's most useful or satisfying: that's concentration again. Using your concentration and mindfulness together makes it easier to be attentive to what's useful to you and ignore what's not, or even to guide a conversation in a given direction when you need to do so.

At about the same time that Socrates was teaching people how to distinguish between what they truly knew and what they only thought they knew, the Buddha formulated his Noble Eightfold Path to reduce suffering. He described a profound insight: about a third of the suffering in human life is inevitable, but we ourselves create the rest of it—the other two-thirds. We can learn to stop doing that.

Suppose you and a friend are talking about a project that you're working on together, when suddenly you hear your inner voice saying, *We'll never get through this. I'm supposed to know what to do and I don't. I bet she thinks I'm a dunce!* Once you have noticed that negative self-talk (which is sometimes almost unconscious), you can change it. You might replace it with a statement asserting that if you persevere, the two of you will figure out what to do. Then you can channel the mental energy you were wasting on negativity into constructive thinking about how to successfully complete the project.

Rhonda Byrne's best-selling book, *The Secret,* says something similar but frames it differently: "Everything that's coming into your life you are attracting . . . by virtue of the images you're holding in your mind. . . . Why people do not have what they want is because they are thinking more about what they *don't* want than what they *do* want."[5] Let's change Byrne's language slightly: what comes into your life you are attracting by virtue of what you pay attention to. Or in the words of Transcendental Meditation teacher Maharishi Mahesh Yogi: "Whatever we put our attention on will grow stronger in our life."

Actually we don't attract *everything* that happens to us. Sometimes fate plays its hand. Unexpected events do happen, occasionally with effects that we would never have anticipated. And in situations where inevitably one party wins and the other loses, both may vividly visualize success but only one wins. In a football game, what might have been a perfect field goal kick may be blown off course by a sudden gust of wind. Even then, however, the kicker is in charge of how he responds to the hand that fate just dealt, and in charge of what he does next.

But perhaps you are getting impatient with all this talk about how the mind works. You may be thinking, *You said this approach integrates both the mind and heart. Where's the heart?*

Where indeed? Let's see if we can find it.

# Messages of the Heart

## The Other Half of Yourself

*If something is missing in your heart—then despite the most*
*luxurious surroundings, you cannot be happy. However, if*
*you have peace of mind, you can find happiness even under*
*the most difficult circumstances.*

THE DALAI LAMA

**TO ATTAIN TRUE CONTENTMENT** and peace of mind, mind and heart have to work together. An apparently clear mind will inevitably make major mistakes when it is linked to a cold, closed heart, just as a warm and caring heart gets into all kinds of trouble when it's connected to a confused and foggy mind. As your movement through the Matrix of Consciousness helps you attain a clearer mind, you can more easily move on to listening to messages from your heart, and perhaps even become kinder in your attitudes and actions. Indian sage Sri Ramana Maharshi taught that the heart, rather than the head, is the true seat of consciousness. He meant not the physical heart at the left side of the chest, but our spiritual heart, and by consciousness he meant not conceptual thought, but pure awareness.[1]

You have probably heard the story Jesus told about the good Samaritan. There's more to it than meets the eye. While Jesus and several others were discussing the principle "Love thy neighbor as thyself," one of them asked him, "And who is my neighbor?"

In response, Jesus said, "A man was going down from Jerusalem to Jericho, and he fell among robbers, who stripped him and beat him and departed, leaving him half dead. Now by chance a priest was going down that same road, and when he saw him he passed by on the other side. So likewise a Levite, when he came to the place and saw him, passed by on the other side.

But a Samaritan, as he journeyed, came to where he was; and when he saw him, he had compassion, and went to him and bound up his wounds, pouring on oil and wine; then he set him on his own beast and brought him to an inn, and took care of him. And the next day he took out two denarii and gave them to the innkeeper, saying, 'Take care of him; and whatever more you spend, I will repay you when I come back.'"[2]

It's easy to see that the Samaritan proved to be the real "neighbor" to the unfortunate Jew who was robbed, beaten, and left lying by the roadside. As the biblical scholars Robert W. Funk, Bernard Brandon Scott, and James R. Butts point out, this story must have shocked Jesus's Jewish audience, "since there was deep and longstanding hostility between Jews and Samaritans rooted in political and religious rivalry." The (apparently Jewish) priest passes the victim by, and then "the Samaritan breaks down social and ethnic barriers" by taking care of him.[3]

Today we could replace the Jew and the Samaritan with an Israeli and a Palestinian, a Sunni and a Shiite, or a Tutsi and a Hutu. The point of the story is reflected in a remark by the Indian holy woman known simply as Amma (Sri Mātā Amritanandamayī Devi, also called the Hugging Saint).

> Love is the very breath of Life. No one would say, "I will breathe only when I am with my family and friends; I won't breathe in front of my enemies." . . . Love and beauty exist within you. Try to express these qualities through your actions and you will touch the very source of bliss.[4]

Both Jesus and Amma were pointing out that acting in ways that help others feel good and evolve in consciousness brightens your own spirit. Acting in ways that harm others injures your own spirit because it deadens you to the places in yourself where you're similar to them. So you put up a wall to block feelings of sympathy with them out of your awareness. You end up with what psychiatrist Wilson Van Dusen called "holes in the personality"—places where you can't see, hear, or feel their pain or suffering.[5]

Here the line between psychological and spiritual questions blurs. Which parts of yourself do you ignore, anesthetize, or annihilate? This is a question that involves your inner spirit. So does the question, "Which dimensions of others do you deaden yourself to seeing, hearing, and feeling?" If you dull your ability to perceive how you hurt either yourself or others, you become a more limited person. Of course you are getting something or other out of it or you wouldn't be doing it. Nonetheless, we can join Jesus in asking, "What does it profit a man to gain the whole world and lose his own soul?" In contrast, by becoming more sensitive to the effects of your actions on yourself and on others, you are nourishing your inner spirit. As you strengthen your internal foundation of clarity, you will act more intelligently and wisely. In so doing you are turning up the light of your soul.

At the deepest level, morality and self-interest merge. Acting in ways that nurture your inner spirit is usually wise, and acting in ways that anesthetize or deaden it is usually unwise. Your physical body also responds to this truth. When you live in a way that respects your deep feelings, you strengthen your immune system. When you are distressed from being out of touch with what matters most to you, your body is not at ease. Being out of touch with your inner spirit creates ongoing stress, lowers the health of your immune system, and increases the potential for disease.

To help people through their earthly trials, all the truly great spiritual teachers have addressed the question of how to avoid being mean-spirited and hard-hearted toward both oneself and others in thoughts, feelings, words, and actions. And many sermons have preached the value of morality. In brief, morality involves questions about good and bad, right and wrong. But that's a deceptively simpleminded summary, because most people think that they or their group is good and right, and the other person or group is bad and wrong—and subsequently transform the other into an enemy. Such disagreements about what is moral and ethical or what is not have consequences as lethal as murder or war. As philosopher Bertrand Russell observed, "War does not determine who is right—only who is left." The labels—*good, bad, right, wrong*—too easily conflict with the facts of real situations. To complicate things, most of us sometimes fail to realize it when we act in ways that are harmful to others (or for that matter, to ourselves). We are too preoccupied with other concerns to realize when we are acting in ways contrary to our own ethics. Often the word *compassion* is something we learn through our own suffering.

The old days of authoritarian morality are passing as more and more people break away from orthodox, restrictive thinking about right and wrong. Morality and ethics must take into account the ways in which the world is changing. For example, a morality that condones wanton destruction of the environment while someone benefits from it is not viable in a world facing ecosystem collapse. A morality that benefits everyone most fully, including future generations and other living beings, has to consider both the immediate situation and the larger context.

The key to a morality that is ideal for both the individual and for society lies in the development of our ability to discern what is actually occurring in any given situation. You can do this by looking closely at the down-to-earth specifics of each real event and at the likely results of a given act or attitude. The crucial questions are: How helpful or harmful is a given act? How beneficial or destructive? How useful or counterproductive? And for whom or what, in what ways, when, where, and under what circumstances, is it useful or counterproductive?

Answering these questions requires honest communication with your inner self, and listening with both your heart and head. This may require you to let go of some of your old ideas. As psychologist Carl Rogers reminds us, "Many people . . . have regarded the facts as possible bearers of disaster, as potential enemies. The facts are *always* friendly."[6]

Both Buddha and the great yogis realized that inevitably we all have thoughts that are potentially helpful and thoughts that are potentially harmful, both to ourselves and to others. Trying to pretend that we don't leads to lying to ourselves, or even to chronic self-deception. Because of this, they suggested methods for observing our thoughts, for stopping ourselves from expressing potentially harmful thoughts in speech or action, and for moving our mind from unhelpful to helpful thoughts. To have the discipline to simply observe unkind thoughts as they rise up in our minds, and then to refrain from speaking them or acting on them, is a powerful force for self-development. It improves the quality of what we offer others and what we receive from them. And it opens the door to replacing the unkind thoughts with more beneficial ones.

If, like many people, you have trouble meeting others in a heartfelt way, don't worry. We all have different personalities with different levels of openness. We also have the option to move toward living in a more heartfelt way as well as a more clear-minded way.

How do we know what's helpful or harmful to another? One good way is to ask. If you can't do that and have to guess, then don't assume your guess is right. Watch and listen carefully to how he, she, or they respond to what you say or do. Remember that each person is unique. An act that's beneficial for one person may be bad for another. Immediate experience with each person in each situation is usually a better guide than listening to the proclamations of authorities.

We encourage you to adopt that same attitude as you read this book, and listen with your heart to everything we say. Compare our words with your own experience. Whether you are just starting out on the path of self-exploration, or whether you are a beginning or an experienced meditator, we invite you to enjoy an inner dialog with us as you read. If something aligns with your spirit and works for you, great. If not, don't be concerned. Our goal is to help you become your own expert in living a joyful life, where laughter and good luck pervade as a result of your choices. The next chapter is about how you can accomplish that.

# Your Inner Guide

## Turning Up the Volume

*I am the Captain of my soul.*

WILLIAM HENLE

THE POWERS OF THE mind are immense, but sometimes we forget that. If you are like most of us, the words and pictures in your mind can sometimes feel like a confusing jumble of thoughts and voices. You might feel pulled in different directions by your own wishes, your struggles to meet others' expectations, or your past beliefs about what you are supposed to do in the present. What then?

In nineteenth-century Denmark, a young philosopher named Søren Kierkegaard rebelled against being forced into the roles and rituals his society imposed on him. An astute observer of the psyche, he noted that when we try to be other than what we deeply sense ourselves to be (to avoid punishment or rejection or to gain approval), we may develop a "shut-up-ness" that turns into a "sickness of the spirit." But, he continued, the capacity to feel despair with our life as we're living it is a sign of our ability to grow. We can take a leap of faith that helps us discover our true selves, our untapped talents, our secret gifts, or our authentic vocations. Then we can nurture those qualities, give them form, sustain them, and perhaps even dedicate them to something greater than ourselves. In so doing, we develop an "inner sustainment," a self-confidence that helps us even in the face of great obstacles.[1]

A century later, Simone de Beauvoir, a leading French writer, placed the right to be true to your deepest sense of yourself and to choose your own path at the heart of her perspective. For her role as one of the founders of contemporary feminism, *Time* magazine, in its millennium issue, called her one of the 100 most influential people of the twentieth century.

After World War I, de Beauvoir's father, a wealthy French lawyer who had left his job to fight for his country, lost his business and told his two daughters that since he could not afford dowries for them, they would have to become career women. In those days, the careers open to women were waitress, clerk-typist, telephone operator, and little else. But de Beauvoir enrolled at the Sorbonne, graduated in 1929, and became one of Europe's premier fiction and nonfiction authors.[2] At the Sorbonne she met existential philosopher Jean-Paul Sartre. They became lifelong friends and lived together for some time. She turned down his proposal of marriage because the role of wife did not suit her. Had she gone along with prevailing custom and denied her unique abilities, she would have succumbed to what Kierkegaard termed "lies of character," or fictions we tell ourselves about ourselves.

Simone de Beauvoir touched the world by example. Her definition of her role as a writer rather than a wife or mother opened the door to self-determination for millions of women. At the same time, she encouraged others to make personal choices that were different from her own.

Karen Horney, a psychoanalyst who wrote at about the same time, coined the phrase, "the tyranny of shoulds." Personal growth, she pointed out, requires distinguishing among others' "shoulds" for ourselves; our own inner "shoulds" leftover from our yesterdays; and our real, present preferences. There is, she said, no good reason why we can't keep on developing and changing as long as we are alive.

The danger in all this is that listening to our authentic self in a one-sided fashion can cause us to be impervious to others' needs and feelings. This is not what either Horney or de Beauvoir meant. They were kind-hearted in their sensitivities. De Beauvoir wrote, "One's life has value as long as one attributes value to the life of others, by means of love, friendship, indignation, and compassion."[3]

When Carlos Castaneda was an anthropology student at UCLA, he went out into the Sonoran desert of the southwestern United States and Northern Mexico to study with an old Indian teacher named Don Juan Matus. One day Don Juan told him,

> A path is only a path, and there is no affront to oneself or others
> in dropping it if that is what your heart tells you to do. . . . Look at

every path closely and [ask]: Does this path have a heart? If it does, the path is good; if it doesn't, it is of no use. . . . One [path] makes for a joyful journey; as long as you follow it, you are one with it. The other will make you curse your life. One makes you strong; the other weakens you.[4]

How would you describe your own present path? Think about your associations with the words *heartfelt, big hearted,* and *open-hearted*. There are also the expressions *heartless, hard-hearted,* and *my heart's not in it*. What does each imply?

How do you know if a direction you are choosing is a good one for you? You can remember Don Juan, and ask, "Does this path have a heart—for me?" And you can ask that either about what you do or the way you are doing it.

What is a path with heart? It nurtures your aliveness and your spirit. It helps you to appreciate each moment and cherish each day. It makes it easier for you to carry out your responsibilities with enjoyment and make the best of what life offers. And it helps you handle hard times and easy times—both the ebb and the flow of the turning wheel of life—with more optimism.

How do you find your own path with heart, and follow Shakespeare's counsel, "To thine own self be true"? Chances are that you won't find the answer on prime-time TV or in a fortune cookie. We believe that the answer can be found at a deeper level of your being. Discerning it requires a subtle kind of listening that goes beyond what reason and logic can provide. Such receptivity is possible in a meditative state, where you learn to turn up the volume on your inner awareness.

As you realize that you are different from every other person, you can let go of judging and comparing and trying to be like someone else. "If everybody looked alike, what monotony!" says spiritual leader and philosopher Vivekananda. "Look alike and think alike—what could we do but sit down and die in despair? We can't live like a row of chipmunks; variation belongs to human life."[5] Ironically, when you truly recognize your uniqueness, you discover qualities you have in common with everyone. "That which is most personal, is most universal," declared Carl Rogers.

The other side of all this involves leaving another person space to be herself, rather than getting irked because she doesn't do what you expect or want. "To love is to understand and feel that the other person is different," says spiritual teacher Swami Prajnanpad. Only when you encourage others to follow their hearts are they likely to do the same for you.

By now you may be anticipating where the portals and paths you will find within the Matrix of Consciousness can take you. You might be wondering, *How do I get ready to actually undertake this inner journey?* It's a good question. Let's take a look.

8

...

# Preparing for Your Journey

## Moving into Meditation

*Meditation is . . . a systematic technique for taking hold of and concentrating to the utmost degree our latent mental power . . . so that we can set forth from the surface level of consciousness and journey into the very depths.*

 EKNATH EASWARAN

**MOST PEOPLE'S MINDS ARE** usually filled to the brim with talking, thinking, or worrying, somewhat like an old storage room full of obsolete junk. Our ability to be aware of what's going on is reduced when our minds are too full, like a computer that has its memory so full of data and programs that it doesn't have enough working memory left over to function well. We need to learn to make our minds more spacious, so that we have enough attention available in this instant to notice and process what's occurring in and around us at any given moment.

As you master the abilities that the cells of the Matrix of Consciousness offer, you will learn to evaluate your thoughts, keep those that are helpful, and let go of those that are not. As you do, you will begin to create an inner sanctuary of quiet, peace, and joy.

To reiterate from the introduction to this book, it is useful to state here that the Matrix of Consciousness contains four basic types of meditation:

**Mindfulness meditation** is a form of attentiveness in which you learn to notice what your mind is doing at any given moment.

**Concentrative meditation** is a different form. While doing it, you learn to focus your attention where you want it. Mindfulness and concentration are two different ways of focusing your attention.

**Adventures in awareness** offer ways to take the capacities and qualities you're developing into your daily life.

**Contemplative meditation**, which includes visualization techniques, involves directing your attention toward a chosen subject of interest to you, in a manner that differs from ordinary thinking.

Mindfulness meditation includes letting yourself become aware of thoughts, feelings, and actions that you haven't been acknowledging. This includes noticing your real reactions instead of telling yourself that you think and feel something else. The ensuing clarity will reduce your tendency to act in self-defeating ways and will help keep your energy focused on what really matters.

Meditation teachers Sharon Salzberg and Joseph Goldstein point out that "mindfulness helps us to see nakedly and directly, being aware of what is going on as it actually arises—not being lost in our conclusions or judgments about it; our fantasies of what it means; our hopes; our fears; our aversions."[1] The next step in mindfulness is that when you do get lost in fantasies, fears, aversions, or other reactions (as of course sometimes you will), notice that you are doing that. Then you can focus on where you are tensing your muscles, the way you are breathing, the mental imagery you are creating, and the statements you are making to yourself. That makes it possible for you to start to let go, one by one, of unhelpful responses.

Concentrative meditation is addressed in detail in chapter 5, "Attention."

Adventures in awareness offer ways to bring the capacities and qualities you're developing in meditation into your daily life. Sometimes they are also a good starting point for relaxing from a stressful day, or giving yourself time to gently move into a more mellow space without taking the time to sit in meditation.

The contemplative meditations give you something different: In our ordinary thinking, many of the doors to little-known sides of ourselves are closed. We distract ourselves from painful memories, hold on tightly to entrenched opinions, or keep up a front that's different from who we are on the inside—or all of the above. These reactions cause unnecessary hardships for both others and ourselves. The process of contemplation helps us clearly see and hear things we haven't realized, or things that we've shut out of our consciousness. You will find meditative ways to address emotional hang-ups that cloud your mind, and also ways to cultivate a warm heart—to make your connections with family, friends, and strangers more enriching for both you and them.

## SETTING THE STAGE

We suggest a twenty-minute meditation every morning, but fifteen minutes will do. (You can set an alarm clock or timer so you don't have to think about the time.) If you would like to do one fifteen- or twenty-minute period in the morning and another late in the day, that's even better. If you want to sit a little longer, go ahead. You may find that your most valuable reflections come when you stop thinking about the clock. Don't try to meditate for hours, however, until you've developed a consistent practice. You might get lost in your mind. Seriously! Would you try to lift a two-hundred-pound weight before you've strengthened your muscles? As a rule, an unsupervised beginning meditator should not meditate for more than forty-five minutes.

By contrast, if you are facing such a busy day that you don't want to take more than five minutes for your meditation, then use that five minutes. Even that brief bit of time can help you feel better and can sustain your involvement and continuity. Five minutes is also good if you feel some resistance to trying meditation at all. If you are feeling hurried, sometimes you will probably tell yourself that it's enough, and other times you just might feel like sitting for a while longer. Five minutes is better than nothing at all, and most of us can spare at least that much time.

If it doesn't work for you to meditate in the morning, then do it when you can. Doing it at the same time each day, though not essential, helps you to develop the meditation habit. What's more important is to do it every day, or almost every day. "Meditation can be done any time, night or day," observes Swami Rama, "but traditionally the best times—when the environment is most conducive to meditation—are said to be early morning and late evening, when the world around you begins to quiet down and you are not likely to be interrupted. . . . However, your schedule and your personal responsibilities will also have a great impact on when you can meditate."[2]

If you prefer to sit on a chair, you will need an upright chair or stool that lets you sit up straight without leaning against its back. If you prefer to sit on the floor or the ground, you may find it helpful to sit on a carpet or a folded blanket or thick towel. And unless you are an experienced hatha yogi, you'll need a cushion—perhaps even doubled over for extra lift. Sitting on its forward edge will raise your buttocks a few inches off the floor. In this position, with your knees angled downward, you'll be able to sit up straight in comfort. Cushions designed especially for meditation are helpful. At some meditation centers you can buy a wide flat cushion called a *zabuton* made especially for this purpose, or you can buy them online. The same suppliers will usually also have a thicker, almost round cushion called a *zafu* that encourages an easy, straight posture while you're sitting on the floor. Also, a feather pillow folded in half will do—or even a folded jacket. If you are outdoors and the ground is clean and dry, a mild slope facing downhill will raise your buttocks enough to substitute for a cushion. You might even find a low rock that lets you sit with your back straight and either your feet flat on the ground or crossed, in a comfortable position.

Ideally, find a quiet place where you won't be disturbed. A tranquil outdoor setting, a room with the door closed, or even a closet will do. Turn the ringer on your telephone off and ask others not to interrupt you. (Not far into the Matrix you'll learn how to meditate amid a noisy, distracting environment when that's where you are, but in the beginning you want the best conditions possible.)

Several of the meditations explicitly say to use a candle to focus your attention. But if you don't have one, you can always substitute some other visual focus. Or you may, like some people, find it helpful to set a lighted candle in front of you regardless of what meditation you're doing.

After you have developed your ability to sit upright and meditate, you might sometimes allow yourself the little luxury of meditating while lying on your back. Or if you are not willing to sit up straight for even five minutes of meditation when you are starting out, or if you have a physical condition that makes it difficult or impossible, you can lie down on the floor, or even in the bathtub. One of our students regularly meditated lying down from day one and found it beneficial.

On the other hand, it's harder to maintain your alertness and to keep from becoming drowsy while lying down. In Zen and many yogic traditions, sitting in an erect posture with a straight spine, and your head pulled back slightly to open the breathing passage, is considered essential. The effort of maintaining that posture helps keep your attention focused. Also, points out Swami Rama, sitting with the spine correctly aligned "allows a certain type of subtle energy to move upward through the body."[3]

Some meditations described here explicitly ask you to do them with your eyes open or your eyes closed. Others leave you an option. "Eyes open" can mean wide open, or half-closed, with your gaze slightly downward just a few feet in front of you. Visualization is easiest with eyes closed.

While you are meditating, release expectations. Let go of your tendency to evaluate and judge. Don't label your meditation as successful or unsuccessful. Every session will be different. One session might reduce stress and distress and help you feel better. Another might cause you to feel like you've entered a realm of extraordinary grace and beauty. Yet another might be difficult. Whether your session on any given day feels great or not, accept it just as it is, like an athlete whose daily training is always a little different. Let go of the idea that you're supposed to achieve anything particular in each session, except for learning and experiencing the new practice.

If you expect miracles from meditation, you'll be disappointed. If you let go of expectations, you'll be rewarded.

As you sit in meditation, you'll notice unimportant random thoughts darting through your mind. Just let go of them as you bring your mind back to the focal point of the day's practice. But sometimes you'll get distracted by items that you don't want to forget as they bubble up into your conscious mind. These may be useful insights, or important tasks. You might want to keep a small pocket notebook and a pen next to you to briefly record these thoughts. Then you can continue with a clear mind instead of worrying about forgetting something.

Set your own pace. If you follow our suggestion of moving through four cells in the Matrix of Consciousness each week, this sixteen-week program will offer you four new elements for awareness each week. But if you want to stay with a given cell for several days or even more before going on, that's fine, too. If you want to accelerate your progress, you can go on to a new cell every day, or even go through two in one day. Do what feels comfortable for you, but if you try to do too much too quickly, your mind can become taxed and awareness can falter.

## FINDING WHAT
## WORKS BEST FOR YOU

The methods described here all share certain basic elements, but also have some differences, like an apple tree that has several varieties grafted onto it. It's all one tree, but you can choose a Red Delicious, a Fuji, a Pippin, or any of several other varieties. "Generally our practice should be whatever calms and relaxes us—whatever works best for the development of stillness and concentration," says Tibetan Buddhist teacher Tarthang Tulku

Rinpoche. "Meditation helps us to be calm and happy . . . to enjoy life, to be cheerful, and to deal effectively with both our physical and mental problems."[4]

Tarthang Tulku's principle applies to this chapter and to everything you have learned in previous chapters. The method that works best for you may not be best for another person. Someone asked Sri Ramana Maharshi, "Which method is the best?"

"That depends on the temperament of the individual," he replied. "One method will prove easy to one person and another to another. There can be no general rule."[5]

Swami Vivekananda adds, "As one practice cannot suit everyone, various methods will be advanced, and everyone by actual experience will find out that which suits him most."[6]

If a certain practice does not work well for you, then set it aside and select a different practice that does. You won't know how well a given method works for you until you've tried it. Once you've tried any given meditation, you'll have a sense of whether it's immediately helpful, whether you need to spend more time to master it, or whether you prefer a different approach.

People's minds work differently. For some, staying with just one method provides a discipline that helps them keep engaged. For others, a minor variation in method from one session to the next keeps them interested. Or one method may work best for you in a certain situation, and another in a different situation. For example, if you feel clear and relaxed when you start to meditate, the Frame by Frame method (cell 29) or the Total Attention method (cell 33) may be just right. But if your mind is spinning, you may need a more complex method like Double Counting (cell 13) or Harmonic Crossing (cell 45).

Whether you follow our suggested program systematically, or begin with the meditative form that attracts you the most, your meditation is likely to be most valuable if you explore its possibilities in depth. "Meditation yields its full significance after the person has gotten into it and not when he is trying to understand it by envisaging it from outside," says Meher Baba. "Be prepared to encounter unexpected states of consciousness; and be willing to go where that line of meditation leads without making any rigid demands based on preformed expectations."[7]

Trying to attain mental balance and peace of mind plays a big role in meditation. One of our students asked whether learning to meditate means that you always have to be calm and quiet. Not at all. Our approach doesn't ask you to lead your whole life with a calm, nonreactive state of detachment from events of the world. Rather, it's designed to help you take the abilities and perspectives that you develop in meditation back into your daily life. If you often feel inhibited and held in, meditation can help you let go of those inhibitions and become more willing to laugh, sing, and dance with life.

This chapter ends as it began, with an observation by Eknath Easwaran, a scholar, meditation teacher, and a disciple of Mahatma Gandhi. He writes: "'Can I meditate?' you may be saying. 'I'm not sure I can do this.' Everyone can do this. It is in our nature; it is what we were born for. By virtue of being human, all of us have the capacity to choose, to change, to grow."[8] Be patient with your progress. Personal growth, transformation, and transcendent states of consciousness aren't something you can make happen on demand. But learning the four forms of meditation taught here, and putting them into active use, is likely to help you live your life with greater wisdom and happiness. Are you ready?

## 9
### ...
# Dancing with Chance
## The Matrix as an Oracle

*If you do not expect the unexpected,*
*you will not find it.*

HERACLEITUS

IN THE MATRIX YOU'LL be able to connect events in your life with messages in the cells. Your first reading of each cell's meaning is only a beginning. In some cells, you will unearth amazing possibilities, since each one is a doorway into a different chamber of your inner consciousness. And each of these chambers is like a sanctuary with passageways that can take you in unexpected and unknown directions. The odds are pretty good that sometimes you will find yourself in satisfying relationships with the world and sometimes in aggravating ones, so messages in each cell can be interpreted in relation to both positive and negative life experiences.

Some cells in the Matrix are likely to offer new perspectives on a situation you've found puzzling. The unseen or improbable can become the possible as you respond with more flexibility, imagination, and creativity. We've seen people consult the Matrix, reflect on what they read, and then say, "I see my dilemma in a totally different way than I did before." A greater depth of understanding can make the difference between handling a problem or opportunity in a way that succeeds or a way that fails.

Once you are familiar with the Matrix of Consciousness, you can use it to invoke the forces of the subconscious. This is what we mean when we say that you can consult the Matrix as an oracle. We emphasize that we are not suggesting that you can use it to predict the future. The ancient Greek oracle at Delphi, high on a sunny mountainside, did not tell people what to do or predict what would happen. Rather, it offered cryptic comments that helped people think about what they had overlooked and see their situations from new angles. Use of the Matrix as an oracle is in that same tradition.

We offer two ways to consult the Matrix in this manner. One uses ordinary playing cards to guide you to a cell, and the other uses three coins, thrown three times in succession. These two methods are described in detail below. Holding in mind some question, problem, or situation that you would like guidance on, use one of the two methods for finding a cell and then turn to its description. Read the text and think about what insights the cell might hold for you in relation to your question. You can also do the meditation or adventure in awareness practice that you find in that cell.

## CONSULT THE ORACLE
## WITH A DECK OF CARDS

Any ordinary deck of cards will do. Shuffle, and without looking at the cards, cut and draw one. In the table below, find which cell to go to by reading across the top line of card suits to locate the suit of your chosen card; then go down the line to find the number of your card. Go to the indicated Matrix cell and proceed as described above.

### CARD ORACLE

| Card Drawn | Clubs | Diamonds | Spades | Hearts |
| --- | --- | --- | --- | --- |
| Ace | Cells 0 and 1 | Cell 2 | Cell 3 | Cell 4 |
| Two | Cell 5 | Cell 6 | Cell 7 | Cell 8 |
| Three | Cell 9 | Cell 10 | Cell 11 | Cell 12 |
| Four | Cell 13 | Cell 14 | Cell 15 | Cell 16 |
| Five | Cell 17 | Cell 18 | Cell 19 | Cell 20 |
| Six | Cell 21 | Cell 22 | Cell 23 | Cell 24 |
| Seven | Cell 25 | Cell 26 | Cell 27 | Cell 28 |
| Eight | Cell 29 | Cell 30 | Cell 31 | Cell 32 |
| Nine | Cell 33 | Cell 34 | Cell 35 | Cell 36 |
| Ten | Cell 37 | Cell 38 | Cell 39 | Cell 40 |
| Jack | Cell 41 | Cell 42 | Cell 43 | Cell 44 |
| Queen | Cell 45 | Cell 46 | Cell 47 | Cell 48 |
| King | Draw again | Draw again | Draw again | Draw again |

If a king is drawn, look at its suit, then draw one more card and note the suit of the second card. Then consult the table below to determine your designated cell.

| IF THE KING IS A | CLUB | DIAMOND | SPADE | HEART |
|---|---|---|---|---|
| AND THE SECOND CARD'S IS | | | | |
| Club | Cell 49 | Cell 50 | Cell 51 | Cell 52 |
| Diamond | Cell 53 | Cell 54 | Cell 55 | Cell 56 |
| Spade | Cell 57 | Cell 58 | Cell 59 | Cell 60 |
| Heart | Cell 61 | Cell 62 | Cell 63 | Cell 64 |

If you'd like a broader exploration of perspectives relevant to your question or situation, you can draw two or three cards and consult two or three cells rather than just one.

## CONSULT THE ORACLE
## WITH COINS

If you prefer an alternative to drawing cards, or don't have cards with you, you can use synchronicity to divine your appropriate cell by using the "coin oracle." To use this method you must have three coins that you throw as if they were dice. Record the results of your throw as OOO (heads, heads, heads), OOX (heads, heads, tails), OXX (heads, tails, tails) or XXX (tails, tails, tails). Then throw them again, once more recording your results. Finally, throw them a third time, and again record what comes up. For example, if your first throw is three heads, your second throw is three tails, and your third throw is two heads and a tail, you would record:

first throw: OOO
second throw: XXX
third throw: OOX

For this system to work, you must toss all three coins and record whether each coin comes up heads or tails three separate times. Once you have recorded the results of your coin toss, find the group of three throws in the table below that matches your results and it will direct you to a specific cell. If your first throw is OOO, you will find your cell in the first column. If your first throw is OOX, you will find it in the second column. If your first throw is OXX, scan down the third column. And if it's XXX, look in the fourth column.

Once you have pen and paper to record your coin values, think about your most important issue or question. Take a deep, relaxing breath, and toss your coins. Next, count the number of heads and tails from your first toss of three coins and go to the matching column of the chart. Then toss the coins twice more and match your results to one of the sixteen combinations shown in that column. In the chart, O means heads and X means tails.

## ORACLE WITH COINS

O indicates heads    X indicates tails

| | Column 1 | | Column 2 | | Column 3 | | Column 4 | |
|---|---|---|---|---|---|---|---|---|
| | 1st toss is 3 heads | | 1st toss is 2 heads, 1 tail | | 1st toss is 1 head, 2 tails | | 1st toss is 3 tails | |
| | The three throws | See cell | The three throws | See cell | The three throws | See cell | The three throws | See cell |
| 1st toss | OOO | 1 | OOX | 17 | OXX | 33 | XXX | 49 |
| 2nd toss | OOO | | OOO | | OOO | | OOO | |
| 3rd toss | OOO | | OOO | | OOO | | OOO | |
| 1st toss | OOO | 2 | OOX | 18 | OXX | 34 | XXX | 50 |
| 2nd toss | OOO | | OOO | | OOO | | OOO | |
| 3rd toss | OOX | | OOX | | OOX | | OOX | |
| 1st toss | OOO | 3 | OOX | 19 | OXX | 35 | XXX | 51 |
| 2nd toss | OOX | | OOO | | OOO | | OOO | |
| 3rd toss | OOX | | OOX | | OOX | | OOX | |
| 1st toss | OOO | 4 | OOX | 20 | OXX | 36 | XXX | 52 |
| 2nd toss | OOO | | OOO | | OOO | | OOO | |
| 3rd toss | XXX | | XXX | | XXX | | XXX | |
| 1st toss | OOO | 5 | OOX | 21 | OXX | 37 | XXX | 53 |
| 2nd toss | OOX | | OOX | | OOX | | OOX | |
| 3rd toss | OOO | | OOO | | OOO | | OOO | |

| | O indicates heads | | X indicates tails | |
|---|---|---|---|---|
| | **Column 1**<br>1st toss is 3 heads | **Column 2**<br>1st toss is 2 heads, 1 tail | **Column 3**<br>1st toss is 1 head, 2 tails | **Column 4**<br>1st toss is 3 tails |

| | The three throws | See cell | The three throws | See cell | The three throws | See cell | The three throws | See cell |
|---|---|---|---|---|---|---|---|---|
| 1st toss | ooo | 6 | oox | 22 | oxx | 38 | xxx | 54 |
| 2nd toss | oox | | oox | | oox | | oox | |
| 3rd toss | oox | | oox | | oox | | oox | |
| 1st toss | ooo | 7 | oox | 23 | oxx | 39 | xxx | 55 |
| 2nd toss | oox | | oox | | oox | | oox | |
| 3rd toss | oxx | | oxx | | oxx | | oxx | |
| 1st toss | ooo | 8 | oox | 24 | oxx | 40 | xxx | 56 |
| 2nd toss | oox | | oox | | oox | | oox | |
| 3rd toss | xxx | | xxx | | xxx | | xxx | |
| 1st toss | ooo | 9 | oox | 25 | oxx | 41 | xxx | 57 |
| 2nd toss | oxx | | oxx | | oxx | | oxx | |
| 3rd toss | ooo | | ooo | | ooo | | ooo | |
| 1st toss | ooo | 10 | oox | 26 | oxx | 42 | xxx | 58 |
| 2nd toss | oxx | | oxx | | oxx | | oxx | |
| 3rd toss | oox | | oox | | oox | | oox | |
| 1st toss | ooo | 11 | oox | 27 | oxx | 43 | xxx | 59 |
| 2nd toss | oxx | | oxx | | oxx | | oxx | |
| 3rd toss | oxx | | oxx | | oxx | | oxx | |
| 1st toss | ooo | 12 | oox | 28 | oxx | 44 | xxx | 60 |
| 2nd toss | oxx | | oxx | | oxx | | oxx | |
| 3rd toss | xxx | | xxx | | xxx | | xxx | |
| 1st toss | ooo | 13 | oox | 29 | oxx | 45 | xxx | 61 |
| 2nd toss | xxx | | xxx | | xxx | | xxx | |
| 3rd toss | ooo | | ooo | | ooo | | ooo | |

| | 0 indicates heads | | X indicates tails | | | | |
|---|---|---|---|---|---|---|---|---|
| | Column 1 | | Column 2 | | Column 3 | | Column 4 | |
| | 1st toss is 3 heads | | 1st toss is 2 heads, 1 tail | | 1st toss is 1 head, 2 tails | | 1st toss is 3 tails | |
| | The three throws | See cell | The three throws | See cell | The three throws | See cell | The three throws | See cell |
| 1st toss | ooo | 14 | oox | 30 | oxx | 46 | xxx | 62 |
| 2nd toss | xxx | | xxx | | xxx | | xxx | |
| 3rd toss | oox | | oox | | oox | | oox | |
| 1st toss | ooo | 15 | oox | 31 | oxx | 47 | xxx | 63 |
| 2nd toss | xxx | | xxx | | xxx | | xxx | |
| 3rd toss | oxx | | oxx | | oxx | | oxx | |
| 1st toss | ooo | 16 | oxx | 32 | oxx | 48 | xxx | 64 |
| 2nd toss | xxx | | xxx | | xxx | | xxx | |
| 3rd toss | xxx | | xxx | | xxx | | xxx | |

For example, suppose you throw two heads and a tail on the first toss. That tells you to look in the second column, which has (OOX) in the first line all the way from top to bottom. Then on the second toss, you throw one head and two tails. That tells you to skim down until you find (OXX). There are four of them in that column, which go with cells 25 to 28. Finally, on the third toss you throw three tails. Looking only in cells 25 to 28, you find that only cell 28 has three tails. So your three tosses have told you to go to cell 28 and read and/or do what you find there.

If you've used the I Ching, you'll see that the system here resembles the three-coin method used in that ancient text. It's simpler, since you throw the coins just three times instead of six, and there are no lines that move or do not move, as in the I Ching.

Before we go on to the Matrix, here are a few useful words about how it's organized.

# 10

# Four Columns

## Four Qualities

*Man need only divert his attention from searching for the
solution to external questions and pose the one, true inner
question of how he should lead his life, and all the external
questions will be resolved in the best possible way.*

LEO TOLSTOY

**THE MATRIX CONSISTS OF** sixty-four cells presented in sixteen horizontal rows,
plus cell zero, which sits independently at the top. Each row contains four cells,
and each cell title represents a universal attribute of consciousness. When you
look at the grid of the Matrix, you see four vertical columns. Each of these represents
one of four qualities of being: mind, body, emotion, and action.

The first column, representing the mind, contains cells with meditations
corresponding to direct awareness and the realm of ideas. The second, or body,
column features cells highlighting techniques that can increase physical awareness.
The third column is connected with emotional states. And the cells in
the fourth column are linked with action. They feature practices that spotlight
active movements and overt behavior. In the last few horizontal rows, some of
the meditation and awareness practices blend two or more of the four qualities.
Intuition and spirit embody the qualities represented by all four of these
columns, much like an alchemical mixture.

Most often, as you traverse the Matrix, you will find that one of the
four dimensions of mind, body, emotion, and action will dominate your
meditative or awareness process. Each can help you expand your consciousness
beyond the boundaries of conceptual intellect alone. In that regard,
the techniques ultimately merge to become stepping-stones to deeper levels
of awareness. They can help you contact and understand your inner spirit,

the soul beneath your perceiving, thinking, sensing, feeling, and doing.
    The qualities represented by each column can be summarized as follows:

**Mind**
Element: Air
Medium: Breath
Activity: Thinking and direct awareness
Purpose: Circulation of ideas and personal evolution
Power: Wisdom
Yoga: Raja yoga

Mental energy helps us comprehend our way of experiencing reality. On an intellectual level, we can reason, discriminate, and understand. While meditating, as we focus on relaxing our breath the mind becomes calm, which enables us to see more deeply into ourselves.

**Body**
Element: Earth
Medium: Physical self
Activity: Maintaining vitality and connecting
Purpose: Security, vitality, and adventure
Power: Moving and touching
Yoga: Hatha yoga

Our body is our vehicle for sustaining life, and our vessel for feeling physical pain or pleasure. Even though we don't have ultimate control over the character of our physique, we each possess a body that we show the outside world and an inner body that we alone can sense. Someone can look good on the outside, but be unhealthy on the inside. How we treat our body can improve or diminish the life force that flows through us, just as our habits of eating and drinking affect the way we feel. When we meet our body from a meditative perspective, we learn more about its subtle nuances and can befriend it with greater knowledge and awareness.

**Emotion**
Element: Water
Medium: Feelings
Activity: Mobilizing passion and opening the heart

Purpose: Love and happiness, self-protection
Power: Attraction and repulsion
Yoga: Bhakti yoga

The emotional spectrum flows from high to low, happy to sad. Emotions are a source of our aliveness, pleasure, passion, anger, and pain. Emotionally based desire or aversion motivates us to move toward our goals or escape from our struggles. To protect our emotional vulnerability we put on an energetic shield of invisible armor. It's a large part of our inner defense mechanism that wards off painful emotions such as grief, fear, or whatever else we don't want to feel. But when love is our foundation and we give our heart a happy voice, our personal world and our relationships can feel safe and joyful. Our emotions help us connect with others and enjoy our world.

**Action**
Element: Fire
Medium: Will
Activity: Doing
Purpose: Experience, exploration
Power: Creating, accomplishment
Yoga: Karma yoga

Action occurs when you affect reality through your will to do what needs to be done. It is an integral part of life that teaches us how we want to be, what we want to do, and where we want to go. People are defined by their activities. When you tap into your will to turn the revolving wheel of life, you are taking action that can take you on the road to accomplishing your dreams. When you experiment with new activities or ways of behaving, you extend your relations with the world. Conversely, stagnation occurs if you become sluggish. Some activities hold soul-deepening value, and others don't. But when you slow your actions consciously and look meditatively at choices, you give yourself a key to finding and accelerating your movement toward your goals.

Body, mind, spirit, and emotion are all interdependent and intertwined in our actions and reactions. All contribute to how we define our reality. To be alive is to draw fully on all these qualities.

Now, the Matrix.

PART TWO

CELLS
OF THE
MATRIX

# Breath

## From Here to Infinity

·····································

*When the breath is slow and silent, the mind*
*becomes more balanced and quiet.*

SWAMI DEVANAND SARASWATI

**YOU CAN AFFECT THE** way you feel by becoming conscious of your breathing.

Gurus and psychologists alike have noted the key role of breathing in our psychological lives. Russian mystic G. I. Gurdjieff said, quite simply, "Breath is life." Think of those times when you've been anxious, angry, or upset in any other way. If you do no more than focus your attention on your breathing, and feel and follow it, you may find yourself becoming less disturbed.

In some cells in the Matrix, you will encounter specific breathing methods to use while sitting, walking, or running. Not only will you find them useful in meditation, you'll also find some of them useful in your everyday life.

## PAYING ATTENTION TO YOUR BREATH

The practice that goes with Matrix cell 0, and which underlies almost everything that follows, is simplicity itself. As the ancient Chinese sage Lao-tzu said, "A journey of a thousand leagues begins with where your feet stand."[1] At this point, taking that first step—becoming aware of your breathing—is all you need to do.

### The Essence
·············
Wherever and however you are sitting or reclining right now, notice yourself breathe. Don't try to change anything. Breathe in, breathe out. During every

moment of your life, this ebb and flow is part of your being. Feel the physical sensation of air coming in through your nose and flowing down into your lungs, then sense it flowing out again.

What does air feel like? Does it have a taste? How long do you inhale before you start to exhale? Can you feel it pass through your nose, your lips, your teeth? Let your mind unite with this rhythmic cycle. Take note of whatever you are naturally doing as you breathe. Notice whether you sometimes hold your breath. If your breaths are sudden and jerky, or shallow and irregular, notice that pattern. Do you pause for a second or two between your inhalation and exhalation? Take a few minutes now to do nothing but become conscious of your breathing.

Discovery is a central element of meditation. You might discover something you do unconsciously, or perceive more clearly something you already know you do. Since your behavior at a given instant often is a snapshot of what you routinely do, meditation helps you observe your own behavior with a penetrating gaze. Once you have a clear sense of what you are doing, you can choose to keep your present patterns and behaviors, or you can change. So this simple practice of discovering exactly how you are breathing provides a model for sharpening your awareness of other things you do as well.

Now that you have become aware of your breathing, continue focusing your attention on your breath. Perhaps your breathing feels perfect just as it is. If so, great. If not, how might you change it? Perhaps you'd like to breathe more deeply, or slow your breathing, or make some other alteration. Go ahead. Don't force anything—let your breathing move in an easy, natural way.

You can let your awareness of your breathing carry you into deep relaxation. At this timeless moment, there is nowhere to go, nothing to do. Release all the business and busyness of your day. If your eyes have been open, close them and float into your inner sanctuary, where you have no worries or concerns. All you need to do right now is sustain your awareness of breathing in, and breathing out.

When you are ready, open your eyes and emerge from your inner sanctuary. That personal quiet space will usually be available to you when you want to go there. You can experiment with returning to it in various environments.

## Feeling Comfortable

Take care of yourself and your special needs. If you have a respiratory ailment like a cold, asthma, or a bronchial infection, take a few extra moments to make sure you are comfortable in your body before working with your breath. If you prefer not to engage in this breathing awareness process for any reason, return to it only when you feel ready.

## Points in the Process

Performing each meditative technique found in the Matrix of Consciousness in a rhythm connected with your breathing provides a focus that helps keep you present in your practice. As you do this, you might remember writer and poet Daniel Odier's comment about breathing and meditation: "All we do is make ourselves concentrate on the breath in the center of the heart. . . . When you inhale, the whole universe inhales with you. When you exhale, the whole universe exhales with you."[2]

·········

# Balance

## The Balance Point

..................................

**FINDING YOUR CENTER**

*When material, psychological, and spiritual dimensions are
brought into balance, life becomes whole, and this union
brings feelings of comfort and security.*

DEEPAK CHOPRA

MOVING INTO PHYSICAL BALANCE can also help you find your mental
balance.

When you feel overly stressed or pushed out of shape, you may feel unbalanced, off-center. By contrast, when you feel balanced and centered, you are
likely to respond with better judgment and more resilience. There's nothing
complicated in this idea.

There is also balance within the moment, and within a given circumstance.
When you take time to center yourself before you go into a situation or respond
to someone's comment, you will usually be more in touch with your self-
confidence, the other person, and your task. By finding your inner balance,
you'll speak and act from a stronger, more resourceful place within yourself.

Conversely, if you are not balanced, life can be hectic. The comment
"She's a bit unbalanced" is slang for "She's crazy." Instead of thinking that
not being balanced is some kind of inherent state, it can be looked at as a
characteristic that can be changed. The discipline of meditation can help a
person move from reacting wildly, to being able to quickly shift, to becoming more centered and focused.

It is difficult to develop balance through your mind alone, because inner
equilibrium is directly rooted in your body-mind connection. Practices such
as hatha yoga and Sufi dancing can be practiced to strengthen one's physical

and mental balance. All martial arts require a well-developed sense of balance; without it, you cannot move effectively in response to your opponent's moves. Actually, the same principle is true on a psychological level. Without inner balance, you cannot respond flexibly to the unpredictability of life, and it then becomes easier to let yourself be the victim of every mean-tempered person or emotional bully who irritates you.

Yogis, swamis, Sufis, and Zen masters throughout the ages have noted the importance of inner balance. Maharishi Mahesh Yogi says, "Balance is the natural state of life, because the basic characteristic of the fundamental element of life, pure consciousness, is complete balance."

Being sensitive to balance can bring a pleasing quality into every area of your life. There can be balance between work and play, between the elements in your home or garden, and in the energies of giving and taking by partners in a relationship.

But don't get too serious and about finding balance, because you can't be balanced if you are too grave—that's very one-sided. Instead, develop light-heartedness and an ability to laugh—and perhaps remind yourself to have fun when you get very, very serious. If you can find your center during difficult times, the scales of balance will tip in your favor. The apparently simple pairing of breathing and movement described below deals with balance in each moment.

## CENTERING WITH GRAVITY

Begin by sitting on a hard or fairly hard seat. Or sit on the floor in a cross-legged, half-lotus, or full-lotus yoga position. If you wish, you can sit on the edge of a raised cushion or a folded pillow to help you keep your spine upright. Or you can sit cross-legged on the floor without a cushion, with your back supported by a wall. Choose a position that is comfortable, one that you can maintain for some time. Swami Vivekananda comments, "the one thing necessary for the posture is to hold the spinal column free, sitting erect, holding . . . the chest, neck, and head in a straight line. Let the whole weight of these three be supported by the ribs, and then you will have an easy, natural posture with the spine straight."[1]

Once you are comfortable, proceed as follows:

### The Essence
After you have arranged your sitting position, abandon it temporarily. Stand up with your feet facing straight forward, about shoulder width apart, and

Half lotus pose                    Full lotus pose

your knees flexed slightly. Close your eyes. (If you feel like you might fall over, do this with your eyes open.)

In your mind's eye visualize yourself suspended from a golden cord that's anchored far out in space. Imagine that your upper body is a pendulum swinging clockwise in a circle. Move your body from your knees upward in as large a circle as best you can manage and still keep your balance. As you do this, synchronize your breathing with your movement, so that you inhale during the back half of the circle and exhale during the front half. This is essential.

Once you are comfortably moving and breathing in a synchronized way, let the circle of your movement gradually get smaller and smaller, as if your body is losing momentum just like a real pendulum. But keep the length of your breathing cycle about the same, still inhaling during the back half of your circle and exhaling during the front half. As a result, your circular movement will slow down as your circle shrinks. Finally, envision gravity bringing your circular movement to a stop.

Now take your seat, on either your chair or the floor. If you are on a chair, sit up straight on the front part of the chair so that there is plenty of space between your back and the chair back. Your feet should be on the ground, about a shoulder's width apart, toes facing forward.

Next, close your eyes again and imagine yourself as a pendulum. Move in a circle as you did before, now moving only from your waist upward. Again begin with a large circle and harmonize your breathing and movement so that you inhale during the back half of the circle and exhale during the front half. Once more, let the circle shrink until you reach a point where you feel perfectly centered in relation to gravity.

## Variations in Technique

From your seated position on a chair, check to make sure your body is completely centered. Do this by leaning forward slightly from your waist, keeping your upper body straight without bending. As soon as you feel off-center in relation to gravity, bring yourself back to your centered place. Breathe out as you lean forward and in as you come back to your center. Then lean backward slightly until you're out of alignment with gravity. Exhale as you lean back and inhale as you return to your centered point. Next lean slightly to your left, exhaling as you do, and then move back to your center as you inhale. Finally, in the same manner, move slightly to the right and then back to center.

Now stand up for a moment, move around a little, and shake yourself out. Sit down again and find your physically centered position using the brief method described just above.

## Feeling Comfortable

Many people feel most centered when sitting cross-legged on the floor or the earth. For others, however, this may be a difficult position. Don't hurt your knees or ankles by trying to do something that you can't do, or that isn't comfortable. The chair method works just fine. It was the preferred meditation posture in ancient Egypt. Even if you're sitting cross-legged, don't force your legs into a lotus posture if your feet and ankles say no.

## Points in the Process

As you continue to notice your breathing, let your physically centered position imprint itself in your somatic memory. Plant in your mind the suggestion that in the future, whenever you feel upset, distracted, or off-center, you can return to this physical position and let go of feeling pushed out of shape. Use the pendulum-swinging-in-a-circle method if you can. If not, use the short method described above. If for some reason you can't even do that, let your body memory of what the centered state feels like guide you.

For example, if you are in a crowd, and someone happens to bump you, you may momentarily become distressed or enraged. That may be a good time to move your focus of attention to your rhythmic cycle of breathing and find your physically centered state. Remind yourself to relax and to let your troubled feeling fade away.

# Relaxation

## Tension versus Relaxation

· · · · · · · · · · · · · · · · · · · · · · · · · · · · · · · ·

### RELAXING POINT BY POINT

*The time to relax is when you don't have time for it.*
SIDNEY J. HARRIS

TENSION AND RELAXATION IN your body can have far-reaching and profound effects on your state of mind and your physical health.

When a mother who is afraid of the water is at the beach with her hand on her daughter's arm, and a big wave breaks, the mother's hand may tighten in a viselike grip of fear. This sends the message *water is dangerous* to the little girl without a single word being uttered. When this has happened several times, the mother's fear may be permanently transmitted to her daughter in the form of a conditioned emotional response, with neither of them having any idea what happened, or how.

Our thoughts, feelings, sensations, and actions are threaded together by a neural network. Physical sensations or muscular activations (often invisible to outside observers) accompany almost every thought and emotion.

A method used in Gestalt therapy draws on such mind-body connections. It involves the therapist noticing an aspect of a client's gestures, movement, posture, or tone of voice, and then asking that person to exaggerate or intensify the action and describe any thoughts or feelings that arise. Awareness of these subtle nuances of action can lead to recognizing conflicts, issues, or inhibitions that have been overlooked or pushed out of consciousness. The meditative element you are about to learn does something similar. The difference is that in counseling, an outside observer brings one's external behavior to one's attention. By contrast, the following meditation makes it easier to notice your internal behavior.

It's only fair to recognize that despite the power of meditative relaxation, it has physical limits. Some kinds of chronic muscular contractions and some kinds of temporary conditions are beyond the reach of inner relaxation. That is why a variety of massage techniques exist. Indian classical artist and ayurvedic scholar Harish Johari suggested massaging the body daily for half an hour. "By rubbing the skin the body becomes heated, which in turn thins the blood and helps it circulate through the system."[1]

*Daily?* you might think. *In today's busy world? Forget it!*

How about weekly? Not like daily, but still effective. Monthly? You're not giving your body much. Never? If you are tense, or if your body protests with occurrences of illness or injuries, you would probably find great value in massage. "Massage is essential for people in all stages of life—infants, householders, elderly, handicapped, infirm, bodybuilders, [and] people unable to exercise," said Johari. He added that it is a must for people who have regular workout sessions or who practice martial arts. Is he overstating the case? Ask the trainer of any professional sports team.

Now here is something you can do for yourself:

## THE TENSION-RELAXATION BODY SCAN

In 1929, physician and psychologist Edmund Jacobson described a means of inducing deep relaxation that involves an internal body scan, in which you notice each point of tension in your body, intensify it for a few moments, and then release it.[2] He found that through this method, many people achieve a deeper state of muscular relaxation than normal.

Jacobson's method is a starting point for what you are about to do. Begin by taking no more than five minutes for tuning in to your breathing and going through the physical centering sequence, as you did in cells 0 and 1. Then continue as follows:

### The Essence

In your physically centered sitting position, focus your gaze slightly downward. Take one finger and push your chin toward the back of your body, to move your head directly above your shoulders. This opens your breathing passage fully.

Next, close your eyes and do a complete inward body scan. From the top of your head, slowly move your attention downward through your entire body. Wherever you notice any tension, pause. For instance, you might discover that your eyes are squinting and the band of muscles around your eyes is tense. Stop your body scan and ask yourself, *Is there anything that I'm squinting about?* Do any mental pictures or verbal thoughts come into your mind? Then squint more—intensify the sensation. See if the exaggeration of your tension brings up any associations or connections. If something important that requires reflection or action occurs to you, make a mental note of it (or jot it down if you have a notebook and pen available).

After noticing whether your tension is connected with any specific mental or emotional content, let go of that tension. Relax those muscles. Feel how good it is to release the tension you've been carrying in that spot.

Continue your body scan downward. Are you clenching your jaw? If so, again check for mental associations. Is there something you'd like to say that you've been biting back, some aspect of yourself that you are unnecessarily clamping down on, or some nagging tension that you're holding in your jaw, mouth, and teeth? Now exaggerate—tighten your jaw more—and see if any associations emerge. Then let go. Relax that spot completely before continuing to scan further downward.

The most common tight spots include the forehead, teeth and jaws, neck, shoulders, forearms, hands, stomach, sphincters, calves, and feet. In your remaining meditation time, be alert to any physical sensations in your body, including those connected with your breathing.

## Feeling Comfortable

Many people tense their shoulders when they sit straight. Notice that you can sit up, yet let that shoulder tension go.

If at any point your body protests that you've been sitting up straight for too long and it's painful, you can let yourself move into any comfortable position that alleviates the pain. As the days go by and you continue your sitting, your back muscles will grow stronger and you will find that you can sit comfortably for longer periods. Less obviously, your "mind muscles" will grow stronger, too.

## Points in the Process

The body scan described above will help you notice when your unconscious mind has been sending you important messages, using your muscles as the medium. Don't overlook them! They are part of the way your intuitive self communicates with your rational mind.

Sometimes tense muscles can tell you that you are holding on to something that you'd be better off letting go of. You may be preoccupied with a possession, a desire, a role, an attitude, another person, or even the past. Physical tension in relation to these thoughts may be a message to let go.

At other times there will be the general message that you are keeping your body chronically tight in ways that serve no useful end. When you find unnecessary tension in your body, remind yourself to release it. With practice, you can get better at sensing where and when you are holding tension, and at relaxing and releasing unwanted stress.

Since it is difficult to be uptight and meditate at the same time, meditation includes letting go of needless tension. Getting better at releasing tension can contribute to feeling better, a stronger immune system, higher energy, and overall better health.

## Variations in Technique

The next time you meditate you can do a body-tension scan without going through the whole progressive relaxation sequence described in this cell. Center yourself using the pendulum method described in cell 1, tune in to your breathing, and do a brief body-tension scan in which you relax all your muscles. We suggest taking six breaths for each of these three: centering, focusing on breathing, and tension scan. When finished, then go on to the meditation practice that you will use that day. From now on we will refer to those three items as the *starting sequence*. Eventually you will add two more items, but that's enough for now. At this point the starting sequence goes like this:

> ### The Starting Sequence, With Your Eyes Closed
> Six pendulum circles for centering
> Six breaths to sense your breathing
> Six breaths to scan for body tensions,
>     and letting them go

If you happen to do these three groups of breaths in a different order than listed here, it's not a problem. Any order will work.

Relaxing deeply from the inside is quite useful when you are getting an injection from a doctor or a dentist or undergoing any medical or dental procedure that may be uncomfortable. Whatever it is, it is likely to feel less uncomfortable if your muscles are very relaxed than if they are tense and tight (and therefore resistant to whatever procedure you are undergoing). Coupled with deep breathing, this kind of physical relaxation tends to be an excellent way to reduce or sometimes even eliminate pain.

# Inner Peace

## Stillness and Tranquillity

. . . . . . . . . . . . . . . . . . . . . . . . . . . . . .

### A CANDLE OR A FLOWER

*You get peace of mind not by thinking about it or imagining
it, but by quieting and relaxing the restless mind.*

REMEZ SASSOON

FOCUSING YOUR MIND ON a single object makes it easier to notice where
your attention travels to and what it does.

If you are like most people, you'd probably like to attain a state of inner
peace. Achieving that requires finding a way to let go of agitation. But
most people in our fast-paced world don't know how to do so. Exploding
in frustration at minor obstacles, losing it, and feeling like we can't get
worries out of our mind are widespread conditions. Moving from those
states toward greater inner peace becomes more likely when you have a
method to achieve it.

One such method to develop a clear, calm mind is with us not only
when we are meditating, but also as we meet people and go about our daily
lives. Clarity comes when we break through the limitations of the restless
mind into an expansive, more embracing mind. Then our mental process
flows in a harmonious rhythm and is more available to help us focus on
what is truly important.

A Zen koan is a special kind of riddle that also aims at achieving this
goal. It cannot be answered by ordinary reasoning. It has to be addressed
in a different way. We have to extend and deepen our capacity to be receptive and endeavor to widen our mind. And to do that, says Jakusho Kwong-
roshi, a Zen master and the abbot of Sonoma Mountain Zen Center, "we
have to be both present and empty. It's like this glass I'm holding. It must

be empty to receive the water."[1] For most of us, in our ordinary conscious-ness, our minds are filled with talking, thinking, or worrying, whether expressed out loud or silently. If our minds are like an old storage room full of obsolete junk, how can we have space for new possibilities? Our ability to be aware and awake in this moment is reduced when our minds are too full.

Although clearing out useless mental junk is an important element of peace of mind, it is not the only element. You can cultivate inner silence and still be far from peace of mind, because you may be full of reactive tensions that cause agitation. These can be as simple as unfinished tasks or conflicting demands that are tugging at you. Or they can be as complicated as going through a divorce, suffering the death of a loved one, or bearing the burden of deceit. All these can cut you off from part of yourself. When they do, you become less than you want to be. Your mind becomes more tangled, more wary, and less at peace.

By contrast, you can develop a mental discipline that lets you be open to the world with an attitude of inner peace. Also, your inner dialog plays a strong role in your ability to find inner calmness. If your mind is filled with anxiety, guilt, or other negative states, your reality is not going to be that of tranquility. To feel happy during a severe thunderstorm you have to be in a good state of mind. You can't control the thunderstorm, but you can affect the way you communicate with your own mind.

Interestingly enough, the commandment "Thou shalt not kill" appears in some form in every spiritual tradition. Kwong-roshi points out that besides its meaning of not killing others, it also means "Don't kill your own life force." This precept, he continues, is life giving: "It comes from that intrinsic part of yourself that longs to live in a full, deep, and mean-ingful way."[2] Whether we try to follow dissolving footsteps in the sand and go where our spirit leads, or take tangible steps in setting goals that give our life direction, our ability to find peace is dependent on our outlook.

A broad approach to finding peace of mind is to speak and act in ways that create life-giving circumstances that make inner calmness easier to attain. A narrower approach is to find a discipline that directly trains your mind to be more peaceful. Physical centering, sensing your breath, and let-ting go of body tensions that serve no useful purpose, all included in your starting sequence (found on page 70), can help you do that. Now we'll add another meditative element to those three items: focusing your mind on just one external object. This practice helps you to notice what your mind is doing in any given moment, and to recognize when your attention is centered in the present and when it is not.

# A CANDLE OR A FLOWER

A darkened room, if one is available to you, is an excellent location for this meditation practice. You will need a candle. Set it five to ten feet in front of you and light it. If you sit on a chair, put the candle on a table at about eye level. If you sit on the floor, put it on the floor. (In either case put something under the candle so it doesn't drip wax where you don't want it. That may seem too obvious for words, but you will want to eliminate the distraction of *Oh, my favorite rug/table!*)

If you don't have a darkened room and a candle, a single flower in a vase will do. Actually, anything that is visually distinct from its background will work. If you are outdoors, you might choose a tree branch or a distinctive rock. For convenience, we will assume that you've chosen a candle. If not, each time we use the word *candle,* mentally substitute whatever object you have chosen for this exercise.

## The Essence

Find your inward center, tune in to your breathing, and release useless tension. Then open your eyes and focus on the candle. Watch it intently. Imagine that after meditating you will have to draw a detailed picture of it, so inspect it carefully. At the same time, continue to remain aware of your breath.

Each time your mind drifts off to something other than the candle, gently pick up your attention, bring it back, and set it back down on the candle again. This may happen many times, or just a few. Don't try to push other thoughts out of your mind. When you notice that your attention is somewhere else, just bring it back to your focus of concentration. Continue watching the candle until the end of your meditation period.

After you have finished, stand up and give yourself the gift of two or three minutes of informal yoga. This refers to comfortable stretches in which you place your attention on harmonizing your breathing and your movements. (Let your body tell you how it wants to stretch and move.) Ideally, end every session with such a period of slow stretching.

## Variations in Technique

Some people find it useful to imagine that their thoughts, feelings, and sensations assume the form of white clouds floating through the mind. If this works for you, each time you notice one of those clouds, let it float away and return your attention to the candle or flower.

## Feeling Comfortable

Holding an erect posture takes effort. Your back might get tired. Your legs may hurt. As your mind drifts, your body may slump, so that you have to bring yourself back into the proper posture time and again. But this straight-spine position allows deep breathing and stimulates your nervous system to help you stay alert.

When you slump, notice how you feel. Hold the position as long as you like (even exaggerate it if you wish), continuing to note the sensations in your body. When and if you're ready, return to your centered posture. With regular practice, soon you'll probably find that you can easily sit in the upright position for the entire session.

## Points in the Process

Mastering the skill of actively noticing what your mind is doing rather than being totally caught up in it makes it easier to let go of worries, obsolete concerns, and miscellaneous random thoughts. It's the first stage in cultivation of that faculty that yogis call the Witness—the observer within who notices what you are doing, as you do it. Often, once you see what your mind is up to, you can choose to continue that or to do something else. Stated differently, your Witness consciousness is two-pointed attention. One point of your attention is doing whatever you are doing, and the second point is noticing that you are doing it. This second point of attention is capable of releasing heavy concerns and moving toward greater peace and inner freedom.

# Patience

## Impatience versus Presence

· · · · · · · · · · · · · · · · · · · · · · · · · · · · · · · · · · · · · · · · · ·

### MOVING MUDRAS

*Don't push the river—it flows by itself.*

FRITZ PERLS

FINDING THE MOST FITTING pace of action and nonaction helps you feel good, think clearly, and act effectively.

"Hurry sickness" has been called the psychological blight of our time. Often we try to do more than we can, or do it faster. "Now is not enough," becomes our attitude and "Let's move on" our watchwords. When this is chronic, life can start to seem hollow, because we are so busy thinking about what is next that we miss the magic of this moment.

Many observers have offered thoughts about patience:

**John Ciardi, American poet and translator:** "Patience is the art of caring slowly."

**Arnold H. Glasgow, American humorist:** "You get the chicken by hatching the egg, not by smashing it."

**Barbara Johnson, American literary critic and translator:** "Patience is the ability to idle your motor when you feel like stripping your gears."

**Rainer Maria Rilke, German poet:** "Be patient toward all that is unsolved in your heart and try to love the questions themselves."

Such observations have been made all around the world. A Chinese proverb says, "One moment of patience may ward off great disaster. One moment of impatience may ruin a whole life." The I Ching adds, "Whatever endures can be created only gradually, by long-continued work and careful reflection." A Dutch proverb quips, "An ounce of patience is worth a pound of brains." As those sayings suggest, impatience can cause bad judgment and big mistakes.

On the other hand, the advice to be patient can serve as a defense of injustice. In that case, patience is not a matter of waiting with the hope that conditions will someday improve, but rather of watching alertly for a good opening to act. A different but related kind of patience is involved when you keep going even though the going is slow. Being patient need not mean doing nothing: as Thomas Edison once remarked, "Everything comes to him who hustles while he waits."

Most especially, be patient with yourself. You make your life harder when you make the impossible demand that you should do or be more than you can at this moment. Likewise, you'll help others around you feel better (and often, act more effectively) when you let go of your impatience with them.

By sharpening your ability to notice what is occurring in and around you, meditation makes your world more interesting. That, in turn, makes it easier to be patient. It also increases your ability to hold back until the best moment for action has arrived. "Sleeping on it" before firing off an e-mail or making a big decision is typically a good idea. Similarly, in meetings, waiting for the optimal moment to give your input may be more effective than immediately jumping in.

If you are usually impatient to get on to what's next, or tend to shoot from the hip, cultivating patience can be of great value. On the other hand, if you tend to procrastinate and delay, then acting promptly may be more productive.

## THE MOVING MUDRA

A mudra is an Eastern term for a hand gesture that represents an idea or state of mind, or a specific position of your body. Perhaps you've seen a statue of the Buddha sitting cross-legged with his palms turned upward on his legs, and his index finger and thumb touching. This hand position, called the *jnana mudra,* symbolizes opening the heart to the wisdom of heaven. Another popular mudra is the *atmanjali,* or the prayer mudra, with the palms together and fingers pointed upward in the familiar gesture of prayer. It is used in many spiritual traditions to indicate communion with the divine. In India and Japan it is also used as a sign of respect or gratitude.

Today you will be practicing a mudra meditation that can help create a calm, clear mental state. As you focus on your hands, you'll be encouraged to move your fingers subtly in rhythm with your breathing to keep your mind from drifting.

In this meditative practice, begin with the starting sequence. That is, for six breaths each:

+ Check your physical posture and find your center.
+ Sense your breathing.
+ Scan for unnecessary body tension and let it go.

Also, even though it is not part of the starting sequence, for now include using a candle or a flower as a focus for your attention, as explained in cell 3.

Now we'll add one more element. *Good grief,* you may think. *Aren't I doing enough already?*

Probably not. If you are like most of us, you're still just beginning to learn to bring your attention under conscious control. Today's mudra practice makes another useful contribution toward that end.

## The Essence

Whether you are sitting on the floor or in a chair, place your hands against your waist, palms facing upward, then slowly slide them forward and stop at a point where they're resting on your legs. Now touch each of your thumbs to the tip of the first or middle finger of the same hand, forming a small circle. This is the jnana mudra shown on page 79.

With your hands resting comfortably on your legs, palms upward, return your attention to your breathing, letting the thumb and fingertip of each hand separate ever so slightly (about one-eighth of an inch) as you inhale, and touch together as you exhale. Separating, touching. Separating, touching.

Now watch the candle (or other focal object) and bring your attention back to it when you notice that your mind has wandered. As you do, continue to let your fingers separate slightly each time you inhale, and touch when you exhale. Feel your mudra's beneficial, calming effects.

## Feeling Comfortable

If the mudra described above doesn't seem to suit you, here are other options:

Jnana Mudra

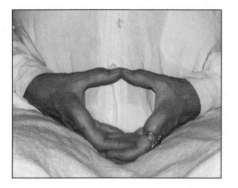

Zen Mudra

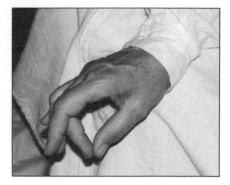

Invisible Mudra

***Zen Mudra.*** Look at your hands, palms toward you. Cover half of your
right hand with your left hand, so that your left fingertips end where
your right fingers emerge from your palm. Touch your thumbtips to
form a circle. Then rotate this hand position forward a quarter-turn and
hold it in front of your bellybutton or just below it, with your forearms
resting on your legs. Let the tips of your thumbs separate slightly (about
one eighth of an inch) as you inhale, and touch as you exhale. When you
notice that your thumbs are drooping and your mudra looks more like a
bean than a circle, you'll know that your attention has drifted off. (The
empty space within the circle formed by your fingers, palms, and thumbs
can remind you to keep some receptive emptiness in your mind.)

***Invisible Mudra.*** If you are meditating in a public place, you may want
to look inconspicuous. If so, you can form the jnana mudra described
above and then turn it upside down. Your wrists or the base of your
thumbs will be supported on your leg or the arms of a chair, with your

knuckles facing upward and your thumbs and fingers pointing downward, hidden from view. Let your thumbs and index fingers open and lightly touch, in rhythm with your breathing. Even in a crowded waiting room, no one will notice.

## Points in the Process

*Aha!* you may be thinking, *the plot grows clear. More of my mind has to pay attention to my meditative practice and less is available to go wandering here and there.*

Exactly. From now on, forming a mudra in which your fingers separate and touch in rhythm with your breathing will become step number four in your starting sequence. Unless stated otherwise, keep using one of the Moving Mudras until the end of your session.

In daily life, when you feel impatient, unless you truly have to finish what you are doing with the greatest possible speed, pause for just one minute and go into your mudra-and-breath combination with the intention of releasing some of your hurry and impatience with the breath. Let a focused presence in the now take its place. You can almost always spare that single minute.

## Variations in Technique

If you find the slight separation and touching of the thumbs and index fingers as you breathe to be distracting rather than helpful after you've tried it for a couple of weeks, then use a basic mudra instead. In this, you simply hold your hands motionless in your chosen mudra position.

·········
# Flexibility

## Rigidity versus Agility—Doubt versus Certainty

····································

### COUNTING BREATHS

*To be truly ignorant, be content with your own knowledge.*

CHUANG-TZU

## MENTAL FLEXIBILITY

SOME TIME AGO I (Victor) moved my things from the second drawer to the top drawer of our bathroom cabinet. I still sometimes open that second drawer to look for those items. Old habits die hard. Think about how much harder it is to challenge mental habits that don't give you a clear signal when you're on the wrong track!

The human mind tends to endlessly repeat the same patterns of thought, feeling, and action. As a result, it's easy to end up locked into the same old mental grooves for years or even decades, even when those grooves are just plain wrong or destructive. By contrast, in the film *The Bridge to Terabithia*, the character Ms. Edmonds made a conscious effort to avoid getting stuck in old grooves. She remarks, "I do try to keep an open mind and you'd be surprised what finds its way in there."

Flexibility and freedom are closely related. If you are so locked in to your ideas about something that you are unwilling to reconsider them, even when you come across new information, you're sure to make mistakes. This doesn't mean that you have to doubt yourself. Rather, you can be confident of your ability to use ideas constructively, and then think flexibly enough to choose the best course of action now.

Ralph Waldo Emerson recognized this. In his essay "Self-Reliance," he said, "A foolish consistency is the hobgoblin of little minds." Walt Whitman,

Emerson's contemporary, said, "Do I contradict myself? Very well, I contradict myself. I am large. I contain multitudes." Wilson Mizner, American playwright and raconteur, said, "I respect faith, but doubt is what gets you an education." Real science is based on doubt. A good scientist is always willing to question so-called certainties. For more than a thousand years in Western civilization, such an attitude was forbidden by most secular and religious authorities. As a result, creative thought and inquiry stagnated for a millennium.

Yogic and Buddhist philosophies hold that most of us are caught in the chains of *maya,* or illusion. The inner freedom of liberation or enlightenment includes casting off those chains. Long ago Buddha remarked,

> Don't believe in anything just because it's spoken and rumored by many. Don't believe in anything just because it's written in your religious books. Don't believe in anything merely on the authority of your teachers and elders. Don't believe in traditions just because they've been handed down for many generations. But after you've watched and analyzed, when you find that something agrees with reason and is conducive to the benefit of everyone, then accept it and live by it.[1]

In short, test every belief against your own direct experience when you can.

## INSISTING THAT YOU ARE RIGHT INHIBITS LEARNING

Most of us at least occasionally tie our self-esteem to being right. We don't like to be contradicted. Ironically, most of us also think of ourselves as being open-minded. The problem is that if I always think I'm right, and discourage others from disagreeing with me, I'm sure to end up right about less and wrong about more. The attitude that I am right and you are wrong stops us from finding out whether what we think we know is really so.

Although it is easy to assume that a concept captures the full truth of a situation, it never does. It's all too easy to get lost in the language. As semanticist Alfred Korzybski pointed out, "The map is not the territory, and the word is not the thing."[2] Actually, words and concepts are never more than abstract representations of the truth of life's underlying realities. They're like the Zen expression "A finger pointing at the moon is not the moon." We need to remember that any word or concept is, like the pointing finger, not the thing it is describing.

Language is a train of metaphors. Your moment-by-moment awareness is your most direct contact with what's happening inside you and outside you—with what exists, how it exists, and when and where it exists. French phenomenologist Maurice Merleau-Ponty called it your "first opening" on the world, before your ideas have a chance to intervene.[3] This state is also known as "beginner's mind" in Zen.

Meditation helps us break out of our old ruts and discover that first opening through which we can touch reality directly, at least for a fleeting moment. It helps give us at least a glimpse of what's really going on before we can distort it with our thoughts. "The essence of life is its fluidity, its ability to change, to turn and take a new course," said Laura Archera Huxley, philosopher Aldous Huxley's wife and a musician, self-help author, and psychological counselor.[4]

The word *knowledge* is sometimes a misnomer. Knowledge may be right or wrong. Each of us has some correct and some incorrect ideas, facts and bogus facts stored in our minds, usually with the assumption that they're all correct. As a result, it's easy to end up stuffing new information into erroneous old beliefs, attitudes, and metaphors, as Jesus recognized when he advised against putting "new wine into old wineskins."[5]

It's a major step forward in consciousness to become truly open to new possibilities, rather than cavalierly disregarding them if they don't fit into the framework of our old assumptions. It's also a step forward to realize how easy it is to think that we know what another person means when we don't. People often get into arguments about abstract principles without realizing that they're talking about different concrete realities. The line, "Of course I may be mistaken . . ." can be extremely useful. Others will usually respect you more when you are open-minded rather than when you try to look important by insisting that you are right.

## COUNTING BREATHS

This concentrative meditation helps you discipline your attention and perceive when you are hanging on to beliefs that may or may not be correct. When you meditate, you learn to notice in real time how you color what you are sensing, seeing, hearing, thinking, and feeling. Each new breath can include the thoughts: *I don't have to hang on to what I thought before. As I breathe out, I can let go of my potentially mistaken "certainties." Then I can discover what the next breath brings.* With this attitude, even when you shut the door on a new realization that threatens limited or mistaken old concepts, you can watch yourself do so as you do it.

Now place a candle or other focal object a few feet in front of you. Sit up straight on your chair, or cross-legged on a cushion on the floor. Go through your starting sequence: find your center; focus on your breathing; release body tension; and form your Moving Mudra. Continue with the Moving Mudra until the end of your session.

## The Essence

Following your breathing, silently begin counting your breaths on each inhalation, beginning with *one,* leaving your exhalation empty to notice what's going on inside you and around you. Count your breaths in this way up to ten.

Now take one full inhalation and exhalation, in which you do no more than notice whatever you are aware of. After that "empty" breath, begin counting breaths again, starting at one and going up to ten, just as before. Whenever you lose count and drift off, return to the last number you can recall and go on from there. If you lose track of where you drifted into reverie, start over again. Continue counting your breaths in this manner until the end of your meditation session.

Perhaps you will be able to count up to ten for ten rounds, which adds up to 110 breaths (and probably a few more where you lost count). How many breaths can you count?

When you have finished, you are likely to find your mind clearer and more focused than usual, and your contemplative thought process more open, efficient, and creative.

## Feeling Comfortable

Perhaps you are not so fond of this Counting Breaths meditation. If so, no matter—later we will describe other meditation styles for you to use, and you can apply much of what you are learning here to those styles, minus the counting.

When you are done, if you're sitting cross-legged and your feet or ankles are numb, massage them for a minute or two before getting up. (If you try to get up while they have no feeling, you could fall.)

## Points in the Process

When people first start to sit in meditation, it's common to feel bored, or uncomfortable in a psychological sense, entirely apart from any physical discomfort. This can go on for days, weeks, or even months. (Some people never experience this, some move through it quickly, and some require time to work through it.) You may feel driven by strong urges to get up, walk around, talk on the phone, or do anything except to keep sitting there.

What's going on? In everyday life, when your body complains, usually you move in a way that gives you relief. Likewise, when you feel anxious, usually you move your mind in ways to distract your attention and help you avoid the discomfort. But in meditation, your response to each urge to do anything other than to keep meditating is to continue to sit, feel whatever you feel, and notice what occurs in your consciousness.

This simple awareness without action or distraction will help you gain greater inner freedom. This practice can reduce restlessness, self-doubt, self-criticism, and self-defeating actions. Looking inward without judgment, sometimes even if only for a second or two, helps you avoid being driven by your own mentally and emotionally conditioned responses that fit your past but not your present. Then you can choose to think, act, and even feel in new ways that fit your life situation now—ways that are consistent with the more centered, thoughtful person you are becoming.

*In three words I can sum up everything I've learned*
*about life: it goes on.*

ROBERT FROST

**LIFE WELL LIVED CONSISTS** of alternating between moving in directions and pausing to reflect on what to do next.

Almost everyone, at one point or another, realizes that some habit or attitude won't work for him or her anymore. When the habit or attitude is an important part of your life or self-image, such a realization is an existential crisis. You discover that you just can't go on in the same way. It can be like a splash of cold water in your face that says *Wake up!* It can feel like psychological death—and in a way it is. It's the death of what was. It's time for something different.

Little in life goes on forever. Impermanence is a basic fact of our existence. Life is partly about continuing, and partly about endings and new beginnings. It's about letting go of what *was* without causing unnecessary pain to ourselves or others, while cocreating *what comes next* with the people and resources available to us.

As you well know, no one can undo and redo the past, however much we sometimes might like to. As the Persian poet and philosopher Omar Khayyám writes,

> *The Bird of Time has but a little way*
> *To flutter—and the Bird is on the Wing. . . .*
> *Whether the Cup with sweet or bitter run,*

*The Wine of Life keeps oozing drop by drop,*
*The Leaves of Life keep falling one by one. . . .*
*The Moving Finger writes; and, having writ,*
*Moves on: nor all your Piety nor Wit*
*Shall lure it back to cancel half a Line,*
*Nor all your Tears wash out a Word of it.*[1]

The sand in the bottom of an hourglass is the past, the sand in the top is the future, and the narrow point where the grains drop through is this very moment. Tomorrow soon turns into yesterday. Thinking about what you might have done differently has value only in helping you think deeply about your values and behavior, and in guiding you relative to what to do next.

Endings and beginnings include:

+ Coming to terms with the loss of relationships/situations we value
+ Releasing or letting go
+ Finding ways to cope with unpleasant or challenging realities
+ Relief at newfound freedom from troubles that have fallen away
+ Discovering and creating new opportunities

Life unfolds. As the wheel of fortune turns, sometimes it takes us into places and spaces in our psyche we never dreamed of. We can handle these transitions well or badly. Handling them badly is dramatized in countless songs, movies, and TV shows. Handling them well includes tilling the soil of your soul so that the seeds of what comes next will have fertile ground in which to sprout and grow. Being fully here in each new moment reveals possibilities that you are apt to miss when your mind is still caught in, or hanging on to, the past. But remembering what you have learned from your previous experience means that you might not have to learn those lessons again. The new beginnings thus open to you. Many may include possibilities you could not see before, and doors that you never knew existed, let alone knew how to open.

Nature's cycles mirror the cycles of change in our lives. Tides rise and fall. Sunset turns to night, and then dawn awakens. Buds become flowers, and then die. Green leaves turn red and gold or brown, then fall to earth. "There is something infinitely healing in the repeated refrains of nature," [2] writes American marine biologist and nature writer Rachel Carson. In this we can feel the power for renewal and rebirth that is latent in every one of us.

Even a meditation session has a beginning and an ending. Cell 2 dealt with the beginning, in the form of the starting sequence. This cell deals with the ending of a meditation session, as you bid your formal practice time good-bye—for now.

# THE YOGIC SEAL

This activity is a way to end your session, and to begin what comes next. It is also a reminder that every day has many small endings and beginnings. You bow in respect to everything around you that has shared your meditation time, and if you are meditating in a group, you bow to everyone. As well, you bow to what is ending in your life, in gratitude for whatever it held for you, and you bow to what is beginning, with whatever adventures it might hold.

## The Essence

Whether you are sitting cross-legged on the floor or sitting upright in a chair, put both arms behind your back and clasp your right wrist in your left hand. Then slowly and gently, beginning with your head and on down through your torso, bend forward and gradually unstack your vertebrae from the top downward until you have bent over as far as you comfortably can. Notice any points where you are holding tension in your back and see if you can release some of the tightness in each place, allowing you to bend a bit deeper. But don't *push* yourself further forward, because that might hurt your back.

If you do hatha yoga or are flexible, and you are sitting on the floor with your hands behind your back as described above, you may be able to touch your forehead to the ground. This yoga position, or *asana,* is called the Yogic Seal. If you are on a chair and your back is quite flexible, you may be able to touch your shoulders to your knees. We repeat: don't try to push yourself here—just release.

Then gradually straighten up, starting at the bottom of your spine, with your head and shoulders still bent over, stacking your vertebrae on top of one another, one by one, until your entire back is straight, and then straighten up your head.

(If you prefer, you can use any other kind of bow you wish, such as holding your palms together in atmanjali, the prayer mudra, described in cell 4.)

## Variations in Technique

Once you are leaning as far forward as you wish to go, hold that position for several breaths. With the first breath, just focus on your body.

With the second, breathe out the past and breathe in the future. That is, in your mind's eye, release what was, and imagine a breeze blowing it away. Then breathe in your hopes and dreams for renewal and growth.

With the third breath, feel the emptiness of your exhalation turning into energy for rebirth, opening a channel to connect with what comes next. Then sit up. Once you are sitting, spread your arms upward and outward fully, with your palms facing forward and fingertips outstretched, as you deeply breathe in a reawakening to the spectrum of visible and unseen possibilities before you. If you wish, you can even stand up for that gesture of renewal—feet about twice your shoulder width apart, with your gaze tilted slightly upward, letting your whole body enjoy the stretch.

## Points in the Process

If you have read the text for each of the cells from 0 through 6, but haven't done all the activities, be patient with yourself. In the beginning, learning to sit silently in meditation can be challenging. Benefits come when you persevere. Doing no more than sharpening your ability to observe inwardly and outwardly, without feeling like you have to do anything more, is a valuable beginning.

# Contentment

## Dissatisfaction versus Enjoyment

· · · · · · · · · · · · · · · · · · · · · · · · · · · · · · · · · · ·

**JUST NOTICING**

*We are disturbed not by events themselves, but by the views that we take of them.*

EPICTETUS

**LETTING GO OF YOUR** conditions or requirements for certain outcomes can change dissatisfaction into contentment.

You probably know some chronic "dislikers"—people who tend to be cross and discontented regardless of what happens. And you may know others who usually manage to be in pleasant spirits even amid setbacks and troubles. According to Zen master Dōgen Zenji, on the last night of his life Buddha said, "Those who are content may sleep on the ground and still consider it comfortable; those who are not content would be dissatisfied even in heaven."[1]

Contentment is related to how you think and feel about what exists. What is, is. You may be able to change it or you may not. But you do have the ability to affect the way you think and feel about it.

A common way we make ourselves unhappy is by mentally insisting that a given event or moment in our life should be different than what it is. Since life is what it is, that's a guaranteed recipe for unhappiness. Russian mystical teacher G. I. Gurdjieff spoke of the "conditions" we set in order to allow ourselves to feel okay about our reality. Suppose you have a blind date. You set up some condition in your mind about what your partner for the evening is supposed to look like. When your date doesn't meet your expectation, no matter how interesting and kindhearted he or she may be, you consider the evening a loss. And doubtless you'll communicate it to the other person, whether overtly or covertly. So you both have a lousy evening when you could have enjoyed each other's company. Psychologist Albert Ellis gave this process the colorful name "musturbation." That is, you hold rigid ideas about how things "must be" in order to find them acceptable (even when it's impossible) and cause yourself needless grief when they're not that way.[2]

Letting go of such "musts" opens the door to a more fulfilling world. Holding on to them keeps you in a dark, gloomy little mental room in which each day you close the curtains to keep the sunshine out. So be attentive to noticing what you require in order to let yourself feel good (or at least okay) about your life and world.

This doesn't mean that you should blind or deafen yourself to harmful conditions that you can change. On the contrary, you want to look for whatever you can do to make life more pleasant and rewarding.

The Stoic philosophers of ancient Greece and Rome, including Epictetus, sought to give human beings a stable basis for ethics and inner peace in the face of a chaotic and sometimes hostile environment. Theirs was no self-indulgent philosophy. On the one hand, they maintained that we can learn to become indifferent to the vicissitudes of fate. On the other hand, we must hold ourselves and other people ethically responsible for every action. But in any case, the way you feel results in large part from the view you take.

## JUST NOTICING

This basic mindfulness meditation creates openings for constructive change. You can learn to be less disturbed by numerous events that bother you now. The best starting point is to notice your disturbed reaction as it occurs. Once you are fully aware of what you are doing, you are better able to choose whether to continue that reaction or to act differently.

If you are like most people, when you begin a meditation session, you're likely to be sensitive to events around you. (That's why you try to find a fairly quiet, secluded place to meditate.) Doors banging, voices in the next room, loud music playing, airplanes flying overhead, dogs barking, people walking in and out—all this and more can be bothersome. *Jerks!* you may find yourself thinking, as your body tenses up. *They're interrupting my meditation!* Actually, these "disturbances" offer you a chance to start letting go of irritation that is potentially under your control, both in meditation and in daily life. In some meditation centers there are even intentional "controlled disturbances" to help you focus. Gongs and chimes that occur unexpectedly at intermittent times are meant to slice into the moment and remind you to keep your attention in the present. You can use real-life "disturbing" events the same way.

## The Essence

Begin by placing a candle or other focal object in front of you. Go through your starting sequence of centering, breathing, releasing tension, and forming a Moving Mudra. Go on to counting your breaths (as you did in cell 5). Then add Just Noticing, as described next:

Be alert to any noisy or attention-grabbing events in the environment around you—events that until now would probably have disturbed your meditation. This time, when such an event occurs, mentally reframe it simply as, *That what's happening.*

Perhaps a car backfires nearby and you inwardly jump. Notice as it occurs: *Car backfires—Oh—I jump. That's what's happening.* Before long, everything that is going on becomes part of your meditation. Whatever happens is what's happening. Events occur and you notice them. *Oh yes, noisy! That's what's happening.* At this moment, that's what is. Let your Moving Mudra and your breath-counting remind you to notice what's going on both outside and inside you without getting caught up in it. Fingers separate and touch as you count to the rhythm of your breathing. Accept whatever events are going on around you as part of your meditative reality, as long as they don't endanger you or others. If you feel disturbed, then notice yourself feeling disturbed, and how—that's part of what's happening. Also notice anything you may be doing mentally or physically to perpetuate your disturbed feelings. Potentially disturbing events, including your own reactions, become part of the fabric of your meditation. *Ah, I'm noticing that and responding in this way.* This "just noticing" is the essence of mindfulness.

## Feeling Comfortable

When you find yourself unusually disturbed by some event in your environment, or by some thought or feeling that arises in you, shift your mind to noticing your somatic (body) reaction. Let go of any physical tensions in your body, just as you did in the starting sequence at the beginning of your session. Then continue to just notice.

## Points in the Process

At this point you are consciously developing two different forms of attentiveness: your concentration and your mindfulness. You have already begun to develop the two-pointed attention of actively witnessing what your mind is doing rather than getting totally caught up in it. Now you are also witnessing what's going on outside and around you as part of your meditation. If you're bothered by those events, witness feeling bothered, too. As you do, you're cultivating another new option for responding that you'll be able to use in daily life as well as in meditation. The Witness can reduce your stress and increase your composure and peace of mind. *Ah, so this is what's happening!*

## Variations in Technique

As you learn to meditate more deeply, you are likely to notice details of outer events that formerly eluded you, and also how the voices in your head affect your reality. You can carry this newfound attentiveness into daily life. For instance, you are tapping your fingers impatiently as you sit on a park bench waiting for a friend to arrive. Then you shift into your new attentiveness skills, notice exactly what you are telling yourself that feeds your irritation, and you pull your attention out of your mental-emotional whirlpool of irritation and bring it into perceiving your environment. You hear a pair of crows calling each other and then in the distance a pair of lovers laughing. (Those sounds were there the whole time.) You notice a shaft of sunlight through the trees, and in the course of a few minutes you see it move slightly as Earth turns on its axis. Suddenly a voice startles you. It's your friend coming along the path. You became so interested in your surroundings that you forgot you were waiting!

Another day you may be cooling your heels in a room, waiting for an interview that will determine whether you'll get a promotion. Your stomach feels like it's tied in a knot. With greater awareness in the moment, you can release at least some of your tension. Perhaps you'll become fascinated with the beauty of a painting hanging on the wall. When the door opens, you're composed and alert.

# Focus

## Zeroing In

**ONE MOVE AT A TIME**

*One who does too much often does too little.*

ITALIAN PROVERB

**A SIMPLE SHIFT IN** how you do what you do can pull you out of hurry and worry, and into calm appreciation of your moment-by-moment experience.

Multitasking is pervasive in today's life. You may be talking on the phone, taking notes, and scanning your e-mail, all at the same time. We tend to think that we can do all these things well at once. Recent research, however, has shown that when we add an extra task to what we're doing, our performance on all our tasks slows down. A well-documented example is that talking on a cell phone while driving leads to slower reaction time in emergencies. Multitasking can also lead to feeling hurried, harried, and harassed. Since trying to do several things at once makes it harder to do any of then well, you may fumble, curse, and feel the jitters as you try to do too much at once. Paying attention to more than one thing also makes it more likely that you'll forget where you put something, or forget to do something important. Paying full attention when you put an item in its place is one of the best ways of making sure that later you'll remember where you put it. This requires training your mind.

Sharpening your ability to focus your attention allows you to perform the same activities as before, but with clearer perception of the situation and your actions. With only that change, an activity can feel radically different.

Finally, knowing what you're doing with your attention helps you keep your conversations in focus. You notice when you start drifting away from what you needed to talk about, or when the other person starts (unconsciously or intentionally) to divert the conversation from what you want to deal with. Tracking where a conversation is going and being able to guide it where you wish is a valuable skill.

An ancient Chinese peasant embodied the kind of focus involved in total presence in the here and now so well that his story has been passed down through the centuries. In the Zen tradition, a master, or roshi, chooses a successor (or successors) by assessing who has the greatest realization of Zen consciousness. The time came when Hung Jen, the Fifth Chinese Buddha Ancestor, had grown old and needed to choose his successor. He presided over a monastery of several hundred monks in which the senior monk was brilliant and knew the scriptures deeply. Senior monk was sure he himself would be the next master. But there were two problems. He had a very big ego. Thus caught up in his self-importance, he saw others as being inferior to him and had not truly grasped the inner meaning of Zen. Meanwhile, in the kitchen, a firewood cutter and laborer named Hui-neng worked peeling potatoes and husking rice. Hung Jen noticed that Hui-neng was completely focused in each moment as he carried out his tasks, seldom hurrying and never worrying about whether he or others were better or worse. Each instant of his work was a moving meditation. When monks came to him with questions about the sutras (the Buddhist scriptures), Hui-neng grasped and explained the spirit of each passage perfectly, even though he couldn't read. *This is my true successor*, thought Hung Jen. But how to accomplish the succession?

Hung Jen announced a poetry contest in which anyone who aspired to succeed him could compose a verse. Senior monk penned a poem about polishing our "mind-mirror" so brightly that it perfectly reflects any image that falls on it, and posted it on the wall. Then Hui-neng composed his own verse, which said that there is no mirror for dust to collect on in the first place. He had someone write down his verse for him and anonymously posted it. Other monks crowded around and judged his verse superior. That night Hung Jen, the master, went to the rice-hulling shed where Hui-neng slept, gave him the patchwork robe and begging bowl that symbolized the transmission of authority from one master to the next, and told Hui-neng to leave and go into hiding until the time was right for him to take his place as the Sixth Chinese Buddha Ancestor.

Sure enough, senior monk flew into a rage when the transmission was announced. Mistaking the symbols for the truths they represented, he set off to find Hui-neng to take the robe and bowl from him, thinking that possessing them would make him Hung Jen's successor. After some months, however, senior monk realized his error, and Hui-neng returned to preside at the monastery.[1]

## ONE MOVE AT A TIME

More than thirty years ago, psychologist Lawrence LeShan pointed out in his classic *How to Meditate* that trying to attend to several matters at once can cause us to feel harried and harassed.[2] When you find yourself in such a state, the following everyday practice can alter your consciousness almost instantly. It might end up saving you much more time than the minute or two you take to do it. Just two or three minutes is enough to try this right now.

### The Essence

Starting from a sitting position, stand up at your normal pace, take an item from your purse or pocket or pick up some item lying nearby, do something with it (such as running a brush through your hair), and then sit back down.

Next, close your eyes and mentally review what you just did.

Then open your eyes and do exactly the same thing again (or reverse the sequence, if an item ended up somewhere other than where it began) with this difference: make just one movement at a time. For instance, lean forward with your torso. Move one leg into position to stand up, then the other leg, and then push yourself up. Next, move your arm sideways toward your pocket, then downward into your pocket, and so on, pausing for an instant between each distinct movement. You may be amazed at how many movements go into such a simple sequence of actions. You are also likely to feel more focused, centered, and present by the time you have finished making just one movement at a time.

### Variations in Technique

You can try Hui-neng's moving meditation yourself. Perhaps you are washing dishes. As you wash the first few, let your mind drift. Then pause, focus your full attention on each movement you make and each moment of perception (like light reflecting on the bubbles in the suds, and the sensations of your hands in the water), and stay in this state of mind as you wash the dishes that remain. Is your experience different? How well can you stay focused? In this cell and some others, you will find methods to calm your energy and focus your mind amid your daily activities.

## Points in the Process

Next time you feel frantic and scattered, remember the techniques you just tried. You can use them to calm your mind and body.

CELL 9
. . . . . . . . .

# Contact

## Connection and Withdrawal

. . . . . . . . . . . . . . . . . . . . . . . . . . . . . .

**SNAPSHOT BREATHS**

*"True Together" means that people live together
harmoniously in accord with their true natures, yet also
benefit from each other's self-realization.*

CONFUCIUS

**THE CHARACTER AND QUALITY** of the contact you make with others and with yourself affects your relationships, effectiveness, and state of mind.

Have you ever looked into a tide pool at the ocean's edge and seen the bright green tentacles of a sea anemone waving back and forth as it scans for any tiny morsel of food that floats by? If you reach down and touch one of those tentacles ever so lightly, they snap closed and the anemone suddenly looks like a spotted barnacle in order to avoid getting eaten by something bigger. The anemone has no problem with contact and withdrawal. It has a clear sense of when it wants to make contact and when it wants to withdraw.[1]

Human life is more complicated. Our environment is sometimes ambiguous. The effects of contact with others are sometimes unpredictable. As a result, we may stay closed in situations that offer something valuable, or remain open when it's dangerous to do so. Or we may get stuck partway open and partway closed, unsure about which contacts we want to make, and which we don't.

The character and quality of our contact can make the difference between a life that offers a succession of rich harvests and one that's a hard row to hoe. If many of your interactions early in life were painful, for example, you may have some important relearning to do. *How can I reach out in ways that others will appreciate?* you might wonder, and *How can I know with whom I want to interact and with whom I don't?* The answers to such questions may not come easily.

When reaching out leads to pain or punishment, you are likely to withdraw. That's healthy. It's a problem, however, when contact has consistently led to discomfort. Then, anxiously anticipating punishment, you may begin to contract your muscles against the impulse to reach out as soon as you feel it. As Freud's student and colleague Wilhelm Reich pointed out, inhibition gets etched into your body, locked into chronic muscular contractions.[2] Your natural ebb and flow of expansion and contraction is interrupted, preventing natural expressions of your aliveness.

But since many of life's encounters don't have that kind of history, you probably want to be able to reach out without letting your fear of contact inhibit you, or your desire for contact blind you. It's useful to sharpen your ability to form a relatively accurate first impression of others, but also to be willing to let go of that initial snap judgment if contradictory information comes along later.

Long ago Confucius saw that reciprocity is part and parcel of social life. That is, we tend to act toward others as others act toward us, or expect us to act. When I expect a friendly response, often you respond just as I thought you might. When I expect you to do me wrong, you are apt to sense that and be guarded toward me in return. If I'm antagonistic toward you, you'll probably act the same way toward me. Almost any attitude can be a self-fulfilling prophecy.

The meditation below can help you develop greater sensitivity and awareness of how you make contact. It can also make connecting with others a more vibrant and vivid experience. Being able to focus sharply and clearly on a simple sensory object is related to perceiving other people clearly.

## SNAPSHOT BREATH MEDITATION

When you take a photo, you probably frame your visual world a little differently than you usually do. You are less likely to look at everything at once, unless it's a broad landscape shot. Rather, you focus on just one item or one small part of your visual field for your photo. Such framing is a metaphor for what you will do now with your mind alone.

### The Essence
Keep your eyes open and begin your starting sequence: Centering, breathing, letting go of tension, Moving Mudra . . . Then, with your next cycle of

breath, find an object to focus your attention on. It doesn't have to be a good picture, but just a small, well-defined object. A splash of sunshine on a wall, a dirty spot on a rug, someone's shoe, the tip of a tree branch—almost anything will do. Look at this object for just one full inhalation and exhalation (as though you are looking through your camera's viewfinder and taking a snapshot).

With the next breath, move your attention to something different or let something else capture your visual focus. This might be as simple as looking at one leg of a chair during one breath and a different leg with the next one. With each cycle of breath, shift your attention to a different object. Count your breaths at the same time (even though that's not the main task here), up to the tenth breath. Then repeat the process for another ten breaths, and so on, for the rest of your session. Stay with this Snapshot Breath meditation for at least five minutes.

If the object you look at brings up a thought, witness the occurrence of the thought, then bring your attention back to the object. Notice how your attention can wander even in that brief period of just one breath.

## Variations in Technique

You can use this same method with your other senses. For example, close your eyes and with each breath notice a different sound. With one cycle of breath you might listen to birds chirping outside the window; with the next, the teapot whistling; with the next, someone's steps in the hall, with the next, the beating of your heart; with the next, one of the internal "ringing" tones inside your ears, and so on. Or you can pay attention to a different sensation in your body with each cycle of breath. You can even mix and match, noting whatever sight, sound, or kinesthetic sensation captures your attention in any given cycle of breath.

## Points in the Process

This useful technique for grabbing hold of your consciousness helps develop mind control, moment-by-moment awareness, and the ability to concentrate. It can be calming when you feel very distracted.

Once you have mastered this method, it's useful for starting your sessions. Ten such Snapshot Breaths are an excellent bridge from everyday consciousness into meditation, and then from meditation back into everyday consciousness. We suggest adding them to your starting sequence at the beginning, and also using ten Snapshot Breaths just before the Yogic Seal and informal yoga at the end (or whatever form of ending you prefer). So at this point here is the complete starting sequence:

> ## The Complete Starting Sequence
> Six pendulum circles for balance
>
> Six breaths to sense your breathing
>
> Six breaths to scan for body tensions
> and let them go
>
> Add the Moving Mudra to your
> breathing
>
> Ten Snapshot Breaths

## Feeling Comfortable

We enjoy using this method for an entire session when we are meditating in a natural setting, such as beside a creek or in a meadow or the woods. In such places, focusing on a different visual object or sound with each breath for the entire meditation can be fascinating. It's amazing how many plants, fish, insects, and other little creatures will show themselves after you have been very still and quiet for a time.

# Stress

## Holding Tight versus Letting Go

. . . . . . . . . . . . . . . . . . . . . . . . . . . . . . .

**EMERGENCY MEDITATION**

*Meditation teaches you how to manage stress;
reducing stress enhances your overall physical
health and emotional well-being.*

MARA CARRICO AND THE EDITORS
OF *YOGA JOURNAL*

HERE YOU WILL COMBINE elements from previous cells into a method you can use in daily life when you are at the point of "losing it."

Almost everyone occasionally feels so stressed out that he or she can hardly cope or function. By contrast, unstressing means restoring the mind, emotions, body, and spirit to harmony and wholeness.

Stress is part of life. Acute stress is a normal response to an emergency. Some of your stress reactions help you cope with danger, like the fight-or-flight response when a threat appears. All living organisms, from plants to people, have stress alarm systems that help them function. If things get dull, you may even actively seek out experiences that will cause some stress, like climbing a mountain or going to a scary movie. A hard-fought game of basketball or tennis can be both stressful and fun.

At the same time, chronic tension can point to ways your lifestyle is unbalanced or fragmented. If stress occurs too often and for too long, it can turn into chronic stress, or stress gone bad, in which you don't relax between stressful events. If part of your body is chronically tense, and it's not due to your work or posture, it may mean that you need to adjust habits or attitudes that cause unnecessary stress.[1]

Too much to do and not enough time to do it is a stressor that affects most of us at times. Heavy ongoing responsibility is another source of stress. Decision-making stress, the pressure of having to weigh many options and make a choice quickly, is yet another. Suppressing anger in response to extreme frustration or put downs can be as stressful as flying into a rage with veins popping out of your neck. Even your own behavior can be a stressor, such as when you act in ways in which you embarrass yourself. Stress responses such as chain-smoking, constant worrying, drowning your troubles in drink, or getting into frequent arguments, can make existing problems worse.

Discovering how you create unnecessary stress in your life can be a help in letting go of it. Often your total organism is wiser than your conscious mind, which can keep pushing you even when you need to take it easy. If you drive yourself so long and hard that you get sick, your body is telling you that you'd better put your Very Important Business on hold, and rest. In such a way, your body can be a helpful friend. It's always possible to learn to be more effective at sidestepping highly stressful situations, and at handling stressors that you can't or don't want to avoid.

Remember that stress is your reaction—what you do in response to the stressor. You can hear this in a teenager's comment about something that disturbs his father—"Hey, Dad, don't get all pushed out of shape about it!" The situation is what it is. To a large extent, Dad's reaction is his own doing.

We know now that a breakdown can become a breakthrough. Stress can illuminate a way to restructure unhealthy life patterns. Mind and body can work together to create exhaustion and illness, or good health and good spirits. That's a big part of what *psychosomatic* (the mind-body connection) means.

With the following practice you are likely to raise your awareness of where you hold tension in your body. Perhaps you will even become aware of the feelings that have become transformed into an emotional suit of armor that blocks responsiveness to either external or internal events. This "muscular armor," as renowned psychoanalyst Wilhelm Reich termed it, protects you to some degree against physical or emotional pain, but also reduces your capacity for pleasure.[2] If you don't learn to release your stress, it can get worse. You may feel anxious and depressed, or, as documented by scientific studies, you may develop such stress-related illnesses as hypertension or other physical disturbances.

## EMERGENCY MEDITATION

With just some of what you have already learned, you can handle many of those times when you feel on edge, when everything seems overwhelming and you just don't know how you can make it through. This basic Emergency Meditation takes about three minutes.

Doubtless you are familiar with the advice that when you are really angry and afraid you might do something you'll regret later, count to ten. You will do that here, but in a special way that draws on what you've been learning. You might try it now, in your present relatively relaxed state, as a rehearsal for when you truly need it. This is meant not just for when you are angry, but when you are extremely upset in any way. Use it for any situation gone awry, or any time you need quick relief.

## The Essence

Sit comfortably and close your eyes. As you inhale, count one, and notice everything that is going on in your mind and emotions. As you exhale, let the one—and everything else in your mind—fade away. Empty your mind as completely as you can. As your mind empties, notice any physical tension anywhere in your body and relax that part of your body as fully as you can.

On your next inhalation, count two, and again notice all that you are thinking and feeling. Your thoughts may consist of words, voices, mental pictures, or all of those. Let your breathing slow and deepen. Then as you exhale, once again let go of the number, emptying your mind and emotions as fully as you can. As you finish exhaling, scan your body for physical tension—perhaps you'll notice something you overlooked on your first breath—and let that tension go. Continue in the same manner. Count three on your third inhalation as you listen to your inner chatter and notice the pictures in your mind. Then let these words and images and your tension go as you exhale. Keep on in this manner. With each succeeding breath, let yourself become more relaxed, more deeply centered in your breathing, and more fully present in just this moment. Allow yourself the gift of completely releasing, at least for a moment, your overwhelming feelings of being worried or disturbed. At some point between your first breath and your tenth, you may discover that you have crossed a threshold into your inner sanctuary.

You can count to ten in this manner in a minute and a half or less. If you wish, you can repeat the process once more—but only once. Those three minutes should be enough for you to regain enough composure to cope with your situation and state of mind. The process itself is fairly straightforward; the trick is to remember that you have this resource available to you whenever you may need it—and to use it.

## Points in the Process

When you have finished your ten (or twenty) breaths, open your eyes and look around. If you are still in the situation that provoked your unsettling emotional response, you may want to give yourself a few minutes of time out from it if you can, until you have calmed down completely.

. . . . . . . . . .

# Visualization

## Mental Pictures, Symbols, and Metaphors

. . . . . . . . . . . . . . . . . . . . . . . . . . . . . . . .

### SYMBOLIC EQUIVALENTS

*Visualization adds a new dimension to our perception of the world and gives us a new perspective with which to view our ordinary reality.*

TARTHANG TULKU

VISUALIZATION HELPS US FORM ideas and perceive what is occurring in our inner world.

Some years ago I sat on a log meditating at dusk. For days I had struggled in vain to solve a particular problem. Suddenly, as I sat silently, not consciously thinking about it at all, I saw a mental picture of an answer—and a nanosecond later heard a sentence in my mind that described in words what I'd just "seen." Only because I was paying close attention to the events in my mind did I notice the translation of the picture into words.

Sometimes it happens the other way around: we hear a verbal description of something and then form a mental picture of it.

In the early days of Western psychology it was widely assumed that all thinking included mental pictures. Indeed, there was controversy about whether "imageless thought" could occur at all. Carl Jung, one of the field's great thinkers and also a prolific artist, was fascinated by the mind's ability to visualize. He studied mental images in great detail. His work with universal symbols and archetypes led to the realization that thoughts often take the form of "mental movies." When we take time to notice what we project on our inner movie screen, we can both watch our mental movies and see how we use and misuse our ability to visualize.

We misuse our ability to visualize by:

✦ Lumping together people, ideas, or things that are actually quite different
✦ Confusing mental pictures with the realities behind them
✦ Doubting or criticizing the power of our thoughts

We use it constructively by:

✦ Vividly picturing something we want to remember
✦ Creating "bridges of meaning" among events that appear different
✦ Bringing more poetic and creative dimensions into our lives
✦ Visually imagining outcomes we want, or images that help us feel good
✦ Healing emotional wounds with positive imagery

Both concentrative and mindfulness meditations can help you understand the functions of your visualizing mind, including dreams, symbols, and metaphors. This understanding emerges as you quiet the normal chatter in your mind, allowing you to better notice your mental imagery and compare it with the reality to which it refers. When you see yourself getting lost in one of your mental pictures, tell yourself *Stop!* Ground yourself with your starting sequence and then return to noticing what your mind is doing. Don't be surprised if you see the same old mental movies that you play over and over—but now with the ability to recognize them as such, instead of being completely caught up in them.

Understanding our symbols and metaphors can help us break old mental habits by allowing us to see through our old ideas, or see more deeply into their implications. Suddenly you may see the light and view an entire situation differently. The hidden structure of a condition or event may be revealed. You may perceive connections, similarities, and differences that you couldn't see before.

Perceiving your metaphors as such can do much to demystify and clarify your thinking. "When they're strung together, metaphors form stories, myths, and narratives," says Gestalt therapist Carl Hodges. "Every culture has such metaphors, which typically are in the background of our mind. We're influenced by them without realizing it. But you can bring them into the foreground of your awareness, and ask, 'Do I believe this metaphor, this myth? Do I want this story to be my story?'"[1]

Our personal mental pictures, metaphors, and myths imply something vague and partially unknown or hidden. They bring messages from the unconscious to the rational mind. These symbols are often keys to discovering feelings or preferences that we haven't yet acknowledged. They are a door to the personal unconscious, which by Jung's reckoning includes everything that you know but are not now thinking about, things that you once were conscious of but have forgotten, and things that your senses recognize but your conscious mind has not yet noticed. The personal unconscious also includes those things that you feel, think, remember, want, and do involuntarily and without noticing. Our personal unconscious can point to new realizations about what's valuable and meaningful to us.[2]

## SYMBOLIC EQUIVALENTS AND OTHER ACTIVE IMAGINATION METHODS

Jung's concept of "active imagination" consists of various methods for waking up your drowsy imagination in order to venture into less-explored reaches of your consciousness. In the following practice, you can experience one of these techniques.

### The Essence

Choose an image from a dream or a life situation that calls out to you. This may be an attractive image, an unsettling situation, an event that appears puzzling or inexplicable, an apparent dead end, an opportunity that beckons, or . . .

Sit or lie back comfortably and let your mind become like a blank movie screen. Visualize the image you have just chosen on that screen for thirty seconds or so, or longer if you wish, keeping an awareness of your cycle of breathing as you do. Then allow that image to fade away and allow another one that feels somehow related to it to appear on your inner screen. When you have a clear sense of that mental picture, again let it dissolve and let another appear. Here's the key: don't try to make any particular kind of image appear. Let whatever emerges from within you arise, however strange and unrelated to your first image or those that followed it may seem to be. The last thing you want here is to lock yourself into your expectations and preconceptions.

Your goal in this inner contemplation is to open yourself wide to unheard and unrecognized messages from parts of yourself that you may have been ignoring or minimizing. As you do this, notice any messages from your body—like interruptions of breathing, muscular tightening, or accelerations of heartbeat— that may alert you that something is especially important.

When the flow of images wanes after a few minutes, mentally review the parade of pictures that appeared in your mind and write down just one sentence that seems to hold the gist of what they are saying to you. Underline it. Then if you want to write more, go ahead.

Finally, sit up, find your center, sense your breathing, and begin your Moving Mudra. Take three quiet minutes (or longer if you wish) to become aware of any further messages that your mind, emotions, or body may send you.

## Points in the Process

In the latter part of the Matrix of Consciousness you will find a number of specific methods in which visualization plays a central role. Visualizing desired results, or visualizing images that help you feel good or heal emotional wounds, can be a wonderful use of your imagination. "Some look at things that are, and ask 'Why?' wrote George Bernard Shaw. "I dream things that never were, and I say, 'Why not?'"

. . . . . . . . . .

# Choice

## Pathways, Preferences, and Self-determination

. . . . . . . . . . . . . . . . . . . . . . . . . . . . . . . . . .

**NARRATING YOUR ACTIONS**

*Life is a permanent crossroads. It is not given us ready-made, but every one of us has to make it for himself. It is untransferable and each of us has to live our own.*

José Ortega y Gasset

EACH OF US IS thrown into a life situation by circumstances outside our control, but from there on we shape our destiny, observed existential philosopher José Ortega y Gasset.[1] Even when your options for action are limited, you can still choose how to think and feel. Your choices about what you say and do define you.

In a sense, in each moment, with each new choice, you are creating yourself anew. Once you recognize this, you free yourself from the assumption that you have to continue to be as you were yesterday. You can choose to act as you've done before, or inhibit old impulses and make different choices.

No one articulated this view more clearly than Jean-Paul Sartre:

> What is not possible is not to choose. If I do not choose, that is still a choice. . . . We each draw our own portrait, and there is nothing but that portrait. . . . A man is no other than a series of undertakings. . . . Nevertheless, when one says, "You are nothing else but what you live," it does not imply that an artist is to be judged solely by his works of art, for a thousand other things contribute no less to his definition as a man.[2]

Your destiny, Sartre is saying, is within you. This view does away with excuses, which limit us by causing us to disown our strengths and our potential. Even when you choose an advisor, you can probably guess something about what course of action he or she is likely to suggest.

José Ortega y Gasset relates choice to both thought and action. We act in the truest sense, he maintains, only when we also reflect on what we are doing. And our reflection has real value only when expressed in action. But our thought must be our own. Throughout history, many authorities and powers-that-be have wanted to stop us from thinking so that we would follow their agendas without questioning them. But through direct awareness of what is going on, and reflection on our potential choices, we can be true to our own intelligence and intuition.

Tibetan Buddhists have a method for putting this outlook into practice. On hearing you describe yourself in limiting terms, they suggest that you start your statement with the words, "Up until now." And so, "I always give in to what other people want me to do instead of listening to my own inner voice" becomes "Up until now I have always given in to . . ."[3]

Those three words can be profoundly liberating. Look deeply into the truth of each moment. In this very instant you can choose an action, a path, and a destiny of your own that uniquely fits you in the situation now. You don't have to be as you've always been before. This is especially important in families or other groups in which people are pigeonholed into old roles and expectations. Today and from now on, you can choose to think, feel, and act in ways that fit your present rather than your past.

This is more than just a strategy for coping with problems or hang-ups. You may be quite successful, but perhaps you've come to a place where you're no longer satisfied. You might find yourself saying, *Now what?* Remember those words, "Up until now, I . . ." Then you can ask yourself, *Do I want to keep on doing this, in this way?* New doors that you never noticed before may swing open.

There are always others ready to tell you what to do if you ask them. But you don't have to ask—or follow their suggestions—even if your usual habit is to look outside yourself for guidance. Many people don't realize that much of the time they look outside themselves for instructions on what to do. If you've been trained to do as others tell you, then in order to hear your own inner voice you'll have to retrain yourself to follow your own nature. After all, as actress Katherine Hepburn once noted, "If you always do what interests you, at least one person is pleased!"

# NARRATING YOUR ACTIONS

Describing what you are doing as you do it makes it easier to be fully conscious of your actions and fully present in choosing what to do next. This present-moment consciousness is implicit in a traditional Japanese tea ceremony. In Kyoto, Japan, we sat with several guests while a tea master arranged her utensils. She beat the thick green tea into powder with a special brush. With precise, patient movements, she lit a small stove, boiled the water, prepared the tea in a prescribed manner, and then at last set a small ceramic cup before each of us and poured the steaming tea. But none of that was the crucial element.

What made the event different from any we had ever experienced was the quality of total attention that the tea master devoted to each movement, action, and gesture. The preparation and service of the tea was like a perfectly choreographed dance in which the slightest moment of inattention would lead to a fall. The tea master's attentiveness had a riveting quality that drew everyone into silence and awe. The effect was such that once the tea was served, we raised our cups in both hands and drank it with the same quality of attention with which it had been prepared.

A method for learning to focus your attention in such a manner involves dividing your attention so that part of your mind notices and narrates what the rest of you is doing. Try this:

## The Essence

Choose a physical activity that involves moving and performing some action(s). As you carry it out, silently report your activity to yourself: *Now I am walking across the kitchen floor. Now I am reaching up and getting a glass from the shelf. I am placing it beneath the faucet. I am turning on the cold water tap . . .* Move and act in your usual way, but pay very close attention to each thing you are doing, and describe it.

Each time you notice that you are acting mindlessly—that is, you realize that your mind has drifted off and you are no longer narrating what it is you are doing—let go of those other thoughts. Return your attention to silently reporting your actions.

## Variations in Technique

If you're alone, or with someone who doesn't mind hearing your narration, you might say your "Now I am . . ." sentences out loud rather than silently.

## Points in the Process

In each instant, you are choosing what to do at that moment. With each thought you can choose to do something differently than you might ordinarily have done. Moment by moment, you are creating your reality and making a choice about which possibilities to express in your behavior.

Narrating in this way makes it easier to inhibit old patterns, because you realize what you are doing as you do it—or even as you begin to do it—rather than acting automatically. Then, with this clearer view of your actions and their probable results, you choose to act in ways that fit this unique situation now.

## CELL 13

· · · · · · · · · ·

# Faith

## From Despair to Hope

·························

**DOUBLE COUNTING**

*In the midst of winter, I found there was, within me,
an invincible summer.*

ALBERT CAMUS

HOPE AND FAITH ARE related yet different. You can cultivate both.

Emmanuel Yeboa combined hope with faith to overcome great difficulties. He was born with a shriveled, useless right leg, in a small town in Ghana, into a poverty-stricken family that lived in a dirt-floor hut without beds, water, or electricity. Early in his life, his father abandoned Yeboa's family.

In Ghana, many such people are put out in the streets with a bowl to beg. But Yeboa's mother had faith. She had enough faith in her crippled son to carry him two miles to school and back each day until he was old enough to hop there by himself on his good leg. At age thirteen he left for the capital city of Accra, where he worked shining shoes. Before his mother died at age thirty-seven, she said, "Don't let anyone put you down because of your disability."

To change perceptions of the physically challenged, in 2002 Yeboa got on a bicycle and rode it one-legged 373 miles across Ghana. With the fame he gained, he obtained support to fly to California, compete in the Challenged Athletes Foundation triathlon, and have his bad leg amputated and fitted with an artificial leg. After he returned to Ghana, he led a successful fight to pass a bill that offers the disabled free or reduced-rate transportation, accessibility to public places, and other benefits. Yeboa's faith helped him persevere when there seemed to be no hope at all.[1]

Both hope and faith are responses to life's uncertainty. Will we get

114

what we want? Will we find the strength to succeed in our journey? How will we respond when events don't go as we wish? The line between the two is soft and filmy rather than sharp and hard. Hope for a specific outcome can be woven into a broader tapestry of faith.

It seems like it would be wonderful if all our hopes could be fulfilled. But we live in real life, not fairy tales. In recognition that we're unlikely to have all our hopes satisfied, Epictetus reminded us to have various projects and interests, so we don't get hung up on just one. "A ship should not ride on a single anchor," he said, "nor life on a single hope."

Hope and faith go hand in hand with a spirit of adventure. Life is unpredictable. Outcomes are uncertain. Yet even when storms and heavy seas require us to take a wayward route, we can sail on.

Faith has several meanings. For some people it is almost synonymous with a specified religion, or strong belief in it. Here we emphasize a different usage, as in the dictionary definition: "belief in, devotion to, or trust in somebody or something." Faith can help you appreciate your strengths and guide you to realize your dreams. It's your "yes" to yourself and the world, in both easy and difficult times. Faith makes constructive use of energy that otherwise might fuel worries and anxieties. It includes a sense that we will usually find answers to our questions when we truly need them. In addition, adds religious scholar William Cantwell Smith, faith includes an ability to respond to a situation in a deeper manner than it seems to offer at first glance—"to see, to feel, to act in terms of a transcendent dimension."[2]

Like hope, faith is linked to effort. It's usually a mistake to think that things will turn your way without your doing anything about them. If you don't invest the effort needed to bring about the ends you seek, success is unlikely. As former president Jimmy Carter wisely said, "My faith demands that I do whatever I can, wherever I am, whenever I can, for as long as I can, with whatever I have to try to make a difference."

Hobart "Red" Thomas, an existential psychologist in the Rogerian tradition, has studied what he calls the *nadir experience.* It's those times when people feel like in some way they've hit rock bottom, and faith turns into doubt. Even though most of us want to avoid such experiences of despair and nay-saying, Thomas found that they can be a source of growth, renewal, and rebirth. Feeling cut off from our hope can provoke badly needed questioning of what we are doing and how we are doing it. By contrast, when all goes well, we're apt to stay stuck in familiar patterns that may not fit new circumstances. Our times of doubt, despair, and defeat are an essential part of life.

"Doubt," theologian Paul Tillich remarked, "is not the opposite of faith, it is one element of faith." It forces us to challenge our past patterns, habits, beliefs, and mistaken certainties. Combined with despair, it can lead to unexpected insights and essential lessons about what to do differently or better next time. As religious philosopher Martin Buber observed, "All journeys have secret destinations of which the traveler is unaware."

Finding our strength during times of despair is essential, and meditation can help us better understand our plight, remember our faith, and move our thoughts toward hope. Our capacity for faith, like our capacity for hope, endures only when we nourish it. "To keep a lamp burning," said Mother Theresa, "We have to keep putting oil in it."

# DOUBLE COUNTING

Double Counting meditation brings greater attentive focus than you have previously attained, and continues your development of moment-by-moment awareness of what your mind is doing.

The mind can be like a wild horse that has to be trained before it can be ridden. This meditation will help you tame your mind, just as using a bridle and reins can help you tame a wild horse. In turn, sharper focus can help you recognize recurring thought patterns. As you become more aware of your thinking process, you will have more ability to think and act in ways that encourage hope and faith, even during troubling times.

## The Essence

Begin with the starting sequence: Centering, breathing, letting go of tension, Moving Mudra, Snapshot Breaths. You will need to concentrate to correctly keep your focus on this breath-counting pattern. Move into counting your breaths, as you learned in cell 5, silently counting each breath with your eyes open. With each inhalation, count your incoming breath with a number, in sequence, from one to ten. Then, on each exhalation, repeat the same number for each of ten breaths. For example, as you are sensing each breath, you will "hear" yourself silently saying: "ONE" as you inhale (and a quieter *"one"* as you exhale); "TWO" as you inhale (a small, quiet *"one"* as you exhale); "THREE" as you inhale (a small, quiet *"one"* as you exhale); "FOUR" as you inhale (a small, quiet *"one"* as you exhale) and so on up to ten. Except for these numbers, let your mind be as empty as possible.

When you begin your second sequence of ten breaths, again count from one to ten on the inhalations. With each exhalation, you will count a "quieter" more unobtrusive "two." Your second series of ten breaths will be like this count: "ONE" as you inhale (small, quiet *"two"* as you exhale); "TWO" as you inhale (small, quiet *"two"* as you exhale); "THREE" as you inhale (small, quiet *"two"* as you exhale); "FOUR" as you inhale (small, quiet *"two"* as you exhale); and so on up to ten.

Then begin a third sequence of ten breaths, counting from one to ten on the inhalation and counting a "quieter" more unobtrusive "three" on each exhalation. Like this: "ONE" as you inhale (small, quiet *"three"* as you exhale); "TWO" as you inhale (small, quiet *"three"* as you exhale); and so on up to ten.

In summary, you will hear yourself silently saying the number that changes with each breath on the inhalation, and the number that stays the same for ten breaths on the exhalation, before increasing the latter number by one for the next ten outgoing breaths.

After each series of ten breaths, allow one full inhalation and exhalation with no counting. Try to let your mind be completely empty except for sensing your breathing, and let any thoughts that appear just float away.

Continue breathing and counting in this way, with an empty breath after each series of ten breaths, until ultimately you are counting from "ONE" to "TEN" on your incoming breaths and *"ten"* on each outgoing breath. After these 110 breaths, your session is finished. Each time you notice that your attention has wandered, return to the most recent numbers you can recall and continue from there.

## Feeling Comfortable

At this point some people get lazy. *Oh, that's too much work. I want an easy meditation.* Our minds can be like a lazy horse as well as a wild horse. We have to train our minds as well as tame them.

This takes just a little more effort than basic breath counting, but it's easy compared to many of the things you have to learn in life. You can do it. If it takes extra practice to get comfortable with this meditation, be willing to go for the gold and take the extra time you need. In your busy world, this valuable practice will take less time than it often takes waiting in line for a morning cup of coffee. The reward is worth the effort.

# Security

## Vulnerability, Alertness, and Self-assurance

· · · · · · · · · · · · · · · · · · · · · · · · · · · · · ·

### YES AND NO

*You truly possess only whatever will not be
lost in a shipwreck.*

MOHAMMED EL GHAZALI

**YOU CAN STRENGTHEN BOTH** your inner sense of security and your ability to cope with life's outer uncertainties.

Most things in life are impermanent, observed such diverse spiritual teachers as Buddha, the ancient yogis, and the authors of the Hebrew scriptures. Circumstances arise, continue, then pass away. Uncertainty is part of life's reality. Much of our suffering comes from wanting things that are changing to continue as they were. Our ability to end suffering is strengthened by our ability to accept, and perhaps even enjoy, the reality in which we live now.

When you hear the word *security,* perhaps you think of locks, fences, police, firefighters, guns, tanks, and soldiers. Or you may think of a judge telling police they can't enter your house without a writ of habeas corpus; or of legislators signing gun-control legislation; or your retirement plan; or an insurance policy; or an investment portfolio. Or your mental picture of security might be of a partner, friend, or family member who loves you truly, unconditionally, and dependably. Such pictures or intellectual associations tell you something about what triggers your own feelings of security or insecurity.

All the items just mentioned are about outer, external security—not inner security. We have a friend whose impressive gun collection was of no use at all when his inner insecurities led him to act in an overbearing manner that caused his wife to leave him. All things being equal, however, someone who is fairly confident that his outer needs will be met is likely to feel inwardly more secure than someone who is pessimistic. Our dictionary defines *insecure* as "without safety." Other definitions are: "not safe from danger, unprotected, feeling more anxiety than seems warranted, in suspense, up in the air." One common example is when someone feels very insecure about his or her future.

Insecurity can interfere with good functioning in various ways. It's hard, for example, for an insecure woman to feel beautiful. We have a friend who is constantly buying new cosmetics because she's convinced that she never looks good enough, even though she's quite lovely with no makeup on at all. And you've probably read about extraordinarily attractive celebrities who have eating disorders because they feel inadequate.

Both real and imagined threats to security can throw a monkey wrench into the gears of your mind. They can cause you act in ways that make things worse rather than better, such as when jealousy leads to restrictive demands that eat away at a relationship, making the jealousy a self-fulfilling prophecy. When insecurity takes the form of a chronic feeling that your physical or emotional survival is threatened, it can lead to acting in desperately grasping, or even cruel or violent, ways that ignore other people's needs and feelings.

Insecurity also affects how others act toward you. It tends to lead to defensive interactions with others. If you are afraid you are worthless unless everybody likes you, you're setting yourself up for a loss. When you appear insecure, you are making yourself an easy target for anyone who's looking for one. By contrast, developing your ability to feel more secure helps you become better able to communicate from a strong, centered inner place where you can get your needs met, even in challenging situations.

At this point you might be wondering, *How can I let go of old mental habits and emotional reactions and feel more secure?*

One step is to become an astute observer of what's going on around you. As actress Mae West put it, "A dame that knows the ropes isn't likely to get tied up."

You can also sharpen your ability to do things well. Security is related to a sense of effectiveness, to feeling competent in handling the curves life throws you.[1] When you think you can get what you need even in tough circumstances, you start feeling more secure. If you're a wallflower, for instance, you can improve your social skills. Your increasing self-confidence in one area is likely to start spilling over into other realms.

The centering point of inner security is to feel like for the most part you have no need to defend yourself. Then instead of going into a full-fledged fight-or-flight response to negative verbal barbs, you can let the remarks pass by like arrows that miss their target. Security also includes the ability to defend yourself physically, verbally, and emotionally when that's necessary.

Paradoxically, we feel more secure as we learn to accept impermanence and insecurity. Notice the form that your own insecurity takes: the thoughts, the feelings, the physical sensations. As you become an attentive observer of your insecurity, its grip grows weaker.

With that said, the following adventure in awareness contributes to your personal empowerment.

## YES AND NO

This helps you protect yourself from demands and influences that are not what you want, and take advantage of those that offer something valuable. Perhaps you feed your vulnerability by agreeing to requests that you ought to refuse. Many people have a hard time saying no. This can cause big trouble. As children, many of us were not supposed to refuse requests from powerful others like parents or teachers. Now, as adults, our insecurity, fears of not having another's approval, or just our well-learned difficulty saying no can have unwanted negative results. Examples include giving in to what your friends want you to do when you know you shouldn't, going along with a scheme you're uneasy about, having sex even if you don't want to, or even getting bilked by a con artist. You may want to say no, but end up giving in instead.

By contrast, some children and teens respond to demanding adults, and to a society that demands compliance, by rebelling and developing a habit of saying no to almost every request or offer, even when it would lead to something enjoyable or rewarding. If that sounds familiar, then your challenge is learning to let yourself say yes. Here you can discover whether *yes* or *no* comes more easily to you, and practice the opposite response. This can be surprisingly liberating.

### The Essence

Ideally, find a friend who is willing to spend a few minutes doing this with you. (If you can't, try it standing in front of a mirror, being watchful of your body language, doing this exercise by yourself—minus another's response.) Stand facing your partner. One of you says, "Yes!" and the other replies "No!" Continue this for three minutes. Then reverse roles. Use everything in your repertory of gestures, expressions, and tonalities to change the other's mind. Afterward, discuss whether *yes* or *no* was easier for you, and what went on inside you while you were saying each of the words.

## Variations in Technique

If you tend to be a "yes" person, as you go through a day you can experiment with refusing both explicit requests and ignoring implicit ones. "Can you make change for this bill?" someone asks. "Sorry, I can't," you reply, even if you do have change—just for today's practice, speaking with a secure voice. Focus on feeling confident within yourself when you respond.

For practice, you can even talk to the TV, the radio, or to various objects. As you flip through channels or stations, with each one say out loud, "No, I don't want to watch you now," or "I don't want to buy that." Or as your glance falls on the broom, "No, I prefer not to sweep the floor right now." If you tend to be a "no" person, do the opposite, if feasible.

## Points in the Process

It's okay if you need to change your mind. If you've agreed to something and are haunted by an uncomfortable feeling about it, you may be able to go back and say, "I'm sorry, but I need to change yesterday's 'yes' to a 'no.'" That can be a challenge, but the knot in your stomach may tell you that you need to do it. Feeling comfortable within yourself, your sense of self-worth, and your security may depend on it.

Changing a *no* to a *yes* is usually easier. When you are uncertain about whether to agree to something, "I don't think so" or even "No, thanks" can buy time. Later, changing that to, "After thinking it over, I'm willing to . . ." almost always brings an enthusiastic reply: "That's great!" In many (though of course not all) matters, the opportunity is still there tomorrow or the next day.

Also, notice how you say your "yes" or "no." If "no" comes easily to you, then making your refusals more tactful, gracious, and considerate of the other person's feelings may be important work for you. But if you usually tend to give in even when you don't want to, you need to make your statements strong enough that others don't think that you are indecisive and your answer is something that can be manipulated into a "yes." Learning to be strong, firm, gracious, and tactful all at the same time isn't easy. But it's worth the effort.

**CELL 15**

· · · · · · · · · ·

# Integrity

## Deception versus Honesty—Duplicity versus Sincerity

· · · · · · · · · · · · · · · · · · · · · · · · · · · · · · · ·

### REPLAYING YOUR DAY

> *My grandfather once told me that there are two kinds of*
> *people: those who work and those who take the credit. He*
> *told me to try to be in the first group; there was*
> *less competition there.*
>
> INDIRA GANDHI

**INTEGRITY IS A COMBINATION** of honesty, sincerity, and decency in our interactions with others and with the world. Unless you are a saint, you are probably like most of us who have room for at least a little improvement in this area.

We recognize integrity in a merchant or craftsperson whom we can depend on to fix a product perfectly or replace it if it doesn't work correctly. We recognize it in someone who follows through on what she says, with actions that correspond to her words. We see it in someone who goes out of his way to help another, even at the cost of personal disadvantage. We recognize its absence when someone pretends that her actions are better than they are, or tries to create a self-image that makes her out to be more generous or important than she really is.

The distinctions between integrity, honesty, and sincerity are hazy, for they overlap. An anonymous pundit declared, "Do not repeat anything you will not sign your name to." Henry Ford remarked, "Quality means doing it right when no one is looking." And a Chinese proverb says: "Laws control the lesser man. Right conduct controls the greater one."

Integrity includes refraining from pretense. It means not pretending that you care for someone more deeply than you do in order to get something

123

you want; or that shoddy work is good work, when you know you can do better. It includes having a clear sense of your values and acting in ways that support them. It includes acting as you would like others to act, or as you expect or ask them to.

"Integrity is doing what's right and not doing what's wrong," is a common definition, but it's only a good beginning. Then there's the next step: integrity also includes being willing to consider the possibility that you are mistaken about some of what you've believed to be right and wrong. And it includes seriously considering the views of others, just in case you might learn something that could change your beliefs about a previous assumption. Closing your ears to what others think and feel, either to feel like you are an authority or to avoid questioning your own views, is a delusional imitation of integrity.

Integrity includes sincerity. Carl Rogers, one of the great psychologists of the twentieth century, expands on this. He says: "I have not found it helpful or effective in relations with others to try to maintain a facade; to act in one way on the surface when I am experiencing something quite different underneath. When one lives behind a facade he must always have his guard up, lest the facade be pierced."[1] Rogers used the term *congruence* for "an accurate matching of experience and awareness." An angry man who denies his anger, such as someone who verbally spews toxic insults and then defends himself by saying, "I was just pointing out the facts," is thus incongruent.

Increasing your ability to be aware of what is truly going on inside you, and to communicate it, contributes to integrity. For most people, this does not occur overnight. Learning to recognize your own double messages, for instance, when you say one thing with your words and another with your body language, is not so easy. Sometimes self-deception is a habitual blind spot in awareness. Meditation can be a big help in this, because it makes it easier to perceive yourself as you truly are. In the spaces between your thoughts, some of the discrepancies between your thoughts and actions are likely to become glaringly apparent.

Integrity has nothing to do with your place and position in life. As we've all seen, kings and presidents can be liars and cheats, while those of humble station can be straightforward with themselves and others. In the corridors of high finance, Warren Buffett, CEO of Berkshire Hathaway, acknowledges this: "In looking for people to hire," he said, "you look for three qualities: integrity, intelligence, and energy. And if they don't have the first, the other two will kill you."

We're all better off when those who hold power in government or business set a good example for everyone else by acting with integrity. As Alexander the Great said, "Upon the conduct of each depends the fate of all." But when those in power fall short, we can keep our self-respect when we act with integrity ourselves.

Having integrity doesn't mean never making mistakes, or being faultless. To the contrary, it includes a willingness to look at your mistakes, and taking responsibility for them, rather than covering them up and pretending that you are more virtuous than you are. Integrity includes recognizing and admitting when you haven't acted as well as you might like. From that you can learn and then take the next step.

## REPLAYING YOUR DAY

This practice, described by G. I. Gurdjieff's student, the British intellectual A. R. Orage,[2] is done just before you go to bed at the end of your day.

### The Essence

Sit for a few minutes, close your eyes, and pretend that you are viewing a movie of the day's activities from start to finish. Start with your first memory of when you woke up in the morning. Watch your day unfold, just as if you were living it over again. (*I see myself getting out of bed, walking into the bathroom, and picking up my toothbrush* . . .) You can use your mental fast-forward whenever you wish. Notice where you have a clear memory of what you did, saw, and heard, and where there are blank spots—periods where you don't remember anything else until a few minutes later. Finally, notice any emotional reactions you feel at any point. (You may feel these emotions directly or notice them through your mind or body.)

The first time I did this exercise, I was surprised to discover large gaps in my memory's record of the day, blank spaces where I could recall nothing. There I was, brushing my teeth, and the next thing I remembered, I was about five miles down the highway on my way to work after I had already passed through two towns. The rest of the day continued in that manner, a combination of memories and blank spots.

Soon I realized that the gaps in my memory were periods when I hadn't been paying attention to what I was doing in the first place. I had been lost in my mind. Anything I didn't see or hear because my mind was elsewhere didn't get noticed. Then later, naturally enough, I couldn't recall the details of the situation that I had never encoded in memory to begin with.

By contrast, if I am paying attention in a given moment, I'm more able to remember it later. To have a clear, sharp memory of any event, I have to focus and keep my attention on it at the time.

Integrity comes in when I've acted in a way that makes me feel uncomfortable. Since I don't admire what I did, I distract myself from thinking about it. When I replay my day, I am likely to notice those uncomfortable feelings. Integrity includes admitting them to myself (in a nonblaming way) and thinking about what I'd prefer to do the next time a similar situation comes along—in contrast to justifying what I did so I can tell myself that I do no wrong. Such awareness contributes to clarity of mind.

In such situations, as you become more aware of what your mind and emotions were doing in regard to the event, it gives you more strength to act with integrity and thwart negative situations.

# Karma

## Carelessness versus Responsiveness—Denial versus Responsibility

. . . . . . . . . . . . . . . . . . . . . . . . . . . . . . . . . . .

### RIPPLES IN A POND

*All actions plant karmic seeds, which may not bear fruit for years. . . . The real job . . . is to recognize these karmas and their effect on [your] being. From this awareness comes the knowledge required to raise [your] level of consciousness.*

HARISH JOHARI

YOU CAN CHOOSE TO think and act in ways that encourage, or discourage, the qualities you would like to cultivate.

In Hindu tradition, your actions are like arrows that once shot from your bow, come back to you eventually, in this life or the next. If you act unjustly, at some point you will meet your bad karma. If you act in a kind, generous, and truthful manner, your next incarnation should be better. And if your actions are truly virtuous, you may even get off the revolving wheel of karma, end your cycle of birth and death, and merge into ultimate cosmic bliss.

Some Buddhists hold a similar view, while others claim they have no knowledge of what occurs beyond this mortal existence. Many Christians and Muslims believe that virtuous behavior can get you into heaven after death, while acting badly may send you to hell to burn. "You reap what you sow" is what many profess. Since we ourselves have no first-hand knowledge of what comes after death, in these pages we shall limit the concept of karma to the effects of our actions within this lifetime.

Metaphorically, karma means that our actions create effects that radiate outward, like ripples from a pebble dropped into a pond. Such effects can make the lives of others better or worse. They also react back on us, in both the very next moment and also the more distant future. And our actions affect the way others respond to us. At any time, writes Sanskrit scholar Judith Tyberg, we are the sum total of our previous thoughts and acts, and the builder of our future.[1] We are the result of what we have done in our yesterdays. We create our tomorrows and affect what happens to others in their tomorrows. This is more than a simple cause-and-effect relationship. The chain of events and feedback loops set in motion by our words and actions often have unforeseen or unforeseeable consequences.

When you handle an encounter in a way that leaves someone feeling cheated, deceived, intimidated, or put down, you are setting yourself up for mistrust and possible retaliation when by chance you meet again. Someone who treats you in a thoughtless or cruel manner is doing the very same thing. When such situations occur, they set waves of consequence in motion. That's karma.

Acting badly creates ripples that can close pathways to happiness. It can make people mean, callous, and anxious, as it pushes away good feelings. By your actions, you create a mental and emotional state that's your own personal heaven or hell. Novelist Edith Wharton commented that "people pay for what they do, and still more, for what they have allowed themselves to become. And they pay for it simply: by the lives they lead."

Even though it's a very human response, looking forward to getting revenge on someone who has been unkind toward you usually shuts down your openness to life. If you can invoke feelings of compassion for the heartlessness that causes an imprudent person to act in a mean, uncaring way, you are on a path to creating good karma instead of perpetuating a negative cycle. But of course this isn't easy, especially when you are angry at what someone did to you or to someone you love.

Although it would be nice to think that the universe either rewards or punishes us in direct relation to how good or bad our actions are, karma is not always that simple. Sometimes people get away with murder. And some people who live virtuous lives are dealt harsh challenges by the hand of fate.

Buddha found a way to deal with such events: "For a wise man, there is nothing to be called bad. Any adversity of life provides a step for his growth, provided he knows how to utilize it."[2] So if you have to experience a negative situation, contemplating what lessons you are learning through it may illuminate truths that will help you make better choices and create better karma in the future. While the Golden Rule, "Do unto others as you would have them do to you," sounds wise, it's sometimes hard to follow. Most of us can at least understand why we should try to follow the "silver rule" that Confucius emphasized: "Do not do to others as you would not have them do to you."

It's dismayingly easy to forget that we are the products of our previous choices. But when you blame your present actions on the excuse that what happened to you in the past made you who you are, you are forgetting that you are choosing what you say and do now—even when you're reacting to what someone else has done.

Dainin Katagiri-roshi, the founding abbot of the Minnesota Zen Meditation Center in Minneapolis, states that karma is a particular kind of energy you create in your life and the lives of others. He points out that what you did in the past is less important than what you do now and from now on:

> Through karma you can understand what your destiny is. Destiny itself has no solid form; it's something you can create. . . . Freedom means that in the next moment you can manifest your life in a new way. . . . You see, "I can change my life!" Many things come to you, and you are not what you were. At that time you turn over a new leaf.[3]

Recognizing that you are creating or affecting your karma includes accepting responsibility. Sometimes your choice of actions has just a short-term effect. At other times it can reverberate through your whole way of being at a deep level—and have equally powerful effects on others.

You are probably capable of justifying, disowning, or hiding from yourself the effects of almost anything you do. But how can we improve ourselves or our karma if we're in denial? "When we ignore unhappy feelings we miss an opportunity to change them," notes tantric scholar, poet, and artist Peter Marchand.[4] You can become more responsive to your feelings, the effects of your behavior, and the options each situation holds. When you cause some kind of harm, whether intentionally or accidentally, you might be able to undo it, fix it, or transform the relationship between you and others involved instead of walking away without looking back. That can change bad karma into good karma. You also may find that acting with integrity, kindness, and a clear mind brightens your inner spirit and helps you feel better.

## RIPPLES IN A POND

In the Symbolic Equivalents exercise in cell 11, you began to add contemplative meditation to your repertoire. Here you will take one more step along that path. You will use the abilities you've started to develop through mindfulness and concentration to create a larger pool of consciousness in which your thoughts float in and out of your mind, rather than dominating your awareness.

## The Essence

In this contemplative meditation, begin as usual with the starting sequence (see page 101). Then when you continue as described below, try to maintain an awareness of your breath and the sounds around you in the background of your consciousness.

Close your eyes and remember a recent event that involved you and another person, or several others. As specifically as you can, visualize what you did and remember the words you spoke. Focus on your own reactions and actions rather than on what evoked them or whether they were justified. Recall how your words and actions affected both you and the other(s) who were involved. Do you feel good or bad about the kind of energy that your choices and actions caused? What kind of karma do you think you might have created?

Next, extend your mind to consider possible longer-term effects of your actions in that situation. Can you find any useful lessons, or anything else that might be positive?

As you do this, don't just think about the situation. Watch the play of energy in your emotions and the sensations in your body, such as tensing or relaxing your muscles. What does your body tell you about your feelings? Let your associations float gently through your mind rather than making your thoughts about the situation into something that feels like hard work.

## Variations in Technique

Next time you are in a situation where you have distinctly different choices about what to do, notice how both you and those around you react as you speak and act. Be sensitive to what the potential karmic effects of your words and deeds appear to be at that very moment.

## Points in the Process

Look inward to find understanding of how you are shaping your world by what you're choosing to say and do. Try not to get lost in your thoughts, or emphasize negative karma. Such awareness, claims meditation teacher Joseph Goldstein, "helps us understand our own particular life story, with all its joys and difficulties, with a deep and genuine respect."[5]

# Adventure

## Outer and Inner Exploration

### DOUBLE COUNTING WITH EYES CLOSED

*Plunge boldly into the thick of life, and seize it where you will, it is always interesting.*
JOHANN WOLFGANG VON GOETHE

THROUGH LARGE AND SMALL adventures you can discover more of yourself and a larger world than you previously knew.

The solid reef was in the middle of a large lagoon, almost completely enclosed by a coral atoll. I was swimming around it underwater, enjoying a remote tropical paradise. Suddenly, about ten feet away, a huge shape appeared: an immense shark with a mouth about three feet wide. Terrified, I swam away like a bolt of lightening. When I stopped to look back, the shark had disappeared—it may have been as startled by me as I was by it. At that time it would have been hard to believe that on future occasions I would actually go diving to watch sharks that have a reputation for not bothering human beings.

Different people are attracted by different adventures. Some like rock climbing, surfing, snowboarding, football, skydiving, or even wrestling alligators. Others prefer social adventures, such as connecting with new and different kinds of people and cultures. Dating services arrange "networking adventures" to help you meet a potential lover or mate. Some people choose work in which they face social and physical challenges, like police officers and firefighters. All these are forms of outer adventure.

In addition, our everyday life holds an alluring promise of countless mini-adventures. Some include taking time from our busy day to look carefully at nature's creations, or at artwork that you might usually pass by. Such momentary explorations also include exchanging a few friendly words with people you meet in the course of the day instead of just looking right through them. Sometimes just a few words can take you into another person's reality that differs radically from your own. All these kinds of large and small adventures can enrich your life.

Odd as it seems, some who vigorously pursue outer adventure are timid about inner adventure. As St. Augustine once remarked, "People travel to wonder at the height of the mountains, at the huge waves of the seas, at the long course of the rivers, at the vast compass of the ocean, at the circular motion of the stars, and yet they pass by themselves without wondering." By focusing only on outward pursuits, the treasures that can be found through inward seeking are often lost, hidden by a fog of not looking or listening.

Indeed, some people compulsively pursue outer adventure to keep themselves from thinking about what lurks behind locked doors in their minds and hearts. Others are intrepid explorers of their inner worlds. Even when these people seem to be sitting motionless they may be following their mental and emotional highways and byways to places where most people seldom venture.

Each person needs to look into his or her own soul to determine what inward or outward adventures they personally find most worthwhile to pursue. What looks unappealing to one person may be attractive to another.

Almost every moment can be a new adventure that arises out of what went before, if you are attentive to life's possibilities. Are there adventures that you'd welcome, but are missing because swirling thoughts keep you from noticing what's right in front of you? This next meditation can help you achieve a clarity of mind that makes it easier to perceive invitations to adventures that you otherwise might pass by.

## DOUBLE COUNTING WITH EYES CLOSED

You can think of this experience as analogous to the adventure of exploring a cave. In this case, the cave consists of chambers of your own mind. This meditation is similar to Double Counting (cell 13) with one important difference: while doing this technique, keep your eyes closed. This allows you to rest your eyes while you refresh your spirit and explore your inner visual world.

The apparently small change of closing your eyes and inwardly visualizing the numbers as you do Double Counting meditation can lead to a dramatically different experience than doing a similar meditation with your eyes open. This meditation can take you to an inner place where the outside world, and perhaps even your body, almost disappears from your mind.

## The Essence

Begin with your starting sequence (see page 101). Then close your eyes and silently count *one* on your first inhalation. Let your mind empty as your exhale.

Silently count *two* on your second inhalation and again let your mind empty on the exhalation. Continue to count in sequence with each breath as you inhale. Let each number dissolve as you exhale. Keep on in that manner, counting to ten. While counting, keep your eyes closed and inwardly visualize each number as fully as you can while you count it. There's no right way for the number to look. Don't try to make it look any special way or color, but rather notice whatever shape and color—and perhaps even movement— it assumes. If you can't visualize the entire number, then try visualizing just the top little bit of it (or the bottom little bit.) If your mind is unwilling and you're not visualizing at all, don't feel stuck. Using your inner voice, silently say the number to yourself, listening with your inner ear. How "loud" does your inner voice say the number? In what kind of voice? After you have completed ten breaths, take a completely empty breath, not trying to visualize anything at all.

After your first ten breaths, again silently count from one to ten, with one difference. This time you'll add an additional number to each breath and mentally "see" it, too. As you count, visualize each new number as you inhale, and also place a small number two in the lower right-hand corner of your mental movie screen. After those ten breaths, again allow yourself a full cycle of inhalation and exhalation without consciously visualizing or counting.

Continue in this manner. During each set of ten breaths, visualize the number that goes with that group of ten in the corner of your mind. On the third set of ten, besides visualizing the number of each breath in the middle of your mental movie screen, you will also visualize a small number three down in the corner with every one of those ten breaths. During the fourth set of ten, see a small number four—and so on. With every breath, you will visualize two numbers: a large one in the center of your eyes-closed visual field that reflects the breath you are counting, and another number in the corner of your eyes-closed visual field that identifies the set of ten breaths you are counting. Keep doing that until you reach a large ten and a small ten. At that point you will have consciously counted a hundred and ten breaths.

You may be amazed at what you can observe with your inner vision (and perhaps hearing). Instead of just one number, you may see a line of them dance across your visual field; your number may be upside down, it may turn cartwheels, change color, or burst into tiny pieces, like fireworks. You'll most likely find that the appearance of your numbers changes in accordance with the state of consciousness you are in when you sit down to meditate.

Also, as you are watching the numbers, let part of your mind remain attentive to your posture, breathing, and mudra. If the sounds and sensations of the world around you, or of your physical body, disappear or almost disappear, just enjoy your inner adventure.

## Variations in Technique

Instead of letting your mind empty on the outbreath, you can continue to visualize the large and small number on each breath until you've exhaled completely.

## Points in the Process

With your eyes closed, it is possible to venture into a state of consciousness in which you are quite removed from your outer surroundings. When I was learning this meditative form, I had to take my car for servicing. While waiting for it, I sat outdoors with my back against the wall near the garage door. Engines were starting up nearby and cars were driving in and out. As I went deeply into this inner state, the sounds of the cars became more and more remote. At last the visualization of the numbers became so dominant in my field of consciousness that the automotive noises completely disappeared. After some time, when I began to move out of meditation, the cars and the garage all reappeared.

Next time you get anxious or fearful at the dentist's or doctor's office during a procedure that doesn't require your active involvement, try Double Counting with Eyes Closed. As you go deeply into your meditation, the dentist or doctor and office may start to feel more and more remote, until they become no more than the tiniest dot in the corner of your consciousness until it's time to "wake up." You may even find that your fear or anxiety fades away.

This meditation also can help you gain a clarity that will make you more discriminating about which adventures you truly wish to embark upon.

# Health

## Energy and Vitality

· · · · · · · · · · · · · · · · · · · · · · · · · · · ·

**WALKING AND BREATHING**

*Health is the greatest of human blessings.*

HIPPOCRATES

**TO MAINTAIN GOOD HEALTH,** keep both mind and body in a harmonious state.

The brain is the seat of sensation as well as thought, concluded Alcmaeon, a Greek physician who practiced at the end of the sixth and the start of the fifth century BCE. He realized that the brain stores and arranges perceptions and is responsible for memory and beliefs. At his medical school in Croton, he taught a holistic, rational, observational approach to disease. Like modern holistic health practitioners, he believed that health and illness result from the balance or imbalance of the body's systems.

The next cutting-edge figure in ancient medicine was Hippocrates, born in the fifth century BCE into a family of priests and physicians on the Greek island of Cos. Still honored in the Hippocratic oath taken by physicians today, Hippocrates understood that the natural healing process that each of us is born with is central in helping us to maintain our good health and ward off disease. He agreed with Alcmaeon that the brain is the seat of the intellect, and added a deeper understanding of how it also affects our emotional states, making us delighted or sorrowful, happy or unhappy. His approach to holistic healing included healthy food, exercise, rest, fresh air, massage, baths, music, and visits with friends. Many of his observations are as valid now as they were then.[1]

Even earlier, around 3000 BCE, scholars in India were giving instructions for living in a harmonious manner. "The Sanskrit term *Ayurveda*," states

135

Harish Johari, "is a combination of two words: *ayu* (life) and *veda* (knowledge)."[2] That ancient healing tradition holds that good health is advanced by an appropriate balance of the interacting energies that exist in our physical, mental, and emotional constitution.

Living according to the elements of good health identified in ancient India and Greece is just as important today as it was thousands of years ago. The air you breathe, the water you drink, and the food you eat affect your health in major ways. The kind and amount of your physical activity improves or retards the smooth working of your body, mind, and temperament. Inner balance affects your outer balance, and outer harmony affects your inner harmony.

Exercise energizes your body, but your movements are also influenced by your environment, your own awareness of it, and your choices of what you absorb from it. All these can positively or negatively affect your emotions as well as your health. For example, taking too much of a powerful drug can kill you. Too much alcohol in your body can send your quality of life spiraling downward. A smoking habit will probably raise the price of your life insurance. If you choose to leave a smoke-filled room and go outside to breathe fresh air, however, you're saying yes to better health.

The contributions of exercise to good health are well documented. Exercise is an antidote to stress, as it stimulates the vital life force that flows throughout your body. It can lift your mood and recharge your energy. "Exercise," says Deepak Chopra, "has a quantum effect, regardless of how much or how little you do, by giving the body a chance to restore subtle patterns of functioning."[3] Because it strengthens your body, it can also boost your self-esteem. If you're trying to lose weight, it's an important component of a successful program. It also helps your mind relax. When your mind is tranquil, you can more readily dive deeply into inner stillness.

Here you will learn a form of meditation that can help you amplify your ability to sense your environment and to look at your inner nature in relation to how your body moves physically through space, one step at a time. You can use information you gather from this practice to become more aware of how your body feels as you listen to the rhythm of your breath, your movements, your internal voices, and your interior choices.

## WALKING AND BREATHING

Walking meditation combines exercise, breathing, relaxation, and concentration. In some meditation centers it is used alternately with sitting meditation. The meditations we describe here can be used wherever you happen to be. Keeping your walking and breathing synchronized keeps your attention focused in your moment-to-moment experience. The moment you notice that your walking and breathing are not coordinated, you'll know that your mind has wandered into daydreams, worries, or memories, giving you a signal to bring your attention back to the present.

## The Essence

In this exercise, we define one step with one foot as a *half step*. We call a step with one foot and then a step with the other foot a *full step*. If possible, please take one full step now.

In two full steps, your feet move left, right, left, right. Take two full steps with your incoming breath and two full steps with your outgoing breath, counting as you do: "one-ne, two-ooo" on your inhalation; and "one-ne, two-ooo" on your exhalation (count silently or aloud, as you wish). Repeat this combination of walking, breathing, and counting with each breath. As you continue walking in this manner, feel your breath move into and out of your lungs. Also internally sense the movement of your muscles and body, and feel the soles of your feet connect with the ground. Let your arms swing loosely (unless you're carrying something).

The important thing is to keep your walking and breathing synchronized. Each time you notice that they're not together anymore, stop completely for an instant. Then start walking while counting breaths again.

As you walk in this way, tune in to your experience of yourself and the world around you. With this walking pattern, many people report feeling a heightened sensitivity and awareness to their environment as well as to internal sensations. You might use this walk when you have plenty of time to get to where you're going. Since it looks like an ordinary slow walk, no one around you will know you're doing anything unusual and you can do it anywhere. (It's especially pleasant in pretty, natural places.) Try this for at least five minutes now, and then try the variation below for another five minutes.

## Variations in Technique

Perhaps you would like to make good time when you are on your way somewhere, and you'd like to feel centered and focused rather than harried and frazzled when you arrive. Even while you're getting there, you can be present in your here-and-now experience. Using the definition of a full step given above, take four full steps with each incoming breath, and four full steps with each outgoing breath. Carefully stay with this pattern. Focus your attention in your body, breathing, counting, and on the environment, as described above.

If you have a smaller lung capacity, you can do three full steps while breathing in and three full steps while breathing out. Also, many people find three half steps inhaling and three half steps exhaling a good rhythm for jogging or running.

Some traditions offer other breathing patterns. For instance, in a Balinese walking meditation you take three full steps on the in-breath and five on the out-breath.

## Points in the Process

To stay healthy, you may already belong to a health club or have a good exercise regimen like running, cycling, swimming, or even taking a brisk daily walk. Perhaps you do hatha yoga, which "make[s] one firm, free of diseases, and light of limb," according to the Sivananda Yoga Vedanta Center.[4]

Most yogic postures, and many other exercises, too, involve a rhythmic alternation of positions. When possible, try coordinating your movements with your breath. As you move in one direction (like stretching your arms upward toward the sky), inhale deeply. As you move in the opposite direction (like bending forward to touch the ground), exhale completely. With each breath, be attuned to your physical sensations. Listen to messages from your body and go only as far as it's ready to move at a given moment, on a given day. Go no further. (Sometimes you can move just a bit further by letting go of tension that you're holding. That's fine. But don't try to push yourself beyond that.) Too many people, including even yoga teachers and exercise trainers, have injured themselves by pushing too far, too fast.

No one can feel your body from the inside but you. In coordinating your breath and movement, you are your own teacher and trainer. When in doubt, be cautious. Since any kind of physical movement is an opportunity to listen to what your body is telling you, you might learn something new. Try to keep your awareness in the present moment, where opportunity for optimal mind-body-emotion integration exists.

# Envy

## Jealousy and Comparison

**JUST SENSING**

*When you learn about yourself, watch yourself, watch the
way you walk, how you eat, what you say, the gossip, the
hate, the jealousy—if you are aware of all that is in yourself,
without any choice, that is part of meditation.*

JIDDU KRISHNAMURTI

YOU CAN USE ENVY as a tool to help you be present with each event and
moment as it is.

Envy and jealousy both make you feel "less than." Even though the
potential to experience these emotions lives within the human psyche, few
of us enjoy such feelings. They can make us feel just a little bad, downright
miserable, or despairing. Even though they often occur together, envy and
jealousy are not identical.

Envy arises from comparing ourselves with others: *How do I stack up?*
It's a social comparison in which you feel diminished because another person has something you covet, or more than you do (regardless of how much
you have). Social psychologists call this *relative deprivation*.[1] The "some-
things" might be material, relational, or personal qualities. You might feel
resentful, angry, or even aggressive toward the person you envy.

On the other hand, you might admire that person and feel motivated
to try to get the same kinds of things she has. With envy, you can ask
yourself, "Am I inspired enough by what this person has achieved that I'm
willing to invest the effort to attain similar ends?" If not, you can work
on recognizing that emotionally as well as intellectually, and let go of the
thoughts and feelings that cause you grief. Strive to free yourself of such

comparisons, to accept and appreciate yourself as you are, and to enjoy your life as it is.

Part of the trouble with envy is that often it has no end. "If you desire glory, you may envy Napoleon," commented philosopher Bertrand Russell, "but Napoleon envied Caesar, Caesar envied Alexander, and Alexander, I daresay, envied Hercules, who never existed."

Jealousy includes another element: the fear of losing someone, or being abandoned by them. Someone else is getting the affection or attention you desire, and you feel deprived and upset as a result. You don't get precisely what you want, and probably also feel "less than" the other person who is getting the love or admiration you crave. In either jealousy or envy there might be something you can do to get what you want, or it might seem, or actually be, hopeless, and you might feel helpless.

With jealousy, when you have your wits about you and the time seems right, it may be useful to talk it through with the person whose affection or attention you're afraid of losing: "Erica, when I see you with Jacques, it looks to me like he's coming on to you. My stomach knots up, and I go into a panic." Erica may be completely surprised, and able to ease your anxiety, or she may make it a point not to act in ways that feel threatening to you. Or you may discover that she really is moving away from you and toward Jacques, and you're better off handling that sooner rather than later. Or you might learn that your tendency to feel threatened and jealous is out of control and something you need to work on to avoid causing yourself and others more grief in the future.

Such reactions often have their roots in early childhood, when one person thinks another is getting more love, attention, or goodies from parents, siblings, teachers, or playmates. Such reactions can go beyond what's normal to become a major source of problems, especially when they become a habitual way of responding. "The person who is [recurrently] jealous is typically insatiable in insisting on fidelity, domination, succor, and victory over all rivals," says experimental psychologist Richard Lazarus. "The jealous person is . . . forever resentful at the imagined or actual deprivation."[2] Many such situations are quite complicated. Emotions, for example, usually come in clusters. Jealousy, pride, betrayal, humiliation, pain, grief, anger, and desire for power over others can all get mixed up together. In such cases we have to deal with them as they come—all at once.

Amma expanded on the theme of jealousy when one of her followers asked: "I try to follow your counsel to practice regular meditation in order to find inner peace, but even after all these years, waves of anger, jealousy, and other troubling emotions over which I seem to have no control sometimes overwhelm me. What can I do?" Amma replied,

> It's difficult to completely eliminate such troubling emotional states, because we have been living in the world for such a long time. Since childhood, our brother grabs something from us and we cry, and so on. We have developed unhelpful habits so deep seated that we cannot easily get rid of them. These firmly entrenched old habits have become our character.
>
> Even so, just as we control our hands and legs when we're walking or driving, we can control our mind. At first when you tell the mind not to do something, it will do exactly what you don't want it to. Try ten times, and you may succeed once. But keep on and you can go beyond. Suppose you want to be an M.D. It takes at least seven years. By the time you're a doctor, you will have become old. It also takes a long time to learn to control your mind.
>
> Try making one kind of vow once a week. For example—for one day, vow not to be angry, or at least to release your anger as soon as you feel it.
>
> The first time you will fail. But don't give up. Try again. You may fall down. Then get up and walk, continue your journey. If you fall down, don't just lie there because it is so comfortable. Keep on and there will be a time when control of your mind and emotions will be in your hand.[3]

When jealousy and envy are so extreme that they interfere with a person's life, counseling or therapy can be useful. But since these powerful emotions can at times cause trouble for almost everyone, meditation and awareness techniques to handle these negative states of mind can be useful for most of us.

Envy and jealousy have this in common: They are both ways in which you tie yourself up in knots. These knots make it harder to get what you want and harder to feel happy with what you have and who you are. And often these knots or feelings of envy or jealousy occur again and again. The Spanish proverb "Envy is thin because it bites but never eats" applies just as well to jealousy.

With both envy and jealousy, instead of swimming in a pool of negativity, try to evaluate which thoughts are useful, which are not, and endeavor to let go of the latter. Focus on appreciating what is present and valuable in your life. The awareness activity described below is a good way to handle both these states in the moment in which they occur.

# JUST SENSING

This is for use when either envy or jealousy grabs and squeezes you tightly in its grip. By itself, it does not bring about a long-term transformation of your tendency to go into one of those states, but it helps you learn more about your relationship with these emotions and may help you feel less distressed in the moment. Combined with other attentive techniques, its practice can reduce their hold on you.

## The Essence

When any event triggers your envy or jealousy, whether it's something happening right where you are, something you've heard about, or even something you've read or seen in the media, try the following suggestion from Laura Archera Huxley.[4] Move your attention away from your thoughts and your emotions and focus as totally as you can on the physical sensations in your body and nothing else. For the moment, don't worry about the event that triggered your uncomfortable feelings. Just notice where you're tense. Is your heart racing? Do you feel the blood coursing through your body? Are you clenching your jaws or making fists?

Notice whatever you can about the posture and gestures you've moved into—your skeletomuscular system and the internal sensations of your organs and nervous system. Keep your attention on the totality of your physical being until the peak of activation in your body subsides. You will know this happens when your body becomes less tense and you relax physically. (This method is sometimes useful with other disturbing emotional states as well.)

## Points in the Process

When you determine where your emotions live in your body, you can learn more about them. Laura Huxley claims that "it is by communicating with the feeling in the body that we liberate the energy encapsulated in that emotion and free it for our own conscious use. . . . [You can] trace a response within your body to any emotion you may experience." If you have a hard time recognizing the physical connections of a psychological or emotional experience, she continues, "then say to yourself, 'if this emotion were to become a bodily feeling, let's imagine where it would be.'"

Every emotional response includes thoughts, feelings, sensations, muscular responses, and internal bodily reactions. Often some of these are unconscious, or largely so. By sharpening your awareness of them, you can paradoxically gain both greater freedom and greater self-control. The messages from your body will probably unveil emotional blocks that emerge as knots of stress. That gives you information that lets you trigger those reactions less often and release them more easily when they occur.

# Courage

## Facing Fears

**STEP-BY-STEP**

*Never interrupt someone doing something you
said couldn't be done.*

AMELIA EARHART

**EKNATH EASWARAN TELLS THIS** story about his teacher, Mahatma Gandhi:

> One evening at Sevagram Ashram hundreds of people had gathered for
> the nightly prayer meeting. . . . This evening a cobra was seen gliding
> toward the gathering. . . . A ripple of panic began to sweep through the
> crowd, and there was danger that some might be trampled if the terror
> spread. But Gandhi quietly showed a sign not to move.
>
> Gandhi was seated on the platform. He wore only his dhoti or loin-
> cloth; legs, chest, and arms were bare. While the crowd held its breath
> and watched, the cobra made its way straight for Gandhi and slowly
> began to crawl up over his thighs. There was a long moment of silence
> in which no one dared to move or make a sound. Gandhi [showed no]
> trace of fear. Slowly, quietly, [the cobra] crawled away, leaving everyone
> unharmed.[1]

Gandhi was not born brave. He had been a small, meek child. A wise
family servant, Rambha, came to his aid. "There is nothing wrong in admitting your are afraid," she told him. "But whenever something threatens you,
instead of running away, hold your ground and repeat the mantram Rama,
Rama, Rama, over and over again in your mind. It can turn your fear into
fearlessness."[2]

As an adult, in his first court appearances as a young attorney, Gandhi was fearful about public speaking. He overcame that fear and became a captivating speaker who galvanized huge crowds. He bravely endured beatings and imprisonments in his struggle against apartheid in South Africa and then in the campaign for India's independence.

Most great spiritual leaders have been courageous in some way. Jesus had the courage to keep teaching even when threatened with death. Buddha, born into the luxurious life of a prince, had the courage to abandon his claim to the throne and become a wandering beggar, and almost died of starvation in his spiritual quest.

People differ in their ability to face threats courageously. Former European heavyweight boxing champion Henry Cooper said he could not recall ever having been afraid of anyone, but such fearlessness is rare.[3] In a study carried out during World War II, only 1 percent of several thousand airmen reported no fear during combat. Fearless soldiers were most admired, but those who carried on despite their fear were also respected.[4] Like them, for most of us courage lies not in having no fear, but in acting despite our fear.

Social support can also bolster courage, as when Martin Luther King Jr. led nonviolent marches for integration in the southern United States despite attacks by police and vicious dogs. In that context, King remarked, "Our lives begin to end the day we become silent about things that matter."

The power of King's statement becomes clear when we look at the "courage of authenticity." Such courage, notes psychotherapist Rollo May, exists when you listen to your inner self and speak from the center of your being. (This may take time to learn if you've spent most of your life being told how and who to be.)

It takes courage to challenge old ways that lead you and others into error, and to hold your ground when others urge you to follow a path you sense is wrong. Russian author and Nobel Prize winner Solzhenitsyn "stood up alone against the might of the Soviet bureaucracy in protest against the inhuman and cruel treatment of men and women in Russian prison camps . . ." writes Rollo May. "[When] we blind ourselves to the other's suffering, we cut off our empathy with the person needing help. Hence the most prevalent form of cowardice in our day hides behind the statement 'I did not want to become involved.'"[5]

"Social courage," in May's words, is "the courage to relate to other human beings, the capacity to risk oneself in the hope of achieving meaningful intimacy." He continues, "Such risk is inescapable. We cannot know at the outset how the relationship will affect us." Social courage requires facing two fears. One is the fear of being abandoned, which can lead to trying so hard to please the other that one's self is lost. The other is the fear of losing one's independence, seen in those who, in May's words, "seek to keep the back door open to beat a hasty retreat in case the relationship becomes too intimate."

Summoning up the courage to follow your dreams can widen your horizons and connect you with new people and places. But many of us doubt our abilities when obstacles appear on our path. If the voice of fear is too loud when you think you may not succeed, you might not even try. To attempt something and fail and stand up again and carry on without losing heart isn't easy. But you just might find a reservoir of strength you didn't know you had.

It also takes courage to restrain yourself and avoid plunging ahead rashly when the universe sends you a message that says the best course is to stop or wait—especially when others are trying to push you on. As Winston Churchill said, "Courage is what it takes to stand up and speak. Courage is also what it takes to sit down and listen."

Fortunately, some kinds of courage can be learned by becoming well trained in coping with threatening situations. Courage can also be learned by repeated success in handling such situations. In this sense, competence and confidence shade into courage.

Courage, and even fearlessness, can also be developed through inner work. In your mind you have an opportunity, while in a safe environment, for repeated mental exposure to a given kind of danger, real or imagined. In contemplative meditation, as you face troubling thoughts and feelings, quietly witness them with detachment instead of either getting emotionally caught up in them or distracting yourself from seeing and feeling them. Whether in action or meditation, the I Ching reminds us that as you work to summon and strengthen your courage, "Perseverance furthers."

## ONE STEP AT A TIME

Like most personal qualities, courage is not something that a person has no matter what. It consists of a series of acts, one after another. You may have been timid in the past, but if your next act is brave, and the next one, and the one after that, you begin to redefine yourself.

In many cases you don't have to challenge a major fear all at once. You can confront it a little at a time, and then, with each step, gather greater courage for the next one. Psychologists have developed several approaches to learning to act courageously. One element most of these approaches have in common is to repeat an event that resembles the one you are fearful about. Another is learning to act in a way that is incompatible with your old fear response. An example is physical relaxation, which inhibits the tenseness that occurs with fear. Still another is the practice of graduated tasks related to your fear, as described below.

From early childhood onward, much of our learning occurs as we watch others and imitate their actions. A useful starting point may be to watch a movie or video of someone successfully doing what you are afraid to do. (This is called *vicarious modeling*.)[6] Another step is to go into an environment where you feel uncomfortable, accompanied by another person who is at ease there. Or watch a real person successfully do something you've been afraid to try. (The person doesn't have to be an expert—"good enough" will do.) Can you join him or her in doing together what you've been afraid to try alone?

Another effective method involves repeated small steps in the direction of carrying out a full-blown fear-arousing activity. The key is to make each step small enough that it's not much more daunting than the previous one. You can use this approach with many different kinds of fears, including social fears like asking someone for a date (for example, having drinks together is less intimidating than inviting someone to dinner), or the fear of talking to authority figures (you might start with a receptionist and end with the company president). This approach is known to strengthen your courage with anything that you are willing to do on your own. The following real-life example provides a demonstration.

## The Essence

A woman who was afraid of driving in traffic asked for help. Usually she only drove around the small town where she lived, on back streets when possible, but she wanted to become courageous enough to drive anywhere, anytime. I asked her to make a list of about twenty different driving situations that ranged from "just the tiniest bit fear-arousing" to "terrifying." Next, she was asked to cut the list into small strips and rearrange them in order from least to most disturbing. For each item, she closed her eyes, visualized the event, and listened to her body for an inner message about how disturbing it felt. She was also asked to give each item a number from one to 100 that represented the Subjective Units of Disturbance—SUDS—she felt as she visualized it. (Subjective Units of Disturbance is a term in trauma therapy that refers to how upset each item causes you to feel, expressed as a number you select.) In one case, the numbers she gave to two items were so far apart that she wrote a new intermediate item to fill in the gap. Her list of items was almost like a staircase, with each stair reflecting about the same increase in fear as the previous one.

With encouragement, she started to actually perform the items one by one. She began with the easiest driving task, stayed with it until she felt fine with it, and then progressed to the next one. Her most intimidating item was to drive around in San Francisco's financial district at rush hour. Ultimately, she succeeded in this real-life desensitization of her driving fear.

To summarize:

1. Identify your fear.
2. Make a list of about twenty different situations or actions that some-how resemble what you are afraid of, or afraid to do. Make these *very* specific, not vague or general.
3. Cut up the list so that each item is on a separate strip of paper.
4. Assign a SUDS number to each item. Then rearrange the items from least to most fear-arousing.
5. Check to make sure the increase in fear from each item to the next is about the same. If any step in this process is too large, add intermedi-ate items to create smaller steps. (This may lengthen the number of items on your list.)
6. Starting at the bottom (lowest SUD), actually do each item on your list. You might need to do some of them several times before you feel comfortable enough to be ready to go on to the next step. (Congratulate yourself after you complete each step!) Gradually work your way up to the most challenging situation.

In this process, as Czech playwright, writer, and politician Václav Havel observes, "It is not enough to stare up the steps; we must step up the stairs."

## Feeling Comfortable

If you have a phobia, or an intuitive sense that a fear feels too intimidating to handle by yourself, by all means consult a professional psychologist or counselor who has specific expertise in treating fears.

CELL 21
· · · · · · · · · ·

# Sound and Silence

## Words of Power

· · · · · · · · · · · · · · · · · · · · · · · · · · · · · ·

**MANTRA PRACTICE**

*When a particular mantra is repeated, you develop that
aspect within you. . . . When that quality becomes more
and more impressed upon your mind, you begin to
perceive it outside as well.*

Swami Satchidananda

**DELIBERATE SILENCE AND THE** repetition of selected sounds can help develop
specified qualities and maintain inner balance.

A reclusive holy man named Gopi Giri Baba who lives in a remote
Himalayan cave was asked what practices he follows. He replied that he does
only *japa,* a term for repetitious chanting or writing of a sacred mantra. "I
chant my mantra continuously to reach the 'Illuminated point,' which is like
a star in the sky," he said.[1]

Giri Babaji follows an ancient tradition that proclaims that seeds of awakening lie dormant within divine words. By continuously repeating a sacred
sound, the inner self begins to resonate with the power of its vibration. In
discussing this tradition, Harish Johari says that mantra is a combination of
the word *man,* meaning "mind," and *tra,* which means "freedom and protection." Putting these together, mantra represents the mind's power to be free.
When liberated from worldly worries and in tune with the essence of the
mantra, the "I-consciousness merges with the mantra and the aspirant can
reach a state of *samadhi* or bliss consciousness."[2]

As Gandhi showed, a mantra can also be a supportive anchor in daily
life. When he and his supporters were jailed and beaten during their nonviolent political campaigns, he constantly repeated his mantra to keep

himself from giving in to rage, despair, or the impulse to retaliate.

Although you may not want to live in a cave, you might find it useful to shut the door to the noise of the outside world while you take time to nurture your inner self. Of course this isn't always easy amid today's hustle and bustle, but chanting a mantra, or repeating it silently to yourself, can be an effective way of doing that, especially when such words of power are adapted to your own path, whether its focus is spiritual or material.

Another discipline used to foster self-control or communion with the divine is the practice of intentional silence. In Western monasteries and Eastern meditation halls alike, maintaining silence for half a day, a day, a week, or even longer has a long tradition as a path to enlightenment. Such realized masters as Sri Ramakrishna, Sri Ramana Maharshi, and Neem Karoli Baba gave up speaking entirely and communicated only by writing on chalkboards. Sri Ramana Maharshi said, "Silence is so potent. Silence is the loudest form of prayer."

## MANTRA PRACTICE

Strange as it might seem, a certain kind of "inner sound" can make it easier to move toward "inner silence." A mantra or word of power can help you be present, enjoy a sense of peace and inner stillness, and at the same time help your mind stay focused on the direction in which you want to move. Use of a mantra adds an automatic contemplative element to the concentration and mindfulness that you are already practicing. The effect can gradually spread harmony and strength through both your mind and your actions.

These sound patterns can even help heal emotional or physical problems. The vibrations of mantra, writes Deepak Chopra, "gradually lead the mind out of its normal thinking process and into the silence that underlies thought. As such, a mantra is a very specific message inserted into the nervous system."[3] Eknath Easwaran says that a mantra "can transform what is negative in the personality into what is positive: anger into compassion, ill into good will, hatred into love. By calming the mind, it gradually integrates divided and opposing thoughts at a deeper and deeper level of consciousness."[4] Swami Rama adds, "Mantra is a rare friend indeed, which helps one whenever it is needed. . . . By remembering the mantra constantly, the aspirant creates deep grooves in the unconscious, and then the mind flows spontaneously in those grooves."[5]

Often a mantra embodies an intention that, through repeating the mantra over and over, moves into the forefront of your consciousness. Another kind of mantra may or may not have an obvious meaning, but rather is based on a sound vibration that resonates with your soul's purpose and helps you evolve toward your goal. Such a mantra, it is said, can be imparted to you only by a qualified teacher or guru who knows you personally. Some meditation teachers who have the ability to see deeply into others select a mantra for each student based on keen observation of the student's needs and tendencies.

A word of caution here: some organizations authorize advanced students to select and distribute mantras using specified guidelines. Our experience with this procedure has been mixed. Rely on your own intuitive reaction to any teacher who might be giving mantras. Do you trust this person? Does this mantra feel right after you've given it a fair chance? If not, let it go and seek other instruction.

Teachers such as Ram Dass and the mahayogi Pilot Baba report good results with mantras when people choose them themselves. You can use any word or phrase that fits your needs. For example, if you struggle with self-ishness, *metta,* meaning loving kindness, or *karuna,* meaning compassion, might suit you.

Many, like these two and the widely used syllable *Om* (pronounced *ah-oom*), are based on Sanskrit, an ancient language that is no longer actively spoken. Sanskrit is fascinating because it has many more terms for highly developed states of consciousness than any living language. (Given that reality, it's easy to give credence to stories of a lost golden age, perhaps encompassing the alleged lost civilization of Atlantis, which even Plato, 2,500 years ago, spoke of as having existed in the distant past.)

The very sounds of Sanskrit words are said by some to have an inherent effect such that using them is more powerful than using their English counterparts. We've seen no research on this, and some people find that a word in their native language works better for them. In English, you might choose such terms as *letting-go, nonjudgment,* or *perseverance.*

Below we have provided a few more words (or sometimes two together) that can serve as mantras. We've also listed their Sanskrit equivalents. Think about your needs, intentions, and life direction. What do you want to develop in yourself now? As you read the list, see if you feel drawn to one of these. Please feel free to substitute equivalent words from your own religious or cultural tradition or from your own language. If the mantra doesn't feel good to you, it probably won't work for you.

# A FEW MANTRAS[6]

| Sanskrit Word | Pronunciation | Some Meanings in English |
| --- | --- | --- |
| ahimsa | (ahheemsuh) | nonviolence, harmlessness, noninjury |
| amitaabha | (ahmeetahbhah) | divine light, unmeasured splendor |
| ananda | (ahnaanda) | delight, cheerfulness, happiness, pleasure, joy, bliss |
| anirveda | (aneervaydah) | self-reliance, self-confidence |
| anugraha | (anoograh-hah) | loving-kindness, benefiting |
| bhoga | (bowgah) | enjoyment of each moment, joy, pleasure |
| daana | (daynah) | giving, gift, charity, bestowing |
| dharma | (daarmah) | duty, practice, custom, the teaching, observances |
| dhira | (deerah) | self-composure, strong-minded, persevering, bold |
| dhirataa | (deerahtah) | courage, strength, fortitude |
| gandharva | (gawndharvuh) | harmony, agreement |
| jaana | (jahna) | awareness while acting, knowledge |
| karuna | (kahroonah) | compassion, empathy |
| ksema | (k'saymah) | safe, secure, comfortable, at ease, prosperous |
| moksha | (mowkshah) | release, liberation, salvation, deliverance |
| prajaa | (prajah) | insight, wise attitude, understanding, prudent |
| sankalpa | (sahnkahlpah) | determination, will |
| satya | (suhtya) | truth, reality, that which actually exists |
| seva | (sayvah) | service, selfless service |
| shanti | (shawntee) | peace in action and of mind, averting pain, tranquillity |
| shunyata | (shoonyawtuh) | sublime eptiness |
| sumati | (soomahtee) | kindness, benevolence, good disposition |
| tapas | (tahpahs) | austerity, asceticism, purification |
| titiksha | (teeteekshah) | patience, endurance, forbearance |
| upazzanti | (oopahzahntee) | tranquillity, calmness, soothing |
| vaaja | (vahjah) | active, energetic, vigorous, swift |
| vajra | (vazhrah) | robust, diamondlike, thunderbolt |
| vyaakhyaa | (veeyahkhah) | clarity of perception, relation, explanation |
| zakti | (zhaktee) | energy, ability power |
| zara | (shaahrah) | fluid, creek, essence, real meaning, main point |
| ziila | (seela) | integrity, ethics, moral conduct |

## The Essence

Some teachers have their students repeat their mantras in coordination with their breathing, while others do not. In *Matrix Meditations,* all mantras, Mantra Passages (see cell 25), and counting practices are done in rhythm with your breathing. Select a mantra from the list of words above (or another that you prefer). When you sit to meditate, go through your starting sequence as usual. Then as you inhale, repeat your mantra to yourself, and as you exhale, let your mind empty. Repeat this sequence with each cycle of breath. Notice whatever you hear, see, feel, or sense in the empty space of your exhalation. When your mind drifts off, bring it back to your mantra and continue repeating it in rhythm with your breath for about fifteen minutes. When you have finished, end with the Yogic Seal.

Chanting your mantra out loud and breathing slowly may help to create a hypnogogic state (a relaxed, almost sleeplike quality of consciousness) in which your central nervous system will automatically follow the melodic tune of your inner pied piper. Your consciousness and your physical being merge with the vibration of the sound.

If (and only if) you chant your mantra out loud, chant on the exhalation and make your inhalation the empty part of your breathing cycle. (This directly reverses what you do when you repeat your mantra silently.)

As you meditate, your mantra can not only help cultivate a specific quality, but can also help you continue to develop your inner Witness—the pure awareness that watches what you do, as you do it.

## Feeling Comfortable

For the next few days, focus on this Mantra Practice. As you do so, you might find that you'd like to change your mantra. By tuning in to your own inner needs and noticing how well a specific mantra fits your situation and state of mind, you can find one that works for you.

## Variations in Technique

Many people find the mantra *so hum* useful, says Swami Rama. It means, "My inner self is united with universal consciousness," but its effect is due less to its meaning than to helping the mind experience inner silence. "Mentally hear the first part, the softer sound, *so,* with the inhalation, and the second part, *hum,* during the exhalation," instructs Swami Rama. "Simply sit quietly and let the sound repeat itself with each breath, allowing the flow of breath to remain serene. . . . The mantra is only heard mentally; it is not repeated aloud. . . . As meditation progresses, there should be a deepening sense of quiet and stillness. No dramatic phenomena are required."[7]

If you choose to make the syllable *Om,* said to represent the cosmic sound of the universe, your mantra, it is intoned either silently or audibly on the outbreath. "Om, shanti, shanti, shanti" (peace, peace, peace) is often spoken or whispered aloud at the end of a meditation.

## Points in the Process

Another form of mantra meditation, well known in the West, is Maharishi Mahesh Yogi's Transcendental Meditation, or TM.[8] Some people like that approach because you can sit in any comfortable position rather than sitting with an erect spine. With TM, even if you fall asleep while meditating, it's considered alright.

When you have mastered the sitting meditations found in the Matrix, meditating in some other comfortable posture instead of sitting up straight will be an option for you, too. But please remember these three points:

First, if you have the energy to sit up straight while meditating, do so. (In regard to this cell, for most people, sitting or lying in a relaxed posture while doing basic mantra meditation is a fallback position—pun intended. But you may also want to use your mantra while going about your everyday life when appropriate.)

Second, always intone your mantra (whether silently on the inhalation or out loud on the exhalation) in rhythm with your breathing.

Third, when you select your own mantra, you can keep it for a lifetime if you wish. Or use it only until you have developed the quality it represents, and then choose another. You can use different mantras for different situations. And you can even put two or more together to make a compound mantra.

Also, you can do your mantra meditation just as easily with, for example, a word that comes from Christian Gregorian chanting, Native American chanting, Arabic chanting, or chants from any other tradition. Use a chant, prayer, or affirmation that works for you.

# Sensation

## Pleasure and Pain

· · · · · · · · · · · · · · · · · · · · · · · · · · ·

### FIGURE-EIGHT BREATHING

*Taste, touch and smell, hearing and seeing are not merely a*
*means to sensation, enjoyable or otherwise, but they are*
*also a means to knowledge.*

ST. THOMAS AQUINAS

JUST AS SOME OF the many authors of the Bible directly contradict one another on certain points, so also Hindu, Buddhist, Muslim, and Christian teachers of past and present express contradictory views about sensation and pleasure. Some Hindu scholars advise withdrawing the senses from contact with the world as fully as possible. Others teach methods of developing them to sense far more than most people realize is possible. Some Buddhist teachers enjoy marriage and family life, while others encourage solitude and celibacy. Even in tantra, where sexual love is considered divine communion, there are the right-hand and the left-hand paths. The right-hand path, "where meditation is key," applauds strict control of the senses.[1] The popular left-hand path includes the enjoyment of sex as a ritual of worship. Sometimes overlooked is the importance of incorporating a meditative awareness of your partner's breathing and responses, and your own, into that ritual.[2]

Ancient philosophers held equally diverse views about the senses and the body. Plato and some others disdained the senses and held that reason alone was the high road to truth. Aristotle, by contrast, believed that the best way to find truth is to look, listen, and measure, using all our senses fully.

Sensation and pleasure are not identical, but they are connected. Aristippus, founder of the Cyrenaic school of thought, proclaimed pleasure to be the greatest good. He held that the keenest pleasures are physical or sensual, and judged almost everything by how well it can evoke physical delight. His goal was not to conquer the desire for pleasures by asceticism, but to enjoy them without becoming enslaved by them, and to distinguish between those that endanger us and those that don't. In that spirit, he declared that we need to find our pleasures while being "neither the master nor the slave of any man." Since in his view, wealth and luxury could produce pleasure but were not inherently pleasant, it might be better to be poor and free than wealthy and choked with cares. His greatest gift to his daughter Arete, he said, was that he taught her "to set a value on nothing that she can do without."[3]

Epicurus, born fourteen years after Aristippus died, professed a "practical wisdom." He compares pleasures to pains, accepting pains that lead to greater pleasures and rejecting pleasures that lead to greater pains. This principle, he held, is the best foundation for every act of choice and avoidance. He also saw the pleasures of mind and body as related. The mind feels delight at the body's well-being and enjoys tranquility or relief at the removal of pains and cares. If we learn to enjoy simple food and plain surroundings, he said, we free ourselves from sources of pain that plague many people.

Present-day experimental psychology approaches sensation from a different angle. It carries out systematic studies of how we sense and perceive our world, and what makes our perception more accurate or less so.

Like a skilled painter or photographer who sees details that many people miss, you can train your senses to be more alert.

We now turn to an advanced breathing method that we call Figure-Eight Breathing. This method helps you breathe more deeply, feel more awake and alive, and use your internal sensations to gain useful information. After learning to do this, some people tell us, "It's almost as if I had never breathed before."

## FIGURE-EIGHT BREATHING

This breath pattern increases somatic awareness, and encourages deep relaxation and letting go when you're in a safe environment. It also provides almost instant feedback when you lose focus in your meditation. It is referred to more poetically in an ancient Chinese text titled *The Secret of the Golden Flower* as "The Circulation of the Light."[4]

You may already know the difference between chest breathing and diaphragmatic (belly) breathing. If not, try this. You will start by lying on your back, on a rug or bed or even soft grass, in the hatha yoga Corpse pose. In this position, your arms are by your sides just away from your body, palms facing up and your feet slightly apart. Close your eyes. Then place one hand on your stomach and the other on your chest. Notice as each rises and falls. If the hand on your chest rises and falls more, you are chest-breathing, as most of us usually do when awake. If the hand on your stomach rises and falls more, you are belly breathing, as most of us do while asleep. Next, consciously chest-breathe, and then belly-breathe. Feel the difference. Then read on to continue to the next step.

## The Essence

To make this easier to learn, it's described here in three stages.

> *Stage One:* Lying on your back, imagine that you are inside a large number eight that's resting on its side, horizontally. As you inhale, imagine that a moving stream of light traces the figure eight by coming in through your navel, crossing your torso, and traveling upward just beyond your back. At that point it curves forward and stops motionless at a spot somewhere above your head for about three seconds. As you start to exhale the light continues by traveling downward in front of your body until it's just above your navel. Once again, it crosses through your body and emerges from your pelvic floor before traveling downward outside the back of your legs. Below your feet it curves forward and hesitates for about three seconds beneath your feet. Then the point of light curves and moves upward just beyond the front of your legs until it reaches the point where it's ready to enter through your navel and repeat the cycle. The full pattern traces a lying-down-on-its-side number eight (see the drawing on the following page). Since a horizontal number eight is also the symbol for infinity, you can think of this meditation as breathing in harmony with infinity.
>
> *Stage Two:* Now go through the pattern again, imagining that air travels upward along the front of your legs and enters through your navel to fill your stomach. As you do, let your stomach actually fill with air. When your stomach is full, let air move into your chest, filling your lungs as well (equivalent to the stream of light traveling upward along your back, in the description above, as it forms the figure 8), until both stomach and chest are filled. At that point, remain motionless for about three seconds, with your chest and stomach both full of air.

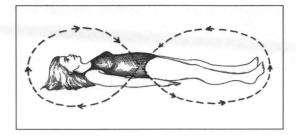

Your breath should have, metaphorically, "reached the very top of the figure 8." Next, begin to exhale, holding the air in your chest and using your stomach muscles to compress your stomach and empty the air from it. Your breath, or your visualized figure eight, exits your lower body ("traveling downward outside the back of your legs"). When your stomach is empty of air, gradually discharge the air from your chest until you've exhaled completely. Keep the air completely emptied from your chest and lungs for about three seconds.

Notice the curving, serpentlike feeling of this breathing pattern, in contrast to the straight up-and-down feeling of ordinary breathing. Now do it again. Continue to do this lying down until you can do it well.

*Stage Three:* Sit up, either cross-legged on the floor or erect on a chair. Go through the starting sequence (see page 101). Then move into the same breathing pattern you did while lying down, except that now the figure eight, or infinity symbol, is standing on its end, vertically, as an eight normally appears. Envision the top of the eight above your head and the bottom below your feet.

Once you are comfortable with this pattern in a sitting position, breathe for several minutes using it. Finally, move to ordinary breathing, then return to the Circulation of the Light. Sense how your body feels with straight up and down breathing compared to this Figure-Eight Breathing meditation. Continue with the latter until you are ready to stop. End with the Yogic Seal.

## Feeling Comfortable

Whenever you are learning a new skill, it takes time to acquire a level of comfort. This includes the practice of an unusual breathing technique. Be patient. Soon it will be a familiar companion that can help deepen your meditation. Some people find breathing in this manner inherently rewarding. One great advantage is that if your attention wanders, you'll find yourself lapsing back into ordinary breathing. So when you're doing Figure-Eight Breathing and notice that you've lapsed into ordinary breathing, it's a reminder to focus your attention on your breathing again.

## Variations in Technique

You can use Figure-Eight Breathing as a stand-alone meditative practice or combine it with other practices. From now on, in whatever meditation you are doing, you may use either ordinary breathing or Figure-Eight Breathing.

# Self-acceptance

## Liking Yourself

### FROM AWARENESS TO ACCEPTANCE

*You can search throughout the entire universe for*
*someone who is more deserving of your love and*
*affection than you are yourself, and that person is*
*not to be found anywhere. You yourself, as much*
*as anybody . . . deserve your love and affection.*

BUDDHA

AS YOU REPLACE CRITICAL thoughts about yourself with realistic self-awareness and appreciation, you brighten your spirits.

In a conversation with psychologist Stanley Krippner, inventor Buckminster Fuller remarked that as a child, his poor eyesight made everything look fuzzy. At the age of four he was fitted with a pair of eye-glasses. Suddenly the world came into focus! Fuller speculated that getting those glasses "might have accounted for his lifelong conviction that even if ideas and relationships seemed fuzzy to him at first, they would eventually become clear." This outlook became a guiding principle that led him to success in many endeavors.[1]

Most of us, according to Krippner and fellow psychologist David Feinstein, unconsciously create a sort of personal mythology that guides our lives. Such a mythology highlights some potentials and inhibits others. Not everyone's personal myths are as fortunate as Buckminster Fuller's, say Krippner and Feinstein:

A limiting personal myth may have muted a desirable quality since your childhood. A man's tender emotions are eclipsed by images of his

160

father's machismo. A woman's mistrust of others may have been family policy when she was young. . . . A woman who gained her parents' praise and approval through high achievement destroys a marriage with unrelenting workaholism. A man whose rebelliousness kept his spirit alive amid childhood oppression is trapped in frivolous power struggles as an adult.[2]

A personal myth that is out of synch with an aspect of the real you is likely to cause distress and pain. So is one that does nothing to inspire you or help you discover deeper meanings in your life. Finding yourself in an existential crisis in which you feel *I can't go on living this way* may mean that it's time for you to change a fundamental guiding myth.

We maintain such myths by talking to ourselves in ways that are consistent with them. It's painful when these messages from yourself to yourself tell you that you are not okay, that you are unacceptable or inferior in some way.

Psychiatrist Aaron Beck asked clients to report the thoughts they had each time just before they felt bad about themselves. He found that many sent themselves messages that said pretty much the same thing, time and time again. He labeled these messages *automatic thoughts*. They were rapid sequences of self-talk, in words or visual images, that linked negative feelings to the events that triggered them. "These thoughts did not arise as a result of deliberation, reasoning, or reflection," says Beck. "The thoughts 'just happened,' as if by reflex. They . . . were difficult to 'turn off.'"[3]

Beck couldn't quite pinpoint why one particular woman felt anxious in therapy sessions. When he asked her to direct her attention to her thoughts about what she was saying while she spoke to him, she reported this sequence:

"'I am not expressing myself clearly . . . He is bored with me . . . He probably can't follow what I'm saying . . . This probably sounds foolish.' Subsequently, [she realized that she] had the same types of interactions with other people. . . . Even though she was actually quite articulate and interesting, she had continual thoughts revolving around the theme of her being inarticulate and boring."[4]

You probably have some automatic thoughts yourself. They might have been programmed into you by others, or may be responses you developed to cope with circumstances. Either way, they became part of your identity: *This is who I am,* you are essentially saying to yourself. You might feel embarrassed about such self-talk. But as Gestalt therapist Erving Polster points out in *Every Person's Life Is Worth a Novel,* even qualities you think are not so good can be fascinating. "People are often the last ones to recognize the drama in their own lives. They marvel at the adventures of others, but don't look inside to see that their own lives hold just as much possibility. . . . No one can escape being interesting."[5]

Your recognition of a limiting personal myth or story as such, rather than as reality, might filter up through your meditation, or perhaps occur in a flash of insight in the middle of daily life. Gestalt therapists Joseph Melnick and Sonja March Nevis note that "if we need to change something that does not work well for us, we paradoxically have to bring it into awareness and get to know it well; then and only then can we change."[6] If you don't or won't recognize it, you have no alternative. To change something, you have to realize that you are doing it. Then at least you have a chance to act differently.

This approach to recognizing messages you habitually send yourself, and to bringing about enduring, positive change, grows out of developing a clear awareness of what you are doing with your mind, emotions, and body at each moment. Instead of trying to change in preconceived ways, you discover who and how you are. This is related to Sri Ramana Maharshi's self-inquiry process in which you ask yourself, again and again, *Who am I?*

The answer is not a conceptual statement, but a journey of realization in which, moment by moment, you find out what you are actually experiencing and doing at this moment, and how you're doing it.

A contrasting approach is to try to live up to who you think you should be, or to create positive new stories about yourself to replace old ones that portray you as defective. For some people this works, at least for a time. Positive affirmations can give the surface layer of your self-image a boost, and even help get you through a crisis.

But that approach also has its limits. It can turn out to be another layer of conceptualization stuck like a Band-Aid on top of old feelings. When this occurs, it interferes with developing the awareness that expands your inner freedom. The ways you picture yourself, the stories you tell yourself at deeper levels, and the emotional reactions engraved in your muscle tensions and breathing patterns may remain untouched. When the Band-Aid comes off, it's easy to come crashing right back down into intense feelings of being inadequate or unacceptable.

Instead, you can change specific ways of acting that cause trouble, yet also honor yourself as you are rather than thinking you have to become different or better. Shunryu Suzuki-roshi, who founded the San Francisco Zen Center, notes that the Samyuktagama Sutra says there are four kinds of horses: excellent ones, good ones, poor ones, and bad ones:

> When we hear this story, almost all of us want to be the best horse. If it is impossible to be the best one, we want to be the second best. . . . [But] you will find that the worst horse is the most valuable one. In your very imperfections you will find the basis for your firm, way-seeking mind.[7]

## FROM AWARENESS TO ACCEPTANCE

During your next formal meditation, alert your inner Witness to notice instances of judging yourself. Do you hear any voices saying that you are unacceptable in any way? Do any images arise that make you feel "less than"? Let yourself notice how you are looking at yourself, and then return your attention to the focus of your meditation. Afterward, continue as described below.

### The Essence

The next step after doing the activity mentioned just above is to take that same meditative focus into daily life. Let your inner Witness form the intention to notice each time you say something out loud that paints an uncomplimentary picture of yourself. Notice each time an unspoken thought portrays one of your acts or qualities in a bad light. Notice even the times when you just wince or grimace or tense up at something you say or do. If you make a mistake, it doesn't mean you're a bad person. Go easy on yourself. If after a day or two you find very little that you don't like about yourself, be grateful. Perhaps you've deepened your understanding of others who are harder on themselves. You can go on to the next cell.

If, however, you find that instances of feeling less than okay are common, then start to count them. But don't go on thinking about them or get lost in self-judgment. Just notice, count, and let go—freeing your attention to do other things. You might find it useful to have a counter like those used to tally purchases at grocery stores, or an old golf score counter that resembles a wristwatch. If you can't find a counter, use the pen in your pocket or purse to make a mark on an index card or piece of paper each time you judge something about yourself as bad.

At the end of each day, add up your total. Keep a daily tally. At first, the total might rise from day to day. Don't worry—this only shows that you are becoming more aware of your criticisms of yourself. After about a week, your heightened awareness will probably lead to making fewer such critiques and your daily totals will probably start to drop.

Your objective is simply to observe your self-critical behavior. As you do so, without getting fully enmeshed in it, you'll likely begin to get outside of these patterns. You'll probably find changes in your self-evaluations occurring naturally. As you watch your negative mental pictures and judgmental stories about yourself, without either quickly looking away or getting caught in ruminating about them, you may start to contact the you who is free from self-criticism. You'll also be developing a broader ability to be aware in the moment without mixing in judgment or comparison. (Continue with this practice for as long as it feels valuable.)

### Points in the Process

As you start to recognize recurrent self-critical feedback, you can become an observer rather than being wholly identified with your self-judgments. As you let go of them, you'll more easily see your positive qualities. The goal is to free yourself and to honor and appreciate the true you.

Apply the same principle to your meditation. If you judge a session "good" or "bad," notice the judgment, then let it go. Each session is simply as it is.

### Variations in Technique

If a narrow focus on awareness and letting go of your self-criticisms does not work well for you, you can expand this practice. Also take note of your good qualities. Each time you notice or think of something about yourself that you like, compliment yourself. Appreciate your actions and qualities. (Just make sure your appreciation is real.) In so doing, you balance what you don't like (your negative appraisals) with what you feel good about. This boosts your self-esteem. Accepting your own nature is a steady path to feeling good.

## Feeling Comfortable

For roughly one person in twenty, the process of counting judgments, described above, doesn't work. If after ten days you find yourself becoming more and more self-critical, you might be that one in twenty. If so, for now focus on other meditations and awareness methods that work better for you. If at some point in the future you feel ready to come back to this, you can do so then.

**CELL 24**

··········

# Shadow

## Unseen Sides of Yourself

······································

**MESSAGES FROM DREAMS**

*All things move within your being in constant half embrace,*
*the desired and the dreaded, the repugnant and the*
*cherished, the pursued and that which you would escape.*

KAHLIL GIBRAN

**VERONICA HAD TERRIFYING NIGHTMARES** in which shadowy figures were chasing her or shooting at her. A friend asked, "In your daily life, is there any way in which you give away your power?"

"Why, yes. Since I often give in to others when I don't want to, people take advantage of me."

"I suggest," her friend said, "that you work on standing your ground. If another person keeps pushing, repeat courteously but firmly what you're unwilling to do, such as, 'Perhaps you didn't hear me. I just said no!'"

"That's scary for me."

"So are nightmares. Do you want to get rid of them?"

"Yes."

"Then try it."

Veronica experimented with her friend's suggestion. She began asking for what she really wanted and refused unwelcome requests tactfully but decisively. As she became stronger in her waking life, she became stronger in her dreams. Within two months, the chasing and shooting dreams were gone.

Long ago she had learned to keep still and do what she was told, so she buried the ability to stand up for herself in her Shadow side. Someone else might do the opposite. The Real Bad Dude who flaunts his adversarial nature might push his gentle, caring side into his Shadow. As these examples show, it's a misconception to think of our Shadow as being just that side of ourself that we think of as bad or wrong. The Shadow includes all the aspects of our being and potential that we don't acknowledge, or don't want to recognize—whether positive or negative.

Carl Jung, who first applied the term *Shadow* to these unrecognized sides of the self, was willing to say "I don't know" about events in the mind that he didn't understand. There are always shadowy elements inside us and outside us, he said, lurking beyond the boundaries of our understanding. Honoring our unconscious, and exploring it as we might explore a labyrinth of caverns, seemed to him the only way to heal the splits that torment humankind.[1]

Everyone has a Shadow. It includes your unconscious psyche, and those sides of yourself that you know exist but try not to show. It includes items you don't allow yourself to think about and realities that don't fit within the boundaries of your personal myths and stories. It includes your unrecognized dark side—the side of yourself that you fear or dislike and try to keep out of your awareness—as well as the potential to develop valuable dimensions of yourself that you've neglected. It contains your most selfish impulses, and also your potential for the altruistic feelings displayed by the world's great souls.[2]

At a young age almost everyone is taught to be good, to know the difference between right and wrong. Our invisible emotional lessons are more subtle. Many people have learned that certain feelings are okay and others are not. At its extreme, this can lead to living out a *dominant emotional theme* (a characteristic way of feeling) while numbing your other emotional dimensions. An example is the self-righteous man who flies into rage at the most minor irritations, while continually provoking others into acting in ways that give him excuses to be "justifiably" angry. Another is the woman who locks herself into following her mother's view of feeling distressed about almost everything. She goes through life as a "sad-eyed lady of the lowlands" while pushing every light and bright inclination into her Shadow.

Every emotion has a function. To think, *I should never feel this way* makes you less likely to recognize a feeling that actually exists. By contrast, when you are willing to recognize what you do feel, you can work on letting go of unhelpful, painful, or even remorseful feelings. With greater understanding of how your "light" casts a shadow, you can stop yourself from being driven by emotions that may incite you to act in unwanted ways.

One way we keep parts of ourselves in our Shadow is by distracting ourselves from seeing motives that we prefer not to admit exist in us. We sometimes disguise unwanted motives as something else. We've had students following spiritual disciplines of the East and others following spiritual paths of the West who viewed themselves as having transcended their negative sides. Their denial was palpable.

A grave problem with such an attitude is that when you keep what's potentially destructive or self-destructive in your Shadow and don't admit it to yourself, you are all too likely to project it onto others, and then try to eradicate it there. The more committed you are to viewing yourself as only good and positive, the larger and darker your Shadow is apt to be. The more tightly you try to bolt down the lid on your Shadow, the more likely it is to erupt spontaneously into your consciousness when you least want it to: "I don't know what came over me," or "I wasn't myself." In this sense, to some degree we can all relate to Dr. Jekyll/Mr. Hyde. By contrast, when we acknowledge as much of our Shadow as possible, we're less subject to being buffeted by its forces like leaves blowing in the wind.

We do not suggest that you will ever know everything in your Shadow. But you can come to know those aspects of it that hold the greatest potential value for yourself. You can also come to know those parts that could be most disruptive and destructive—and sidestep them so you can act from other motives that are better for both you and others. Through reflective exploration of your dreams, you can contact and reintegrate your unrecognized parts.

Through the following guided dream work, you can allow your inner reality to flow into your conscious awareness with greater fluidity and appreciation. As you do so, a captivating dance of light and Shadow will illuminate your path more clearly, like a candle in the darkness, to help you bring your underused potentialities into reality.

## MESSAGES FROM DREAMS

"Whatever fearful and terrifying visions you may see, recognize them to be your own thought forms," says *The Tibetan Book of the Dead*. Impulses and figures from your Shadow may float up into your awareness during any meditation. Take note of them when they do.

You can also access these figures more directly, through dream symbols. Dreams can help you contact both accepted and disowned parts of yourself. They can help you hear messages from your inner self.

For this contemplative meditation (an adaptation from Fritz Perls' therapeutic dreamwork),[3] begin with a memory of a dream—or a waking fantasy. Some people easily recall their dreams in great detail. Most, however, forget at least half the content of a dream within five minutes after waking. Some don't recall their dreams at all. But everyone dreams, and with practice, most people can learn to record and remember their dreams.

Set an alarm for a few minutes before you usually wake up. Its jarring noise can slice right into the middle of a dream, so the awareness of your dream will be vivid when you first awaken. Keep a pen and notebook or a voice recorder by your bed and record your dream immediately. (If you use a voice recorder, you may want to transcribe it later.) Give each dream a title: this is indispensable for identifying and remembering your dreams in the future.

## The Essence

Before you start to meditate, read or listen to your recording of your dream or fantasy. Then close your eyes and replay the record of your dream as vividly as you can, as if it's happening right now, from start to finish. Then contemplate it in the following manner:

First, go through the dream and imagine yourself as each person, object, or being in it—identify with each one. With each identification, mentally finish the statement, *I am . . . I feel . . . I can . . . I want . . . I don't want . . .* Use any or all of these lines that fit, or any others that might occur to you. For example: *I am a child who can't find my house. I feel lost and afraid.*

Second, create a one-line statement that sums up the dream's message as a whole, or the message of a scene that stands out. After that, for about five minutes treat the dream or fantasy as if it were a candle flame on which you are meditating. Each time your attention drifts away, return it to the dream. As you do this, listen to anything the dream or fantasy tells you.

## Variations in Technique

You might use this awareness technique: Get a notebook and a pen. Choose two elements of your dream or fantasy that feel like they have some relation to each other. Give each a distinct name, and then write out a dialog between them, using free-association. Write everything that comes into your mind as fast as you can, without stopping to think, quickly moving back and forth between the voices. For example,

Girl: "House, where are you? I don't know where you are. I feel panicky."

House: "I won't tell you. You'll have to find your own way. I don't care if you find me or not . . ."

Continue writing your dialog quickly until your energy wanes. Free-association writing like this leaves no time to pause and censor. Insights may emerge that would not be found in ordinary writing, in which you stop to think before composing.

## Points in the Process

Dreams can reveal what is occurring in your life and how you feel about it, dramatizing inner truths, feelings, and conflicts. They open revealing windows of fresh insight on life situations or relationships. They send dramatic messages that can shake you out of self-deception or warn you of dangers. They can alert you to something that's unfinished or emerging in your life. Recurrent dreams, or a series of dreams with a similar theme, call out to you to pay attention to something that's unresolved, or that you're not dealing with effectively. They can tell you about your Shadow, and about paths that are wise and unwise for you to take. Sometimes they remind you of important things that you've forgotten and may need to remember. They can even help you make decisions.

Most dreams hold symbolic rather than literal messages. You have to decode them for yourself, or find others who can offer guidance in doing so. Some books offer suggestions about the meaning of your dream symbols, but no book can tell you definitely what they mean. Finally, as you explore a dream, you may find it useful to explicitly ask yourself, *Is there a guiding message here? If so, what does it lead me toward—or away from?*[4]

*You are what your deep driving desire is. As your desire is,*
*so is your will. As your will is, so is your deed. As your*
*deed is, so is your destiny.*

BRIHADARANYAKA UPANISHAD

**DISTINGUISHING BETWEEN WHAT YOU** truly need and what you want, or think you want but can get along without, can make your days more satisfying and less stressful.

The Brihadaranyaka Upanishad, oldest of the ancient yogic texts called the Upanishads, was written more than three thousand years ago. Its incisive remarks about the role of desire in our lives have been a central feature of yogic thought since that time until our own. It is especially salient now, with commercial come-ons of every kind bombarding us and suggesting that only if we buy product X can we be happy.

The Upanishads contain two main themes related to desire. One is connected to its role as a motive. The other is its heavy emphasis on renouncing desires and trying to reach a totally desireless state.

Later, in the Yoga Sutras, written about 300 BCE by Patanjali,[1] we find "passionlessness" described as a goal that we ought to seek. At times he seems to suggest that getting free of desire and its associated affect—all feelings of pleasure or pain—is the only manner in which we can we reach a state of serenity and, ultimately, joy. If this sounds difficult, that's because for most of us it is.

It also leaves no place for people who enjoy living passionately, like Zorba the Greek, famous for his contagious, life-loving zeal. For Zorba, to laugh, love, cry, and dance zestfully was what life was all about.[2] In our own observation, the ideal of trying to be passionless may be fine for some people, but would drive others to utter madness. For many of us, even controlling our emotions appropriately seems easier said than done.

Several centuries after Patanjali, Shankara, who lived from 788 to 820 CE, clarified matters by noting that not all desires are created equal—nor is all renunciation. In his classic *Crest Jewel of Discrimination,* Shankara is most concerned with letting go of selfish desires that harm others, and with the harm you do to yourself when you make yourself insensitive and uncaring.[3] He astutely recognized that renouncing all desire would quickly lead to major problems, such as a quick death. Desires for food, water, and other basic needs are innate. They become a problem only when we neglect them, or come to believe that we need far more than we really do. Tantric scholar Harish Johari says,

> Desires are natural, and as long as we are embodied, we will have them. . . .
> The more we try to suppress [natural desires], the stronger they become. . . .
> Since Tantra accepts desire as the prime motivating force of the universe, it
> does not ask its aspirants to renounce desire. Other spiritual sciences advise
> the avoidance of desire. . . . Yet one is left with the paradox that to achieve
> desirelessness, one must have a strong desire—to be desireless![4]

Desires can be classified into four groups. *Ordinary desires* are those things we want for ourselves or for those close to us, which, when fulfilled, don't have much intentional impact on anyone else. *Selfish desires* are those that, when fulfilled, keep others from getting what they want, or cause them harm—and we know it. With *hostile desires,* we have an active intention of harming another person or their interests, whether in a small way or a large one. With *altruistic desires,* we actively intend to befriend and benefit others—usually others who are outside our close circle of family and friends.

Two hundred years before Patanjali, the concept of the Four Noble Truths came to Buddha as he sat beneath a pipal tree in Bodh Gaya. The second Noble Truth holds that self-centered craving, and desire for that which we are unlikely to get, causes much of the avoidable suffering in our world. We ourselves create this suffering. Driven by desires and cravings, we grasp in futility at the constant, changing flux of life as if it were something fixed and stable. Through unrelenting cravings for things we don't really need but think we do, we make ourselves unhappy.

Philosopher Archie Bahm suggests that the essence of Buddha's philosophy is that desire for what will not be attained ends in frustration; therefore, to avoid suffering, avoid desiring what will not be attained. However, notes Bahm, "it is natural to want more—at least a little more—than one gets. . . . Secondly, one cannot always anticipate precisely what will be attained."[5] Bahm also points out that since effort of will or strength of desire itself often influences the outcome, we ought to desire strongly enough to assure adequate effort. But desires are not equipped with antilock brakes, so they often overshoot their mark. In general, the stronger the craving, the more bitter the frustration. If you can let go of desires that are unlikely to be fulfilled, and the conditioned states and views that often cause them, one cause of your suffering falls away.

A key insight here is to gain a greater sense of which of your desires are rooted in deep needs. The Dalai Lama advises: "Develop a strong desire to refrain from harming others, either physically or verbally."[6] He also suggests that we keep our desires close to our true needs. So even if we try to dissolve the mental and emotional energy that we've attached to disposable desires, it's important to honor our true deep needs. As the I Ching notes, "Any merely superficial ordering of life that leaves its deepest needs unsatisfied is as ineffectual as if no attempt at order had ever been made."

Some people want to feel stronger and better able to take care of themselves financially in the world. Some are looking for more self-respect, respect from others, or both. Some want to feel that they are contributing something of value somewhere, somehow. These are not flickering shadows of desire that will float away on an afternoon breeze.

You don't have to put down material things as inherently not spiritual. Sri Aurobindo, a revered spiritual master, said, "Material things are not to be despised—without them there can be no manifestation in the material world."[7] The point is to know what you need, and to direct your energy toward getting it. The next meditation is a means to help you with this process.

Now is a good time to look inward and assess your desires and needs. Perhaps you'd like to change some of your ways of thinking and acting so that they're more fulfilling and less frustrating. In the following practice, you will be reflecting on what you truly want and chanting or repeating silently to yourself, in a precisely specified way, phrases that support their fulfillment. For instance, if your desire is to reduce stress, your focus will be on repeating words and phrases that will help you relax.

# MANTRA PASSAGES

Using the Mantra Passage is similar to a mantra meditation, but instead of repeating just one word, you'll be using a phrase or a sentence, using a distinctive method of coupling words and breathing. Multiple-word mantras have been used since ancient times, and are still widely used to attain desires, change behavior, and free the mind from problems. This Mantra Passage meditation can help you affix the power of a mantra's message firmly in your mind.

For the most part, multiword mantras of no more than about ten words tend to work best. One example is *Aum gang ganapataye namah—aum.* It is a Tantric mantra chanted to invoke the elephant-headed god Ganesha to help bring peace of mind and remove obstacles.

Choose a relevant passage and keep it in your consciousness for as long as it helps you develop the understanding, attitude, or quality it addresses. Swami Rama, who was one of the first Indian yogis to allow himself to be studied by Western scientists, did this with *No matter where you live, live cheerfully.* He found that it never stopped being useful.

For now, let's suppose that for your mantra you've selected some words from a poem by Rabindranath Tagore: "[May] all my desires ripen into fruits of love." (Having faith in your words will give you the impetus to use the Mantra Passage.) If you don't care for that passage, here are several more:

> Prayer by St. Theresa of Avila: "Where there is hatred, let me sow love."
> Pete Catches, Sioux medicine man: "All nature is in us; all of us is in nature."
> "Success will find me; I will attain my goal!"

You may also choose a beginning quote from any cell, or use any other relevant line you like.

## The Essence

As usual, begin with the starting sequence. Continue as you did with your single-word mantra meditation, with this difference: Using Tagore's passage, above, on either your first inhalation or exhalation—whichever is easiest for you, subvocally say the word *May.* Empty your mind during the other half of your breathing cycle. On the next breath, subvocally say *all.* On the third breath, inhalation, *my.* With the fourth breath, *desires.* Continue in this fashion, until you have finished the Mantra Passage with the word *love.*

Next, take an empty breath, and then start over again with the same sentence, again saying it one word at a time, with each word on a successive breath. Go through the entire mantra at least ten times in this way. As in previous practices, end with the Yogic Seal or any other closing gesture of respect or devotion you prefer.

Throughout the day, keep your Mantra Passage in the back of your mind. Be alert to moments when it might illuminate something you are doing, feeling, or thinking about. It may cast a whole different light on some of your actions and projects, letting you see them from a new angle.

## Variations in Technique

Begin with your starting sequence. Still your mind as much as possible. Move into awareness of your mantra passage. You can repeat it to yourself on either your incoming or outgoing breath, whichever is most comfortable for you. Then with each breath, starting with either the inbreath or the outbreath, run the entire passage through your mind. Empty your mind of thoughts during the other half of your breathing cycle. Continue in this manner for about ten minutes.

## Points in the Process

While you are meditating, don't try to think about the passage. Use it as a focus of concentration, like a candle flame. The meaning will sink in all by itself, and any reflections you have will bubble up out of your depths on their own. If your mind drifts elsewhere, take note of whether there is a message regarding something you need to think about, and then return your focus to your Mantra Passage meditation.

You can use a multiword mantra just as many people use one-word mantras, keeping it with you for as long as it feels relevant. Also, you might start collecting inspirational lines when you read or hear them. If you have a selection of lines for contemplation at hand, when you are ready to meditate you can skim through them until you find one that fits your mental state. Or you might put them in a bowl and pick one at random. You just may find that your Mantra Passage meditation brings about a radical change for the better in your attitude and actions.[8]

*Listening is a magnetic and strange thing, a creative force.*
*The friends who listen to us are the ones we*
*move toward. When we are listened to, it . . .*
*makes us unfold and expand.*

KARL MENNINGER

**DEEPLY WANTING TO HEAR** another person, coupled with listening attentively, can bring about a remarkable enhancement of your ability to communicate.

Carl Rogers, psychologist extraordinaire, had the remarkable ability to carry on a dialog in which he said little more than "Uh-huh" or "Oh?" as another person spoke at length. He never interrupted. He almost never argued. He heard the other person's inner world, and the other person sensed it.

As Rogers showed, effective listening requires a close attentive focus on the other person's words and feelings. In a sense it is a concentrative meditation in which the other person is the candle flame. Just as in sitting meditation when you are mindful of your inner voices, in listening well you become mindful of someone else. Your attentive practice of silent contemplation can help you as you talk with others.

Most people like to think they're good listeners. In reality, most of us are not. We start talking, and very quickly our own thoughts and feelings interfere with truly hearing. These include our beliefs and reactions, our judgments and evaluations, and our ideas about what to say in return. A person may get so involved in rehearsing a reply that she misses much of what her counterpart is saying. Or she'll interrupt so he can't even finish. This is apt to cause resentment, and he might even tune out anything she says. If she keeps shifting the spotlight from his interests onto her own, she's not listening, and he'll feel it. A major component of listening is to keep the spotlight of your attention focused on the other person—not on your own concerns.

Someone's manner and attitude can make it easy or difficult to communicate with them. An attitude of truly wanting to hear as fully as possible, and listening deeply, is important in gaining true understanding. When that's lacking, there's a good chance that people will distort what is said with their own preconceptions and biases.

Rogers pointed out that even when a person's attempt to understand is off the mark, if she's sincerely trying to understand the other person's meaning, and he can feel that, it means a lot. Her sensitive listening tells him that she cares about his feelings and concerns.

When a person truly listens, she is actually saying, "I want to hear you clearly and accurately." Whether her attention wanders for an instant, or whether her counterpart is not communicating clearly, is not so important. If she doesn't quite get the message, she can let him know she wants to hear, and ask questions to help her grasp what he is trying to say.

When another person feels truly heard, he often tends to feel greater freedom to express his true self. "When I . . . let him know that I have heard his own private personal meanings," says Rogers, ". . . it is as though he were saying, 'Thank God, somebody heard me. Somebody knows what it's like to be me. . . .' By that one simple response he is released from his loneliness; he has become a human being again."[1]

## BRACKETING

A structured process that can help you take a major step toward hearing something of another person's world is called *bracketing*. This involves using your inner Witness to notice each reaction that arises within you as you listen, and then mentally placing brackets around that thought, feeling, or sensation, and setting it aside so you can continue to focus on the other person. You can return to your own reactions later, after you have heard his or her experience. You can learn to bracket using the following methods:

> You notice yourself starting to react with an emotion, a disagreement, an
>     opinion, or an attitude. You may even start to express that reaction, in
>     words, gestures, posture, or body tension or relaxation.

You tell yourself inwardly, "That reaction is going to interfere with hearing this person."

You mentally put brackets around your entire response and set it aside until later—or just let go of it.

You return your attention fully to the other person so you can truly hear the events in his or her world and his or her experience of them.

When our students do this exercise, we ask each of them to bracket their reactions as they listen to the other person talk about something of major personal interest for twenty minutes. Afterward, many say, "It was so hard for me! I had no idea how much my own reactions interfere with hearing another person. Bracketing is so useful."

It's alright to ask questions as you listen in this way. And yes, it's alright to disclose your own experiences that are related to what the other person is saying—in just a sentence or two, while keeping the spotlight on the other person.

After the person has finished talking, you might want to explicitly sum up the major theme or themes you seemed to hear and then check out your perception: "It sounds like you felt like you were on an emotional roller coaster between incredible highs and lows. Is that how you experienced it?"

If the answer is, "Not quite," then you can ask the other person to restate the theme. You don't have to make this hard work. A relaxed and receptive attitude will help your listening.

## FOUR POTENT PHRASES

The four phrases stated below are for actual use in your everyday conversations. Using these lines helps focus your attention on the other person's feelings and concerns. As long as you clearly capture the meaning of each phrase, feel free to replace our words with your own language.

### The Essence

When appropriate, insert one or more of these phrases or your equivalent as you listen to another person. You'll probably find it useful to make them part of your everyday conversational repertoire.

1. "Please say that again in different words. I want to make sure I understand you correctly." A closely related line is, "Will you please repeat that? My mind drifted for an instant and I really want to hear you."

2. "You seem to be saying . . . Is that right?" An alternative line is, "I think I heard you say . . . Am I getting what you mean?" When you are right, a person will know he is being heard. Sometimes he might also hear meanings and feelings that he was conveying but had not consciously realized. When you are wrong, be willing to let go of what you thought another person meant.

3. "I'm guessing that you feel (intend, want, etc.) . . . Is that right?" It's all too easy to get caught in a sticky web of assumptions about what's going on within another person. The simple word *guessing* is crucial. What's important is that you verify your guesses, rather than being committed to automatically assuming that they are right.

4. "Please give me a concrete example of what you mean." Misunderstandings occur when you and I think we're talking about the same thing but actually we're not. We can stay lost in a fog of abstraction or metaphor without ever hearing anything of the other person's real experience, and never even realize it. This phrase moves a dialog from generalizations to specifics, and leads you from your imaginings to real events that underlie another person's feelings and beliefs.

These four lines, or variations of them, let the other person know you are present and interested. They invite the other person to add depth and detail to his or her remarks.

## Points in the Process

Sometimes listening is not easy. Every message—our own or someone else's—contains both an explicit meaning and an underlying feeling tone. The words we hear can illuminate or disturb, elate or deflate us. Because words and sounds have such a vibrational and energetic quality, it's usually better to spend more time listening to words that inspire us and less to words that drain us.

TV interviewer Larry King leaves us with this thought: "I remind myself every morning: Nothing I say this day will teach me anything. So if I'm going to learn, I must do it by listening."

**CELL 27**

..........

# Loss

## Grief, Sadness, and Recovery

..............................

**SITTING LIKE A MOUNTAIN**

*It is the law of heaven to make fullness empty*
*and to make full what is modest; when the sun is*
*at its zenith it must . . . turn toward its setting, and at*
*its nadir it rises to a new dawn. . . . This heavenly*
*law works itself out in the fates of men.*

I Ching

SEVERAL KEY INSIGHTS AND a contemplative meditation can soften losses and contribute to your inner strength and your ability to move on to new projects and stages in life.

At times we all face loss. We may see a field of wildflowers where we played as children turn into asphalt and concrete. Sometimes we lose money, property, or possessions, or face failure in our enterprises. We lose games, athletic contests, or fall from fame into disgrace. Through life-shattering experiences we can lose our faith in what we have believed. And as we confront loss from the deaths of those we love, and ultimately our own demise, we may have to revise our beliefs about who and how we are. We need ways to face such losses without making them even worse, and without losing heart.

Long ago in India, a woman's son died from a bite from a poisonous snake. In denial, she refused to believe that he was dead. Carrying him in her arms, she pleaded with guru after guru to heal him—all in vain. At last she came to Buddha. "Sister, I will heal him under one condition," he said. "I need some medicine. You must bring me a seed of black mustard from a household where no relative or loved one has died—no mother or father or child, no brother or sister or cousin or dear beloved friend."

The woman went eagerly to beg a mustard seed from household after household. Everywhere she told her story, she heard a similar story of loss and grief in return. She could find no household that had not mourned. As she retold her story over and over, and heard from others about their losses, she came to realize that the whole world shared her suffering. Finally she began to live with the fact of her child's death.[1] Since that time, because of its healing effect, the custom of exchanging personal stories about heart-rending losses has spread throughout India.

Although death is the most potent form of loss for many people, unrequited love often takes second place. In such cases, as sages have noted throughout the ages, there is a difference between physical loss and psychological loss. A girl whose boyfriend is cheating on her may lose trust. It takes a brave soul to ask what's missing in the relationship and find a way to set it right. A man who finds that his wife is having an affair may angrily threaten her. It may take a long time before he realizes that a better solution is to ask her to join him in visiting a marriage counselor. Sensible action can prevent some losses like these before they happen, but not always. During such times we can only try to not torment ourselves and do what we can to restore our lost sense of what had been.

Other losses are less obvious. You might lose the feeling that you have to be right, or some idea about how you are supposed to be. Zen master Jakusho Kwong roshi describes a time when he twisted his ankle and damaged a ligament:

> I had to use crutches for four months. . . . I couldn't sit full lotus as I always had done. One of my students loaned me a beach chair [but] part of me was afraid someone from Sotoshu Headquarters would arrive unexpectedly and see me sitting California Zen in a beach chair. I had to [sit] not as I wanted to sit but as I had to sit. . . . All of my opinions about people sitting in chairs, or [other positions] dissolved. It was as if a large window opened for me.[2]

Søren Kierkegaard goes one step farther. "Every other loss, that of an arm, a leg, five dollars, a wife, etc., is sure to be noticed [but] the greatest danger, that of losing one's own self, may pass off quietly as if it were nothing."

When an irrevocable loss occurs or is about to occur, it helps to grieve. Grief involves reconciling yourself to live with what is, however much you may want what was to continue. Grief always involves sadness. Sometimes it reaches the extreme of depression—especially in a case like that of the breakup of a marriage in which the partners have lost any clear sense of who or how they are outside the relationship. In the beginning, a grieving process often includes shock or denial. This is often followed by resentment or anger. That can give way to despair or depression, resignation, and then, hopefully, acceptance and recovery.

Grief also includes putting aside our emotional inhibitions and letting ourselves feel fully. We now know that healthy crying has positive physiological effects. This is an important insight for men who feel like they always have to keep up a stoic front. Similarly, women who usually bury their anger beneath tears often find it healthy to let themselves feel angry about circumstances that led to their loss. If you deny those feelings, they're still there, eating at you. As you work through the feelings of loss or frustration, you become more able to feel whole and move forward through life.

By feeling and facing your sorrow, even though it may be difficult, you escape the trap of hanging on to your grieving, and perhaps letting it control you. There is a time to grieve, and a time to let grief become an honored part of your past, so you can be open to what life's next moment brings. Out of grief new life is born. David Brazier observes, "The time of loss is an enlightenment. At such a time we are forced . . . to perceive reality in a more naked fashion. . . . After such a rebirth . . . one has opened up to the condition of the whole world."[3]

Everyone's personal losses exist within a larger reality of impermanence. The ability to perceive all beings coming into and going out of existence, day after day and year after year, was one of the insights acquired by Buddha as part of his enlightenment. The shock and pain of loss can be eased somewhat, noted Buddha, by remembering that everyone and everything in this world is impermanent. Moments arise, and then are gone. People and things and situations move into our life, and then pass out of it.

Much of the suffering that often comes with loss results from wanting what was to continue, even when it can't or doesn't. Not long ago a relative of ours died. His wife sent cards to all the family with a wonderful picture of the two of them smiling at each other as they had a drink together, and the caption, "It's been fun!" She chose to focus on her appreciation of the five wonderful decades they had spent together rather than on her loss. Her card truly reflected the spirit of impermanence.

The less we realize the truth of impermanence, the more tightly we grasp at the constant, changing flux of life as if it were something stable and fixed. We may have a poignant desire for that which is impermanent to endure beyond its time. As we begin to acknowledge impermanence, says Buddhist teacher Sylvia Boorstein,

> sooner or later we see what the Buddha saw. We see the truth of change. We begin to understand how fragile life is and how, most surely, we will lose [what] is dear to us. At some point, in some way, we ask ourselves . . . "Is there some way I can do this life with my eyes open and my heart open and still love it? Is there a way not to suffer?"[4]

In autumn, leaves fall from trees and bushes and flowering plants to enrich the soil in an annual ritual of renewal. In springtime, buds swell and new leaves appear. In orchards, gardens, and our lives, there are times of falling away and times of new growth. Nature instructs us about how to live with the seasons of our lives.

But in life's projects, loss may be a splash of ice-cold water that jolts you into trying something different, something that works this time around. Think about the I Ching's comment that "in such times of shock, presence of mind is all too easily lost: the individual overlooks all opportunities for action and mutely lets fate take its course. But if he allows the shocks of fate to induce movement within his mind, he will overcome these external blows with little effort."[5] The method below may help you carry the heavy energy of loss with less weight on your soul.

## SITTING LIKE A MOUNTAIN

This contemplative meditation is especially useful in times of loss, despair, or both. For it to work well, you have to sit up straight, whether you are sitting on the floor or on a chair. Feel your body in strong, solid contact with the ground or chair, like the base of a mountain firmly rooted in the earth. Close your eyes and double check to make sure you are sitting with an upright and balanced posture. Perform your starting sequence and proceed as follows.

### The Essence

Imagine yourself to be a massive granite mountain. You have been sitting in this spot for millions of years, and you will be here for millions of years to come. Clouds cluster around your peak. Up to the snow line you are covered with forests and meadows in which animals live and graze. Sense yourself as this great mountain, immovable, as strong as anything on the earth. Take a few minutes to feel the blowing of gentle breezes, the sun bathing your meadows with its warmth, and refreshing streams of cool water flowing through them. Throughout your visualization, continue to sense your breath, whether the air around you is quiet or the wind is strong.

Now feel the wind picking up. Soon a storm is upon you, howling through the trees, drenching your lower slopes while driving snow falls on your peaks. Trees sway wildly as animals take shelter behind boulders or in canyons. Feel the full force of the storm against you and blowing past you. All the while, know that you are immovable and eternal, strong and resilient. At last, feel the wind dying down, the snow and rain stopping, the animals coming out of hiding, and the wildflowers opening again. End with relaxed breathing and the Yogic Seal.

Here's the key part: next time you feel emotionally distraught from loss (or for that matter, from any other difficult event), wherever you are, adopt a solid, straight-backed sitting posture and go into this Sitting Like a Mountain meditation. Affirm that you can handle whatever life throws you—and that after the storm you will still be standing strong. In time, the clouds covering the sunshine of your happiness will move on and you will find a new sense of opportunity, openness, and freedom.

## Variations in Technique

After you have done this meditation, it can also be useful in everyday situations that have nothing to do with loss. When you are at the point of getting angry or defensive about something that's occurring, you can remember your "mountain" self. As you become one with your inner mountain, you don't have to respond at all. Instead, feel the strength of your immense composure as that storm blows through.

## Points in the Process

There is the danger when someone you love dies, or the two of you go your separate ways, of losing valuable parts of yourself that emerged in the presence of that person. So it is important to find new ways for those parts of you to keep on living.

When you find yourself sifting through memories of your time together, instead of focusing on the sadness of loss, focus on gratitude for the good times. Let happy memories fill you with good energy. When sadness is strong, acknowledge it, but don't dwell on it to the point where it interferes with your ability to be here now. As Lao-tzu wrote, "The sage . . . trusts his inner vision [and] allows things to come and go."

## CELL 28

· · · · · · · · · · ·

# Judgment

## Beyond One-upmanship

· · · · · · · · · · · · · · · · · · · · · · · · ·

### AN INTERNAL FRAME OF REFERENCE

*Let whoever among you is faultless
throw the first stone.*

JESUS

**MOVING FROM MALIGNING OTHERS** to accurately stating your personal likes and dislikes clarifies your thinking and leads to nonjudgment.

Jesus spoke the preceding words to a crowd of men who intended to stone a woman who had committed adultery. When they heard him, the passage continues, "one by one they went away . . . and Jesus . . . said to the woman, 'Where are they? Has no one condemned you?' 'No one, sir,' she said. Jesus replied, 'Nor do I.'"[1]

This story expresses one of the major themes that runs throughout Jesus's teachings. It is also found in his explicit principle, "Pass no judgment, and you will not be judged; do not condemn, and you will not be condemned; acquit, and you will be acquitted . . . for whatever measure you deal out to others will be dealt to you in return."[2] And in reference to the process that today's psychologists call *projection,* Jesus advised someone who was busy criticizing another to "remove the great plank in your own eye" instead. In so saying, he astutely recognized the tendency for people to see and condemn in others those very same qualities they dislike and don't want to acknowledge in themselves.

The tendency to judge others as bad, wrong, inferior, defective, sinful, or uncool is widespread. The Tibetan Buddhist master Chogyam Trungpa says, "Disparaging people is based on showing off your own virtue. You think that your virtues can only show because others' are lessened." He notes that this can apply to meditation: "You might have better training . . . and say, 'Somebody's attention span . . . is shorter than mine; therefore, I am better. . . . Fundamentally, these are all ways of saying, 'That other person is stupid, and I am better than he is.'"[3]

None of us is faultless or without some bias that impedes our vision. Making matters worse, many of our judgments of others are hypocritical. We stand on quicksand when we make snide remarks about how others are not so hot. It's all-too-easy to manufacture self-serving excuses to justify your put-downs.

Why is the tendency to judge others—often very harshly—so widespread? Let's look at some probable causes.

First, judgment is an evaluative faculty that helps us survive. Every day we make evaluations of which item, person, or course of action will help us achieve our goals, and which will not. So it's easy to slide into a put-down of whomever or whatever is less helpful, and into uncritical admiration of whomever or whatever is more helpful.

A second reason is the tragically destructive dynamic of self-righteousness. Simple, unadorned righteousness is acting in a way that benefits others, our community, or environment. Self-righteousness is entirely different: it is making up a self-serving excuse for looking down on others and treating them poorly. This usually takes the form of a conviction that we are "better than" them. From there it's a short step to telling others how they are "less than" we think they ought to be. In this situation, people act in ways that harm while pretending to be fully justified in doing so. History's greatest butcher, Adolf Hitler, made "Gott mit uns" (God is with us) his slogan while murdering millions. Other parallels are easy enough to find. As H. G. Wells said, "Moral indignation is jealousy with a halo."

Author and founder of the integral movement Ken Wilber speaks of "deepening" our consciousness rather than "raising" it.[4] This helps us to avoid the trap of judging ourselves as "higher" or better than others while denying the existence of aspects of ourselves that we consider "lower." The attitude that "my consciousness is higher than yours" plays a big role in the kind of religious one-upmanship that says, "Our way is better than theirs." The same dynamic occurs in political correctness (of the Right, Left, or center) that stops people from perceiving what's really happening when it doesn't fit their labels and preconceptions.

The third explanation for the widespread tendency to judge others as less than ourselves is because it helps us feel superior. If at some level a person doesn't like something about himself, when he puts you down he can feel a little better. When done crudely, this takes the form of gross intimidation, like the school bully who picks on weaker children. When done cleverly, it leaves others feeling bad without knowing quite how they were put down. (One sneering word in a cutting tone of voice may suffice.) Bizarre as it seems, such tactics were glorified in a popular twentieth-century book, *The Theory and Practice of Gamesmanship and One-Upmanship,* which described many subtle ways to make other people feel inferior to you. Actually, one-upmanship works only as long as the victim and bystanders buy into it. As Eleanor Roosevelt observed, "No one can make me feel inferior without my permission." The naked truth is that one-upmanship is inherently a very low-consciousness activity.

Just as you would prefer to avoid being the victim of others' judgments, you can avoid making them the victim of yours. You can start becoming more aware of such inclinations, and try letting go of whatever tendency you have to speak and act in ways that make others feel wrong, bad, or inadequate. Your words have power, and coupled with actions, can cause people to either feel better or worse.

On the one hand, when you focus on the good in people, your kindness brightens the lives of others, and tends to brighten your own life as well. On the other hand, being a chronic critic and habitual judge tends to make you harder, more hostile, and more brittle—and that's probably not what you want. Lao-tzu says,

> *When a plant is living, it is soft and tender.*
> *When it is dead, it becomes withered and dry.*
> *Hence, the hard and rigid belongs to the company of the*
>   *dead;*
> *The soft and supple belongs to the company of the living.*[5]

To acknowledge and appreciate people and things as they are is soft and supple. To scorn them with a judgmental eye and tongue is hard and rigid. The habit of criticizing and condemning is a harsh wind blowing through life. If you tend to be judgmental, even when others say, "You really told him!" they'll also be wary of being your next victim. They'll close down somewhat in order to be less visible targets when you turn that same attitude in their direction.

By letting go of this tendency, you can ease whatever hardhearted feelings you may carry with you. In so doing, you move toward feeling better within yourself and in the wider world around you.

In your inward journey, notice your judgments and put-downs of others just as you were attentive to your judgments of yourself in the From Awareness to Acceptance meditation (cell 23). When you are able to notice such reactions without getting fully enmeshed in them, you are likely to find that some changes in your attitudes and self-talk occur by themselves. Just notice. If you go on to mentally criticize yourself for judging, notice that. When judgments float through your mind that you are unwilling to let go of, acknowledge them, too. We all have a few—especially about people who have caused great harm to other people, places, or other beings we love. Long ago, when asked whether she ever got angry or upset, Theresa of Avila reportedly replied, "What do you think I am, anyway, a saint?"

## AN INTERNAL FRAME OF REFERENCE

Carl Rogers offers a highly useful alternative to a judgmental stance. He suggests that our awareness of our experience, and our perception of others and the world is most accurate when it is expressed from an internal frame of reference. For example, I never truly know that "He's a jerk" or "She's a really great gal." All I know for sure is that they seem that way to me—or more accurately, that I have certain feelings about them—with opinions attached. This is sometimes called "I-language." It acknowledges that in the last analysis, I speak only for myself.

### The Essence

In both meditation and daily affairs, each time you find yourself labeling anyone or anything as *good* or *bad, positive* or *negative,* reframe it in terms of your own feelings: *I like . . . I dislike . . .* or even, *I detest . . .* or, *I'm amazed by . . .* or however else you feel.

During contemplation, framing your thoughts in this manner will illuminate your inner critic and move you toward a more accurate perception of yourself and your world. This shift broadens your realm of awareness from just a positive or negative judgment to your whole spectrum of feelings, which may include ambivalence or several feelings at once. If the voice of your inner critic is harsh, magnifying your awareness of that voice gives you the power to soften it and become kinder to yourself.

In conversations with others, this will give you a stronger position. When someone attacks your statement, you can reply, "You may feel differently. But at this moment that is the way I feel." You are perceiving and speaking your truth, from your own internal frame of reference. As you absorb this reality, you may start feeling less of a need to challenge others when they state their likes and dislikes. This can help you hear them more deeply instead of getting caught in argument.

## Points in the Process

Can downsizing your judgmental attitude really have a significant effect? Try it and see. One of Carl Rogers's students who was working on awareness of his inner judge commented: "I feel less rigid, more open to the world. And I like myself better for it."[6]

Nonetheless, if you are the victim of another person's criticism, and others around you admire the one-upper's put-down, it can leave you feeling bad. It's useful to have some psychological judo moves available to help you respond in a healthy manner. On a one-to-one level, sometimes total silence combined with eye contact that bores into the other person will jolt him into recognizing what he's doing. Sometimes a simple honest response is effective: "When you talk to me that way, I feel like having nothing to do with you. Is that what you want?"

When all else fails, and if you are in a situation that allows this method of last resort, a useful response is to shift the spotlight to the other person, identifying what he or she is doing in a negative light. "Are you always so hostile, or just having an especially bad night?" Your tone of voice can make clear that this is not retaliation. A statement of this sort moves the focus from you to the other person's antagonistic or inconsiderate behavior. It's apt to make the put-down artist clam up fast. You don't have to be anybody's doormat. Ideally, you leave the door open for mutually respectful future interaction. This is can be a delicate balance.

If the one-upper doesn't fall silent, change the subject, or move to a friendlier mode of interaction at that point, but instead continues to be negative, you can step out of the win-lose structure of that interaction. Disengage by turning your attention to someone else or walking away. Breathe deeply and liberate yourself from that entanglement. Then you can be receptive to what happens in the next moment of your life.

# Presence

## Awake in Each Moment

· · · · · · · · · · · · · · · · · · · · · · · · · · · · ·

**FRAME BY FRAME**

*This moment will never come again.
The moment that you are living right now is [an]
opportunity to make your life vividly alive.*

DAININ KATAGIRI-ROSHI

**EACH MOMENT IS WHERE** past and future meet. Be truly present as life unfolds from one moment to the next, and problems tend to drop away.

Kapil Adwait was an Indian Air Force pilot who flew many daring missions, and then became the pilot for the prime minister of India—India's equivalent of a pilot for U.S. Air Force One. In his midthirties, he began to feel that, "there must be something more, a new frontier to explore." He left the Air Force, trekked high into the Himalayas, and studied with advanced yogis. He became remarkably adept, learning to slow his body processes down to the point where at one point he was buried in the ground for two weeks and emerged alive in perfect health. These abilities have been confirmed by scientific testing. He is now called Mahayogi Pilot Baba.

Even though he has accomplished these and other remarkable feats, he encourages appreciation of "everyday miracles":

> Sunrise, the world is waking. Birds start to chatter. People stir, the dew sparkles, the flowers release their fragrance. A baby cries. A mother responds, and there are the smells of a meal being prepared. Truly all things great and small are in the service of this message.[1]

The "message" to which Pilot Baba refers is that living a rich, full life is based in part on our ability to be fully present in each moment. When we are aware and responsive, we discover what to do next. Beyond any method, technique, or discipline, the very essence of mindfulness is to "be here now"[2] with yourself, with another being, or with any situation. Life unfolds in each instant. If you are not quite here, you might miss it—whatever *it* is.

Incisive Western thinkers acknowledge that same reality. "What often escapes notice are those simple events which give context and continuity to life," says Gestalt therapist Erving Polster, who relates this incident:

> One person, for example, asked me what interesting things I was doing lately. Although I knew he wanted to know about bigger things, I told him how I had especially enjoyed walking across my house that morning to get a glass of water. The feel of my soft shoes against the wooden floor, the view outdoors as I passed my living room windows . . . and the pleasures of just drinking water . . . mattered more at that moment than anything else.[3]

When truly present, you have the best chance to act in a way that fits both you and your life's situation. By contrast, when your inner chatterbox is turned up high, others may feel like you're impervious to their ideas and feelings. When so many messages come from your internal noise generator, you have little attention left for them—and may not even realize it.

"In the transient stream of time, moments appear and disappear," says Katagiri-roshi. Presence is being in this moment, "before you try to bring any concept or idea into it . . . while letting past moments drop away."[4] Long ago, continues Katagiri-roshi, "Dōgen Zenji said that if you want to say something about what a moment is, say that moment is arising. The Japanese term for arising is *ki*. Ki is a kind of energy, always coming up, like spring water bubbling up from under the ground."

Being attentive to what's bubbling up is a way to avoid being so single-minded about your program that you miss some important feature of what's occurring in the present. Instead of being caught in our programs, whether or not they fit the circumstances, we need to respond to the real situation.

It's misunderstanding to think that being fully present in the moment means ignoring past and future. Your present includes your memories of your past. Spanish poet, philosopher, and novelist George Santayana wrote, "Those who cannot remember the past are condemned to repeat it."

Santayana's statement applies to ordinary people as well as heads of nations, companies, and other major enterprises. Even when you attend closely to what's occurring in the present, it's often useful to remember what worked in the past and what didn't. And, points out social psychologist Philip Zimbardo, being *present with the past* is prized by some people and cultures, especially in conversations about their collective past with friends and family: "Remember the time when Uncle Giovanni . . . ?" In countries with oral traditions, stories of the past help transmit the culture.[5]

On the other hand, old habits and expectations from the past can eat away your ability to be present. Life can become like an old movie that you replay again and again instead of responding to what's unique and alive now. Likewise, if your future is based wholly on past programs and expectations, it's likely to feel rehearsed and less interesting.

But there is more than one way of relating to the past. In The Time Paradox, Zimbardo and his coauthor John Boyd quote Roman poet Martial, who wrote, "To be able to enjoy one's past life is to live twice." They report their discovery that people who view their past positively tend to function better in the present than those who view it negatively. They suggest asking "Who was I?" and then replying with twenty different answers. Next, they suggest, "List three significant negative events that have occurred in your life." With each of those three, go on to ask, "What positive messages can be taken from these events?" Finally, they suggest that you answer the question, "How can these [three] lessons improve your future?"[6]

Acting now in ways that help bring about a positive future is also important. We all know people who are so committed to having a good time now that they don't do what's necessary to prepare for tomorrow. Almost all of us at least occasionally give in to temptation because it feels good now, as we push future consequences into a dark corner of our mind.

One of our students tried both present and future orientations in turn:

> I just wanted to have fun. But "living as if there is no tomorrow" led to very poor decisions involving drugs and sex. Then I did a 180-degree turn and focused completely on the future. I rarely had quality time with friends, family, or myself. My friends dropped away. I was successful and miserable. Finally I found a balance. I tried to live each day as if it were my last, but also as if I would live forever. That was difficult at first, but now it comes more easily.

In thinking about all this, we were puzzled at the apparent contradiction between a "get it all and do it all now" present focus that neglects the future, and the positive qualities of the here-and-now presence developed by meditation. Zimbardo provides clarity. He calls an "I just want to have fun" outlook a present hedonistic time orientation, and the kind of presence developed by meditation as a holistic present orientation. In the expanded perception of the holistic present, past and future are closely interconnected in our consciousness without diminishing our ability to be focused in the here-and-now. This state of consciousness includes truly being in the moment and also includes being thoughtful about how your present acts affect the future.[7]

Your present exists in and of itself. It's also the focal point of past and future. Each day you make choices about which scenes you'll step into and which you won't. Those choices affect the nature of your future, and your presence in the now. Zimbardo found people who are good at both reaching their goals and enjoying the pleasures of the moment can switch from one time perspective to another, according to which one fits the situation best.

## FRAME BY FRAME

Just as Dōgen Zenji noted that each moment arises from the previous one, each breath arises from the preceding breath. In this practice you attend closely to all that occurs in and around you during each cycle of breathing.

In the television age we've grown used to watching brief clips of events flash onto the screen, one after another. Since many are shown for just about the time it takes you to inhale and exhale (or even more briefly than that), you can think of whatever you notice during each cycle of breath as analogous to one of those video clips on TV.

You are most likely also familiar with the old way of making movies, which consists of taking a series of still pictures or frames on a roll of film. In action sequences, each frame is just a little different from the one before it. When the frames move past the lens of the projector, it looks like you are watching a smoothly flowing sequence of events. In a sense you'll be recreating that process in this meditation. You are to notice what occurs in your consciousness "frame by frame," as if you were sitting in the editing room inspecting a filmstrip, one picture at a time.

### The Essence

As usual, begin with your starting sequence (see page 101). After that, as you sit quietly meditating with your eyes open, carefully notice whatever you see, hear, or sense during each cycle of inhalation and exhalation. Metaphorically, let each breathing cycle become a "frame of consciousness" that is analogous to one frame on a filmstrip. Observe both external and internal events intently.

For instance, as you inhale at the beginning of one frame (one full cycle of breath), a fly buzzes through the room. *Oh! A fly,* you may think, and then witness yourself reflecting, *I don't have to be judgmental—I can just notice it.* During your next cycle of breathing, you sense a bead of sweat rolling down your cheek. *I could wipe it away,* you think. Then—*No, I'll just notice the sensation,* and at that point you finish exhaling—another frame.

As you inhale again, you notice a bird alight on a branch outside the window, and feel a moment of pleasure at the tiny scene. Then you hear the bird chirp as your out-breath ends. And on to the next breath, and the next frame of awareness.

Each cycle of breathing is its own miniature mind movie. It's remarkable how full and rich the events of one breath can be. Your entire meditation becomes a succession of separate frames of consciousness, with some events extending through several frames, or many, and some occurring within a single frame.

When you've done this mediation for about ten minutes—or fifteen if you wish—finish with ten Snapshot Breaths and the Yogic Seal or an equivalent acknowledgment of completion.

## Feeling Comfortable

Within one frame of consciousness, you might notice how a certain thought helps you feel better or worse, and choose whether to keep thinking about it or to move your attention somewhere else. Your meditation may consist of a hundred tiny such "mind movies," each complete with sounds and sensations.

In this mindfulness practice, mental, emotional, and sensory events that used to be automatic and unnoticed will probably become more visible and audible. Your whole internal world will begin to be a movie you can watch. You are discovering a way to maintain focused awareness even amid complex events.

## Points in the Process

With this meditation you may sometimes have a harder time keeping your attention focused in the present moment, especially if your mind is resisting like a wild horse. One approach is to watch your fountain of thoughts from the perspective of witnessing self as part of your "mind movie." But if you feel like the moments of witnessing are too few and the thoughts too overwhelming, it's perfectly all right to move into a more structured practice, like Double Counting or Mantra Passage, right in the middle of your meditation session. Trust your sense of what's working for you.

## Variations in Technique

You can take this meditation into your everyday reality. It can transform your experience of where you are and what is occurring—even if just for a few minutes—in fascinating ways.

# Respect

## Disregard and Domination

· · · · · · · · · · · · · · · · · · · · · · · · · ·

**MATCHING WALKING**

> *Do you know what is better than charity and fasting and*
> *prayer? It is keeping peace and good relations between people,*
> *as quarrels and bad feelings destroy mankind.*
>
> MUHAMMAD

**SHOWING TRUE RESPECT FOR** others opens new possibilities, helps others feel better, and improves relationships.

*Respect* is a small word with large implications. It means avoiding remarks that include any kind of put-down, whether blatant or subtle. It also means avoiding sending any nonverbal message with your body language, words, or tone of voice that another person is less than you are. It means showing in your attitude and actions the same degree of respect for the garbageman that you would give the CEO. As in the Golden Rule, it means acting toward others as you would like them to act toward you. Harish Johari puts this in spiritual terms as "the ability to perceive the divine grace in all existence."

Respect does not go quite so far as kindness, which involves doing something beneficial for another person with no thought of personal gain. Opening a door for another is a small act of kindness. Waiting for them to come through first, regardless of your relative social status, is an act of respect.

Recognizing your common humanity with every other person, and letting that govern your words and actions, defines a broader attitude of respect. Everyone is someone's son or daughter, someone's mother or father, sister, brother, or dearest friend. Every person has hopes and fears and feelings just like you—even those who are on the other side in politics, war, and other conflicts.

Many people try to make us forget this—especially those whose vested interests in disrespecting others bring them gains. Looking down on others has the convenient feature of providing an excuse to take advantage of them. If you think someone is a bad person in some sense, it's easier to convince yourself that it's alright to cheat him, steal from him, or keep him in a subservient position. And there's always that smug self-satisfaction of letting him know that you are better than he is. That's a basic cause for a lot of gang wars and murders: "The SOB didn't give me any respect!"

One financial magazine written primarily for the wealthy often includes remarks about how people low on the economic totem pole are inherently undeserving. Comments such as "Status is everything" help generate the view that "people like us deserve to be respected and people who are less well off do not." That classist attitude, and the behavior that goes with it, is a major source of the schisms in society today.

Oftentimes schisms are blatant. Classism, sexism, racism, and ethnic prejudice have ancient histories and all exist to some degree within our psyches. They are also entrenched in every rule, regulation, and custom that makes members of one group subservient to those of another. Such schisms victimize the group of lower status—such as laws and customs that treat men and women unequally in regard to everything from sexual transgressions to disposition of property upon death or divorce.

Disrespect for people from cultures other than our own is also widespread. It often takes the form of arrogance and hubris. Interpersonally, that includes put-downs, disregard for others, acting as if they are stupid, or bad, and so on, ad nauseum. Until recently, for example, "civilized" peoples ridiculed hunting and gathering peoples as "savages." Now anthropologists are trying to understand other cultures from the inside, on their own terms. The results are startling. Very often such peoples are not only more advanced in their understanding of the natural world than most so-called civilized people, but are also more psychologically secure, integrated, and caring.

Early theories of Western "superiority," says anthropologist Johannes Fabian, were a rationale that justified colonialism and imperialism. That theory gives us a pretext for imposing Western ways on others. Fabian observes that today, "what are opposed in conflict are not the same societies at different stages of development, but different societies facing each other at the same time."[1] The honest way to meet someone from any culture, he says, is as one person to another, face to face—in the same time, with the attitude that the cultures of each are equally valid and valuable. All of us can learn from one another. Today, anthropologists have abandoned the terms *primitive* and *advanced,* and are saying that diverse peoples who have developed different sides of their cultures share our world at every moment. That's true respect.

There is also respect for nature. When hunter-gatherer cultures began to give way to agricultural civilizations, suspicion of "untamed" nature began to take root. When the Industrial Revolution arrived, this trend accelerated. Natural ecosystems were viewed as obstacles to the juggernaut of civilization and urbanization.

Now the winds and tides of our understanding are shifting. Signs are everywhere that to disrespect nature is to ride an express train toward disaster. Cataclysms of resource exhaustion, extreme weather events, and ecosystem collapse have already begun in some parts of the world. Unless we learn to live with a respectful attitude that recognizes all of us as an interactive whole, our world is in deep trouble. This is part of what Lao-tzu meant when he spoke of living in harmony with the Tao, the "Great Way" of nature and the universe.

Developing a respectful attitude includes showing respect for others whose intentions oppose your own. A friend of ours, in his years on the local school board, often opposed others who had different views. Yet he did not antagonize them, but rather, remained unfailingly respectful even in his opposition. He assumed that they were all people of goodwill who sought similar ends, even though their views about the means were different. As a result, he was well liked and respected by almost everyone, and others were glad to support him when they could.

This attitude, points out Meher Baba, goes a step beyond "the principle of equality, i.e., that one person is equal to any other single person in respect to claims, rights, and worth." He points out that "in spiritual infinity all comparison is out of place. There is no smaller or greater, or hierarchy of claims, privileges, rights, and valuations."[2]

In all this, it is crucial to recognize that respecting another person does not mean respecting yourself less—quite the contrary. Respecting oneself is a necessary step on the ladder of self-actualization. As the I Ching notes, "Truth and strength must dwell in the heart, while gentleness reveals itself in social intercourse. . . . To render true service of lasting value to another, one must serve him without relinquishing oneself."[3]

Even in times of difficulty when you can't get any respect, you can learn to respect yourself regardless of what others may think of you. But that's harder if you've been looked down on all your life. So the principle that it's easier to respect yourself if others respect you generally holds true. And if you respect others, it's easier for them to respect themselves. So when someone looks like they're having a hard time of it, treating them respectfully may have life-saving value—theirs or yours.

Sometimes knowing more about what another person is going through makes it easier to respect them. In the following walking meditation, you'll get a sense of that.

## MATCHING WALKING

In this exercise it is possible to discover a way in which you are not better or worse than someone else, but different and unique. It allows you to feel something of what it is like to be another person. You will abandon your usual way of moving and walking, and imagine inhabiting another person's body by trying to experience his or her way of moving as fully as you can.

### The Essence

You and another person must mutually agree to do this exercise. One person becomes the "walker" and the other the "matcher." In an outdoor or indoor public space such as a sidewalk or hallway, you, the matcher, will walk side by side with the walker. You will try to walk just like the other person and in doing so, learn something about what it is like to be that person.

Observe the other person's movements in detail. As you begin to walk, change your walk so that it matches hers. Notice how her legs move, whether her feet point straight ahead or outward, whether her arms are at her sides or swinging (and if they're swinging, with what rhythm), whether she looks straight ahead or downward or around, whether she glides smoothly or strides purposefully, etc. Do your best to match each detail of her walk until you feel like your walk is as much like hers as possible.

Avoid conversation, which takes away from the experience, but two kinds of comments can be useful. The walker can offer feedback, such as: "Bounce a little more with each step. Look from right to left rather than downward. Don't swing your arms quite so much. Take shorter steps and hold your chest up." As the matcher, you can mention how you feel being in the walker's body, so to speak, and what sensations you are experiencing, like: "I feel more grounded and more attentive to my surroundings," or, "I feel taller when I walk like you."

Continue to walk like that person for several minutes. As you do, move your attention toward noticing the sensations within your own body. What feels different? Are there points in your body that feel uncomfortable? Are there points that feel more comfortable, and better, than when you walk as you usually do? If so, make a mental note of it.

## Feeling Comfortable

After you have a clear sense of how you feel as you walk like the other person, return to your usual walk and compare your sensations. What did you discover? Some people have profound insights. One woman said, "I just learned how my usual walk causes chronic tension in my lower back. I'm changing that aspect of the way I walk right now!" A realization like hers could have a long-term impact on your health as well as your attitude. You may even realize how you or your partner carries self-respect or the lack of it in subtle body language.

## Variations in Technique

You can do something that resembles this without a partner. Find a warm memory from your past, when someone was very good to you and showed you respect at a time when you needed it. Feel the strength it gave you until it brings a smile to your face.

Continue to remember this feeling as you move and walk. With each breath, step deeper into the feelings and qualities of self-respect and respect for others. How do you feel as you walk? You may even want to exaggerate this way of walking.

Remember the feeling of this movement. This memory lives deep inside you. You can draw on it whenever you feel the need to feel better about yourself and your situation. Perhaps you can even share your strength with someone else who needs it.

# Limits

## Possibilities and Boundaries

· · · · · · · · · · · · · · · · · · · · · · · · · · · · · · · ·

**THE FLOW OF AWARENESS**

*He is wise who acts without lust or scheming*
*for the fruit of the act;*
*His act falls from him; its chain is broken;*
*Melted in the flame of my knowledge.*
*Turning his face from the fruit, he needs nothing. . . .*
*He acts, and is beyond action.*

BHAGAVAD GITA

YOU CAN LEARN TO move beyond flexible limits, handle inevitable limits without feeling crushed, and use your own thoughtful choices as a guide to a better life.

Each of us, from birth to death, faces limits beyond which we cannot go. If you are hiking a mountain path, stepping a few inches past the edge could send you into a thousand-foot free fall. Appropriate respect for that kind of a limit equals survival. Every day we live within the boundaries of our limits. Limites and limitations result from:

+ Restrictions in our inherent capacities
+ The constraints of situations
+ Lack of the skills or knowledge needed to go farther
+ Lack of the courage, imagination, or motivation to move beyond them
+ Our own, self-imposed best judgment

Certain limits keep us from getting something we want, or doing what we would like to do. Often, that's a small problem, since life offers many possibilities. Certain other limits, by contrast, loom large. If they feel abrasive or persist for too long, they can become a problem.

With its discerning wisdom, the I Ching says,

> In nature there are fixed limits for summer and winter, day and night, and these limits give the year its meaning. In the same way . . . if we live economically in normal times, we are prepared for times of want. . . . But in limitation we must observe due measure. If a man should seek to impose galling limitations upon his own nature, it would be injurious. And if he should go too far in imposing limitations on others, they would rebel. Therefore it is necessary to set limits even upon limitation.[1]

Some limitations exist only because we think they do. Inspirational speakers are fond of sayings such as: "Limits exist only in our minds. You can do or be anything you want if you set your mind to it." German philosopher Arthur Schopenhauer remarks, "Everyone takes the limits of his own vision for the limits of the world."

Educator Hobart "Red" Thomas points out that people are often so intimidated by apparent limitations that they never find out what the limits really are. "Again and again," he said in a lecture to one of our classes, "while other people stand back and say, 'This is as much as we can do here,' I've 'pushed against the wall' of what appeared to be possible, and found that I could go farther and accomplish more." By going far enough to find out what the limits really were, rather than stopping where most others did, he created a remarkable experiment in education in the form of a "School of Expressive Arts" that combined psychology and the arts that enriched many students' lives. But when a new college president allowed him to go no further, he accepted that reality.

Among the limits we face are those we were born into. You may have chosen some limits yourself, because they seemed the best option at the time. You may hold a job that requires you to do disagreeable things, but if you need to keep the job, you do them. You might like to do other things that are outside the limits of your job description but are prohibited. These restrictions may or may not be problems, depending on your attitude and on the consequences of doing or not doing them.

A different kind of limitation exists when you lack the skill, knowledge, or credentials needed to accomplish what you want to. In many cases, if you are willing to take the time, you can learn what you need to know, or get the credentials that are needed to become more than you could have been within the confines of previous boundaries. That may require giving up certain other things you want. If you're young, it may require redirecting your efforts in order to discover what you need to know. If you're older, it's likely to require letting go of the idea that you "ought to know it all by now," and adopting the open-minded attitude of the student. Whatever your age or experience may be, if you want to make a change, look for those advisors who can point you in the right direction or teach you what you need to know. You are never too young, too old, or too cool to learn something new.

Sometimes we can be only as creative in overcoming limitations as circumstances permit. Once you recognize the limits of a situation, you can accept being the best you can be in spite of them. You don't have to beat yourself over the head about being unable to do what's not possible. That same mental and emotional energy then becomes available to use in alternative ways. Perhaps a different perspective can help you find ways to go around whatever blocks you are experiencing, or provide an opportunity to be kinder to yourself.

Limits are also related to ethics. Moses brought down the Ten Commandments from Mt. Sinai. Patanjali formulated the Yamas and Niyamas, the ethical precepts that comprise the backbone of the Yoga Sutras. The Buddha's Eightfold Path (of helpful and beneficial conduct) and his Paramitas ("wholesome states" or "things to be encouraged") guide us to move in wise directions, away from detrimental choices. All these guidelines send messages that help you to choose wise ways of acting and avoid wrong paths.

Being attentive, moment by moment, to what is occurring in your body, mind, emotions, and with the people and environment around you, can help you make wise choices about which limits you want to observe and which you wish to move beyond. The following awareness technique is a way to help you do that.

## THE FLOW OF AWARENESS

In this method, you will be taking meditative consciousness into your everyday activities. You can do it anytime and anywhere you have a spare minute. Called "The Awareness Continuum" by Fritz Perls, Ralph Hefferline, and Paul Goodman, who developed it,[2] this practice can be done either as a formal sitting meditation or as a daily awareness activity.

## The Essence

Start by describing your awareness in each moment. Silently in your mind begin each sentence with the exact words, *Now I am aware of* . . . (Not *Now I am aware that* . . . The word *that* tends to tilt your mind away from direct awareness.) For example, you might say: *Now I am aware of the shaft of light shining on the dark carpet. Now I am aware of feeling nervous. Now I am aware of feeling a sharp, jabbing resentment toward my boyfriend,* and so on. Describe specific details of events. Avoid generalities.

You may think, *The things I'm aware of in the now are so simple.* That's the point. There is great value in being aware of the obvious. (We often overlook a great deal of it, making ourselves oblivious to the obvious.)

If you start to daydream as you report your awareness, then describe that: *Now I am aware of remembering an event that occurred on my way home yesterday. Now I am aware of wondering how my job interview will go tomorrow* . . . These comments refer to your present process of remembering or imagining. In this instant, identifying your thoughts about past or future is a present act. If you go into describing the details of your memory or fantasy, however, you're moving out of present awareness.

Mentally repeating the words *Now I am aware of* . . . at the start of each sentence helps keep your focus in the present. Because the mind often moves faster than even silent speech, several things may slip through your head since your last "now" statement. Just be mindful and report what you are aware of at the instant when you formulate your sentence. Ignore the intervening items that are now in your recent past. Do this for seven minutes.

## Variations in Technique

You can use the Flow of Awareness in rhythm with your breathing. With each cycle of inhalation and exhalation, silently say, *Now I am aware of* . . . , and finish the sentence with your awareness of what is dominant in that cycle of breath, while letting the rest of what passes through your mind dissolve away.

## Points in the Process

While you were watching the flow of your own awareness, which sources of information did you favor and which did you largely ignore? Are you most attuned to sensations in your body? To sights and sounds around you? To your feelings and emotions? Or to memories and imaginings? Discovering which kinds of events you tend to notice can open a broader field of awareness. It allows you to actively attend to the kinds of events you often overlook. And as you become more present, you can sense which thoughts put you in mental handcuffs and which thoughts set you free.

During the next week, guide your attention toward noticing your emotional reactions (however subtle they may be), or to tension, relaxation, and other sensations in your body. You will be consciously broadening your range of self-monitoring. The goal is to have every emotional, sensory, and mental source of information readily available, so that at each moment you can hear and select the message that's most relevant. This expanded awareness will enhance your ability to make wise and meaningful life choices.

## Feeling Comfortable

As you become more conscious of the reality of your present moment, you can more easily observe your comfort or discomfort zones and notice your red-light boundaries, or your opportunities for growth. You might also see how you can cause yourselves needless grief when you imagine that real limits don't exist. On the other hand, you may find that some limitations exist only because your beliefs give them power.

We can all draw inspiration from the combination of acceptance and transcendence of limitations demonstrated by educator and author Helen Keller, who was born both blind and deaf: "I seldom think about my limitations, and they never make me sad. Perhaps there is just a touch of yearning at times; but it is vague, like a breeze among flowers."

# Communication

## Priorities, Leveling, and Tact

· · · · · · · · · · · · · · · · · · · · · · · · · · ·

## FOUR-LEVEL COMMUNICATION

*Say what you mean and mean what you say. Ask for what you want but know you will not always get it. . . . Be open to receiving feedback and listen to it carefully because you might learn something about yourself.*

VIRGINIA SATIR

**FAMILY THERAPIST VIRGINIA SATIR** was one of the twentieth century's leading communication experts. She suggested that we treat people as if they are already as we would like them to be, rather than condemning or blaming them for falling short of our expectations. Based on the idea that there should be mutual respect in relationships, the methods she described for improving communication make it easier to avoid misunderstandings.[1]

Satir sums up her basic communication concepts in her concept of "The Five Freedoms." These are the freedom to:

* See and hear what is here, instead of what should be, was, or will be
* Say what you feel and think, instead of what you think you should
* Feel what you feel, instead of what you think you ought to
* Ask for what you want, instead of always waiting for permission
* Take reasonable risks in your own behalf, instead of choosing to be only "secure" and not rocking the boat[2]

These Five Freedoms encourage you to be yourself and actively take responsibility for your actions and feelings. They lead to honesty and integrity in communication. If you experiment with using them, they can help you learn to create and follow necessary limits, let go of unnecessary limitations, and find nonblaming ways to express your love, appreciation, and resentments.

Satir found that one particular communication pattern is usually apparent in healthy communication. She called it *leveling*. Its basic statement is, "I'll level with you about how I'm really feeling and what's going on with me here . . ." This is saying something straight out, with no equivocation. Of course it's useful to level with others in a thoughtful and respectful way. That was recognized in the ancient Chinese proverb, "The swiftest horse can't overtake a word once spoken."[3] This proverb points to the importance of tact and consideration.

Delving yet deeper into Chinese tradition reveals another kind of wisdom. Yang, considered the principle of initiation, is often seen as masculine, outgoing energy. Yin, considered the principle of completion, is seen as feminine, restraining energy. Dynamic communication is symbolized in the perfectly balanced yin-yang symbol. It points to a person's clear, honest statement of feelings from his or her internal frame of reference (yang), stated in a tactful way that's open to hearing the other person's feelings and perspectives (yin). Acting together as a continuous, circular flow of energy, yang and yin complement each other.

The interdependent connection of yin and yang symbolically indicates that people have mutual as well as personal interests. If you are insincere with others, they will most likely sense it and keep you at a distance. By contrast, true friendliness, integrity, and honesty are also likely to be returned in kind, as they create good feelings.

Not everyone is sincere. Part of astute communication is developing your sensitivity to occasions when others might try to take advantage of your goodwill. Diplomacy at such times means keeping your integrity while being careful to leave no opening for them to take advantage of you.

In India, the importance of good communication has long been recognized in the section of Buddha's Eightfold Path entitled "Wholesome Communication," which is comprised of basic ethical values: tell the truth, don't gossip, avoid comments that make others feel bad, and so on. Buddha's crucial principle was to be mindful of all your motives and the likely effects of your words. Pause to reflect before speaking, so that your words are most likely to achieve the outcome you seek.

There are many communication styles that often sabotage these ends, notes Satir. These include *blaming* or pointing a finger at someone while denying your own responsibility in the matter ("It's your fault"). *Computing* involves insisting that you are only being logical while denying your own feelings and the validity of anyone else's. *Placating* is trying to make everything alright with everybody, while ignoring and neglecting your own needs, wants, and feelings. *Distracting* involves saying or doing something that's conveniently unrelated to the main issue at hand, which usually changes the focus and prevents agreement on anything.[4] If, like most of us, you occasionally use at least one of these patterns, the inner Witness you are developing through meditation can help you become more aware of your tendencies. Before long you may notice that you are about to act in one of those ways. With awareness comes the choice to stop yourself before you do so.

## FOUR-LEVEL COMMUNICATION

Confused communication is common when one or more of the people involved wants several different things from the interaction. That's as true of friendly, casual conversation as it is of agenda-oriented communication such as business meetings. The following process can bring greater clarity to your communications.

### The Essence

When talking with someone you can ask yourself these four questions:

1. What is the main point of this person's explicit message? (What is he or she trying to say?)
2. What emotional tone underlies the message? (How does the person feel at this moment, as far as I can tell?) This may involve picking up on obvious "vibes," or listening to subtle currents of emotion.
3. What is the person's main priority here? What does he or she want most in this interaction? (For example, "I want you to like me" or "I want to get this done efficiently.")
4. Are there any possible double messages here? (These are messages that contradict each other, such as when a person's words say one thing but her body language or tone of voice says something else.)

You can also ask these questions about yourself, to help you realize what messages you are sending.

Which of the four questions above is most important varies according to the situation. For instance, two people might be on a dinner date in which the explicit conversation is only tangentially related to such unspoken priorities as *What happens later in the evening?* or *Does this relationship have a future?*

Or in the workplace, your employee comes up with a design for a project. Getting your okay or suggestions for improvement may be the explicit agenda. Beneath that, the emotional priority may be a desire for approval—such as wanting acknowledgment or appreciation for her efforts.

## Feeling Comfortable

If one person is intent on saying his piece without reference to the other's reactions, the latter is likely to shut down. On the other hand, if a person is so anxious about how the other might react that he is unclear, he is unlikely to be heard or get what he wants.

## Variations in Technique

Several comments can help you find out whether the other person is hearing you accurately. These include:

> **"Perhaps I was unclear. Let me say that differently."** When something is expressed in two or more different ways, the odds of misunderstanding shrink.
>
> **"Please tell me what you hear me saying."** Here you are asking others to reflect back your meaning, to check on whether they have heard what you were trying to say.
>
> **"I'm still trying to get clarity. I'd like to hear your thoughts on this."** You are saying that you are interested in the mutual exchange, of a dialogue, rather than in broadcasting your monologue.
>
> **"I'm aware that I just interrupted you. You were saying . . . ?"** In other words, "Sorry for the interruption. This time I'll bite my tongue and listen. Please try again."

It is often useful to explicitly consider what's missing in a message. If any of the questions *Who? When? What? Where?* or *How?* are unanswered in a person's statement, their absence is like an arrow pointing to what you will probably want to ask next. Likewise, when you hear yourself leaving out such details, you'll know that the other person will hear you better if you fill them in. Deep communication brings us closer to the heart, where empathy and compassion dwell.

## Points in the Process

Your own statement, or another person's, may be made not only by words, but also by demeanor. "By behavior we do not mean a particular way that you ought to behave, but rather the natural expression of yourself," says Shunryu Suzuki-roshi. "We emphasize straightforwardness. You should be true to your feelings, and to your mind, expressing yourself without any reservations. This helps the listener understand more easily."[5]

Sufi master Hazrat Inayat Khan highlights the connection between developing your inner spirit and communicating in a deep way with others. "The task to be accomplished is . . . harmonizing with one's fellow-man," he says. "[This includes] speaking to everyone in his own tongue, answering the laughter of one's friends with a smile and the pain of another with tears, standing by one's friends in their joy and their sorrow."[6] As we do these things, we share a common ground with others and find soulful bonds where our spirits connect.

# Wholeness

## Fragmentation versus Integration

· · · · · · · · · · · · · · · · · · · · · · · · · · · · · ·

**TOTAL ATTENTION**

*You should work with your greatest obstacle first—whether
it is aggression, passion, pride, arrogance, jealousy, or what
have you. . . . We simply work on any highlight or problem
that comes up in our mind directly and straightforwardly.*

CHOGYAM TRUNGPA

**EVENTS USUALLY WORK OUT** better when you consciously strive to develop
better communication.

In the meditation hall at Sonoma Mountain Zen Center there is a standing, fourteen-foot-tall carved wooden statue of the Asian goddess of compassion. She is called Kannon in Japan; Kuan Yin in China; the goddess Tara in
Tibet, and Avalokiteswara in India. Above the face of Kannon, the goddess
wears a crown that has ten smaller faces arrayed around it. These portray
each of the major conditions of human existence, as described by Jakusho
Kwong-roshi:

> The first three faces are similar, calm in appearance, and peaceful.
> As you move sunwise from right to left around the crown, the faces
> become more and more ghastly, reflecting our agonizing states of suf-
> fering, fear, anger, and hopelessness. . . . It would be difficult for the
> first three faces on the statue to see the ones on the sides and even more
> difficult for them to see the ones in the back, just as it's difficult for us
> to see or really to face these things within ourselves. . . . Kannon wears
> all these faces on her crown; they are a fact of living.[1]

All these faces are different aspects of each one of us. When we try to deny them, or lose our sense of their connections, we *dis-integrate*. We become, in a sense, fragmented people who are collections of bits and pieces. And as Sigmund Freud pointed out, keeping the connections between different sides of yourself out of your awareness requires quite a bit of mental energy.

Many psychologists and spiritual teachers have drawn attention to the phenomenon in which we act like we are completely different people in different situations. Sufi teacher G. I. Gurdjieff referred to the "Little I's" inside us. Jungian psychologist Roberto Assagioli spoke of "subpersonalities." Or we can call them the different characters within ourselves. Carl Jung compared these subselves to a collection of masks that we put on for different people and occasions.

(An interesting activity involves cutting out pictures from magazines and newspapers that reflect different aspects of yourself and then taping them together into a collage. Then as you look at your collage, or even describe it to a friend, you can think about whether any of those sides of yourself are getting too little or too much of your energy.)

Illusions about ourselves can cause us trouble. Incorrect stories about how we are and what we do are usually not easy to give up. Even a story you told just yesterday, to just one other person, can be hard to let go of. Abandoning a picture of yourself that you've held in your mind for years, and recognizing a different reality that underlies it, can be a tough job.

Nonetheless, for many people there ultimately comes a point where we have to choose. You can chain yourself to a lifestyle that requires an inflexible personality and be cut off from much of your own inner world, or you can begin a process of rediscovery. At times such personal rediscovery occurs slowly, piece by piece. At other times, you may find yourself plunged into a profound "Aha!" experience in which your whole self suddenly seems different, as if a cover is abruptly removed from some aspect of who you thought yourself to be. Either way, the deeper self-perception that emerges usually leads to more aliveness, better use of personal power, and less stress.

Allowing yourself the flexibility to try new ways of being in the world can be exciting, intimidating, or both. It can also involve discomfort. After all, your old self-perceptions and self-imposed limitations are familiar and comfortable. But challenging them can enrich your life. As your different sides, or "characters," start communicating more effectively, you'll less often find that one part of you has gotten you into a situation that another part can't handle—or regrets.

As you become more integrated within yourself, you could find that an old relationship no longer fits the person you are becoming. If that is so, you may no longer want to stay in a failed relationship just because it feels safe. Or you and your partner may seek and find new ways to bring adventure and aliveness into what has become a stale relationship. In a good marriage, family, or workplace, people have room to grow and change. They need to be able to reshape their roles.

But as Kannon's eleven faces make clear, moving toward a more flexible, enlivened way of living does not mean that life will always be sunshine and roses. "If our awakening is to be complete, our unknown possibilities must also contain the knowledge of human suffering, impermanence, and danger, for wholeness is the measure of our attainment," points out mythographer J. L. Walker.[2]

Carl Jung used the term *individuation* for the process of discovering, expressing, and harmonizing the varied conscious and unconscious components of the psyche. He chose this term to emphasize that we can continue to develop our capacities and expand our consciousness in diverse directions even as we develop better communication within ourselves.[3]

As Jung identified it, this communication includes the "personal unconscious," where we keep "all more or less intentional repression of painful thoughts and feelings." By his definition it also includes all that we know but are not now thinking about, and that we were once conscious of but have largely forgotten. And it includes all that our senses perceive but our conscious mind does not choose to notice. It includes whatever we think, remember, want, and do, and that which is taking shape in us and will come to consciousness at some point. He differentiated the personal unconscious from the "collective unconscious," in which inherited, universal themes exist in all of us. In some spiritual traditions, becoming a whole self implies a deep realization of being part of a universal self that unites all living beings.

In a famous old Japanese story, a tea master said something that offended a samurai, who challenged him to a duel. The samurai was an expert swordsman; the tea master knew almost nothing of sword fighting. They took their places. The tea master held his sword above his head with the same total attentiveness that he gave to preparing tea. The samurai lifted his sword and waited. A minute passed—then two—then three. At that point he laid down his sword, bowed to the tea master, and apologized for the challenge.

"Why didn't you attack?" an onlooker asked.

The samurai replied, "I could see no opening," The tea master's attention was so complete that the samurai saw him anticipate his slightest moves.

He was not just wholly present, but also present in his wholeness. In the tea master's total focus, there was no space for contradiction. He had to perceive and move as a completely integrated being. This story shows that being whole is linked with our ability to be attentive in the moment. When mastered, the meditation that follows can bring great presence to varied life situations.

## TOTAL ATTENTION

This apparently very simple practice is actually quite demanding, since it requires your utmost focus. (When you truly meditate in this way, you approach the spirit of the Zen practice of *Shikantaza,* or "just sitting," with complete presence in the moment. Some Zen practitioners follow that practice in retreats that last a day, or several days, or even several weeks.

### The Essence

Begin with your starting sequence, including ten Snapshot Breaths. Continue to sense your breathing as your anchor for keeping your attention focused in the moment. There is no counting, no mantra, nothing but your total attention on whatever is happening within you and around you during the meditative period. Try not to let anything escape your attention. If an ant crawls across the floor, notice it. If you've lit a candle and it flickers, notice it. Like a samurai, be alert to the slightest movement, ready to counter it—or to mentally bow in respectful greeting. Be aware of any sound outside you or inside you, any sensation in your body, or any thought that crosses your mind. If the desire to make love with someone occurs to you, notice that. If your attention is rooted in a great calmness, or if you feel an undertone of nervousness, observe that. (You might even find yourself sweating from the effort of maintaining such an intense degree of attention for the entire meditation period.) Do this for at least fifteen minutes.

Finish your practice with ten Snapshot Breaths and the Yogic Seal or an equivalent closing posture. If you have time, informal yoga is a good addition to this sequence.

### Feeling Comfortable

Total Attention meditation is simple because there is so little to do. It is difficult because it is hard to be completely attentive to what is happening in each instant without your mind drifting. Don't expect Total Attention to be easy. After you have tried it, you may even find that for now, it's too hard. You can choose to come back to it in a week, a month, a year—whenever you are ready. (But then one day you may find yourself slipping into it when you least expect it. Your other meditative practices may help you become ready without your realizing it.) So try it now. If it seems difficult, or if you feel impatient or frustrated, that's alright. Just notice the precise form your impatience or frustration takes (i.e., your specific thoughts, feelings, and sensations)—and there you are, moving toward greater insight into yourself.

## Points in the Process

When focusing outwardly, it may seem distracting to also notice your interior processes. While you are meditating, says Shunryu Suzuki-roshi, "do not try to stop your thinking. Let it stop by itself. If something comes into your mind, let it come in, and let it go out." Just notice each moment. Krishnamurti adds, "Be aware of every thought and of every feeling, never to say it is right or wrong but just to watch it and move with it. In that watching you begin to understand the whole movement of thought and feeling."[4]

## CELL 34

. . . . . . . . . .

# Freedom

## Outer Autonomy
## and Inner Freedom

. . . . . . . . . . . . . . . . . . . . . . . . . . . . .

### THE CRYSTAL CAVERN

*In the truest sense freedom cannot be bestowed;*
*it must be achieved.*

FRANKLIN D. ROOSEVELT

**INNER AND OUTER LIBERATION** go together. You can find your own freedom only if you search within, and do not rely just on what others say.

Sri Aurobindo was one of the few great yogis who challenged the dominant yogic tradition that if one attains personal liberation, others will become liberated, too. Along with Gandhi, he worked with the masses to gain India's freedom from Great Britain. Both held that inner and outer freedom must go together. In the Buddhist tradition, there has been great emphasis on helping others attain personal liberation once you have attained your own. In the West, the emphasis has been just the opposite. Most Western thinking has been concerned with political freedom. Here we will make Western views our starting point, and then move to the inner freedom that makes outer freedom possible.

Today, when you hear politicians speak grand words about "protecting our freedom," your first thought might be, *How are they trying to hoodwink us now?* And in the economic realm, despite the widespread ideal of freedom, if you take a test for an entry-level job in many businesses, the "right" answers are most often those that portray you as someone who will obey orders without question and would never dream of thinking for yourself. It can be a confusing double standard.

Despite those inconvenient realities, it is tempting to think that once attained, freedom is guaranteed. But it's all too easy to let it slip away, little by little. We may trade it for security, or fail to insist on protections for our liberty because of the risk such action sometimes seems to carry. Benjamin Franklin wrote, "They that can give up essential liberty to obtain a little temporary safety deserve neither liberty nor safety." Sometimes, however, the "giving up" is so cleverly disguised that it's almost invisible. James Madison astutely noted that our freedom is more often taken away quietly by the fine print in legislation and regulations than in any other way. "There are more instances of the abridgment of the freedom of the people by gradual and silent encroachments of those in power than by violent and sudden usurpations."

Martin Luther King noted that "freedom is never voluntarily given by the oppressor; it must be demanded by the oppressed." Brazilian educator Paolo Freire points out that the nature of oppressor consciousness is to transform everything and everyone into an object of its domination. When oppressors move to the side of the exploited and join in the struggle for liberation, he points out, they "believe that they must be the executors of the transformation. . . . Leaders of a struggle for freedom cannot think *about* the people, or *for* the people, but only *with* the people."[1] Sociologist, psychoanalyst, and social psychologist Erich Fromm adds that historically, "classes that were fighting against oppression at one stage sided with the enemies of freedom when victory was won and new privileges were to be defended."[2]

Often overlooked is the effect of our own freedom on the freedom of others. If I'm committed to my own freedom to do as I please, I just might forget to notice the ways I knowingly or unknowingly take yours away because it happens to interfere with mine. What looks to me like freedom to do what I want might look to you like domination. I may sincerely believe that I should be free to do as I wish even when it exploits or intimidates you. In so doing, I may blind and deafen myself to the callousness of my own attitude.

Such callousness or imperviousness is highlighted by French poet, journalist, and novelist Anatole France's comment that "rich and poor alike are equally free to sleep under the bridges of Paris." (They are not equally free to sleep in the rich man's house, however.) Where does such an attitude come from? Often it is learned in the family and passed down through generations, such as when one spouse insists on making all the rules without listening to their partner's needs, thoughts, and feelings. Or the parents are so overbearing that their children have little chance to develop a sense of independence or self-determination. Becoming aware of your own dominating, insensitive attitudes in your family, workplace, or friendships is a first step toward letting go of them and respecting others' freedoms.

Our consciousness and behavior are simultaneously determined and free. Some of our behavior patterns are formed early in life and turn into compulsive, habitual responses that haunt us until we come to terms with them—if we ever do.

Nonetheless, at every moment we have another new chance to think or act differently than we have ever done before. We have never previously been in this present situation at this moment, where great potential may exist. Psychologist Kurt Lewin coined the term *life space* for the free-ranging territory our mind has available for roaming. It consists of the physical places we've been, and everything we know about through conversations, education, reading, and the media. When we increase our freedom, we expand our life space.

We each, however, have to wrestle with our inner dictator. This is that part of you that holds on tightly to old perceptions, beliefs, and ways of acting, so that there's not much room left in your mind to respond in new ways. The inner dictator is stronger in some people than in others. Yours may push you to take the role of abuser or victim, tyrant or slave (among many other possibilities). If you are a tyrant, your inner dictator has of course decreed that it is "all for the other person's good," and that your own motives are entirely benevolent. It is possible to be extremely skillful in such self-deception. At the other extreme, you may be confined in a jail cell or a hospital room but be gifted with an inner freedom that allows your mind to roam the seven seas and the skies, as Gandhi, Martin Luther King, and Nelson Mandela did while imprisoned, and so expressed in their writings.

How can you increase your inner freedom?

If you don't realize what you are doing, you can't do anything else. Shunryu Suzuki-roshi offers a starting point: "Know what you are doing at any particular time." He also says,

> Our everyday life is like a movie playing on the wide screen. . . . When the movie stops and you don't see anything anymore, you think . . . "I will come back and see another show . . ." Maybe you are discouraged because there is nothing good on right now. You don't realize the screen is always there.

The screen, he continues,

is something you always have. The reason you don't feel you have it is because your mind is too busy. Once in a while you should stop all your activities and make your screen white. . . . Without this kind of foundation your . . . practice will not work.[3]

Pilot Baba links freedom to meditation in two different ways: "You have to have some practice to develop your perceptions and become receptive, to be open." But he also cautions against dependence on the practice: "Don't depend on any technique. A mantra or whatever. It is given to you to go beyond. You do not want to become the slave of the technique."[4] Once you have developed your meditative skills, you can use a specific method or not, as fits your situation and state of consciousness.

Inner freedom illuminates a key pathway for growth. Human nature avoids being aware of what is uncomfortable. But since we can't affect or change what we are unwilling to perceive, such avoidance impairs our freedom. As we become aware of and let go of that unwillingness and avoidance, our enhanced perception leads toward what Sri Aurobindo calls "the integral freedom of the spirit."

## THE CRYSTAL CAVERN

Here you have a chance to discover how you might be diminishing your own freedom, and what you can do about it.

### The Essence

After your starting sequence, close your eyes. With each breath, feel yourself relaxing. Imagine that you are in a small crystal cavern filled with lovely, diffused light. Mentally gather your entire present life experiences into it— everything you are doing, thinking, and feeling. For a few minutes just watch your life unfolding in front of you.

Next, as you look around, notice a magical mirror on the wall. As you gaze into it you will see or hear one story that you are telling yourself about yourself that is distorted. It might involve some sort of exaggeration, or minimization, or self-deception, or concern about an element that is missing or minimal in your life, or a matter that involves the life of someone else you know. (This could include doing something you are not doing that could benefit you, or letting go of something you are doing but would rather not, or taking care of an unfinished commitment, or doing a routine task in a more fulfilling way.)

Next, imagine a doorway that leads out of the cavern to your freedom in a sunny outdoor scene. As you try to step through it, think about the insights that came to you while looking in the mirror. If you succeed in walking through the door, continue your journey, and envision yourself putting your insights into practice. If you can't get through this door, continue to sit in the crystal cavern and contemplate your life and what you might do with the message or image in the mirror. (You can repeat this contemplative meditation whenever it feels appropriate.)

## Points in the Process

Although freedom and love are seldom thought of as closely related, there are connections. Amma says, "Love and freedom are not two; they are one. They are interdependent. . . . Only in the state of love will the beautiful, fragrant flower of freedom and supreme bliss unfold its petals and bloom."[5] When we add love to our perception of mental restrictions, whether forced or voluntary, whatever lack of inner freedom we may be feeling seems to relax its tight grip.

# Worry

## Uncertainty and Anxiety

### IMAGING AND CALMING

> *Mental problems feed on the attention you give them. The more you worry about them, the stronger they become. If you ignore them, they lose their power.*
>
> ANNAMALAI SWAMI

WORRY AND ANXIETY SOMETIMES reflect inner conflicts that need resolution, but many times they have little basis, and can waste a great deal of time and energy.

Mark Twain remarked, "I've seen many troubles in my time, only half of which ever came true." Worrying can be purposeful, but often it is not. Psychologist Fritz Perls called anxiety "the gap between the now and the later."[1] The same could be said of worry. In both, our present is dominated by serious concern about the future. Worry tends to be more an activity of mind, while anxiety is an agitated whole-body response. This includes constricted muscles and a change in breathing—either holding the breath or rapid or erratic breathing. But often *worry* and *anxiety* are considered synonymous.

Either one can be acute or chronic. Acute worry is a temporary response to a troubling possibility. It comes quickly, is intense, and when its cause is gone, is over. Chronic worry is an ongoing personal style of being in the world. You probably know some worriers. It's not uncommon for a worried expression to be etched into a person's face (another thing to worry about!), revealed in his gestures, or in the way he holds his body. Chronic worry causes ongoing physical tension, which is bad for your body. Most people would like to be free from the pressures of chronic worry and anxiety and have a more relaxed existence—even those who, out of habit, make worry the center of their life.

There is a difference between normal and neurotic worry and anxiety. Normal anxiety is a response to a genuine danger that something bad will happen—or that something you want to occur won't. One kind of neurotic anxiety is an unrealistic response to a possibly unreal danger. This happens when we are anxious about situations that resemble painful events in our past that can cause us to panic, even though they pose no real threat in our present.

We also can have anxieties about how we view ourselves in relation to others, or when we give up our authenticity. Existential anxiety is a sign of conflict about some way you are defining yourself, or being in the world. Something just doesn't feel right. The conflict might, for instance, be between an old role and an emerging new realization, or between compliance with what everybody around you does and your own sense of what's right.

Concern about how others will react to what we do, points out Amma, is a source of both worry and anxiety. In that case the source of our worry or anxiety is not our action itself, but rather what others think and feel about what we do. We worry about the negative judgments others might have of us.[2] You might be anxious because you don't know the answer to something or you feel inadequate. If you want to respond but hold back out of concern about how you'll be received, you become anxious. "Will I get applause, or will I get rotten eggs?" To realize that having rotten eggs thrown at you is "not a catastrophe, but just an unpleasantness," says Perls, "is . . . part of waking up."[3] And just like stirring from a dream, awaking from your anxiety can be exhilarating.

The other side of anxiety is adventure. Life lived fully is an unfolding journey from the old and familiar into unknown new territory. Anxiety can be an expression of suppressed emotional excitement and a longing for passion. This excitement energizes you to do something. Next time you feel anxious, try reframing the way you feel as, "I'm excited!" and see if that fits better.

In this spirit, Chogyam Trungpa writes about one day when the Tibetan yogi Milarepa went into his cave and "was confronted by a gang of demons. . . . But they would not leave until he ceased regarding them as 'bad' and opened to them, saw them as they were. This was the beginning of Milarepa's period of learning how to subjugate the demons, which is the same thing as transmuting the emotions. . . . They became dakinis, or the energies of life."[4]

Transmuting anxieties into something positive is comparable to the alchemists' dream of turning base metal into gold. The magic of this formula is within reach when your worry or anxiety inspires you to find ways to make things turn out as you want them to. Tantric scholar Peter Marchand notes that

> there is a thin line between worrying and planning ahead. . . . Often people do not make proper plans for dealing with a particular problem even though they worry about the problem very often. . . . Whatever worrying thought comes up, we must evaluate if the subject has been properly studied and appropriate action has been planned. . . . If a plan already exists, we must stop ourselves from going over it repeatedly. . . . No amount of planning can forestall all potential obstructions.[5]

In a similar spirit, philosopher Bertrand Russell suggests handling a specific worrisome matter by doing all you can to make the situation work out as you want it to until there's nothing more you can realistically do. Then put it out of your mind as completely as you can by giving other matters your full attention. When another moment arrives in which you can actually do something to affect the situation, do so. Then again turn your attention elsewhere, leaving less of it available to worry.[6]

## IMAGING AND CALMING

This practice is especially useful for specific anxieties that shade into fears. The procedure is directly parallel to the Step-by-Step meditation described in cell 20, except that it includes a major calming and relaxing element, and the word *anxiety* is substituted for *fear*. As you "step up the stairs" in your imagination rather than in reality, you will begin a new course of action. (The essence of the method was developed by psychiatrist Joseph Wolpe in the United States and psychologist Hans Eysenck in England as a treatment called "systematic desensitization" for phobias and traumatic fears. We have adapted it here into a meditation to reduce troubling anxieties.)[7]

## The Essence

Get comfortable. Remind yourself that you are in a safe place and relax. Make a mental note that you can return to your safe, comfortable place at any time.

1. Identify your anxiety.
2. Make a list of about twenty different situations or actions that somehow resemble what you are anxious about. Make these very specific scenes—not vague or general.
3. Cut up the list so that each item is on a separate strip of paper.
4. Assign a SUDS (Subjective Units of Discomfort) number to each item. Then rearrange the items from least- to most anxiety-arousing.
5. Check to make sure the increase in anxiety from each item to the next is about the same. If any step is too large, add intermediate items to create smaller steps.
6. Sit, recline, or lie comfortably, and think of the place where you feel most comfortable, safe, relaxed, and at peace. It might be a sunny beach, a springtime hillside, or . . . (Close your eyes and let your safe place come into your mind now.) Go there mentally, and then go through a complete relaxation sequence until you sense no physical tension in your body at all.
7. Open your eyes and read the item on your list with the lowest SUDS rating. Using the staircase metaphor, we'll call this first item "step number one"—the lowest step on your staircase. Then close your eyes and scan for body tension. If you feel any at all, mentally return to your comfortable safe place and consciously relax again until the tension is gone. Again visualize the item with your mildest discomfort rating see whether any tension returns. If so, go back to your safe, comfortable place and relax again. Repeat this alternation until you can visualize that first item on your list and feel no physical tension.
8. Open your eyes and read the item on your list with the second lowest SUDS rating—the "second step on your staircase"—then continue as in number seven, above. Once you can visualize this item and feel no tension, proceed to the third item (the third step on your staircase). With each item, alternate between visualizing the anxiety-producing

item and visualizing your comfortable safe pace until you feel no trace of physical tension when you visualize the former. Continue in that manner until at last you reach the item with the highest SUDS number on your list (the top step on your staircase). This is likely to take a number of sessions. How many will depend on the length of time it takes you to do each step. Don't expect to get through more than three or four items in a single meditation. If you get stuck with an item, i.e., if you can't relax completely, add one or two new intermediate items between the previous one and the one that's causing you difficulty.

## Variations in Technique

Maxwell Maltz, a plastic surgeon who developed Psycho-Cybernetics, a practice of positive thinking and the visualization of success that he developed to help his patients and others feel better about themselves, comes at worry from another angle. If you insist on worrying, he suggests, try *constructive worry*. Maltz recommends that you imagine the possibility of the positive event you'd like to see happen "so clearly that it becomes 'real' to your brain and nervous system. So real, in fact, that the same feelings are evoked as would be present if the [events had already turned out as you wish them to]."[8]

## Feeling Comfortable

A different strategy is to become interested in your own process of worry. When you feel anxious about what *may* happen, shift your attention to *what you are doing now*. Go into your Witness mode and notice exactly what occurs in your mind, emotions, and body. When you find that you are tensing up physically or forming unhelpful mental pictures, relax the muscles that you've been tensing. And, as Maltz suggests, you can replace worrisome imagery with more positive images, and talk to yourself in a more encouraging way.

## Points in the Process

If you worry a lot, when you watch and listen to your inner world, you are likely to hear subliminal monologues like, *I just know I'm going to do a lousy job, and I'll never get that promotion.* Or perhaps, *How can I compete with all the pretty women in my boyfriend's office?* You may discover that you keep up a constant chatter of statements that trigger anxieties. When meditating, you can more easily hear them and see the mental pictures and mind movies that are often hidden behind your foreground thoughts. And you can sense the muscular tension or relaxation that goes with these messages. As you become more adept at such inner noticing, you can take this new awareness, and your increased ability to relax your body through mental scanning, from your meditation into your daily life. You will be better able to act effectively and to avoid the results noted by philosopher Michel de Montaigne: "He who fears he shall suffer, already suffers what he fears."

# Anger

## Hostility and Aggression

**EXPRESSION AND RESTRAINT**

*No one deserves to be the victim of someone's anger. If anger arises, you say, "I am angry now, I will talk to you later." And you empower the people around you to say to you, "You are angry now, let us talk later."*

SWAMI DAYANANDA SARASWATI

**THE DESTRUCTIVE EFFECTS OF** different kinds of anger and aggression can be reduced when we grasp their root causes and heal the disturbing connections within ourselves.

Despite laws and customs that discourage anger and aggression, many of us are drawn to movies in which we can watch bombings, shootings, and other forms of hostile attack. Oddly enough, even though we can eagerly get lost in such diversions for hours, very few people like to be yelled at, insulted, or called names, much less assaulted. Many of us feel emotionally injured when even mild criticisms or suggestions are directed our way.

Our hunter-gatherer ancestors needed to be aggressive if they wanted to survive. In today's society, similar aggression can get us thrown in jail for mayhem. Still, aggression sometimes serves self-defense, and our anger helps us mobilize it. We may need to be able to respond strongly to others who are characteristically aggressive. In the absence of alternatives, someone who has learned to stifle most of his or her anger and aggression may appear weak and powerless in the face of provocation. But alternatives exist.

In his *Rhetoric,* Aristotle says, "Anger may be defined as a belief that we, or our friends, have been unfairly slighted, which causes in us both painful feelings and a desire or impulse for revenge." When anger includes a craving for revenge, it is strongest when the injury against us is greatest, such as the killing or maiming of a friend or family member. This phenomenon is quite clear when watching both sides of the ongoing antagonism between Israel and Palestine. (For some people, revenge is all they think they have left to live for.)

Unless you constantly live in Christ Consciousness, when others act toward you and yours in a hostile or inconsiderate way, it may well provoke your anger. Also, we are likely to get angry at ourselves when we've "done something stupid" that harms us or those we care about. In all these cases our ego is hooked, and we feel anxious and insecure.

We are also likely to get angry at ourselves when we're actually upset with someone else but don't dare express our anger at her, so we "retroflect" it back against ourselves instead, or direct it onto an innocent third party. For example, in the former case you want to strangle someone for what she said but instead you tighten up so you can hardly speak, thus "strangling" yourself. In the latter case, your boss humiliates you at work, so you come home and scream at your wife or dog, displacing your anger at your boss onto them. Or if you are angry at yourself or your circumstances, you might look for someone else who can serve as a scapegoat to blame instead.

People also get angry when some aspect of themselves that they don't want to recognize is brought to their attention and they feel helplessly disempowered. *Why did my boyfriend tell me that I'm too fat? And he must be crazy because he said that in front of my family!*

If you are like most people, you've probably never learned the difference between clean anger and dirty anger. Clean anger is your statement of how you actually feel, from your internal frame of reference—for example, "I'm upset because you . . ." After the other person has responded, you might go on to say what you want: "When we are out on a date together, I'd like to be the center of your attention." In clean anger you are talking mostly about how you feel and what you want, with brief reference to what the other person did to trigger it.

Dirty anger mixes up your irritated feelings with blaming and belittling the other person. It usually provokes defensiveness, escalation, or both.

Expressing your anger cleanly is no guarantee that someone won't get upset by your words, but it makes it less likely, or tends to lessen the degree of upset and increases the odds that you will find a successful resolution. When the other person is angry and you argue with them, that's usually a ticket to escalation. But if the other person's anger is due to an obvious misinterpretation of something you have done, and they're not too enraged or too committed to their position to hear you, you can try to correct the misinterpretation.

Pure anger is an emotion; aggression is some kind of an attack. And yes, you could argue that screaming at someone enough to intimidate them is not just anger but an aggressive expression of anger. Part of the challenge of handling anger is to avoid escalating it into aggression and, worse, violence.

Well-meaning but frequently counterproductive advice about dealing with anger and aggression suffers from the widespread lack of understanding that their dynamics are fundamentally different in different people. We can handle anger and aggression better only when we see the different patterns in people. It's easy enough to say, "Let go of anger and become inwardly calm and serene." For many people that's exactly what they need to do. For others it's not. When you hear about mass murderers, often their neighbors say, "Why, I can't imagine! He was always the mildest-mannered person! I never saw him get mad about anything."

How can that be? The answer lies in the three patterns that most often govern expressions of anger. We see one pattern in people who fly off the handle easily. If these people feel hurt, they tend to bury it and get mad instead (a common pattern for men). (When we realize that their anger often masks deeper feelings of hurt, it can be easier to accept.)

A second pattern is chronically hostile people who live off their anger. Every minor frustration or insult is an excuse to become enraged. If these people go through an hour without getting pissed off at someone or something, they don't feel alive. (Research has shown that such chronically angry or hostile people are several times more likely to die of cardiac arrest and other circulatory diseases at a young age.)[1] A milder form of this pattern includes people who are easily irritated and express it frequently. For these people, "Don't sweat the small stuff" is excellent advice. This means learning to face irritating circumstances with composure—"No big deal," or "Forgive and forget." Someone gives you a dirty look, and instead of boiling over you shrug your shoulders as you realize that it's his problem, not yours.

The third pattern is an inability to express your anger when it is appropriate to do so. At some point, probably during childhood, you learned that getting angry is unacceptable and you would get punished or beaten—perhaps severely. So now, when others abuse, cheat, dominate, intimidate, or insult you, your tendency is to clench your teeth, hold back, and drown your anger in tears (a common pattern for women), or perhaps respond with a phony little submissive smile. Such held-in anger turns into simmering resentment or even hate. The term *frozen rage* has been applied to bottled-up anger when the underlying feelings go unexpressed. Some learn to express their denied feelings as *passive-aggressiveness,* in which they find clever ways to "knife someone in the back" when it's least expected. Others have emotional explosions that are far out of proportion to the event that triggers them, such as the "straw that broke the camel's back."

People in this third group characteristically need to go through a process of emotional relearning in which they realize at a deep emotional level that the punishment received in the past for expressing anger no longer is a threat. Then they can start to recognize and state their anger as an earnest form of communication. Only then can they move on to the stage of genuinely letting go of anger.

Whatever your pattern, if you feel your anger is too much for you to deal with on your own, it could be a good idea to consult with someone skilled in anger management.

Unless you are nearing sainthood and have no issues with anger, chances are that you may occasionally question how to better deal with it. We offer the following methods in the hope that they may guide you in making your peace with this powerful emotion.

## EXPRESSION AND RESTRAINT

The following practices offer opposite modes for dealing with anger, and fine-tuning mental balance and emotional control. If you always bury your anger beneath tears or logic, you need to learn to contact it and express it—at least to yourself. But if you express anger easily, or too easily, you can benefit by becoming watchful of your automatic angry responses and follow Peter Marchand's suggestion that anger may be reduced when you "regularly meditate, to give love and care to all existing beings without discrimination . . . and remain alert."[2]

### The Essence
. . . . . . . . . . . . . . . . . .
*Expression:* Swami Dayananda Saraswati's comment at the beginning of this cell suggests cooling down before discussing a grievance, to prevent "the inappropriate expression of anger." He goes on to say, "By controlling its expression, you have given yourself the space to process it. Write out all that you are angry about, in the language in which you are most comfortable, then destroy that paper. In the process of writing you will discover certain

things that will give you more insight into and more compassion towards yourself. That will help heal the underlying pain, and as a result, anger will diminish."[3]

If writing about your anger doesn't work, you might borrow a method from Gestalt therapy by placing an empty chair in front of you and pretending that it's the person at whom you are angry. Since the person isn't really there, you are free to say whatever you wish. Later, if you are so inclined, you can actually approach the person and find out whether there is any chance of dialog. Perhaps there is something you need to say to clear the air. Can you say it in a way that makes it possible for the person to hear what's important to you, so that you both have a chance to heal the rift?

*Restraint:* Swami Rama says, "When you hold on to your anger, it becomes like a ball and chain." Learning to let go of this intense energy is very useful.

If you express anger easily or often, at this very moment close your hands into fists, knuckles pointed upward. Imagine that you are holding your angry feelings in them. Next, open them, palms downward, and visualize your angry feelings simply falling toward the ground and blowing away in the breeze. Shake your hands lightly, and feel whatever is left of the anger fall away as you do.

Also, when possible, sit in contemplation when you are angry. Notice your annoyances and investigate these thoughts. What mental pictures form in your mind? What words or sentences are creating your feelings? Where are you tensing your body? Next, do your best to stop thinking about your anger. Bring your awareness to the present, count your breaths, release physical tension, and see what you experience. If you still feel angry, continue to observe what your mind and body are doing. Filter your feelings through the light of heightened awareness. Don't let angry feelings take hold of your situation—or overtake you.

## Variations in Technique

When people get extremely angry, often they can't think straight. Anything said to them tends to trigger an escalation of their anger. That is why allowing a time-out to cool down can be useful. You might remain silent, try to stay centered (perhaps either go into Just Sensing, cell 19, or Sitting Like a Mountain, cell 27), and let the other person rant and rave until his or her energy wanes. Remember that people are more likely to get mad when they are tired or stressed. Leave them extra space at such times.

You might also use distraction to change the focus. Distraction from a negative subject to a pleasant topic can change the mood and make anger seem less important.[4]

## Points in the Process

It is usually better to wait to make important decisions when you are not in an irritated mental state. However, sometimes the raging fires of anger can motivate you to do something valuable. The key is not to let *it* control *you*.

# Attachment

## Impermanence and Clinging

· · · · · · · · · · · · · · · · · · · · · · · · · · · · · ·

### COUNTING YOUR COWS

*How many things there are that I do not want!*

SOCRATES

**TAKING TIME TO CONSIDER** what is truly important in your life, and relaxing your grip on what is not, can make simple truths for living a meaningful life more visible.

Socrates felt himself rich in his poverty. Blessed by indifference to worldly desires that meant so much to many around him, "he was incredibly free of the acquisitive fever that agitates mankind," writes historian Will Durant. Following his lead, his student Antisthenes founded the Cynic school of philosophy, which rejected the material desires and trivial pursuits of society. "The essence of the Cynic philosophy," says Durant, "is to reduce the things of the flesh to bare necessities so that the soul may be as free as possible."[1]

But freeing the soul in that manner is not so easy, since everyone is attached to someone or something. Socrates was attached to the pursuit of Truth. Our worldly attachments and our affections for people we love enrich our lives. Even gurus who teach nonattachment perk up when their disciples are nearby. And for better or worse, most of us are attached to one or more of the following: wealth; classy clothes; others' good opinions of us; our self-images (accurate or not); and our usual ways of thinking, perceiving, and acting. We might also be attached to the habit of conforming to the customs of those around us, or the habit of rebelling against them. We may be attached to ideas about how certain other people are supposed to act and create unnecessary conflicts by trying to make them meet our expectations.

Such attachments can open a Pandora's box of misery when we become consumed with their loss. As Buddha pointed out, everything in the world exists in time. And "anything that is *in time*," adds Ram Dass, "is going to pass away . . . because *time passes*."[2] Our permanent reality firmly embraces the law of impermanence.

One philosophic view proclaims that the only way we can truly be happy is to free ourselves from our attachments and the worries that accompany them. If we wish to avoid this extreme, however, there is great value in a healthy respect for simplicity. Simplicity allows us to avoid much of the trouble we get into because of entanglements that we introduce into our lives as the result of our attachments.

How do you live simply? If holding on is the essence of attachment, and letting go is the essence of detachment, we need to become more aware of how this polarity plays havoc with our desires. How does each side of the polarity contribute to our peace of mind, or add to unwanted complexities that disrupt it? If you think about someone who is attached to cigarettes, it's easy to find an answer if you don't smoke: stop smoking! But if you think about someone attached to his or her wife, husband, lover, or child, things are more complicated. Can you truly let whatever you've been attached to float away without fighting the emotional tides of a sense of loss?

The truth of impermanence tugs at each of our hearts. A starting point for letting go is to realize that your desire for something you are not likely to get leads to unhappiness. When letting go completely is more than you can do, or want to do, you can experiment with loosening your firm grip. This process goes together with developing your witnessing mind and watching your identification with mental and emotional states that prevent you from accepting the give and take, the coming and going, of life.

Jesus placed great emphasis on letting go. His statements, parables, and personal way of life are filled with encouragement to let go of greed, hostile or stingy interactions with others, dogmas about the inferior position of women, and obsessive observation of unfair yet rigid rules.

In the Bhagavad Gita, Krishna tells Arjuna that the wise fulfill the duties of life in a joyful manner while knowing that no one can succeed in every endeavor. Gandhi echoed this theme when he emphasized that means are as important as ends. We do our best, then sometimes win and sometimes lose. When we lose we don't have to be attached to winning and thereby create unnecessary suffering for ourselves.

Letting go of attachments by becoming a monk, nun, or sadhu is a long-respected religious tradition, but it's not the path for most of us. The more widespread challenge is finding freedom while living within a society that places value on constantly trying to increase the number of things we're attached to. Swami Satchidananda adds, "A spirit of detachment doesn't mean that you run away from the world and become no good for it. [Rather] you are the best person to do something for the world because you have the proper understanding."[3] This outlook can bring you closer to feeling at one with the river of life that flows into an ocean of perpetual joy.

In your daily life, when you consider letting go of people, activities, or things you've been attached to, keep in mind that you have the right to make decisions in your own behalf. The people who are attached to you may not want to make the same changes you want to make. Emotional struggle often accompanies situations where letting go is a source of ambivalence, but nonetheless you can detach from something—at least temporarily—to try out a lifestyle change or give yourself breathing room. For example, we've known some relationship junkies who found that intentionally staying out of a relationship for several months helped them find themselves and improve their relations with others—sometimes even with the person who was so fearful of being let go. In other cases, detaching from a relationship can start an avalanche of emotions and events that goes out of control. Mutually letting go of counterproductive behavior in a relationship may open it up to a period of rebirth and renewal that's rewarding for both partners.

Tarthang Tulku points out that "there are two kinds of 'giving up' or 'letting go.' There is giving up attachments, and there is giving up because of difficulties and disappointments. The person who has inner strength and openness does not 'give up'—but gives up grasping and attachment, and consequently gains freedom and confidence."[4]

There is also the trap of ego-attachment to the idea of detachment, complete with feelings of superiority about your renunciations. Antisthenes not only gave up all property, but dressed in a cloak so ragged that Socrates joked, "I can see your vanity, Antisthenes, through the holes of your cloak."

## COUNTING YOUR COWS

One day Buddha was sitting with several of his monks when suddenly someone ran up and asked if any cows had passed by. "O, monks, I'm the unhappiest person on earth," he said. "I've lost all sixteen of my cows." He then went off to continue looking for them. Buddha told his monks, "You are very lucky, you don't have any cows."[5]

If you are like many people, you may have more "cows" (things and activities) than you really need or want. Some items might require too much of your time or too much maintenance. In this contemplative meditation, you will evaluate which are truly useful to you and which are more trouble than they're worth.

## The Essence

Complete your starting sequence (see page 101). After you feel calm and focused, imagine that you are standing next to a gate near two empty corrals. For some reason, everything you possess—all your commitments and all your attachments to people, things, and activities, have taken a form in which they look mysteriously like cows, and are moving toward the gate and the corrals. After you open the gate, the cows start walking through it single file. As each cow passes, it reveals itself as what it really is.

The first group of cows is your activities. In your mind's eye, review your normal activities in work or play. As each element of your personal life goes through the gate, notice how your body and emotions respond. The responses may be strong or subtle. Use your mind to look at your activities, and your emotions and physical sensations to evaluate them.

After passing through the gate, each cow goes into one of the two corrals. Activities that your body and emotions tell you feel satisfying, valuable, and meaningful go into one corral, and those that don't feel so good go into the other. When all the cows are through the gate, take a good look at that second corral that contains the less enjoyable items. Let your thinking mind help you look more deeply at those activities again. Might there be some things you really don't have to do that you'd be happier eliminating from your life?

Now the next group of cows moves through. This group represents some other aspect of your life, like your clothing, personal hobbies, or even your friends. Again, let your sensing and feeling self send each desired item into the first corral and each less-preferred item into the second. Every group of activities, possessions, and intentions in your life goes through the gate and into one of the two corrals.

Next, imagine that Buddha has strolled up and that you are having a conversation with him. Tell him why each item in the "questionable-attachments" corral is there. Also in your imaginary dialog, discuss the probable effects of letting go of each item in your less desirable corral. What insights does he have for you?

## Feeling Comfortable

Turning your attention to your "might-let-go-of" corral, think about the effects on other beings of each activity, item, or personal condition if you removed (or largely removed) it from your life. Some kinds of letting-go might cause you or others pain or difficulty you don't want. Others might be welcomed—such as extra activities that you've been pushed to do by someone because of his or her wishes rather than your own desire. Ideally, letting go of unwanted attachments should make things better and easier for you and everyone involved.

## Points in the Process

Do some of your possessions, or your ideas about them, or your commitments to do things, make you close your heart to good feelings? Do some make you more open to experiences of joy and allow you more flexibility in juggling your responsibilities? Would letting go of something cause you to breathe a sigh of relief?

# Attitude

## It's Up to You

· · · · · · · · · · · · · · · · · · · · · · · · · · · · · · · · · ·

**TAKING A STANCE**

> *Those who follow that part of themselves which is great are*
> *great; those who follow that part which is little are little.*
>
> MENCIUS

**THE ATTITUDE WITH WHICH** you meet the world has a far-reaching influence on the character and quality of your reality.

Psychologist Martin Seligman got a much-needed lesson about his own attitude from an unexpected source. "In my garden," he writes, "I was weeding with my five-year old daughter, Nikki . . . actually trying to get the weeding done. Nikki, however, was dancing around. I yelled at her. She walked away, came back, and said, 'Daddy, I want to talk to you.'

"'Yes, Nikki?'

"'From the time I was three to the time I was five, I was a whiner. When I turned five, I decided not to whine anymore. That was the hardest thing I've ever done. And if I can stop whining, you can stop being such a grouch . . .'

"Nikki hit the nail right on the head," admits Seligman. "I was a grouch. I had spent . . . the last ten years being a nimbus cloud in a household of sunshine. . . . In that moment, I resolved to change."[1]

That change in attitude transformed Seligman's professional work. Already known for his research on fears and learned helplessness, he shifted his interests to the study of strengths and virtues and called his new approach "Positive Psychology." Its popularity shows that many recognize the benefits of a positive attitude.

At the opposite extreme is the troublesome yet common attitude of negativity. Negativity exists in ideas about what you can and cannot do, how people may respond, or how a situation will turn out. It takes such forms as feelings of inferiority and harsh judgments that assault vulnerable sensitivities. It appears in self-talk, mental images, and body tension. Early in his career, singer-songwriter Willie Nelson had a tendency to "think negative all the time. . . . I was making myself unhappy and anyone that was around me, I was making them unhappy. And I just decided one day that I didn't want to be that way anymore." He discovered that "just like one negative thought will snowball into a whole big bunch of 'em, a positive thought will do the same thing."[2]

Ancient and modern gurus alike have prescribed positive affirmations to counter negative thinking. In a similar mode, psychologists speak of *reframing* or *cognitive restructuring*. One form of this is trying to reverse your doubts by visualizing yourself succeeding, or telling yourself repeatedly *I can* instead of *I can't*. As Henry Ford put it, "Whether you think that you can or that you can't, you are usually right." Examples of positive affirmations are:

+ Love exists in my heart and fills each moment with appreciation and gratitude.
+ I am successfully using my talents to create prosperity and happiness.
+ I will maintain a healthy diet and lifestyle.

Try thinking now of an affirmation that fits your own needs. (If you find one that's effective, you can even use it in the Mantra Passages meditation, cell 25, if you like.)

Another approach to positive reframing is to look at a negative idea or an event in a fundamentally different way that opens your mind to possibilities you didn't recognize before. Some counselors will listen to a description of a social dynamic that sounds hurtful and then try to tease out what possible positive intention may lie buried beneath the destructive or self-destructive surface behavior. What message isn't getting heard? For example, an overweight woman who kept sabotaging her diets turned out to be afraid that if she became slim, men might make advances, and then she might get painfully rejected again. She was trying to protect her fragile self-esteem—but in a way that had a major downside.

However, once our inner messages to ourselves are identified, we can see ourselves differently and think more positively. Instead of telling yourself *I can't* or that something is *too hard* or *not likely,* you can restructure your thinking to transcend old limitations. The essence of reframing is finding a way to see the good rather than the bad in someone or something.

An attitude you probably sometimes hear mentioned in everyday speech is embodied in the term *small-minded*. It means, roughly, a combination of self-centered and judgmental (and in some cases, self-righteous, too.) When you're small-minded (as most people occasionally are), you do things that are heedless of others. In a sense this harms you, too, since you are reinforcing an egocentric attitude that you don't have to be sensitive to the needs of other people, or that you are better than they are, or that there's not enough of whatever you want for others to share. Shunryu Suzuki-roshi speaks of "big mind" and "small mind." When you're big-minded, you feel good in a way that helps others around you feel good, too. Big mind, says Suzuki, is inclusive. It is present and expansive. It is, most especially, not small-minded. Small mind, as he uses the term, is different from "small-minded," as defined above. It refers to our ordinary state of consciousness in which go we about our daily affairs. "Actually," he says, "big mind includes small mind. . . . When everything exists within your big mind, all dualistic relationships drop away."[3] He adds, "When small mind becomes calm, big mind starts its true activity."[4] At any given moment, just noticing whether you feel big-minded or small-minded can open the way to adopt a more embracing and compassionate attitude.

These comments are intended to help you make the best of wherever you are and whatever you are doing. They don't mean that you should ignore your preferences. Recently, for instance, we went out for a drink with some friends and were on our way into the restaurant when one person said, "I don't like the feel of the music here." So we left and found a place that pleased us all a few doors away. Honoring our inclinations enabled us to have a more pleasant evening. Our preferences can be wise guides to situations in which we feel a resonance or harmony and don't have to work hard to keep a positive attitude. We could have been alright in the first restaurant, but it was easier in the second one.

## MOVING WITH ATTITUDE

One way to get a broader sense of the attitudes that shape your personal reality is to think about different people you know and their varied approaches to life. Take a few minutes to do that now.

Next, place this book on a table or something like it so that you can read it while standing up. Then proceed as follows.

## The Essence

Below is a list of attitudes. One at a time, select at least six of them and "think yourself into feeling" each one. Assume a posture and gesture that expresses the attitude you are focusing on. Then take several steps. See how you stand, feel, and move as you express that attitude. As you do, you'll begin to sense how an attitude exists in your body as well as your mind and emotions. Take at least one full minute, but not more than two minutes, for each word. After each enactment, pause, close your eyes, go inside yourself, and see what you experience in your mind, body, and emotions.

| | | | |
|---|---|---|---|
| cheerful | pessimistic | alert | distracted |
| generous | greedy | blaming | accepting |
| friendly | hostile | compliant | rebellious |
| flexible | rigid | joyful | defeated |

Think about your own characteristic attitude(s)—you may have more than one. How do you feel it in your body? Consciously express it (or them) in movement. What do you discover about how your attitude influences the way you are in your body and your world?

## Variations in Technique

You can use visualization to affect your attitude. (If you are skipping around the cells rather than reading straight through this book, you may want to read cell 11, Visualization, before continuing here.)

Visualization can help you develop a sunnier attitude. Imagine that you reach up to the sky. See yourself touching the sun and bringing it down into your chest. Feel its healing warmth radiate outward, filling your body and your outlook. Then, when you interact with others, remember to let your words and actions express the sun in your heart.

## Feeling Comfortable

Few attitudes are more comforting than optimism. Swami Sivananda offers these thoughts:

> An optimist gets the best out of life. He . . . makes the best out of circumstances and people. . . . The hill is not as steep as you had thought.

The difficulty is not as great as you had expected. Things came out better than you had hoped.[5]

## Points in the Process

Although you can't escape troubles in life, your attitude can help you sail on through adverse conditions, or cause you to sink into despair. Moment by moment, you choose that attitude. Let your mind and heart choose well.

# Trust

## Betrayal versus Loyalty

· · · · · · · · · · · · · · · · · · · · · · · ·

### CAREFREE OR CAUTIOUS?

*He who does not trust enough will not be trusted.*

LAO-TZU

BOTH TRUST AND BETRAYAL have far-reaching consequences. You can cultivate your ability to trust, and your capacity to know when not to trust.

Trust illuminates hope and plays a major role in our decisions. By trusting, you are letting yourself be vulnerable to the reality or unreality of another person's message as he expresses it. You are taking a risk that might lead you to swim in an ocean of love or dive into a pit of miscalculations. You may get what you want, may not get it, or may run into unanticipated consequences. Which of these outcomes occurs depends at least in part on what others say and do. Usually, we're willing to take that risk when reason or intuition tells us that it's safe to do so.

How you relate to the world depends in part on how much you trust or mistrust yourself and others. Three recurring threads of advice found in both East and West are: be careful about whom and when you trust; trust when you can; and deserve the trust of others.

Shakespeare advocated vigilance in his admonishment to "love all, trust a few, do wrong to none." The advice to "trust a few" implies that it is sensible to assess whom you can trust, in what ways, where, and when. He is suggesting that it is prudent to trust some people more and others less. You probably know some people whose word and handshake are all you need, and others with whom you want a written contract that spells out every detail. But determining how much to trust is not only a matter of measuring character. It is also related to experience. "Trust one who has gone through it," says Virgil in *The Aeneid*.

Throughout life, for most of us trust issues occur. On occasion you are likely to meet those who would take you for whatever they can, and you are the only one who can keep yourself from getting taken. At the opposite extreme, there are those who will give you the shirt off their back. Improving your ability to see into people's character and intentions will help with knowing whom you can or cannot trust.

The ability to live and work together requires some degree of mutual trust. Organizational consultant Jack Gibb writes,

> Trust level is a diagnostic cue to the understanding of individuals and groups. . . . When trust is high relative to fear, people and systems function well. When fear is high relative to trust, they break down. [With] trust . . . the creative processes of the person or the system are heightened. Feeling and thinking are both more focused and energized. People act in more direct and effective ways. Consciousness is awakened.[1]

Gibb's statement, "Consciousness is awakened," is a key to being or becoming trustworthy. Trustworthiness includes honesty, integrity, and commitment. They add up to values that stop you from wanting to deceive or defraud, and from engendering distrust that comes back to haunt you. The ensuing trust in yourself enriches rather than impoverishes your soul.

Truth is essential to trust. If you deceive someone, you'll probably be suspicious that others are deceiving you, and will be distrustful. Honesty includes being honest with yourself. If you're not, how can you be honest with others?

Gandhi states: "Trust begets trust. Others are likely to trust you to the degree that you show them they can rely on you. And if you let others know that you trust them, they'll usually try to live up to your trust."

How and what you communicate also affects trust. Showing that you hear another person's thoughts and feelings makes it more likely that they'll trust you. So does a warm attitude and noncompetitive stance in situations involving love, power, and money. In most cases, trust takes time to develop. It seldom comes quickly—especially the deep trust that can develop over time in an ongoing relationship.

Trust usually requires a rough equality of giving and getting. If this balance is lopsided over time, with one person consistently being less trustworthy than the other, trust fades.

All this can be tricky. In relationships it's not uncommon for partners to make commitments they don't fulfill and promises they don't keep. Every unmet commitment or promise, real or imagined, can lead to a decline in trust.[2]

Many violations of trust involve some kind of cheating, as in: "My boyfriend/girlfriend cheated on me." Whether that means an affair, a one-night stand, or something less than that—a kiss, for instance—it's giving someone outside the relationship a special kind of affection reserved for the partner that may cause the partner to feel the harsh chill of betrayal. A commitment to be the other's exclusive partner may be explicitly stated or just assumed. It helps when both partners have the same understanding of their commitment. But even when they do, not all commitments come with guarantees. People sometimes change their minds, or even fall in love with someone new.

Another common breach of trust is cheating someone out of money or goods, such as the borrowed item that disappears, the loan that never gets repaid, the repair job that ends up costing three times the estimate, or the too-good-to-be-true investment in which large sums of money vanish. In a sense, all these events involve a broken promise. Other broken promises can be simpler yet terribly poignant, like the father who promises to take his child to one event after another and never follows through.

If you've lived through many broken promises and commitments, you may expect that someone, or people in general, won't come through. Distrust grows in the unforgettable bog of hurts and disappointment.

Trust or mistrust is first learned in infancy and childhood. Adults who are tuned in to their children's signals, interpreting them accurately and responding appropriately and promptly, help the children become both self-reliant and trusting. Children of parents who are often unavailable or unreliable, and who have no other close adult relative or friend to turn to, often develop mistrust.[3] But whatever your history, at a certain point who you are becoming is your own doing.

## CAREFREE OR CAUTIOUS?

This technique can help you gain clarity about a trust issue by fine-tuning your perceptions and organizing your thoughts. It can offer guidance in building your trust if that feels appropriate.

### The Essence

Trust is a feeling that lives deep inside you. You are the source for your perception of trust, or your lack of it. Either you believe in someone, in your relationship, the future, and whatever your heart holds dear with hope and faith, or you don't. You can't blame anyone else for these feelings, for they belong to you and live inside your mind.

Here you will be making a list of the pros and cons of your thoughts and feelings about a trust issue or incident that's important to you. You'll need pen and paper.

When you are ready, draw a vertical line on your paper to create two columns. Title your first column "Pros: Reasons to Trust." Title your second column "Cons: Reasons Not to Trust." Draw four horizontal lines across the page to divide each column into four sections, and in each column number those sections one through four. Next to the number one in each column, write the word *body*. Write the word *emotions* next to number two; the word *mind* next to three; and the word *spirit* next to four.

Do the following writing activity rapidly, without giving yourself time to second-guess your responses. Write down what you are feeling or thinking at this moment in relation to the pros and cons of trusting the person or situation you are concerned about.

First take several deep breaths and relax. Then write your answers in both the pro and con list without thinking about your replies. When you are ready, you can start. In regard to this person or situation, respond to the following:

First, body: Do you feel physical tension, or any other sensation such as pleasure or pain? Listen to the messages your own body signals are sending. What part of your body are these sensations coming from? What words go with them?

Second, emotions: What are you feeling? Do you want to cry? Are you angry, or happy, or . . . ? Describe your feelings as precisely as you can in both the pro and con columns.

Third, mind: What are your thoughts? Do unexpected ideas about the situation pop up? What does your thinking mind say? What do you imagine the other person thinks in regard to your thoughts? If you have two or more conflicting thoughts, record them both—or all.

Fourth, spirit: Is your inner spirit delighted or tormented? How does it react to the words that you are telling yourself? Do you feel a connection to heaven or hell, glory or surrender? Put at least one thing in both the pro and the con columns.

Be alert to whether you have shut down your receptiveness to a person or situation that reminds you of something painful in your past. Is there a real threat now? If you distrust someone because he or she triggers unpleasant memories about past experiences, you can learn to look at the present with greater discrimination. You can let your past inform you without being chained to it.

When you are done, read what you've written. What do you learn about yourself and how you perceive your trust issue? What has your inner source revealed?

## Variations in Technique

Trust increases in our relationships when we receive the same message verbally and nonverbally. If one person's words and actions send contradictory messages, the other may wonder what's up.

When you hear a mixed message and wonder what it really means, one option is to check it out: "I hear you saying that you want to go to the show, but your voice sounds resigned rather than enthusiastic. Would you rather do something else?" Such mixed signals are common. Their meanings may or may not be obvious, but can be clarified through open communication.

## Feeling Comfortable

We are always making choices about what we will or won't disclose. What we reveal about ourselves to others depends on how much we trust. You are likely to reveal something to another person in confidence only if you trust that they won't use it against you later, whether in a put-down or in some other way.

Self-disclosure is usually related to how well two people know each other. If you and another person have just met, telling that person interesting things about yourself is one way to engage his or her interest. Listening attentively to their disclosures is another. Bit by bit, you feel your way along. For the most part, how much one of you reveals affects how much the other reveals, and vice versa. Trust is gained through sharing mutual experiences of trustworthiness.

# Difficulties

## Obstacles and Danger

· · · · · · · · · · · · · · · · · · · · · · · · · · · · · · · · · · · · ·

**THE RIVER OF TIME**

*Difficulties always come, but they do not last forever. You
will see that they pass away like water under a bridge.*

SARADA DEVI

YOU CAN MINIMIZE THE ways you contribute to your own difficulties,
move through them effectively, and make them a vehicle for your own
evolution.

Obstacles can spur you on or stop you cold. Some people give up easily. Others are driven to exhaustion in their efforts to overcome difficulties.
Some people cause trouble for themselves by moving through certain aspects
of life in a semidrowsy state, paying less than full attention to where they
are or what they are doing. A man who ignores his wife's requests for more
appreciation may think it's not important until she walks out and slams the
door. At the opposite extreme, many try so hard to please others that they
sacrifice what they themselves truly need. For example, a woman can be so
busy worrying about her family that she forgets to unwind from her busy
schedule, and as a result gets easily frustrated because she has no time or
energy for herself.

Most of us create a few, perhaps many, problems for ourselves and others
through our lack of awareness. Also, some people create difficulties by insisting on having things their way regardless of others' wishes or the effects of
their demands and intransigence. This can occur when someone falls into
the egotistical trap of believing that he or she is powerful enough to do
or say almost anything, while ignoring common courtesy, tact, and ethics.
Besides causing many difficulties, such arrogance often creates isolation for

the high flier, since few people want to be around someone who is rude and lacking in social awareness.

Other potentially destructive patterns include indecisiveness when the time for action comes. And there is its opposite: hasty or reckless action when careful thought is needed. Yet another pattern is that of following a rigid agenda with little flexibility in response to circumstances.

Of course, not all difficulties are self-created. Fate throws us some unexpected curveballs, and we have to field them as best we can. To our benefit, shocks of fate sometimes jar us out of old mental ruts into creative rethinking. Such shocks can show us that instead of trying to continue with business as usual, we need to regroup and then change the way we do things.

Many people have faced tremendous obstacles before finally succeeding. What often separates those who succeed from those who don't is the willingness to continue in the face of difficulties. Sages from many times and places advise, "Keep on, and don't lose heart." Oprah Winfrey suggests, "Think like a queen. A queen is not afraid to fail. Failure is another stepping-stone to greatness. . . . Where there is no struggle, there is no strength. Turn your wounds into wisdom." With patience and perseverance, over time many obstacles turn out to be less daunting than they first seemed. Some may even turn out to be blessings in disguise.

At times, however, the forces that obstruct movement are so great that little can be done in the present to bring about the ends you seek. When nothing can be done, it's best to do nothing. "Patience and perseverance," said U.S. president John Quincy Adams, "have a magical effect before which difficulties disappear and obstacles vanish."

There are also times when a judicious retreat is wise, stepping back from what you were trying to accomplish. And there are times when it is best to neither advance nor retreat, but to stand your ground and wait for an opening. The I Ching counsels, "According to the laws of heaven, [the times] show an alternation of increase and decrease, fullness and emptiness."[1] When circumstances are unfavorable for moving ahead, it is wise to be content with producing modest effects in small matters—or in some situations, just with getting out of danger. In such conditions, it's prudent to be cautious, attentive to details that could turn into major problems, and avoid giving yourself too much credit for being able to handle whatever comes up.

Whatever you can or can't do, as Euripides said, "events will take their course, it is no good being angry at them; he is happiest who wisely turns them to the best account." In more recent times, TV host Art Linkletter said, "Things turn out best for the people who make the best of the way things turn out." In short, when given lemons, make lemonade.

Auspicious for those who practice it, the lemonade principle of facing adversity can build mental strength and the ability to roll with the punches. Although you might prefer everything in your life to be trouble-free and to go smoothly, life's highs and lows can help you recognize what is truly important and what's not. Most of us sometimes get unnecessarily upset about minor troubles. Tibetan Buddhist teacher Chogyam Trungpa reminds us that "obstacles are an essential part of the path." You can transform the frustrated energy with which you face them into composure and strength, using difficult times to help your self-development.[2]

People sometimes overlook the satisfaction that comes from facing obstacles, overcoming difficulties, and achieving goals. If there were no mountains to climb, we would never see the view from high up on the trail. "In the end," said Sir Edmund Hillary, "it is not the mountain we conquer, but ourselves."

## THE RIVER OF TIME

Our existence occurs moment by moment. In *Shobogenzo,* Zen master Dōgen Zenji said, "It simply is as it is."[3] Your existence is part of the surging river of life on which you have received the precious, yet uncertain, gift of traveling on the raft of time. In the following practice, you will look at how you manage both life's wild rapids and gentler currents. Center, breathe, and relax as you go through your starting sequence. For as long as you feel comfortable, try doing this contemplative meditation:

### The Essence
Imagine your life as a flowing river from its beginning sources to the bountiful sea. In a small boat, canoe, or kayak, you paddle skillfully to avoid the dangerous waters, while at other times an unseen current grasps your craft and hurls it in an unexpected direction.

As you paddle, review your life and recall both easy and difficult times. How do you most often flow or struggle with the river of life? Do you resist its current even when it insists that you go in a given direction, or do you guide your boat to go with the flow?

Pause at each large or small difficulty that comes to the forefront of your mind and consider what lasting effects it had, or didn't have, on you and on anyone else who was involved. Examine honestly how many of these effects were outside of your control, and how many were self-created.

Now, thinking of your life as that river, what can you do to navigate more skillfully? How can you give yourself permission to make changes more easily and flow with the currents that carry you toward new possibilities? Lastly, gaze downriver at the many moments of your future hidden in the mists, and consider what guidelines you want to follow as you steer your boat through both calm and choppy waters.

## Variations in Technique

A useful suggestion for handling troubles in your life comes from Joseph Goldstein and Jack Kornfield.[4] Identify a mental state that most often causes you difficulty. For the next week, watch carefully to notice each time that state of mind arises. Play the detective as you try to discover how it starts and what internal or external cues triggered it. Pay precise attention to what you do while you are in that state of mind, and to what you do afterward. As you continue to be on the lookout for that quality of mind, you will probably start to be aware of its presence at subtler and subtler levels. Do you find connections with any events in your body?

## Feeling Comfortable

Swami Satchidananda remarked, "With proper understanding, pain and pleasure are the same. Both are lessons. In such a light, pain becomes pain no more."[5] This principle can be applied to the emotional pain of difficult life situations. When you are in emotional pain, a counting or mantra meditation might serve to calm your mind. Then focus on your emotional process. Look at the expectations associated with your challenges. Give yourself permission to release your painful feelings with each breath. With each inhalation, breathe in peace, with each exhalation, breathe out fear; breathe in faith, breathe out worries. The heavy waves of your concerns may lessen and your inner eye may find a way to ease them.

## Points in the Process

It's hard to do much when you're flustered and frustrated. Taking a few minutes out to meditate at such times makes it easier to calm down and pay precise attention to all sides of what's occurring. Then you can respond in a way that fits the circumstances and avoid the trap of wishful thinking that events are as you'd like them to be instead of as they are.

Frequently, with the passing of time conditions change. As you move ahead, be sensitive to what can be achieved at that moment, rather than trying to go beyond where you can possibly go. On the other hand, observed St. Francis of Assisi, at times you can "start by doing what's necessary; then do what's possible, and suddenly you are doing the impossible." Zest for living can coexist with difficulties.

# Ego

## Selfishness, Egotism, and Confidence

. . . . . . . . . . . . . . . . . . . . . . . . . . . . . . . .

**SEQUENCED COUNTING**

*Ego is knowing that "I" exist. The negative side of ego is
arrogance, hardheadedness. The positive
side of ego is appreciation of the self, being thankful
for existence, for being alive.*

SWAMI NIRANJANANANDA SARASWATI

A POSITIVE, REALISTIC SENSE of self is valuable. Egotism, or bigheadedness, can cause trouble.

Every person has some sense of identity that is distinct from everything and everyone else: *This is me!* This personal sense of self—*me, myself, and I*—is one meaning of ego.

A realistic and flexible perception of yourself can serve as a guide to what you can do and what you truly want. But too often, says writer, philosopher, and Buddhist scholar Walt Anderson, the ego is more like "a case of mistaken identity. You go through life clinging to a cheap, twisted, and obsolete concept of what you are, when you are in fact something grand and infinite and mysterious."[1]

Elaborating on the effects of mistaken identity and a rigid conception of self, Swami Niranjanananda Saraswati cautions: "Don't be fixed in one perception, but learn to accept and allow change to happen. . . . The distorted perceptions are corrected, the aggressive ego expressions are redefined, and the new soft you, the new wisdomful you, the new creative you, becomes the new identity. . . . But the moment you fix yourself in a new identity, it will again become distorted."[2]

253

Errors in self-perception also occur because the depths of your being are like a cavern with many chambers. You know some parts of yourself well, while others are almost forgotten. You may even have qualities that you vigilantly keep out of your consciousness because they contradict the way you see yourself. This is true of almost everyone.

A second meaning of ego and egotism (or conceit) is thinking that you are not only hot stuff, but better than most people. This aspect of ego often involves one-upmanship and looking down on others. Boasting about how great you are is a minor example of egotism. Yet when someone puts on airs, then disapproval from others tends to be immediate, whether it's obvious or hidden.

Conversely, there are also people who consistently think themselves as being worse than others. Their self-evaluation, says Sri Aurobindo, "turns sometimes toward . . . a morbid and exaggerated self-criticism; but this too is an ego-structure."[3] Whether we build ourselves up or tear ourselves down, we are constantly wondering, *Am I good enough?* If the answer is no, then either we believe that we are defective, or we act like we are better than the rest to bolster our self-esteem. Either way we are playing a role that's difficult because it's different from who we truly are. "An organized self-deception is thus added to an organized self-ignorance," says Aurobindo. "It is only by going within and seeing these things at their source that we can get out of this obscurity."

The third main form of ego is selfishness. A selfish person takes what he or she wants with little or no concern about the effects on others. Of course you don't want to think that you are being selfish, so your mind is likely to make up a cover story to justify why you're more deserving. Or, if a person is insensitive enough, he may stick out his or her chin and assert entitlement to everything he wants: "I'm NUMBER ONE and I'm out for ME!"

In reality, we're all at least a little egotistical and a little selfish. These qualities lie on a continuum from little to lots. Our challenge is to move along that continuum in a direction that softens the intensity of their influence. To do so, we have to develop a sensitivity to when we're being driven by excessive ego. What thought processes contribute to egotistical behavior? As you see and hear these thoughts, you have the choice of putting your energy elsewhere.

If the ego is too strong, it traps you in small-mindedness and restricts your consciousness. "It is characteristic of the ego," says Meher Baba, "that it takes all that is unimportant as important and all that is important as unimportant."[4] Flaunting your ego does not make you feel more connected to your inner self or to others, but it does contribute to making you more isolated and alienated, even when you think you're cool.

The goal of transcending ego is elusive, like herding dragonflies. We can move toward being less self-centered, more compassionate, and more generous of heart, looking out for the interests of others as well as our own. As you consciously act in ways that are incompatible with selfishness and egotism, your egotism is likely to diminish. Striving to be less uptight and more accepting also contributes to fine-tuning the balance between ego, mind, and heart.

## SEQUENCED COUNTING

The following meditation can move your mind into one-pointed attention in such a way that you have little attention left for egocentric concerns. Sequenced Counting is a method by itself. In its form described in Variation 2 below it is also the first stage of Harmonic Crossing in cell 45. Although it takes mental discipline, once mastered, it can bring great clarity.

The repetitive character of many meditations in general allows your mind to shift into autopilot once they've become familiar to you. On autopilot you can lose your focus even though you're meditating. By contrast, the staggered, sequential changes in your counting while using this method make it hard to mentally drift.

Unless you've been meditating for some time, we recommend that you use this technique only after you've mastered the concentrative and mindfulness meditations that have been described in previous cells, listed on pages xiii–xiv. As you read the description below, be reassured that its practice is easier than it sounds.

### The Essence

This meditation has two steps. Begin with your starting sequence. Then, as you inhale slowly and deeply, count silently from one to five during your inhalation. When you've inhaled fully, find a moment of quiet eternity in your breathing cycle, and then count *one* silently. As you exhale slowly and deeply, count from one to five. When you've exhaled fully, again count *one*. (This full cycle of breath, with counting, will probably take about ten seconds.)

With your next breath, as you inhale slowly and deeply, count silently from one to six. When you've inhaled fully, count *one* silently. As you exhale, again count silently from one to six. When you've exhaled fully, count *one*.

With your third breath, count silently from one to seven. When you've inhaled fully, count *one* silently. As you exhale, again count from one to seven. When you've exhaled fully, count *one*. Like this:

|  | During each inhalation and each exhalation, count to | After each inhalation and each exhalation, count to |
| --- | --- | --- |
| First breath | 5 | 1 |
| Second breath | 6 | 1 |
| Third breath | 7 | 1 |

Now the sequence changes. With your next breath, count silently from one to eight. Here's the change: When you've inhaled fully, count silently, *"one, two"* As you exhale, again count silently from one to eight. When you've exhaled fully, again count silently *"one, two."*

Next count from one to nine as you inhale and exhale, and count *"one, two"* while your lungs are full and again while they're empty. After that, count to ten as you inhale and exhale, and again, silently count *"one, two"* while your lungs are full and empty. These additional breath cycles will follow your five-one, six-one, and seven-one breath counts. Like this:

|  | During each inhalation and each exhalation, count to | After each inhalation and each exhalation, count to |
| --- | --- | --- |
| Fourth breath | 8 | 2 |
| Fifth breath | 9 | 2 |
| Sixth breath | 10 | 2 |

Repeat the entire sequence of six breaths just described for the rest of your session. This session can be as short or as long as you wish, but not more than half an hour.

Changing these two breath counts at two different intervals requires great attentiveness. As you master the technique, you will become less easily distracted. When you do get distracted, you'll notice it more quickly. You are controlling your mind rather than letting it control you. End your session in the usual way.

## Variations in Technique

**Variation 1:** If this technique seems difficult, you can do just the first half over and over for the entire session (counting to five, six, and seven while inhaling and exhaling, with a silent count of *one* when you've fully inhaled and when you've fully exhaled). Do this for as many sessions as you wish, until it becomes easy. Then add the second half, counting to eight, nine, and ten with each inhalation and exhalation, and a silent count of *"one, two"* between each in-breath and out-breath.

**Variation 2:** If you have larger than average lung capacity and well-developed breath control, you can use the pattern described above with a longer count on your inhalation and exhalation and also a longer count when you've fully inhaled and fully exhaled. In this case, on the first breath count to ten as you inhale and as you exhale, and count to three when your lungs are completely full and again when they are completely empty. (This cycle of breath will probably take about eighteen seconds.) Continue as shown in the chart below:

|  | During each inhalation and each exhalation, count to | After each inhalation and each exhalation, count to |
|---|---|---|
| First breath | 10 | 3 |
| Second breath | 11 | 3 |
| Third breath | 12 | 3 |

|  | During each inhalation and each exhalation, count to | After each inhalation and each exhalation, count to |
|---|---|---|
| Fourth breath | 13 | 4 |
| Fifth breath | 14 | 4 |
| Sixth breath | 15 | 4 |

Then repeat the entire pattern for the rest of your session.

## Points in the Process

If you develop some special ability through your practice, beware of too much self-congratulation, or you'll end up in a self-defeating ego trip. Telling others about your remarkable ability in prana is counterproductive. In the Yoga Sutras, Patanjali says: "The yogi does not regard these powers as ends in themselves. Dwelling on them becomes an obstacle." And even when you try to cultivate selflessness, your ego can jump to sing praises of your own importance: "Ah, see how virtuous I am!" Chogyam Trungpa called this tendency spiritual materialism. "Ego is able to convert everything to its own use, even spirituality."[5] But if you anticipate the tendency to get caught up in spiritual superiority, you can alert your inner Witness to be on the lookout for it and avoid feeding it.

. . . . . . . . . .

# Healing

## Body and Mind

.......................................

### YOUR INNER HEALING CENTER

*You can be down, you can even be broken, but there's*
*always a way to mend.*

OPRAH WINFREY

WE EACH SOMETIMES NEED physical, mental, emotional, or spiritual healing. You can find methods that work for you, and help others find methods that work for them.

Jesus was a healer. He placed his hands on the sick and crippled and their illnesses and injuries vanished. There have been many healers since, but none with a fraction of his miraculous power. For guidance about how to heal, we must look to those who do their best without a direct line to the divine.

Among ancient healers of the Western world, the most celebrated was the Greek physician Hippocrates. He emphasized treating the total unique person, not just the disease or injury. Recognizing that nature's own healing power helps the body regenerate, he asserted that the physician's first commandment is to do no harm, and avoid interfering with the body's natural healing power.

In 169 CE, 600 years after Hippocrates, another great healer, Galen, made history as the royal physician to the Roman emperor Marcus Aurelius.

Galen advanced our understanding of psychosomatic problems. This is the term used when events in the mind, emotions, and soul, which comprise the psyche, cause problems in the body, our somatic side. For instance, ongoing mental stress can lead to hypertension, heart attack, and stroke.

Today more and more doctors recognize what Hippocrates and Galen articulated long ago. The necessity of holistic healing is becoming a familiar idea in mainstream Western medical practices. Author and complementary-medicine authority Dr. Andrew Weil makes the distinction that "treatment originates from outside, whereas healing comes from within." He says, "The true purpose of medicine . . . should be to unblock the healing system and allow it to do its work." He suggests that the best way to activate natural healing is often the least invasive and the least drastic.[1]

The practical question is how to bring about such healing. In our global community we are not bound solely to Western medicine. We can research alternative methodologies on the Internet. We can get bodywork and opinions from practitioners who use Eastern traditions, such as acupuncture or ayurveda. And we can meditate, a proven way of accelerating the healing process.

Deepak Chopra reports, "Levels of cortisol and adrenaline are often found to be lower in long-term meditators, and their coping mechanisms almost always tend to be stronger than average." Research by UCLA physiologist R. Keith Wallace showed that meditation "quickly produced profound relaxation, and significant changes in breathing, heartbeat, and blood pressure."[2] Wallace also found that with several markers for biological aging, meditators who had been practicing regularly for several years had an average biological age that was years younger than their actual age. They had fewer medical problems than nonmeditators in thirteen major health categories. This may or may not mean that you will live longer if you meditate, but it suggests that at the least your health and quality of life will be higher.

Meditation can also help heal mental and emotional wounds. As psychological and emotional wounds and physical rigidities that have been invisible to us percolate upward during meditation, we can start to heal them.

Yoga master B. K. S. Iyengar says, "Ninety percent of us are suffering in some way, physically, mentally, or spiritually."[3] Suffering of the psyche often has its roots in past injuries. Without realizing it, a person may have drawn a protective mental curtain across memories of being beaten as a child, sexually abused, or shamefully ridiculed. The energy spent to keep those painful memories at bay is unavailable for healthy use. Blocking out painful memories includes tightening your muscles to create what Wilhelm Reich called "muscular armor." Such armor stops you from saying or doing that which society decrees you must not express. It assists in keeping such emotions as anxiety, rage, and sexual excitement from breaking into consciousness. It appears in the form of muscle groups that are chronically hard and contracted to prevent the free flow of energy.[4] The longer you maintain such armor, which is usually involuntary and unconscious, the more psychosomatic problems you are likely to have. This can show in restrictive body postures, sore and painful muscles (or numbing that hides the pain), or chronic high blood pressure.

Fortunately, such symptoms can be reversed. Through meditation, you can let your awareness flow into areas of your body and psyche that have been off-limits. By becoming more inwardly sensitive to how certain muscles feel, you can start to release chronic contractions. With a more finely tuned mind-body connection, you can release blocked or stagnant energy. Results may vary, but you will probably feel healthier and open to a wider range of physical movement.

The rhythm of frequent meditation also creates an internal momentum that can help you heal. Conscious breathing, relaxation, unstressing, self-acceptance, letting-go of what's gone, being in the now, and mental agility are all helpful tools. They can contribute to preventing injury or illness, to healing, and to becoming whole in body, mind, and spirit. We offer the following exploration to awaken your inner healer and tap a treasury of inner resources to help you be well.

## YOUR INNER HEALING CENTER

You can sit up straight or lie down for this guided visualization. Relaxing your body and releasing tension will deepen this experience. Take at least ten minutes for this—or as much time as you like.

### The Essence

Imagine that you have been given the resources to design and create a healing center. First visualize a location. Let a mental picture of the facilities, inside and out, appear in your mind. It might be a place where people simply go for healing or for personal retreats, or it might have a structured program with remedies and restorative techniques. Allow the design to unfold in your mind. If your healing center has a program, what does it include? If unanticipated ideas or images you wouldn't expect appear, let them become part of it.

Once your center is designed, with each element you've included, ask, *Does this hold a message about some way I might need healing? If so, what is it? And what, if anything, does my center say about how I'd like to help others heal?*

After you've finished your contemplation, you might write a description of your healing center. Also jot down what messages it held for you. And stay open to other messages that may take longer to emerge.

## Variations in Technique

In your mind's eye, see yourself going to a highly regarded healer who can help you. Next, discuss your symptoms. Ask the healer what is most needed for your renewal and well-being. What efforts are required to improve your health? What insights or advice are you given that make the strongest impression? Mentally affirm: *I have begun making choices that enable me to be emotionally, physically, and mentally healthy.* (Also, be open to any message that you ought to consult a real-life doctor about some issue of concern.)

## Feeling Comfortable

If you stay in the same position for a long period as you sit in meditation, sometimes you might feel physical pain in your knees, back, or elsewhere in your body as a result of maintaining the position. Take your attention into the center of the pain. What is its character, size, and shape? Exactly where do you feel it? Does it change and move, or stay the same? Answer these questions with direct awareness rather than words. Next, move your attention to your object of meditation and let the pain recede into the background of your consciousness. Experiment with moving your attention back and forth from your discomfort to your object of concentration. Watch your mind and breath.

This ability to experience pain as a sensation in your meditation without being overwhelmed by it or feeling like you have to change it can be transferred to handling pain in daily life. Although the options for dealing with physical pain are numerous, the practical reality is simple: pain is challenging. If you can use meditation to help lessen its severity, you are moving toward greater wisdom.

## Points in the Process

You yourself may not need healing at this time. Perhaps you are interested in healing methods or feel drawn to healing others. Amma speaks of one who heals as a person "whose legs rush to help the suffering ones, whose eyes shed tears of compassion, whose ears listen to the woes of the distressed, and whose words bring solace to those in pain."[5]

One way to heal others is to become a skilled medical practitioner. But ordinary people without special expertise can also help others. When he identified the wounded-healer archetype, Carl Jung recognized that we have all been wounded in some way, and can draw on understandings from our own experience to help others. Showing someone who is suffering that you truly hear her can be healing in itself. If you have suffered in a similar way, sharing your own related history can be therapeutic. The trap, however, lies in assuming that another's experience is just like yours or that what helped you will help her, too. It may or it may not. Help her discover what she needs, and what she might do.

Sometimes simple acts of love can heal. With the right intention and attitude, almost anyone can offer immeasurable hope and positive energy that can further healing.

**CELL 43**

· · · · · · · · · ·

# Joy

## Happiness and Bliss

· · · · · · · · · · · · · · · · · · · · · · · ·

**YOUR SPECTRUM OF ENJOYMENT**

> *Most folks are about as happy as they make up their*
> *minds to be.*
>
> ABRAHAM LINCOLN

YOU CAN DISCOVER AND let go of the ways you make yourself unhappy, and replace these with thoughts and acts that bring you joy.

Every language has many words for feeling good: *joy, enjoyment, happiness, delight, pleasure, cheer, gladness, bliss, ecstasy.* Just hearing these words is reassuring. We'd all love to be able to go to the store and buy happiness, but it's not for sale. You have to find it within.

Happiness, the dictionary says, is "a state of well-being and contentment," or "a pleasurable satisfaction." Bliss is defined as "perfect untroubled happiness," and "a state of spiritual joy." It is also a synonym for peak experiences and the abiding state that can be reached by letting go of self-created unhappiness and suffering. The other expressions listed above overlap with these words to some degree, and your own sense of how they fit you is probably better than any definitions.

Happiness can be momentary or enduring. You feel it when you obtain something you want or when something good comes your way unexpectedly. You also feel happy when you are doing something enjoyable or worthwhile. And you probably feel happy when you bring others happiness. In Swami Ramakrishnananda Puri's words, "Happiness is like perfume. We can't pour it on someone else without getting a few drops on ourselves."[1]

But knowing what we need to do to feel good isn't always easy. Trying to feel happy when you're not just doesn't work. Stressful experiences, anxiety, discontent, and painful events can all cause us to feel bad. If you or someone you know is having an emotional breakdown, tears may be more healing than trying to be happy. Amma, who gives solace to the masses while cradling them in her arms, does not pretend that life is all joy. "Coolness is the nature of water, and heat the nature of fire," she says. "Similarly, happiness and sorrow are the nature of life."[2]

It is difficult to find happiness by trying. Striving to get what you think you need to make you happy always puts joy just barely out of reach. It's the "Are we having fun yet?" phenomenon: if you have to ask, you're probably not. Writer Nathaniel Hawthorne said, "Happiness is like a butterfly which, when pursued, is always beyond our grasp, but, if you will sit down quietly, may alight upon you."

For many people, it is all too easy to get locked into hectic routines that leave little room for happiness. One cause is a workaholic pattern in which you view everything as a serious responsibility and forget that laughter is an option.

You can, however, increase your ability to be happy, or even joyful. Vietnamese Buddhist master and meditation teacher Thich Nhat Hanh suggests the metaphor of watering flowers: "Cultivating joy means to . . . organize our daily lives so that the positive seeds are watered every day, and the negative seeds are not watered."[3]

How do you water seeds of joy? A good starting point is to notice your thoughts that contribute to making you feel bad, and move your attention away from them. In their place, you can amplify thoughts that make you feel good, and act in ways that help you feel optimistic instead of pessimistic. Notice, for instance, each time you criticize yourself. Even if your self-criticism is warranted, and it may not be, you can still realistically appreciate your good qualities. For personal growth, you have to be honest with yourself about qualities you'd like to change, but you want to put your hope and strengths rather than your weaknesses in the limelight.

Also, notice whether you set limiting conditions for letting yourself feel good. If so, you can let go of those conditions and become more accepting of being in each moment. Observe when you're tight and tense, since it's hard to feel good then, and use whatever tools you know of to destress, relax, and maybe even smile.

We can learn something about watering seeds of joy from Gestalt therapist Stella Resnick, who had a thriving psychotherapy practice, a hectic life, and pervasive feelings of dissatisfaction. "I did yoga," she writes. "I meditated. I exercised.

I became a vegetarian. Why wasn't I happy?" At the age of thirty-four, she closed her practice and moved to a house in the country where she lived alone for a year, read Thoreau, and contemplated her life. She discovered

> how little I knew about how to be happy on a daily basis. I knew how to drive myself to succeed. I knew how to criticize myself. . . . But I didn't know how to take on a day and enjoy it. . . . I suddenly realized: It isn't enough to know what you are doing wrong. You have to . . . learn how to . . . enjoy your life—moment by moment and day by precious day.

With that revelation, Resnick began to awaken to a new spirit of adventure. She gave herself permission to enjoy tiny, simple pleasures that were available in almost every moment. After her year alone, when she resumed her practice, she shifted her focus from what was wrong in her clients' lives to helping people open themselves to more of life's joyful dimensions.[4]

Meditation teacher Sharon Salzberg shares a valuable insight: "It doesn't matter how long we may have been stuck in a sense of our limitations. If we go into a darkened room . . . it doesn't matter if the room has been dark for a day, a week, or ten thousand years—we turn on the light and it is illuminated. Once we control our capacity for love and happiness, the light has been turned on."[5]

The state of bliss feels somewhat different from either happiness or joy. Psychologist Abraham Maslow coined the term *peak experiences* for those moments when we find ourselves transported into states of consciousness where everything takes on an unfathomed sense of beauty and wonder. Such states usually come unexpectedly, as if by grace.[6] You've probably known such moments. It's like walking into an alternate reality in which the everyday environment that we were just experiencing turns into something outwardly unchanged but inwardly transformed. It's a moment of exquisite ecstasy. You may feel an intimate connection with everyone and everything around you, so that boundaries seem to blur and you're just one part of a unitary field of being. You never know when this state will occur.

For me it happened quite unexpectedly one day when I was hiking alone. Suddenly the sky darkened and a massive thunderstorm began. Shielded somewhat beneath a huge old tree, kept dry by my slick rain poncho and wide-brimmed hat, I gathered some twigs and started a tiny fire just large enough to warm my almost-frozen fingers. Suddenly the raging storm and the moment seemed exquisitely beautiful. It was half an hour of timeless eternity. When the rain ended, my state of cosmic bliss drifted away with the clouds. I was back in my everyday world again.

For the most part we can't bring on such states on demand, but we can increase their probability. The following meditation can help sow seeds of increased receptivity to joyful states of mind.

## YOUR SPECTRUM OF ENJOYMENT

Begin with your starting sequence, and do five minutes of a concentrative or mindfulness meditation of your choice to calm your mind. Next, continue with this contemplative meditation.

### The Essence

Remember large and small events that have brought you great happiness, or joy. Think about pleasant events in your recent past. Then think back to your childhood, your teenage years, and your adulthood prior to the recent past and recall your most enjoyable times. Finally, contemplate potential enjoyments that you seldom or never allow yourself.

When your recollections slow to a trickle, scan through those old and recent memories to see which sources of enjoyment are an active part of your life today and which are not. (For instance, perhaps when you were a teenager you spent pleasant, lazy afternoons with friends, but now never do.) In your mind's eye, survey the range of enjoyable experiences that you allow yourself. Then shift the spotlight of your attention to experiences that lie outside that range. Are there past pleasurable experiences that you'd like to make part of your life now? (We recommend discarding any that might cause harm to you or others.) Are there opportunities for enjoying life that you'd like to allow yourself to experience more often than you do? Is there something you'd like to try that you've never done? Finally, choose one neglected source of enjoyment that you'd like to allow yourself to experience this week—and make a commitment to do so.

### Variations in Technique

As in the above technique, recall various memories of happy moments. Now focus on just one or two of your most meaningful events. Take a few more minutes to reflect on the feelings and sensations you experienced in these happy moments. Enlarge these feelings from past happiness and let them saturate your present awareness. They live inside you. At any time, you can recall them to some degree by remembering the moments in which they arose.

## Points in the Process

Contributing to others' joy or happiness can increase your own. Jesus, Muhammad, Buddha, Lao-tzu, Confucius, and all the other great prophets and saints had this in common: They recognized that finding your own happiness, joy, or bliss is just one stop on the path to self-realization, but it is still attachment to ego. *I am the one who must be happy. I am the one who must be saved.* The next step is to help others. Buddha used this metaphor: Once we have built a small boat and crossed the river from samsara (illusion, or your mind going around in circles) to nirvana (in which we discard illusion and live in abiding clarity and joy), the next step is to give up hanging out in bliss and go back across the river to the realm of toil and tears where most people live. There we can build a larger boat to ferry others across, too. He called one who does this a bodhisattva.

# Success

## From Trials to Triumph

• • • • • • • • • • • • • • • • • • • • • • • • • • • • •

**THE MAGICIAN**

*There is no passion to be found playing small—in settling for
a life that is less than the one you are capable of living.*

NELSON MANDELA

**SUCCESS IN DOING IS** achieving external goals. Success in being is presence within yourself. Life is better for most people when they attain both.

Nelson Mandela was the central figure in ending apartheid in South Africa. He says, "In my country we go to prison first and then become President." Imprisoned by the government and assigned to breaking rocks in the yard, he motivated and organized the prisoners. After he was freed, he inspired and organized the nation, illuminated a path to solidarity in South Africa, and created a vision for a better world. All of us can be encouraged by his example, and then seek success in our own terms.

When seeking guidance about how to become successful, we find a cornucopia of sage advice. For instance:

**Henry van Dyke, author, educator, and clergyman:** "Use what talent you possess: The woods would be very silent if no birds sang except those that sang best."

**Vince Lombardi, football coach:** "The difference between a successful person and others is not a lack of strength, not a lack of knowledge, but rather a lack of will."

**Nordstrom's employee handbook:** "Success Rule #1: Use your good judgment in all situations. There will be no additional rules."

**Anonymous:** "As you climb the ladder of success, check occasionally to make sure it is leaning against the right wall."

Some advisors on how to be successful emphasize thoughtful and careful planning, while others hold the view that taking action is the most important thing. Paramahansa Yogananda suggests a judicious synthesis of these views: "Whatever you want to do, think about it until you are lost in that idea. . . . Don't jump into anything at once. Take a step, and then think more."[1]

Many prescriptions for success include paying careful attention to the details of what you need to do to accomplish your goals, and then making sure your work is the best it can be each step along the way.

A different approach described by Maxwell Maltz, M.D., minister and author Norman Vincent Peale, and author Rhonda Byrne (*The Secret*) involves imagining yourself achieving what you want to bring about so vividly that your nervous system almost thinks it's already real. Peale tells the touching story of a couple in which the husband was staying out late at night and wanted a divorce. His wife had recently learned the method of vividly picturing success. Her minister "advised her to hold a mental image of the restoration of the old-time companionship . . . and picture a restored harmony between them." Following his advice, every evening she imagined her husband home reading in his old chair as he used to. She pictured him puttering around the house, and mentally saw them hiking, playing golf, and enjoying each other as they once had. One night he actually sat in the old chair. As time passed, he did so more often, and sometimes read to her as in the old days. They began to hike and play golf together as they'd done in the past. And after three months, when she asked if he still wanted a divorce, he replied, "Don't be silly. I couldn't possibly get along without you."[2]

In reality there are many paths to success. One strategy is right for some people and their goals and circumstances, while another is right for other people. Even in similar situations, the same principles of success aren't equally useful for everyone. What works best for you depends on your own aptitudes, inclinations, and style. There is no single answer to the question of how to find success.

To attain certain goals, you have to carefully consider how to get the skills you need. And then you have to follow your plan of action, which may require great effort and perseverance. In other cases, if you visualize accomplishing what you want to achieve intensely enough, everything you need to do may fall into place.

We have found that some people can surf alternating waves of opportunities and obstacles and make reaching goals look easy. For others, finding success or fulfillment is just plain difficult. We don't suggest that you pretend life is easy when it isn't. As Zen master Dōgen says, honor your present reality *as it is*. Then watch carefully to discover any ways in which you may contribute to creating problems or to constructing opportunities.

In the time-hallowed tradition of offering a list of principles for success,[3] we now offer *Nine Soul-Satisfying Steps to Success*.

**1. *Ask yourself what you truly want to achieve.*** If you try to fit others' definitions of success that don't fit who you are, you impoverish yourself. What are your real aspirations? How hard are you willing to work? What commitments will you make?

**2. *Do what you do with attention and care.*** Martin Luther King said, "If a man is called to be a street sweeper, he should sweep streets . . . so well that all the hosts of heaven and earth will pause to say, here lived a great street sweeper who did his job well." Being fully present in each moment illuminates the opportunities existing in that particular time.

**3. *Take the initiative.*** When possible, initiate and choose rather than react. Move in the direction you prefer instead of following others' agendas. As Jean-Paul Sartre observed, we are always making choices, whether consciously or unconsciously. Become aware of your choice-making process. Own your ability to make choices to further your success.

**4. *Adopt a whole-system view.*** Look beyond simple cause-and-effect relationships and try to identify any feedback loops that may be at work. If you change one thing to fix another, you don't want to inadvertently cause trouble somewhere else, as simple, one-track answers so often do. Another dimension of whole-system thinking lies in the principle called the "high-leverage point." Often there are many actions you could take, but just one that will set other events in motion in the direction you desire.

For instance, one community had ongoing trouble with vandalism after the skating rink closed at night. They tried different hours, more police, and other solutions with no luck. Finally someone had the idea of renting a bus to take the kids home at closing time. Incidents dropped to nearly zero. They had found a high-leverage point. Similarly, you can also identify high-leverage persons. Master craftsman Tai Lake says, "When I walk into a room of fifty people, I'll scan for the two or three I need to talk with. They'll be the ones who can move our whole project forward."

**5. *Formulate realistic objectives by dividing large or long-term projects into short-term subgoals.*** As you succeed with small objectives, your sense of competence rises. As you feel your own effectiveness, you become more confident in tackling larger tasks. For example, when children who were learning mathematics set successive subgoals they could attain, they moved rapidly into self-directed learning.

**6. *Step out of power struggles.*** A power struggle is ego against ego, will against will, like a parent against a two-year-old. The child discovers the magic word, "No," and the parent says, "Don't say no to me." This parent doesn't understand that the child is not challenging him but just beginning to discover herself as an autonomous being. Later this happens again at another level when the child becomes a teen. In our home, work, or social world, many disputes are basically about who wins. The "winning is everything" mentality is counterproductive when you step away from your true goals as you strive to be the winner.

A better approach is to create synergies. The word comes from the Greek *syn-ergo*—working together. The term is widely used for win-win attitudes and solutions in which as we help ourselves, we also help others, and vice versa. "When we choose actions that bring happiness and success to others," remarked Swami Vivekananda, "the fruit of our karma is happiness and success."

**7. *Develop and use your ability to listen carefully.*** Knowing how to truly listen is a skill crucial to success in many matters (see cell 26). Picking up subtle verbal and nonverbal messages allows you to understand those around you and enjoy better communication in almost every situation.

**8. *Be flexible.*** People can become so complacent about an existing structure, procedure, or ideology that they may think it is good even if it is bad, and resist changing it. Because many of us tend to want reality to conform to our wishes, we refuse to shift our approach even when external conditions demand change. Flexibility is needed to discern how to address *this* situation *now*. In reaching some goals, using the latest and best information leads to success. In other matters, the ability to slice through an information overload to find what is essential is more helpful.

**9. *Act within the context of your sense of ethics.*** Be sure to look at the concrete situation, at who or what will be helped or harmed, and how.

Whatever you want to succeed in, take advantage of fair winds and high tides to move toward your goals. Everything has a natural cycle. Just as the moon waxes to full illumination and then wanes to darkness, every situation has its own rhythmic momentum of ease and difficulty.

Looking inward can help you feel the moving forces of the underlying currents in the river of your life, so you can make the wisest choices. The visualization that follows will help you connect more fully with your potential for success.

## THE MAGICIAN

In the tarot, a storybook deck of playing cards, there is a card called the Magician. Dressed in majestic robes, the Magician holds a wand that symbolizes mind over matter. His magic is the mind's power to focus thought and direct the will. He represents the intellect and inner spirit becoming one interwoven force to energetically manifest desire in physical reality.

We each have an inner magician who holds a magical wand that can help us find success. Many people have forgotten that dimension of themselves and drift through life as if they had no magic. In the contemplative meditation that follows, you will meet your own inner magician.

### The Essence

Take five minutes for your starting sequence and a brief period of a concentrative meditation of your choice. Now imagine that you are holding a magic wand. Allow images or words to spontaneously come into your awareness in relation to dimensions of your personal magic. Don't try to make particular images occur, but let them appear by themselves. Some images might point to abilities and interests that you allow less than full expression. Others might show you how you can use your spirit of magic and wonder to achieve either success in doing or success in being. Other images and words will not announce their meaning, and it will be up to you to discern the aspect of your magic that they represent. When the flow of associations slows, let those with the most impact or meaning linger in your consciousness. After this meditation, reflect on what you can do to bring your interests and abilities more alive in your work, words, and deeds. Give the contemplative part of this practice at least ten minutes.

### Variations in Technique

Don't forget to feed your soul. Many people are successful in the outer world but frustrated inside. Your passage to both inner and outer success may lie in changing what you do, changing the way you are doing it, or continuing forward as previously planned. Look deeply within! Can your inner magician illuminate your desires and potential pathways so that you can more easily make favorable choices? "Your vision will become clear only when you look into your heart," observed Carl Jung. "Who looks outside, dreams. Who looks inside, awakens."

## Points in the Process

When traveling the road to fulfilling your ambitions, says motivational speaker Jim Rohn, "the most important question to ask on the job is not 'What am I getting?' [but] 'What am I becoming?'" Reflecting on his question may be invaluable. Paramahansa Yogananda adds, "Success . . . can only be measured by the extent to which your inner peace and mental control enable you to be happy under all circumstances. That is real success."[4]

**CELL 45**
..........
# Transformation

## Transitions and Passages

..............................

### HARMONIC CROSSING

*Like the silkworm you have built a cocoon around yourself.*
*Who will save you? Burst your own cocoon and come out as*
*the beautiful butterfly, as the free soul.*

SWAMI VIVEKANANDA

**IN ORDINARY LEARNING, YOU** change incrementally if at all. Through meditation you can bring about transformation in far-reaching ways.

"I've seen miracles occur because of my changed perceptions," says a man
in his late forties. "Once I started sitting on the floor meditating, within a
year or two my life started straightening out. It changed the workings of my
mind, and then somehow the minds of people around me changed, too."

"What do you do?"

"I'm a construction project manager."

"What changes have you seen?"

"Fights that I was having with my subordinates started disappearing. I
stopped maintaining a rigid stance. I let go of my attachment to winning, and
granted more value to the viewpoints of others. The results are remarkable."

We have all gone through transformations of one kind or another. Going
from childhood to adolescence, from adolescence to young adulthood, from
young adulthood to maturity—these are all transformations. Our perspective and behavior changes dramatically in each stage of our growth.

Some transformations result from life's changes. You get married or
divorced, have a child, or start a different job, and find that in important
ways you just can't be as you were before. What you do with those changes,
of course, is up to you.

275

Many people, mistaking the physical body for the true self, pay dearly for the promise of radical transformation by going to plastic surgeons to have their body or face altered. The ego may be pleased, but unless internal changes accompany the external changes, transformation is thwarted. Likewise, you can say you are going to give up smoking, but unless you adjust the way you think, your desire for a new you will prove fruitless. Yet we are all capable of sudden changes of heart, which can be profound and generate lasting improvements in our quality of life, notes author and psychotherapist David Brazier.[1] Some transformations that result from inner work might be:

*You go from getting easily upset or angered to being cheerful and composed.* Pilot Baba says, "When we feel irritated with something, in dealing with it within ourselves we can become transformed."[2] As we become aware of negative old mental habits, we can release them and look for positive alternatives.

*You go from sleepwalking through life to becoming alert to opportunities.* You can make use of almost anything that happens to shake you and wake you into greater presence in the moment.

*You go from contacting others through programmed responses to touching them with compassion.* Almost all of us can become more sensitive to the truth of our heart. Amma says, "If carried on the head, spiritual knowledge is a burden; but the same knowledge is beautiful if brought into the heart."[3]

For many of us, some transformations are like a seed growing into a fruit-bearing tree. These require a long period of practicing a new way. Sometimes you may undergo a slow and subtle transformation that you don't even recognize until someone points it out. Other transformations occur almost instantly, like a kind of personal earthquake that realigns your soul. Once a transformation has been triggered, it is not uncommon for a person to undergo dramatic visible changes in a few months' time. But don't *expect* dramatic sudden change, or you will cause yourself trouble by comparing your experience to a fantasy of what you think should happen.

Perhaps you have already noticed changes in your consciousness due to your meditation practices. The Sequenced Counting meditation in cell 41 contains the beginning of a meditative method we call Harmonic Crossing. In this practice, you will continue the Sequenced Counting practice and will add to it.

The particular transformations you are working with here are greater composure and increased ability to focus and control your attention and actions. In the contemplative meditations that follow in later cells, the results you gain from this practice can help you make desired transformations in varied aspects of your life.

## HARMONIC CROSSING

The brain produces several different kinds of waves. For most people during sleep, theta waves are strong. During waking consciousness, while doing tasks like math problems that require a lot of thinking, beta waves are dominant. In a relaxed yet attentive state, alpha waves grow stronger. If you were hooked up to a biofeedback machine, you could see a visual display of brain waves on a biofeedback monitor because it's common practice to have brain-wave activity show up as different colored lines.

Most meditative methods cause beta waves to grow weaker and alpha waves to grow stronger. Harmonic Crossing is the only method we have found, however, that with an experienced meditator regularly and reliably leads to an alpha-beta crossing within a fifteen- to twenty-minute meditation session. That is, you start out with weak alpha and strong beta waves. As the strength of alpha rises and the strength of beta falls during meditation, you can actually see on a biofeedback monitor that the one line rises and the other drops until they cross, and ultimately you end up with high alpha and low beta, in a relaxed and attentive state.

If you are highly agitated or upset when you sit down to meditate, you may or may not bring about an alpha-beta crossing. But even so, the meditation will almost certainly help you to become more centered, focused, and relaxed.

### The Essence

The first half of the Harmonic Crossing meditation is identical to Sequenced Counting in cell 41. After your starting sequence, count silently from one to five as you inhale. With your lungs filled, silently count *one*. Then count to five as you exhale. With your lungs empty, again count *one*. Continue as shown in the chart on the following page, exactly as you did in Sequenced Counting.

After your first six breaths, keep increasing by one the numbers you count as you inhale and exhale. And after each cycle of three breaths, increase the number you count when your lungs are full and when they are empty by one. Here's the pattern at a glance.

## FIRST SIX BREATHS

| | During each inhalation and each exhalation, count to | After each inhalation and each exhalation, count to |
|---|:---:|:---:|
| First breath | 5 | 1 |
| Second breath | 6 | 1 |
| Third breath | 7 | 1 |
| Fourth breath | 8 | 2 |
| Fifth breath | 9 | 2 |
| Sixth breath | 10 | 2 |

## SECOND SIX BREATHS

| | During each inhalation and each exhalation, count to | After each inhalation and each exhalation, count to |
|---|:---:|:---:|
| Seventh breath | 11 | 3 |
| Eighth breath | 12 | 3 |
| Ninth breath | 13 | 3 |
| Tenth breath | 14 | 4 |
| Eleventh breath | 15 | 4 |
| Twelfth breath | 16 | 4 |

Any time you lose track of your count, just go back to the last number you can remember and continue.

At this point you may wonder, *Are you saying that this practice consists of just twelve breaths?* Yes and no. That's the basic pattern. For a longer meditation session and greater benefit, however, you can repeat the pattern for twelve more breaths.

### Variations in Technique

If you have larger lung capacity and excellent breath control, you may prefer a longer count on each breath, as in the following chart.

| | During each inhalation and each exhalation, count to | After each inhalation and each exhalation, count to |
|---|---|---|
| First breath | 10 | 3 |
| Second breath | 11 | 3 |
| Third breath | 12 | 3 |
| Fourth breath | 13 | 4 |
| Fifth breath | 14 | 4 |
| Sixth breath | 15 | 4 |
| Seventh breath | 16 | 5 |
| Eighth breath | 17 | 5 |
| Ninth breath | 18 | 5 |
| Tenth breath | 19 | 6 |
| Eleventh breath | 20 | 6 |
| Twelfth breath | 21 | 6 |

These twelve very long, slow breaths, when combined with the starting sequence, are sufficient for a brief meditation session. For a longer session, you can repeat the sequence, or follow it with a contemplative meditation, or with the extended sequence below.

A more advanced pattern goes like this: if you have a greater degree of breath control, you can continue as shown in the next chart. We suggest that you try it only when you are fully comfortable with the pattern immediately above. This is the most demanding concentrative meditation found in the Matrix.

Begin with the pattern just above, starting with a count of ten on the inhalation, a count of three with your lungs filled, a count of ten on the exhalation, and a count of three with your lungs empty. After the twelve breaths that end with a count of twenty-one, continue as follows:

| | During each inhalation and each exhalation, count to | After each inhalation and each exhalation, count to |
|---|---|---|
| Fifth 3 Breaths | 22 | 7 |
| | 23 | 7 |
| | 24 | 7 |

| | During each inhalation and each exhalation, count to | After each inhalation and each exhalation, count to |
|---|---|---|
| Sixth 3 breaths | 25 | 8 |
| | 26 | 8 |
| | 27 | 8 |
| Seventh 3 breaths | 28 | 9 |
| | 29 | 9 |
| | 30 | 9 |
| Eighth 3 breaths | 31 | 10 |
| | 32 | 10 |
| | 33 | 10 |

## Feeling Comfortable

If you've gone through the full sequence of sitting meditations in the Matrix, you can probably do Harmonic Crossing without difficulty. If not, don't worry. Stay with one of the other methods, such as Double Counting or Mantra Practice, that works well for you.

If at any point you feel dizzy or uncomfortable, stop. Move into any position your body requests (including lying down if you wish), return to your normal, everyday breathing, and do a mental body scan to release tension.

## Points in the Process

After you have mastered the Harmonic Crossing pattern, you may want to add Figure-Eight Breathing (cell 22) to it. These two elements can be done at the same time. Loss of your attentive focus in either one is a signal that your mind is drifting.

# Hang-ups

## Complexes and Sanskaras

### REPLAYING LIFE RECORDS

*Life seeks to . . . obtain release from the mazes of
its own making, so that its further creations may
spring directly from the heart of eternity.*

MEHER BABA

BY WORKING THROUGH OUR hang-ups, we can move beyond stuck points and expand our sphere of inner peace.

Juanita began psychotherapy because she didn't like to ride in cars. Her therapist suspected that a traumatic past event lay at the root of her loathing. He asked her to go back through the years in her memory and report each incident related to driving that she could recall. When she reached the age of ten her eyes filled with tears.

"What are you remembering?" he asked.

"I—I'm in the backseat of the car," she said. "My left arm hurts terribly and my little brother is wailing."

"Go on."

"The car is all smashed against a bus, and Mom and Dad in the front seat aren't moving," she said in anguish.

Until that moment she had no conscious memory of the event. She had known only that her parents died in an accident, but had not remembered that she was in it, too. Juanita had a complex about the accident. Her hang-up about riding in cars had a positive function. It helped her block out painful memories of the crash. But it also limited her freedom in life.

Juanita's story points to the potential healing power of awareness through focused attention. Although there is not just one way to work through hang-ups, seeking subconscious clues to unearth their probable origin can often help alleviate the confusion that's usually part of them. Although you don't necessarily need a therapist to help you work through a hang-up, psychologists have studied such events in great detail.

In the nineteenth century, German psychiatrist Theodore Ziehen coined the term *complex* for the mental, emotional, and physical energies that get stuck together in a complicated way. Carl Jung found this concept so important that for a time he called his work "complex psychology." He compared a complex to "a pair of ill-fitting glasses through which one sees situations and other people in exaggerated or otherwise disturbed form."[1] Usually repressed and subconscious, complexes can disrupt our ability to think logically, interfere with our ability to remember, and make us act compulsively in self-defeating ways.

Everyone has at least a few hang-ups. Some of us are walking, talking bundles of them. Easily triggered anger and aggression, or tears and submission, are often driven by an underlying complex. Most anxieties and inhibitions are due to complexes. A complex may result from a single traumatic incident or a series of related incidents. Frequent criticism of a child can produce a criticism complex. A person who has been betrayed by a lover may develop a complex about trust. Someone who nearly drowns may have a hang-up about being on a boat. Having a bad relationship with one's father can create a complex with authority or father-type figures. You can probably think of your own example.

Sigmund Freud studied what occurs in the repression that is often part of a complex. "Repression is not . . . something which takes place once and for all. . . . [Rather it] demands a constant expenditure of energy."[2] He found that whatever we keep out of our consciousness is preserved in the form it had when we repressed it, so that no working-through or healing occurs. He discovered that after a complex has been formed, it acts like a hand that reaches up and grabs on to other related thoughts that might make us recall the painful event. Then we avoid thinking about them, too. In that way, a repressed memory can make other memories unavailable to our consciousness as well.

When we experience a particular complex over and over, it can seem like we are doomed to live with it forever. Even if intellectually our hang-up disgusts us, the mental and emotional energy it triggers can feel like part of our inherent nature. In India, these troubling mental habits are called *vasanas* or *sanskaras*. Some writers use the terms interchangeably. Others use sanskara for the mental trace of a past experience, and vasana for a larger pattern built up of more than one sanskara. Meher Baba, whose thinking draws on both Sufi and yogic traditions, defines a sanskara as "the accumulated imprints of past experience." He says: "Sanskaras or impressions form an enclosure around the field of consciousness. The subtle power of these forces can be discovered when we look inside ourselves, and if we're aware, we can also find them in our worldly activities."[3]

Many of our actions and reactions are determined by cues in our environment that may be as simple as a getting into a car or as complex as meeting a mixture of personalities in a room. When hang-ups that trigger contradictory feelings are aroused, a person is likely to feel at least confused, and perhaps immobilized. An enormous amount of our energy can be spent trying to get out of these complicated mental and emotional mazes. Meher Baba observes, "Life is an effort to attain freedom from self-created entanglement."

But how?

## REPLAYING LIFE RECORDS

When we focus our attention on events in the present moment, including what we ourselves are doing, we increase our awareness and enlarge our sphere of possible actions. This helps us stop creating additional sanskaras that may limit us in the future.

Letting go of limiting emotional habits that we carry from our past, or at least softening their impact, is harder. Long ago, India's yogis and sadhus developed a method for doing so. Ancient writings tell of yogis sitting in caves, replaying the records of their lives. We recommend attempting this advanced meditation only when you feel centered in your well-being. If you feel upset for any reason, you will probably lose the concentration it requires.

### The Essence
..................

#### Stage One: Playing the Life Record

Begin with your starting sequence. Next, move into a concentrative or mindfulness practice of your choice long enough to feel calm and clear. Close your eyes, and mentally go back through the years. Search your mind for your earliest memories to the degree that you can recall them. Slowly, replay the scenes that come through your mind like a series of short movies. If a scene takes the form of a still photograph, look at it briefly and then go on to the next one. Each time you feel any twinge of emotional agitation or physical tightening in your breath or body, stop and take that memory to stage two.

### Stage Two: Releasing Stuck Energies

Replay the emotionally loaded incident in your mind from start to finish. Watch carefully and nonjudgmentally as its details unfold. Be closely attentive to your breathing and body tension. Each time you hold your breath or start breathing faster, stop and focus on your breathing. Once you're breathing normally again, continue. Likewise, each time you notice that you are tensing or tightening some area of your body, stop and let that tension go. Then continue watching your mental scene unfold. Replay this recorded event over and over again until you no longer tense up or go into stressful breathing at any point. When most of the emotional energy around that memory feels fairly calm, you'll be ready to review other parts of your life record. End your meditation when you are ready.

Your stage two concentrative focus on a single impression from your past is likely to be enough for one session. If your processing of the memory feels unfinished, go back and continue it the next time you meditate.

## Variations in Technique

Instead of starting with your early memories, you can start with any period in your life that you want to review. You can also start with any specific disturbing memory or associated hang-up that you want address first. In that case, after your starting sequence go directly to stage two.

You may want to ask yourself whether any changes in your attitude might help you deal better with unhappy memories or unruly compulsions. Are there any mental signals that you can give yourself to increase your feelings of trust or compassion and decrease disturbing thoughts? Take time to validate your positive feelings.

## Feeling Comfortable

You can examine as much or as little of your life as you choose, when you choose. If you come to a memory that feels more intense than you want to handle now, leave it alone and move your focus to other recollections. Sometime when you feel differently, you may want to return to this disturbing memory. In dealing with hang-ups of any kind, remember Jakusho Kwong-roshi's statement that the most important thing is that "we make an unconditional vow not to give up on ourselves."

Many hang-ups that are not so severe can be examined productively within a structured contemplative meditation. But if a hang-up is so severe that you can find no way to handle it by yourself, seeing a counselor or therapist may be helpful.

## Points in the Process

Robert could remember his childhood, but didn't like to. He had a history of being tormented by the schoolyard bullies, often with other children looking on. One evening when he was meditating, an especially painful memory came into his mind. Instead of moving his attention away, he allowed the recollection to unfold. Then he ran it through his mind again and again, while attending to his breathing and body tension. When he was finished, most of the painful emotion attached to it had vanished. He could relax and breathe as he recalled the incident, instead of tensing up and moving his mind away.

Like Robert, when you are working to release any hang-up, large or small, it may teach you something important. As you release pain associated with old memories, you will probably stumble across times when you feel ashamed or embarrassed about something you once did. You might even see what Freud called a "screen memory" fall away. This once happened to one of the authors of this book during such a meditation. It was as if a knife slit the movie screen that Victor was watching (a self-manufactured false memory) in half, and he could see through the opening to the actual reality that had been hidden behind it.

Everything inside you is part of your inner path in one way or another. In Meher Baba's words, you "forge your way toward self-knowledge through the tangles of these sanskaras like the traveler threading his way through a wild and thick forest."

# Love

## Possessive versus Unselfish

**DOORS TO YOUR HEART**

*Accustom yourself continually to make many acts of love,*
*for they enkindle and melt the soul.*

St. Theresa of Avila

**LOVE TRANSFORMS LIFE.** Our love grows richer as we move from conditional to conscious love, and with luck, sometimes even transcendent love.

Love is an uncalculated gift of the heart that brings poetry and magic into surroundings that seemed drab and dreary. In love, your heart sings even though there is no music. It's an opening of your being in which you give deeply of yourself. As souls touch, life feels energized and joyful.

Love is not, however, all violins and roses. To feel the exploding attraction or warm glow of love when it fills you is easy. To keep its magic alive can take some effort. And falling in love involves risk, since you can't be sure where your path will ultimately take you. Most of us don't know where we will or won't find love of any quality, and sometimes even when we've found it, we're still not sure if we have it. And we may be afraid to open up to love because of painful memories from the past. In the midst of passionate romance, knowing that you are becoming vulnerable to unknown forces as you dive naked into the unpredictable currents of love can be frightening. Usually, however, love's alluring charms are great enough to overcome such fears.

Loving and being loved can bring new depths of trust and understanding. In turn, we may reveal more of ourselves than we've ever done before. One young woman says, "My partner's love has helped me love myself, and in return to love him more."

But there's a pitfall in all this. When someone's love awakens our own passion and aliveness, it's easy to assume that these qualities depend on him or her. In response, we clutch our partner tightly. The resulting dependency can be so strong that it feels like the end of the world if the one who loved us has a change of heart and walks out of our life. If our self-confidence is low, we can believe there is nothing to sustain our emotional survival. Overdependence on a relationship can lead to an emotional breakdown when it ends. Piecing a broken heart back together is often accomplished tear by tear.

To complicate matters even more, if a person is a love junkie, he or she will sometimes latch on to anyone willing to have sex, no matter how ill-matched the two may seem. In the game of seducing and being seduced, developing independence and inner strength is a central challenge.

At the opposite extreme, some people who have been previously betrayed, rejected, or abandoned, or who have had a dear loved one die, may become paralyzed by the pain of lost love. In fear of feeling that pain again, they avoid risking becoming vulnerable yet another time. Or, if Cupid's arrow has never come and a person feels unlovable, he or she will have a hard time giving or accepting love. Too much focus on the downside of love creates emotional reluctance and a negative outlook. In turn, these negative thoughts may continue to attract a pattern of negative experiences.

But for those who have faith in romance, the words *I love you* imply a willingness to face potential drawbacks and embrace one's own capacity to love.

In this vale of joy and tears, what many of us assume is true love is actually conditional love. Even when it feels all-encompassing, conditional love is centered on mutual sharing with a strong emphasis on "What can I get?" In such love, one insists that the other meets one's conditions. The conditions that are set, consciously or unconsciously, may be about power: "Do as I say and don't challenge me." Or they may be about identity: "Be who I want you to be and don't even think of questioning my wishes." When a person doesn't meet the set conditions, his partner's love moves into the background and another feeling like anger, grief, or jealousy steps in front of it. Then the person might use manipulation, tears, argument, cold hard silence, expensive gifts, violence, or any other means to get the other to do as he desires. His partner's wants and needs take second place to his own. If one person's needs consistently get met more and the other's get met less, the latter's love may fade away.

Typically both partners have their own conditions. If both have equal power, they can compromise and work things out. But if each is stubborn and insists on having his or her own way, the relationship is apt to be an endless string of power struggles.

Inequalities of power may be embedded in the culture. The male-chauvinist-pig attitude of masculine dominance, stronger in some cultures and weaker in others, defines the man as entitled to make decisions for the woman, the children, or both, regardless of what the other wants. This causes ambivalence and resentment in those who are disempowered. Equality of power nurtures harmony and is an essential part of the most deeply loving relationships.

Another relational pattern involves a mixture of love, jealousy, insecurity, and power. This is called possessive love. One partner's attempts at domination may include trying to control all the other partner's actions, or stopping him or her from growing and changing. This is just one of the many varieties of tainted love.

The more evolved we are, the more closely the love we share with another will match the needs of our partner's inner self. As such relationships endure and mature, we come to accept and even treasure qualities in the other that previously bothered us. Sometimes in love we put up with a lot—but our heart realizes that it's okay.

To grow into mature or conscious love, we have to let go of some of the myths of love. One is that love requires constant closeness. People need time together and time apart. Partners may differ in their desires for closeness, and these needs can change with time. There is also the myth that love must be exclusive. In reality, it's normal to feel different kinds of love toward different people. And the myth that there's just one true love or soul mate for each of us is contradicted by the fact that many people marry happily more than once. Closely related are the myths that people who love each other never disagree, and that true love automatically endures forever. People who love each other can argue and get very mad at each other. People who fall in love sometimes fall out of love. To keep love burning brightly requires that two people work out ways to turn incompatibilities into compatibilities, work together to resolve troubling issues, and share a deep commitment.

Beyond conditional love is conscious love. Conscious love includes making choices that show you are awake, aware, and deliberate with your trust and caring. You offer your best and act in ways that nourish and nurture the other. You let go of your conditions and accept others as they are. Respecting the other's limits and individuality, you listen to his or her needs and try to meet them as fully as you do your own. The boundaries of your egocentric *me* softens into a wider *we*.

Conscious love means letting go of your preconceived scripts for your relationships. That doesn't mean you have to happily accept everything others do. If they have some ability to change, you can ask them to alter the behavior that troubles you—but sometimes you'll be the one who needs to change for the issue to be resolved. (Viewing another person as "good material" that you can mold into being as you want him or her to be is a prescription for disaster.)

In conscious love, you do more than trust, support, and enjoy each other. You genuinely respect each other, including your differences. Even where you disagree, harmony comes from acceptance of your own and the other's ongoing development. It's a precious gift to be able to look at the world through the lens of your partner's eyes. Such relationships tend not to go stale because the relationship itself evolves and those in it change and grow. Jalalu'ddin Rumi sums this up:

> *What then is Love? 'Tis sacrifice*
> *Of self and self's hard will;*
> *He that by selfish will is bound*
> *Can never self fulfill.*
> *Who loves doth reign, and at his feet*
> *This and the next world lie.*[1]

Transcendent love is an unconditional love for other people and living beings that flows effortlessly from a well of inner joy. This kind of passion doesn't worry about sexual attraction, compatibilities, dominant roles, or power issues. It is the selfless love about which Jesus spoke when he said, "Love thy neighbor as thyself." People are magnetically attracted to such love. We recognize great souls who radiate it. One such being, Meher Baba, said, "The mind is the treasure-house of learning but the heart is the treasure-house of spiritual wisdom. . . . Divine love will conquer hate and fear."[2]

But how do we open our hearts to such love? Love for children usually comes easily, and most people adore their pets. But transcendent love for other people doesn't come as easily. What kind of work do we have to do to turn it on, and how can we prepare?

Although there are no easy answers in the unpredictable realm of love, certain forms of mindful meditation can make you more receptive to the voice of your heart. Mahayogi Pilot Baba declares, "The great saints and philosophers have said, 'Develop your ability to love.' So meditation must become a technique to unite the radiant energy of consciousness with the sensitivity and power of your heart."[3] The practice just below can heighten your ability to perceive what your heart is feeling and help you make conscious choices about it.

## DOORS TO YOUR HEART

The murmurings of your heart can inspire you to explore silent truths and find the right answers for your situation. With patience, you can probably find the willingness to bring more love into your life.

### The Essence

Begin with your starting sequence. Sense your breath, and then close your eyes. Visualize a pair of swinging doors in front of your heart. They can be any size and move into any position, from wide open to tightly closed.

Next, let people in your personal world enter your mind one by one. As each appears, take note of the doors in front of your heart. Are they closed, or open? How far? If there is just a small opening with someone, how do you feel about opening your doors more? Is there anyone with whom you are willing to open them completely? What concrete step or steps can you take that will help in doing that? Is there someone with whom you want to close them a bit more? For you, what makes a person lovable?

Come out of this meditation when you feel that it is complete. What has your inner exploration shown you about your willingness to love?

### Variations in Technique

As you go through a day, with each person you meet, friend or stranger, check out how open or closed the doors to your heart seem to be. Be especially attentive to when you feel willing to open them a little more and when you don't.

Let your heart and mind have a dialog to discover what makes the doors close or open. What qualities make you want to open your heart and how easily can you do so? How do you stop yourself from opening those doors? You don't have to have the answers to all these questions. Adopt the attitude of a student who is learning about love from within. Amma makes this sound easy when she says, "Love is not complex—it is simple and spontaneous. Indeed, love is our essential nature. . . . To love means to see and feel life in everything."[4]

## Points in the Process

If you seldom feel open-hearted, you can catch the feeling of it by being near someone who radiates love. Meher Baba has said, "Love is essentially self-communicative; those who do not have it catch it from those who have it. . . . It goes on gathering power and spreading itself until eventually it transforms everyone it touches."[5] You may also open your heart by honoring the positive aspects of the love you find within yourself.

**CELL 48**

··········

# Defensiveness

## Justification and Restraint

···········································

**THREE LITTLE WORDS**

*Seemingly trivial things often have roots in deep emotional experiences. To deal only with the superficial trivia without seeing the deeper, more tender issues is to trample on the emotional ground of another's heart.*

STEPHEN R. COVEY

EVERYONE SOMETIMES SPEAKS OR acts in ways that cause others to become defensive. And almost all of us sometimes become defensive ourselves.

"Defensiveness can be a healthy characteristic that allows the individual to feel no more pain at a given time than is tolerable," says psychologist Abraham Maslow, a leading figure in the late-twentieth-century human potential movement.[1] Sometimes we need to defend ourselves and those we love to nullify a threat. We can cause ourselves trouble, however, when we counterattack, or become so practiced in giving sharp retorts that we respond to things that aren't really threats as if they were. And we get into difficulty when our method of defending is to distort our awareness of what's really occurring, or of what we ourselves are doing.

As we mature, our defensiveness may no longer serve the ends for which we learned it. A child who is repeatedly whipped or beaten usually becomes an expert in defensiveness. A different child might react defensively to avoid withdrawal of love. And most children and adults alike are overly sensitive to criticism, even when intended as nonjudgmental suggestions for improvement.

Defending involves trying to convince ourselves or others that we did something right, whether or not we really did—often with at least a little self-

292

righteousness attached. When people start to explain themselves defensively, often they get so involved in expounding their positions that they hardly hear a word the other person is saying. They are less present, and able to hear the other's thoughts and feelings. They're even likely to be out of touch with themselves, since reacting under stress interferes with inner knowing. Deepak Chopra observes, "[When] you become defensive . . . your life meets resistance. . . . If you just relinquish the need to defend your point of view, you will . . . gain access to enormous amounts of energy that have been previously wasted."[2] The question, of course, is how to stop being defensive. The following communication practice provides a way.

## THREE LITTLE WORDS

This is a powerful everyday awareness method for recognizing and reducing your defensiveness. You can use this approach whenever anyone says something to you that evokes your tendency to explain, defend, or justify your past or present actions. It will increase your ability to see how you perceive yourself and to understand why you are reacting as you do. You can use it whenever you are inclined to correct another person's perception of you, or of something you're doing or did. We advise trying a mock practice during one full meditation session before you try it with others in the world.

### The Essence

When someone makes a remark about you that you think is mistaken and you want to set them right, take a deep breath or two. No matter how you would like to respond, limit your reply to no more than three words. One word might also suffice, like "Well," "Oh," or "Really!" Useful two- or three-word phrases include, "Thank you"; "Imagine that"; "How about that"; "A useful observation"; "I'll consider that"; "Worth thinking about"; and "Ah, so." Avoid responses like "Not really," or, "You're wrong," since they are basically two-word defensive messages that defeat the purpose of this practice.

As you remain silent or utter your one- to three-word response, you will probably find a flood of statements welling up within you that you'd like to say. Your clever mind will supply numerous remarks that would serve the purpose of explaining or justifying or defending yourself in order to protect your self-image or affect the other's opinion of you. But the three-word limit on your verbal reaction gives you time to be thoughtful and watch your own mind's process.

Your concise response also makes your energy and attention more available for assessing your emotional state. When your defensive internal chatter dies down, you can recover your equilibrium and perhaps determine what the person said that pushed your button. You will also find that the other person's comments often lose momentum when they trigger no defensiveness from you. And by using no more than three words, you won't get sucked into a whirlpool of arguing.

## Feeling Comfortable

Sometimes you will feel like you have little choice but to defend yourself. Explaining or justifying can be a useful thing when an officer pulls you over and there's a chance to talk your way out of a traffic ticket. Or if someone levies an accusation, you may fear that you'll lose face if you don't reply. You always have the choice to turn the other cheek, as Jesus suggested. A less noble, yet often effective option if someone insults you is to shift the spotlight onto their insulting behavior. For instance, "Ah, and you're lucky enough to know everything and do no wrong!" Of course, no course of action is right for every occasion, and every situation needs your intelligent assessment before you speak or act.

If you have really done something wrong or stupid, you might look a bit wiser if you admit it. "There is a certain degree of satisfaction in having the courage to admit one's errors," points out public-speaking teacher and self-improvement writer Dale Carnegie. "It not only clears up the air of guilt and defensiveness, but often helps solve the problem created by the error."

## Variations in Technique

In some situations you might just collect your thoughts and feelings and say, "I disagree." Buddhist teacher Pema Chödrön suggests being grateful for painful challenges when they cross our path.[3] When a disparaging remark brings about a defensive stance, it is an arrow pointing to something we need to work on to attain peace of mind, she says. Chödrön suggests that we train ourselves to open our hearts even in difficult situations.

Conflict resolution expert and former judge Jim Tamm suggests that when you find yourself being defensive with people you trust, you can add a bit of self-disclosure, by saying something like, "'Can you go back over that again? I think I'm getting a little defensive and I may have missed your point.' [This] acknowledges your defensiveness, both to yourself and your colleagues, and asks for their help in dealing with it. . . . it not only offsets the damage caused by the defensiveness, it can actually create greater intimacy and a stronger relationship."[4]

Be alert for times when your defensiveness pops up during meditation, as it sometimes will. Detaching from the need for instant resolution creates space for a healing solution.

## Points in the Process

The other side of all this occurs when you push the buttons that trigger another's defensiveness. You can expect other people to respond defensively when they feel their self-image threatened or attacked. Even if they don't say a word, you may see defensiveness in their body language.

Perhaps you'll want to fall silent and think about your motive for using a verbal zinger, even if it's subconscious. It might be best to say something supportive, or move the conversation to another topic if that feels appropriate. We advise avoiding "Why did you . . . ?" questions. They're communication breakers that trigger defensive reactions. You might also avoid telling other people things like "This is how you are." Statements from your personal frame of reference that refer to specific behavior, like "I appreciate . . ." or "I felt offended by . . ." are more useful.

The awareness you gain from the practice of Three Little Words can give you insight into universal emotional reactions connected with defensiveness. If you've felt the anguish of being devalued, demeaned, or threatened, even if someone was "just telling the truth," you know how painful that feels. Identifying with other people's defensive reactions can open you to becoming more supportive if you want to minimize the negative energy flow that goes with defensiveness. This can fertilize seeds of insight, strength, and wisdom that will improve relations with yourself and others.

# Conflict

## Criticism and Opposition

### RESOLVING AND TRANSCENDING

*We have met the enemy and he is us.*

WALT KELLY

**EFFECTIVE METHODS ARE AVAILABLE** to avoid, resolve, and transcend conflicts. Turning opponents into allies requires inner strength and mindfulness.

Conflicts of interest inevitably occur in life, starting as early as the shocking moment when an infant bites the nipple and the mother pulls her breast away. No one likes to be told no to something they passionately want to do. We need wise, effective ways to handle personal differences so that they don't erupt into disputes.

When possible, avoiding behavior that might provoke a conflict is a good starting point. Twenty-five hundred years ago, in the *Tao Te Ching*, Lao-tzu offered these poetic suggestions for harmonious relations:

> *Water knows how to benefit all things without striving with*
> *them. . . .*
> *In dealing with others, be gentle, benevolent, and kind. . . .*
> *In action, choose the right moment.*
> *Do not be contentious and you will not be blamed. . . .*
> *Amid your active life, can you embrace the quiet spirit? . . .*
> *Can you adopt the feminine attitude,*
> *Being open to all things?*[1]

Lao-tzu used water as a metaphor for humility and being able to flow with surrounding forces. By avoiding attempts to usurp power or seem more important or virtuous than others, we avoid antagonisms. His reference to the quiet spirit shows the timeless value of inner calm. And even though he doesn't suggest that men should be more compliant, he notes the importance of qualities often characterized as feminine, such as open-mindedness, nurturance, acceptance, and flexibility.

When conflicts occur, showing mutual respect and consideration can open the door to finding a satisfactory resolution. By contrast, verbal aggression like sarcasm, cynicism, and one-upmanship is almost sure to generate ill will. Perhaps this is why the I Ching advises not to step on a tiger's tail.

It's all too easy to slide down the slippery slope of regarding the "Other" as the enemy and dehumanizing them. "Hating is a tool of exploitation that invites you to a fight," says Pilot Baba, who served in the Indian Air Force in three India-Pakistani wars. In *Faces of the Enemy,* Sam Keen presents an astounding gallery of pictures and posters showing how opponents, especially in wartime, are depicted as monsters of the most terrifying and despicable kind.[2] The "enemy" becomes an incarnation of cruelty, ugliness, and evil, while "we" are clean-cut, honest, brave, honorable, and good. This blinds us to our common humanity. Once we have dehumanized and demonized the Other, we tell ourselves we're justified in squashing them like insects. In the dim recesses of our minds we bury the fact that we are injuring or killing real human beings who have families, just like us.

If we look deeply within ourselves, each of us will discover the violent urges connected with our basic survival instincts, and we will find every aggressive impulse that we detest in our enemy. Since most of us are not great-minded enough to admit that, we project our own vicious urges onto the Other, who could be a neighbor, an opponent on the city council, or the people of another country. In this situation we easily fall into seeing our opponents as evil and ourselves as good. Simultaneously, they are doing the same thing.

Martin Luther King spoke of a different way:

> Let no man pull you low enough to hate him. . . . Returning violence for violence multiplies violence, adding deeper darkness to a night already devoid of stars. Hate cannot drive out hate. . . . Man must evolve for all human conflict a method which rejects revenge, aggression, and retaliation. The foundation of such a method is love.[3]

Mahatma Gandhi behaved in such a way that his enemies were converted into friends. He said, "I object to violence because when it appears to do good, the good is only temporary; the evil it does is permanent. . . . 'An eye for an eye' makes the whole world blind."[4] The conflicts we face in daily life are on a scale quite different from those that Gandhi faced in India's struggle for independence. Nonetheless, his words hold an important message, as he advised "the cultivation of a nonviolent attitude of mind and emotion," which is called *ahimsa* in the yogic tradition.

The best way to resolve a conflict depends on its character. Resolution may take the form of compromise: "I'll give a little here if you'll give a little there." Or it may involve taking turns: "You choose this time and I'll choose next time." Or it may involve defining spheres of influence: "You make these decisions and I'll make those." Or it may take still other forms that emerge from creative problem solving in the moment.

If you want a person to do something other than what she is doing, or want her to do it differently, you need to be honest with yourself and clear with her about your motives and wishes.

People will hear you more easily when your attitude is respectful rather than offensive. "I'm right and you're wrong—and a bad person, too," won't get you very far. Conflicts can be resolved when each person is willing to be flexible and ultimately reasonable. And problems are more likely to be resolved acceptably when both parties take the time for a full and thoughtful exploration of the possibilities. Quite often there are options that have not occurred to either party at the outset.

Sometimes no resolution may be better than a lose-lose outcome. An uneasy truce is better than each side savaging each other. When people can't agree, if everyone is nonetheless courteous and respectful toward the others, life can go on in spite of differences. Future conditions or attitudes may change so that a win-win solution becomes possible.

But don't give up too quickly. A truly open-minded discussion might yet unveil a win-win option. The following approach might help achieve that end.

## RESOLVING AND TRANSCENDING

If you are willing to care about the other person enough to want her to get as much as possible of what she wants, and feel as good as possible about the outcome, you're off to an excellent start. Of course, you want to get as much of what you need to feel good, too.

A simple but widely useful tactic is called the "sandwich." You begin by preceding any criticism, complaint, or request with genuine appreciation for something good the other person or party has done. Then make your request. Finally, follow it with another positive remark. Your complaint or request is thus sandwiched between the two statements of appreciation. This shows that you are not antagonistic, but are focused on a specific issue or behavior.

It is usually wise to avoid bringing up complaints about the past, since that can sabotage a present resolution process. It is also helpful to stay focused on the main source of disagreement, and not enlarge the conflict by introducing extra items.

It's possible that at some point in the process described below, you may discover that you actually don't care so much about what you thought you wanted. In that case, you have found a way to transcend the difficulty. This is letting go of your attachment to having things be your way.

## The Essence

### Resolution Step One: Listen

Sit down facing each other and look silently into each other's eyes for at least one full minute. When you speak, each of you states what you think you want (even though it might be quite different from what the other person wants you to want).

During your discussion, use your best listening skills to hear the other person's wishes, hopes, fears, and suffering about the issue as fully as you can. Adopt the attitude of a tolerant and inquisitive observer. Be sure to consider:

+ All sources of happiness and sorrow for each of you in this matter
+ Whether this is truly important for you now, an agenda left over from the past, or an unnecessary power struggle to maintain your self-image
+ Any impacts on other people and beings besides the two of you

After listening, repeat back the central points you think you heard, so the other person can set you straight if there's something you misunderstood. Then pause for a moment of silent reflection before you reply. When you do, reply from the role of a peacemaker. Then offer your perspective. Ask the other to listen, just as you were willing to hear his or her concerns.

### Resolution Step Two: Explore

Think of all possibilities for creative solutions that either of you can conceive of, even if some seem far-fetched. Identify the elements of what you each want and that mean most to you, as well as those that mean the least.

### Resolution Step Three: Negotiate

This may mean trade-offs, or letting go of lesser concerns in order to get what each of you cares most about. This will probably take some time and discussion. (In this phase, think of yourselves as working cooperatively on the same problem-solving team.) When one of you thinks you've reached agreement, state it clearly and in detail. If the other doesn't agree, continue until both of you do.

Sometimes it's useful to wait a day and sleep on it before you go on to decision making. But not always. Consider the circumstances. It may be better to stay engaged until you reach agreement.

## Variations in Technique

Meditate. Go through your starting sequence. Go into contemplative meditation with your issue as the focus. Don't try to think it through in a linear or logical fashion, but let it float in your mind in whatever way it does. When your attention drifts, note where it's drifted—that may hold some idea that could help with your conflict. Then bring your mind back to the issue as if it were a candle flame. Nonjudgmentally witness your thoughts, feelings, and sensations as you contemplate. (Or if you can't be nonjudgmental, witness your judgments.)

Visualize yourself asking Jesus, Buddha, Confucius, or any great thinker what he or she would do. What insights do you receive? Also, look for the silver lining in your conflict. What useful message or source of insight—of any kind—does it hold?

If during your meditation you felt an internal shift in which you transcended the conflict (such as moving from dislike to acceptance of something the other person does), you probably won't need resolution steps one, two, or three, above.

## Points in the Process

The ultimate act of conflict is war. Before becoming president of the United States, General Dwight D. Eisenhower was supreme commander of Allied forces in Europe during World War II. In his inaugural address on January 20, 1953, he declared:

> Every gun that is made, every warship launched, every rocket fired, signifies in the final sense a theft from those who hunger and are not fed, those who are cold and are not clothed. . . . I hate war as only a soldier who has lived it can, only as one who has seen its brutality, its futility, its stupidity. . . . When people speak to you about a preventive war, you tell them to go and fight it. . . . War settles nothing. . . . Though force can protect in emergency, only justice, fairness, consideration and cooperation can finally lead men to the dawn of eternal peace. . . . The problem in defense is how far you can go without destroying from within what you are trying to defend from without.[5]

Our personal conflicts can also benefit from Eisenhower's wisdom.

# Strength

## Power and Control

· · · · · · · · · · · · · · · · · · · · · · · · · · · ·

**YOU'VE GOT THE MOVES**

*When you are strong, you should be strong. . . . But that*
*toughness comes from your gentle kindness. When you are*
*kind . . . that does not mean you are not strong.*
SHUNRYU SUZUKI-ROSHI

**STRENGTH COMES WITH FEELING** capable and effective in what we do.
Wanting power over others masks a deficiency of inner strength.

Perhaps you've seen runners on a track. Two are neck and neck, with
the third just a step behind. On the last lap, drawing on some inner reserve,
the arms and legs of the runner in fourth place start moving faster and her
stride lengthens. With each step she inches forward until at the very end her
momentum carries her past the leader. She crosses the finish line half a step
ahead. She wins through pure strength—which includes physical strength,
coordination, determination, training, and grit.

Far Eastern traditions identify an energy center called *chi* (pronounced
*chee*) in the area of the solar plexus. The Chinese believe that chi connects
us with the universal life force. In our body, a healthy flowing chi generates
well-being, power, and physical strength. People who train in martial arts
learn how to connect with their chi through breathing and mental focus
in order to generate the inner strength and mind power that's needed for
maximum physical agility. Chi is valued most when it is harnessed for self-
control and for expanding the qualities needed to live a satisfying life.

In the West, a widespread view of strength includes a strong will,
self-discipline, and personal power. The conceptual boundaries between
strength and power are not hard and fast, however, and there are gender

biases as to what people believe makes someone strong or weak. The sensitive, nurturing, softer personal qualities that comprise a woman's strength are viewed by some as weaknesses in a man. What you think about strength is important since your beliefs shape your perceptions. Others' views of you can also affect your perception of yourself as strong or weak. Feeling some degree of personal power and significance appears crucial to a sense of self-esteem.

Power is both related to strength and different from it. Strength is a personal quality. Power is the ability to affect or control other people. In India's tantric tradition, it is viewed, in Harish Johari's words, as the wish "to be somebody who is recognized by others as special, and the desire to be powerful and authoritative, a king of one's own domain [who enjoys] reputation, authority, and status."[1]

Sometimes people crave power to offset a feeling of insecurity, weakness, or inferiority. These qualities contribute to feeling anxious that you won't be able to protect yourself or get what you need. Gaining power, whether through wealth, intimidation, or guile, is one response to that feeling.

A different cause of power hunger, points out Jungian analyst Jean Shinoda Bolen, is a deficient capacity to love. She says, "The quest for power is a substitute for love." Bolen offers an analysis of Richard Wagner's four-opera Ring Cycle, based on Norse mythology, which was written almost a hundred years before J. R. R. Tolkien's three-volume epic, *The Lord of the Rings*. Both Wagner's and Tolkien's stories are centered on a mythical ring that holds enormous power, yet destroys the wearer's soul.

In Wagner's operas, Wotan, the Norse equivalent of Zeus, is driven to sacrifice almost everything to build a palace-fortress called Valhalla. Foremost among these sacrifices is Freya, the goddess of love, youth, and beauty, whom he promises to the two giants who build Valhalla. Bolen writes: "Trading Freya for Valhalla is a metaphor for an interior choice that many men make. They trade away . . . love and youth, the very qualities usually sacrificed by ambitious men. In exchange, they acquire a cynical attitude that they call realistic [and become] obsessed with having control, which power provides."[2]

The ring of power was forged by the dwarf Alberich, who had been humiliated and ridiculed. To gain the ability to create the ring, he had to renounce love forever. Bolen observes that often, "having power over others is an effort to compensate and retaliate for abuse, rejection, and humiliation. . . . Rejection and exclusion . . . make a person feel impotent and unlovable."[3] They can get locked into being hard-edged, and can become impervious to genuinely loving feelings and behavior.

This destruction of empathy and inner wholeness can cause power-driven men to become consciously or unconsciously contemptuous of their wives, who embody qualities that they themselves may have devalued. If love fades, power struggles often take its place. This scenario is not a fantasy, as the pattern of loving relations deteriorating into bitter power struggles is seen frequently (especially in divorce court).

This pattern is not, of course, an absolute. It can occur to a greater or lesser degree, or not at all. And the sacrifice of love for power can be reversed. We know some who have reached their goals of wealth and power and have happy, loving relations with the love of their life.

What, then, are the elements of using your power wisely and enhancing inner strength?

One is relentless honesty with yourself. This includes acknowledging and accepting yourself as you are in relation to your desire or lack of desire for power. Recognizing our greedy sides and admitting to them takes courage. As you integrate the different aspects of your power issues, which may include both admirable values and behavior patterns that you might want to change, your inner strength increases.

A second element of inner strength is strong determination. This is, in Pema Chödrön's words, a "commitment to use our lives to dissolve [our] indifference, aggression, and grasping." She makes this comment more specific in such questions as, "How do we catch our thoughts before they become 100 percent believable and solidify into 'us' against 'them'? Where do we find the warmth that is essential to the transformative process?"[4]

A third element of inner strength is the ability to hear your egocentric voice. In this, your task is to notice extra ego—the *me first* voices beyond those you need to take care of yourself and others for whom you have responsibility. When you notice such a voice, to the degree that you can, let go of it.

A fourth element of inner strength includes empathy, compassion, and presence. This is a willingness to feel another person's pain and suffering, identify with it, and when possible, help that person move beyond it. It requires awareness in the moment, anticipation of where what's occurring now may lead, and readiness to act as needed.

A fifth element of inner strength is self-knowledge.

But how can power or powerlessness be converted into strength? The next exercise is designed to help you find the answer.

## YOU'VE GOT THE MOVES

This adventure in awareness is suggested by Laura Archera Huxley. In this exercise, you pretend to be an animal and explore specific ways in which you do or don't express your strength, and do or don't move. For example, one young woman in a group felt impotent and powerless. When asked to imagine herself as an animal, she became a tiny mouse and acted out that role with members of the group. As she became more aware of her mousiness, she became disgusted with it. Then she transformed herself into a huge, scary bear. She stood on her hind legs, reared above group members, and roared. In the weeks that followed, her mousiness almost disappeared.

Now it's your turn. You can become each of several different animals and explore what it's like to be each.

### The Essence

Imagine yourself as the animal that first pops into your mind, or one that expresses your mood of the moment. Stand up and move as that animal would, feeling yourself to being as completely like that creature as you can. Pay attention to the emotions that accompany doing so. Do this for about three minutes. Then stop. Suggests Huxley:

- ✦ Become this animal.
- ✦ Make the noises this animal makes.
- ✦ Feel as it feels.
- ✦ Think as it thinks.
- ✦ Eat as it eats.[5]

Above all, move as it moves. Pay special attention to which parts of your body are active and which are not, and how, and make full use of this chance to explore the ways of moving that go with being this animal. Next, choose another animal very different from the first one. If you were not a cat before—whether a shy housecat or a powerful lion or tiger—you might become one now. As you move, bend your knees fully as you walk, and stretch your front and back legs and paws as cats do. Let yourself be moved by your inner cat or tiger. Again, after three more minutes, stop.

Now choose yet another animal quite different from your usual way of being. Perhaps you will wish to be an ape, with arms that can move far out to explore your environment; or an elephant; or an animal that lives under the sea such as a dolphin or toothy shark. Or perhaps you'll be an imaginary animal such as a centaur or unicorn, or a phoenix, the symbolic sacred bird of transformation.

After playing the roles of three different animals, contemplate what you just did. Did you use your body and move in ways that you don't ordinarily do? (Many hatha yoga poses, or asanas, are named for animals.) Is there anything from this experience that can add to your sense of strength, power, or flexibility? Do you want to incorporate any insights or new moves into your way of being in your everyday world?

## Variations in Technique

If you have found a special connection with a particular animal, it can become an inner guide for you. In times of difficulty, you can call on your totem animal for guidance. For example, our chiropractor loves bears. She's collected hundreds of bear figurines that tastefully adorn her office. When her strength is waning, she calls on her spirit guide for energizing bear energy and healing thoughts.

## Points in the Process

Either a dominant or a submissive attitude can be considered weak, while a clear stance of mutual respect is strong. Getting caught in power struggles is weak. Responding to each situation as it is, in a present, flexible, and ethical way, expresses strength. So, too, does an attitude of realistic optimism, while staying alert to the yin and yang, receptive and generative forces, at play in any situation.

# Confusion

## Moving toward Clarity

**INNER VOICES**

> *When you are confused, it's like being in a thick fog. Don't think that you shouldn't be confused; just see the fog.*
> JAKUSHO KWONG-ROSHI

**CONFUSION IS ALMOST ALWAYS** linked with inner contradictions. Often you can transform these conflicting thoughts into a pathway for creative thinking.

"Good grief—I'm so confused! I feel pulled this way and that. I'm lost inside my mind, and have no idea what to do!"

Almost everyone sometimes feels this way. Confusion usually combines internal conflict with not knowing enough about concerns that are related to the conflict. You don't see things clearly. When you lack a clear and comprehensive view of what's occurring, it's easy to be in conflict about what to think or believe.

At other times, you might have a clear sense of what you want, while someone else is urging you to think, feel, or do something different. Or several people may have different agendas for you. These pressures can produce uncertainty. Externalized multiple voices, each falsely claiming to know what's best for you, can easily muddle your own understanding.

Throughout history the perspectives of great masters in sources such as the I Ching, the Tao Te Ching, the Bhagavad Gita, the Bible, and the Qu'ran have offered profound insights that can help us attain clarity. Since many of these ancient resources use love as their guiding principle, they point to the value of seeking the truth of your most heartfelt preferences to serve as a compass for navigating toward the right choices. However, if you feel conflicting feelings, thoughts, and motives, with one part of you wanting to do one thing and another part wanting to do another, just listening to your feelings may not be enough.

Ambivalences take many forms. Personal questions about relationships, love, money, career changes, buying or not buying a house, or how to pay credit-card debts can consume a large amount of time and energy. Changing family structures and gender roles can create confusion not just for adults, but for children, too. Contradictory advice about how to raise children or how long to support them puzzles many parents. The time spent sorting through our emotional or financial preferences is often coupled with anxiety and distress. Without reliable and trusted guideposts, uncertainty about the best course of action can become a dramatic inner play of consciousness.

To complicate the situation, not all of the dimensions of confusion are always conscious. We may feel the proddings of our instincts, inherent tendencies, and unconscious mind without knowing where they are coming from. (That is especially true of things we want to avoid seeing.)

Our thoughts, feelings, and inclinations to act seldom travel alone. There is almost always some thought, feeling, or a combination of them (often called a motive) beneath an action tendency. Many of our thoughts have feelings hiding under them. In turn, feelings usually have thoughts attached, and even feelings themselves often travel in pairs, or even gangs of three or more. You may feel pushed or pulled by desires, fears, aversions, or complex combinations of internal states. No wonder our confusion sometimes is so hard to untangle.

Gestalt psychologist Kurt Lewin studied the varieties of inner conflict. He found that confusion connected with two desirable alternatives often tends to be quickly and easily resolved. The closer you get to making your choice, the more desirable it is likely to seem. By contrast, conflicts between two negative options are more difficult, since the closer you get to making either choice, the more salient its negative qualities become. Whether or not to choose something that has both liked and disliked qualities is also difficult. So is a choice between two or more options that have both positive and negative qualities. Such choices are not only difficult but confusing, since you are both attracted to and repelled by each alternative.[1]

If you can relax instead of going into a state of panic, you'll be less likely to feel driven to force your way to clarity prematurely. Stressful decision making is often tense, and your "clarity" might be narrow and rigid rather than truly clear. If you can, it's in your favor to wait until you are relatively free from stress and confusion to make a big decision.

In addition, sometimes a gestation period to mull things over is important. People differ in how long they need to sit with a dilemma or decision to be ready to resolve it. Such a gestation period may include letting go of old concepts, feelings, and inclinations that are no longer useful.

In the following contemplative technique, you will be asked to think of the ideas, emotions, and impulses that surround the subject of your confusion as inner voices. You'll listen to what each different voice has to say until you hear them all clearly and have a panoramic view of your situation. That is called "seeing *through* the fog."

## INNER VOICES

As you identify your inner voices and listen carefully to what each wants and doesn't want, you will reach a point where you can hear each of them distinctly. As you do, you gain a broader and deeper understanding. Once you know what each voice is saying, thinking, or feeling, you will probably have a pretty good view of the situation you've been confused about. You might even find that the fog has lifted and your perplexity is gone. At that point, even if you still don't know what to do, it is likely to be easier to find your way out of what's left of your confusion.

### The Essence

Begin with the starting sequence and several minutes of a counting or mantra meditation to focus your mind. Then move into a contemplative meditation in which you listen to each of the voices that are pushing or pulling you in different directions in relation to your confusion. With each voice, scan through your thoughts, feelings, and the associated physical sensations. Actively listen in turn to hear: the approving and the disapproving voices, the accepting and the nonaccepting, the one that wants or doesn't want this, the one that wants or doesn't want that. With each voice notice the thought, the strongest feeling, and the action tendency that goes with it.

As you contemplate a feeling, try sinking deeply into it to see whether another feeling, or even more than one, underlies it. Do this with each inner voice or opposing opinion or impulse.

If other people are urging you in certain directions, identify their voices inside your head along with those that arise from within you. Also, notice how your body reacts as you listen to each voice. Does your stomach relax or tighten up? Do your jaws clench or relax? What are you doing with your hands? Your toes?

Don't forget to listen for your inner foghorn that sounds when some course of action you are thinking of is likely to be hurtful to you or others. That foghorn is connected to your deep sense of ethics, or your need to protect a vulnerable part of your inner spirit. Of course, you make the choice of whether to heed its warning or to distract yourself by moving your attention elsewhere.

## Variations in Technique

If listening to your body's messages and your thoughts and feelings that percolate during meditation doesn't guide you to clarity, you can write the concerns of each voice on paper. Give each a name, such as My Inner Mom, The Worrier, The Whore Within, My Saintly Self, The Guilty One, etc. Then conduct a written dialog among the various voices. Pretend that they are all having a meeting to find the best solution to your dilemma. Continue your dialog for as long as each voice has something to say to one or more of the others—but no longer than fifteen minutes. (Do this as a free-writing exercise, in which you write each statement by each voice as fast as you can, without pausing to think before you go on to the next one. When your energy for writing wanes, stop and contemplate what you've written.)

## Points in the Process

Although most people think of confusion as negative, it has an upside. It can be an escape from a cut-and-dried, too-well-ordered, perhaps even stifling reality, into more exciting uncertainties and possibilities. Confusion can also be a cauldron for creativity. Think of such painters as Pablo Picasso, Salvador Dali, and other groundbreaking artists. The apparent confusion in some of their paintings can catapult viewers into dramatically different ways of looking at themselves and the world. You can apply this same principle yourself, using your perplexity as a doorway to stimulate your creativity. Not only can you learn to see through the fog, but if you choose, you can let it take you on unexpected life-enhancing journeys.

*Kindness is a language which the deaf can hear, and the blind can read.*

MARK TWAIN

KINDNESS CAN BE EXPRESSED in thoughts, speech, and action. It is impossible to exaggerate its value.

The woman at the airport baggage checkpoint hesitated when the inspector asked her to step back from the conveyor belt. Her delay in complying was a few seconds too long. Suddenly a burly security guard grabbed her and threw her across the room headfirst onto the hard floor. Another security man jumped on her. Then the two pulled her to her feet and roughly twisted her arms behind her back, and one slammed her face onto a counter before he handcuffed her hands behind her back. She whispered afterward, "I was afraid they were going to kill me."

The incident was captured by a surveillance camera and was shown on national TV. The woman did not have a weapon or make an aggressive move. The security team's response would have been more suitable for a masked terrorist with an AK-47. In this case, a less brutal response would surely have sufficed.

This incident illustrates the opposite of a simple act of kindness. We ourselves have encountered occasional airport security personnel who were downright nasty, and others who went out of their way to be considerate. Every day each one of us speaks and acts in ways that fall at various points along a continuum that goes from maximum kindness to maximum cruelty.

Kindness begins with self-awareness and an inclination to be helpful to others. It is furthered by compassionate thoughts and feelings, expressed in words and actions.

At first glance, the following general principle seems like a no-brainer: be kind to others and helpful when you can. This was the very essence of the social teachings of Jesus, Buddha, Confucius, and Lao-tzu. The prophet Muhammad emphasized it again and again. On one occasion he stated, "Kindness is a mark of faith, and whoever is not kind has no faith." Another time he said, "The best of houses is the house where an orphan gets love and kindness." And yet again: "Shall I tell you who is kept away from Hell and from whom Hell is kept away? From everyone who is gentle and kindly, approachable and of an easy disposition."[1]

Similarly, while highlighting the drawbacks of hypocrisy, Jesus repeatedly defended those whom respected citizens looked down on, such as the destitute. Buddha was so overwhelmed by compassion for unnecessary suffering that he abandoned a life of luxury and set out to discover how to reduce suffering. In our time, the Dalai Lama says of kindness, "If you are able to do so, then help others, and if you are not able to do so, at least do not harm others. This is the main practice."[2] By main practice he meant that it is the most important single principle in meditation and action.

How strange that so many people often do the opposite. Consciously or unconsciously, we may act in ways that are hostile, cruel, heedless, or uncaring. With animals like dogs and jackals, the impulse to dominate is innate, but human minds can perceive harmful consequences, and at some level we know there are alternatives to acting like the ruthless alpha of the pack.

What can we do? We can examine the ways in which we are impervious and unkind, so we can stop dulling our sensitivity. We can also contemplate ways in which we are compassionate and kind, so we can expand that responsiveness.

Kindness and compassion are related but not identical. In Sylvia Boorstein's words, Buddha taught that when the mind is at ease it is "friendly, congenial, well-wishing, [and] likes nearly everybody—even people who, because of who they are or what they do, are very hard to like. . . . Friendliness is not hard. We don't need to learn to be friendly. We need to *remember* to be friendly."[3] Usually our friends care about our suffering and will offer help when possible. Kindness comes easily when we love someone. But it's less usual to offer kindness to those with whom we are not involved. Boorstein refers to extending our care to those we don't know as *loving-kindness*.

Joseph Goldstein writes that the "special quality of lovingkindness is the generosity and openness of heart that simply wishes all beings to be happy. . . . It's not offered with the expectation of getting something back. And because it's not dependent on . . . people being or behaving in a certain way, it is not easily disappointed."[4]

Compassion is empathy with others who are having a hard time. It means coming as close as you can to feeling along with them how their situation is. This is different from pity, which is feeling sad because someone is in trouble or pain, but staying emotionally distant from it, and maybe even looking down on that person. Compassion is not great fun. It is more agreeable to look away, think of pleasant events, and keep those who are suffering out of mind. But, says the Dalai Lama, "Even a small act of compassion grants meaning and purpose to our lives."[5]

The feeling of compassion lives next to love within us. One step in sharing compassion is to let another person know you feel something of his circumstances and his pain. This can lighten his burden a bit because he won't feel so alone.

Compassion leads to kindness in speech and action. Kind speech means refraining from remarks that make others feel sad. Plutarch recognized this when he said, "Do not speak of your happiness to one less fortunate than yourself." It costs nothing to utter a word of appreciation or encouragement even to someone you don't like much. Occasionally an act of kindness that seems insignificant to you may change another person's life.

Even small gestures can help. We're reminded of an old story from the *Reader's Digest* about an extreme low ocean tide and a young boy. He was gently picking up starfish marooned on the beach and throwing them back into the sea. A man came along and said, "Look, there are starfish along the beach as far as you can see. You can't save them all." The boy replied, "Maybe not, but I can save *this* one, and *this* one, and *this* one," as he continued returning them back into the water.

The Dalai Lama says, "If you show other people kindness, love, and respect, they will respond in kind: this way your happiness will increase. If you show other people anger and hatred, they will show you the same, and you will lose your own happiness. . . . So, even from a selfish viewpoint, you get better results by respecting [and] serving others."[6]

# RANDOM ACTS OF KINDNESS

Most likely you've heard of this phrase countless times. The innovation here is that you make a commitment to actually carry out the idea during your daily activities.

## The Essence

For one full day, make a point of saying a few kind or sympathetic words, or performing some small act of kindness, every chance you get. These systematic acts of kindness may even improve your communications. During the day also look for at least one occasion, or even more, where you can go out of your way to do something especially nice or helpful for someone—or for an animal, plant, or even your community. If your kindness is completely unexpected, so much the better, since then you are actually performing random acts of kindness. You might consider whether you want to make this one-day practice a regular part of your life.

## Variations in Technique

You can also be kind to yourself. Begin with your starting sequence of centering, slowing your breath, and relaxing. Once you have entered your inner space, scan your mind for a memory of when you experienced an act of kindness that felt like a wonderful gift. Think about how you felt. Take a few minutes to expand the feeling by imagining that good energy flowing through your entire body. Now imagine that these feelings are transmitting light and love to every cell in your body.

After a few minutes of focusing on positive energy that radiates love throughout your body, in your mind's eye think of a time when someone was unkind to you. Remember how you reacted to this circumstance and how you felt in response to the callousness. Even if you felt awful, is there any way you could have been appropriately kind to this person within the context of the circumstances? Was there anything that you could have done to make yourself feel better? Now as you maintain your image of that incident, bring the mental technique described above, of envisioning rays of light and love throughout your body, into the incident. Now how do you feel?

In the future, if you are in a situation where someone is being callous or insensitive to you or another being, you can take better care of yourself. Instead of being stung by their negativity, control your emotions by envisioning yourself surrounded by luminous rays of love. Just as you practiced above, recall your experience of positive feelings expanding throughout your being. You might even feel good enough to respond to unkindness with compassion.

## Points in the Process

Through your experience of others' unkindness toward you or toward those you love, you can deeply understand why compassion is so important.

Walking the path of kindness and showing simple acts of caring can create karmic ripples. My kindheartedness to you may make you want to act similarly to another, and that person in turn may transmit kindness to yet another. If enough of us do this, it can transform the world. As Paramahansa Yogananda observes, "Kindness is the light that dissolves all walls between souls, families, and nations."

# Moderation

## The Middle Way

. . . . . . . . . . . . . . . . . . . . . . . . . . . . . . .

**ONE TOUCH, ONE TASTE**

> *It is the sign of a great mind to . . . prefer things in measure*
> *to things in excess.*
>
> LUCIUS ANNAEUS SENECA

THOUGHTFUL MODERATION IN YOUR actions and appetites opens new horizons to personal satisfaction.

Ram Dass said, "If you are to get out of prison the first thing you must realize is: You are in prison. If you think you're free you can't escape."[1] In response, you might reasonably wonder: *What on Earth does he mean by "you are in prison"? And what does this have to do with moderation?*

We imprison ourselves when we think we must have or must be this or that to feel happy or be acceptable. For example, we can be imprisoned by pessimistic thoughts that who we are and what we have are not enough. We want more—more money, approval, sex, fame, clothes, a bigger house, a newer car, more drugs or alcohol—the list goes on and on. So we end up on an endless treadmill of dissatisfaction.

We are imprisoned by accepting invisible conventional ideas about how we ought to be, like the desire to be as thin as a runway model or as glamorous as a movie star. Similarly, some young people give in to their parents' expectations that they'll go into a certain field even though they feel no attraction to it. And too often, following the herd, a person becomes imprisoned in a faulty vision of how he or she perceives the world to be. It can be devastating when a belief or vision to which we are attached is found to be at odds with our reality.

Even Siddhartha Gautama, who became the Buddha, was a prisoner of the conventions of his time. As a young adult he rebelled against them, left his father's palace, and went into the world to learn how people could be freed from suffering. He sought out noted holy men to discover the nature of truth and practiced with ascetics who pushed their bodies to extremes of self-denial in pursuit of enlightenment.

But after all his wanderings and studies, Gautama still felt far from comprehending the causes and cures of suffering. He found a pleasant spot by a river near the town of Uruvela and resolved to sit there in meditation until he found an answer to his quest. He sat in trance and practiced the most severe asceticism. His clothes rotted. His skin was stretched across protruding ribs. Leaves matted in his hair. Narrating what is said to be the Buddha's story, author and editor Betty Kelen continues:

> One day his hand slid to his belly, and he found himself grasping his spinal column. Feeling around his back for his spinal column, he touched his belly.
>
> Some townsmen came by, and one of them exclaimed, "The ascetic Gautama has turned black!" He was starving to death.
>
> "This is the uttermost," he thought. "Beyond this one cannot go." What was he doing here, trying to conquer suffering while suffering acutely? But despite doubts he persisted.
>
> One day as he sat in meditation, he fell over in a faint. . . . A goat herder came by with his flock, and seeing the holy man inert on the ground, took the liberty of squeezing a little milk from a goat's udder into his mouth.
>
> Revived by the goat's milk, Gautama remained in meditation. Some dancing girls came by, and they were singing a song about a lute: if the lute was strung too tightly, the noises were high and strained; but if it was strung properly . . . beautiful music could be struck from it.[2]

From their song an insight emerged that became part of Buddha's teachings: the doctrine of the Middle Way. He realized that instead of bringing inner peace, his severe deprivations impaired his health and dulled his mind. Like a lute that is strung neither too loosely nor too tight, he said, out of your experience you can find a middle path for living wisely that fits your own nature. Similarly, Greek philosophers considered moderation one of the four cardinal virtues, along with justice, courage, and wisdom.

What's the practical significance of this in daily life? Moderation is the discipline of choosing what is healthy and helpful and avoiding what's not. It is paying attention to what you need to survive, and feel fully alive, without turning excessive demands into conditions for living the good life. It is also making prudent choices in relation to invitations or demands from other people that would lead you to unhealthy extremes.

Gaining a better sense of what holds real importance for you helps you evaluate which desires are most worth pursuing. You will probably find that some decisions and actions lead to dangerous excess and indulgence, so that moderation may seem like a guardian angel. There may also be times when getting and having more of something would lead you to be possessed by your possessions. Letting go of the craving for more than you need is easier when you don't think you have to have all that stuff (of whatever kind) to receive others' respect. After all, the Qu'ran says, "Riches are not from abundance of worldly goods, but from a contented mind." Obviously, living moderately and renouncing excess desires for possessions, fame, or power is easier when you have found other sources of meaning.

Living with moderation does not mean we have to give up the essence of our present way of life. Jakusho Kwong-roshi wisely says, "Properly understood, renunciation . . . does not mean turning our back on the world. It means turning our back on the conditions that cause suffering—greed, anger, and ignorance."[3]

Moderation includes things small as well as large, like the choice between buying two shirts instead of six, eating one cookie or a dozen, or drinking one beer or a six-pack.

## ONE TOUCH, ONE TASTE

In this practice, less is more. Begin by moving into meditative awareness through any method of your choice.

### The Essence

Take a piece of fruit and cut just one slice. Focus your attention completely on that slice. Smell it. Take a tiny bite. Then chew it very, very slowly, with awareness of each movement of your mouth, savoring the taste each time you chew. When it's gone, take another bite and do likewise. Take as long to eat that slice as you would usually take to eat the whole piece.

Next, touch an object near you with the same quality of attention. Explore the texture of a desktop, the smoothness of your cup, the fabric of a chair, or the bark of a tree. Run your fingers over it. Concentrate intently on it.

Now look inwardly at one of your desires. Can you simplify your way of mentally touching that desire and still find satisfaction?

## Variations in Technique

Both Sufi and Zen traditions have sayings that those who know when they have enough are rich. Regardless of your material wealth or poverty, think of at least five different intangible or nonmaterial ways that you are rich. Also, think about your moderate or immoderate actions in daily life. (Acting with moderation is sometimes called temperance in religious literature; the tarot card by this name means essentially the same thing.) Take a page or two (perhaps even in a journal) and jot down these reflections.

Put this note that you have just written to yourself where you'll find it in the future. In a year and again in five years time reread this record of who you are today, and reflect on it in relation to your life then.

## Points in the Process

Acting with moderation is easier when you are present in the moment, and sensitively aware in your tasting, touching, talking, or any other form of acting or experiencing. A little enjoyment can go a long way.

*Transform reason into ordered intuition; let all of
yourself be light.*

SRI AUROBINDO

INTUITION ACCOMPANIES OBSERVATION AND reason as a way of discovering
our self and our world.

In the West, for hundreds of years (thousands if you go back to the
ancient Greeks), reason has been deified as the royal road to understanding.
Meanwhile, intuition has been neglected. Intriguingly enough, many great
scientists, philosophers, and inventors consider intuition indispensable. Here
are a few of their reflections.

> **Albert Einstein, physicist:** "The intellect has little to do on the road
> to discovery. There comes a leap in consciousness, call it intuition or
> what you will, and the solution comes to you and you don't know how
> or why. . . . I believe in intuition and inspiration; at times I feel certain
> I am right while not knowing the reason."
>
> **Henri Poincaré, physicist:** "It is through science that we prove, but
> through intuition that we discover."
>
> **Immanuel Kant, philosopher:** "Neither concepts without an intuition
> in some way corresponding to them, nor intuition without concepts,
> can lead to knowledge."
>
> **Jonas Salk, inventor of the polio vaccine:** "Intuition will tell the think-
> ing mind where to look next. . . . It is always with excitement that I
> wake up in the morning wondering what my intuition will toss up

to me, like gifts from the sea. I work with it and rely on it. It is my partner."

Western culture has been less than effective in training people to use intuitive abilities. As a result, we can overlook or misread many messages that would be obvious to someone with well-developed intuitive sensitivity. In the information age, there is too much data for people to process without relying on intuitive as well as rational faculties. Our intuition or sixth sense brings into play our personal "psychic hotline" to gather information and address questions that elude the conscious mind's attempts to answer them by reason alone. Our instinctive insights are then translated by our conscious minds.

Just as the moon reflects the light of the sun, subconscious impulses are projected on our rational mental screen. For people who perceive themselves as intuitive, this is a natural process, such as when they feel a gut response, or just seem to know something that defies logical explanation. Intuitive people are often sensitive to reading nonverbal energy that emanates from another person, object, or situation. Just as a radio station or satellite transmitter sends inaudible signals that become songs on your radio, the mind sends muted waves of intangible vibrations into physical reality. Highly intuitive people perceive these waves more readily than those who believe they are primarily logical by nature. Some people are afraid to trust in their intuition because it might be wrong, or they think others might view them as nuts. Others fear they'll see something they don't want to, or something that isn't real.

Even if you don't recognize yourself as an intuitive, your ability to use information received subconsciously from beyond the known world of our five senses can be developed. It's not that you'll know the future or the winning lottery numbers. But when you develop subtle awareness skills, you become more alert to the ebb and flow of positive and negative energies within others as well as yourself. When you integrate the sixth sense of intuitive perceptions into your everyday existence, you will improve your ability to take care of yourself and to be more helpful to others, too. Many who use their intuition say, "Listening to my intuition helps me make the right decisions and points me in the direction where I need to go."

How do you validate your intuitive sensing? Direct experience is the best teacher. Much as a child learns to walk by standing up and falling down, the path to intuitive success is one of perseverance. It takes patience—just as you have to develop strong leg muscles to become a competitive runner. Sometimes our sensing is right, sometimes wrong, and sometimes partly right and partly wrong. Through experience you will discover the clues and cues that tell you whether there's a good chance that you're on the right track.

It's useful to check your intuitive perceptions against logic and common sense. One important way to validate them is to ask. Carl Rogers was an expert at intuiting what was occurring beneath and beyond what a person actually said. Usually he was right—but not always. So he would tell the person what he thought he was hearing at a deeper level, and then ask if he had heard accurately. Instead of committing himself to potentially incorrect conclusions, he asked discerning questions and remained open-minded.

Metaphorically, we often see and hear only shades of gray as we move through a world of vivid colors that carry important messages. At first glance, the emotional content that lurks opaquely under the surface of what we and others say often appears to be less important than the explicit meaning of the words we hear. Often, however, it's the main thing that's going on. When hidden currents of emotion and meaning are outside our awareness, we can unconsciously base our views of what's going on in others and in life situations on a narrow and limited pipeline of information. As a result, we misunderstand many situations.

In everyday lingo, "picking up on people's vibes" is an important guide to what's happening with them. When posture, gestures, facial expressions, and the qualities of voice seem to carry information that contradicts or extends what words convey, pay attention. Your intuition may help you discern their meaning. Learning to habitually carry out a quick intuitive scan of both yourself and others when you meet and interact, with special attention to what's going on with both of you emotionally, can guide your questions and understanding.

If you hope to use your intuition effectively, you need to have some measure of hope and trust that you can really do so. If you are a skeptic about this possibility, then forget it—at least for now. Beliefs about the possibility of using your intuition open or close the door to using it effectively. To do so, you have to think it's possible.

When you start to experiment with using your intuition, you may or may not see immediate results. As Paramahansa Yogananda remarked, "By learning to go deep within, you will connect your consciousness with the superconsciousness of the soul, so that with infinite will-power, patience, and intuition you can grow those idea-seeds of success."[1]

# THE INTUITIVE SPHERE

The guided visualization that follows can help you learn to listen to your silent inner guiding voice and strengthen your ability to call on your intuitive capacities when you need them.

## The Essence

Lie down comfortably and go through the starting sequence, omitting the first part about finding your balance through centering. As you relax, focus on sensing your breath. Then concentrate on the energy flowing through the bottoms of your feet. Visualize a white light radiating out through your toes, and picture it turning into a brilliant ray of light that encircles your body seven times until it becomes a soft globe that surrounds you entirely from head to toe. The swirling illumination of the warm, healing light generates a protective wall of energy that keeps you safe.

Once you feel secure in your bubble of light, let it expand so that you can mentally descend a spiral staircase within it. At the bottom is a door. You open it and enter a walkway that leads to a banquet room in which a prophet is sitting at the end of a large table ready to answer any question you ask about some dilemma or conflict. Ask as many questions as you wish, to generate an understanding of possible solutions.

As you approach, let your inner vision be free of conscious rational dictation. Envision your question being answered through some aspect of your intuitive sixth sense. After you receive your answer, let the globe of light and everything in it fade away and return to your normal thinking process.

Consider the answer you were given. What do you think and how do you feel about it? What significance, if any, do you find in it? Write down any messages you received. Note any impressions that seemed out of the ordinary, such as extrasensory perceptions, the feeling of knowing or reading someone else's emotional or mental state, or hearing or seeing anything that suggests knowledge of the unknown. Your subconscious may be giving you direct communication.

## Variations in Technique

For problem solving that can be answered with a yes/no question you can use the following visualization. Rationally consider a problem you are questioning. Once you are lying down or reclining, go into a meditative state and begin your Intuitive Sphere visualization of protective light encircling you.

Within it, use your mind's eye to create and look at an inner blackboard. On the right side of the blackboard is the word *yes*. On the left side is the word *no*. Does your gaze jump to the word *yes* or the word *no* when you ask yourself the yes/no question? Trust your intuition to go to the right answer.

These visualizations can help you develop confidence as you learn to listen to your intuition.

## Feeling Comfortable

In this or any other guided visualization, your mind is completely under your own control. Specifically, this technique is used to familiarize you with using the right, nonlinear, nonverbal side of the brain. For your personal well-being, never force yourself to try to use your sixth sense if it doesn't feel right. Even when using your intuition, you always also have your logical mind to help support your process.

## Points in the Process

Doing no more than maintaining a regular daily meditation practice will probably heighten your intuitive sensitivity to some degree. Whether you're doing a concentrative, mindfulness, or contemplative meditation, you are creating mental space for messages from deep within to take form and emerge. But when your mind is filled with trivial chatter, whether you're chattering to yourself or with others, it's harder for messages from your intuitive faculty to come through. While discussing the concentrative meditation approach called *tratak,* which focuses the eyes and all mental energy on one point, such as a candle flame, Harish Johari states, "Hindu scriptures say that one who practices tratak regularly develops the faculties of intuition and imagination."[2]

# Forgiveness

## Beyond Revenge and Hatred

### WHERE FROM, WHERE TO?

*To err is human; to forgive, infrequent.*

FRANKLIN P. ADAMS

FORGIVING OTHERS IS SIMULTANEOUSLY an act of kindness toward yourself, as it can sometimes also heal your painful memories.

Zen master Ryōkan was outdoors near the house of a friend when he was attacked by a crazed man in a drunken rage. Ryōkan calmly bore the blows until several villagers subdued the drunk. That night a big storm came in, and suddenly Ryōkan, who was staying with the friend, went outdoors. His friend followed and saw Ryōkan go over to the sleeping man who had attacked him and cover him with a straw raincoat. In other incidents as well, Ryōkan showed a remarkable willingness to forgive.[1]

Unfortunately, for many people revenge, complaints, bitterness, and holding on to grudges tends to be easier than forgiving. But such attitudes poison your spirit and trouble your mind. A grudge is an emotional burden. By contrast, forgiveness releases negative energy that was spawned by resentments and lightens your feelings. Forgiveness also helps cultivate a generous mind. "It has been said that the continuation of the species is due to man's being forgiving," says India's great epic, the Mahābhārata. "Forgiveness is the might of the mighty; forgiveness is sacrifice; forgiveness is quiet of mind."[2]

Although forgiving doesn't erase the pain of the past, it can change the way you think and feel now. It lets you write a new and better ending to your story or begin another chapter and make a fresh start. It embodies a merciful response to unjust treatment. Forgiving opens your heart to compassion and involves transcendent morality.

But forgiveness may not always seem appropriate. It may very well be inappropriate when you have reason to suspect that someone will try to harm you. Nor is it appropriate when you are not ready to forgive. People differ in the speed with which they process their thoughts and emotions. It's better to honor your emotional rhythms than to mislead yourself about the reality in your heart. Forgiveness is also inappropriate when you just don't want to forgive, since true forgiveness is a choice freely made. If you feel pressured to utter the words "I forgive you," they won't be genuine—and at some point both you and the other person will probably realize it, making you look hypocritical as well as unforgiving.

There may be something or someone you think you will never forgive. If, for example, you see your best friend killed by bombs or bullets, forgiveness may be beyond you. Hating the perpetrators may be all you have left to stay psychologically alive. But you can wish for revenge and at the same time stop yourself from acting on that wish. Breaking a cycle of revenge and counter-revenge can help put an end to escalating pain and suffering.

If you feel ready to forgive someone, a key element is consciously acknowledging your anger or resentment and its underlying cause, and then loosening your grip on those feelings. Pain usually lies beneath the anger, and some real injury or injustice often lies beneath the pain.

Psychotherapists Robert Enright and Richard Fitzgibbons have identified several phases in the forgiveness process. These are:

- **The uncovering phase:** you think about whether the injustice or injury is causing you unnecessary suffering. If so, the next question is how much of that are you personally creating and maintaining?
- **The decision phase:** you become willing to make a personal commitment to forgive.
- **The work phase:** you try to understand what's going on inside the other person—the "offender." This understanding usually starts in your mind and then may percolate into your heart as empathy and compassion.
- **The deepening phase:** you consider such questions as, *Have I needed others' forgiveness in the past? What was it like for me when I was forgiven? Can I find any value in the pain I endured? Am I motivated to interact in new ways with the offender and with others?* These reflections take you back through one or more of the three earlier phases, but with more depth and insight.[3]

It is also useful to look at what forgiveness is not. Here, too, we appreciate Enright and Fitzgibbons's thinking:

Forgiveness is not condoning or excusing someone's action because of unavoidable circumstances—like when your boss does you wrong but it might cost you your job to make an issue of it. In such a case, remaining silent to avoid trouble is not the same as forgiving. Nor is forgiveness making concessions to another person to get him to stop acting badly.

Forgiveness is also different from reconciliation. You can forgive by yourself. Reconciliation involves you and at least one other person, and it requires a willingness by one or both of you to change offensive ways. Reconciliation works only if those involved are committed to building a sense of trust in the relationship.

And forgiveness is not the same as forgetting. In forgiveness you remember what the other has done, but find a different way to think and feel about it. And forgiveness is not passively waiting for the passage of time to heal the wound. Time may or may not heal. Forgiveness, by contrast, is an active process.

Pardoning others and making things right is doubly difficult when an injurious action is part of an old pattern. Amma tells of a man who felt deeply hurt and angry at his son. One day the son came home completely stoned. When the father questioned him, the son screamed at him and began breaking plates and smashing things. The father threw his son out of the house and didn't speak to him for a year. The father told Amma, "Whenever my heart tells me to forgive him . . . my mind says . . . 'He committed the mistake, so let him come to regret it and seek forgiveness.'"

Amma replied, "Trust that beyond the known cause there was also an unknown cause for the chain of events that took place that day." Upon further questioning it turned out that the man had experienced a terrible relationship with his own father, and he himself had been rude and rebellious. He had suffered deeply and did not forgive his father until days before his death. When he realized that he was recreating the same dynamic with his son, he burst into tears and realized that he was the one who had to reach out in forgiveness.[4]

Jesus took forgiveness to another level when he said, "Love your enemies; do good to those who hate you; pray for those who treat you spitefully."[5] At first glance, his statement may seem puzzling unless you are a saint, since returning love for a verbal or literal slap in the face isn't easy. But Geshe Langritangpa's Tibetan text for training the mind offers a clue to understanding this idea:

*When I see ill-natured people,*
*Overwhelmed by wrongdoing and pain,*
*May I cherish them as something rare,*
*As though I had found a treasure-trove.*[6]

A later Tibetan master, Geshe Sonam Rinchen, explains: "People who are difficult to deal with offer us a precious chance to train ourselves to be loving, compassionate and altruistic, generous, ethical and patient. That is why they are like a precious treasure."[7] As we learn to forgive such people, we become more awake to the spirit of love.

# WHERE FROM? WHERE TO?

The following contemplative meditation asks you to connect invisible dots that link your past and future.

## The Essence

Begin with your starting sequence. Once your mind is calm, focus on events from your past that are related to your present forgiveness issues. Next, focus on the following questions: What is your most hurtful memory? What events in that situation or similar ones resemble any forgiveness issue that concerns you now? Is the hurtful event part of a pattern you can see in a past or present relationship(s)? If so, what might you be doing to invite or perpetuate this pattern?

Next, let your mind contemplate the future. How do you imagine you will feel about this issue in a week, a month, or a year? What do you guess your relationship will be like with those toward whom you feel upset?

Now imagine yourself letting go of your grudges. How do you suppose you will feel if you are successful in forgiving? In contrast, how do you think your relationship with whomever is involved might be if you hang on to your grudge? Which would you prefer?

As your mind moves among present, past, and future, be attentive to your breathing, how you hold your body, and any body tension. Remind yourself to breathe through tension and release any tightness you may feel.

## Variations in Technique

While you are inwardly calm, perhaps even just after the above practice, you might find it useful to brainstorm conflict resolutions. Even if you have no intention of forgiving, be open to messages and possible solutions that offer a way to reduce or release anger or hurt feelings and that reduce the chance of having your pain restimulated.

## Feeling Comfortable

Don't rescind your forgiveness. As actress Marlene Dietrich said, "Once a woman has forgiven her man, she must not reheat his sins for breakfast."

## Points in the Process

Forgiveness doesn't always have to be explicit, or require the words "I forgive you." It can be conveyed implicitly, as in Ryōkan's act of covering his assailant with a raincoat in a storm. Some people find it helpful to envision a fountain of love sprouting from a spring deep within them.

. . . . . . . . . .

# Tolerance

## Intolerance and Self-righteousness

. . . . . . . . . . . . . . . . . . . . . . . . . . . .

**VIVE LA DIFFÉRENCE!**

*What is tolerance? . . . Think for yourselves and let others enjoy the privilege to do so too.*

VOLTAIRE

**TOLERANCE IS AN INDISPENSABLE** key to peace of mind.

Tolerance serves as a cure for its opposite, intolerance. It leads toward harmony with others, whereas intolerance includes negative attitudes and actions that create opposition. The value of tolerance can be best understood once you experience the sharp sting of prejudice or discrimination. Prejudice, an attitude composed of harmful thoughts and feelings in regard to you, some group, or a member of it, often involves discrimination, which is an overt behavior that includes exclusion, unfairness, or injustice of some kind. Prejudice and discrimination can be based on race, ethnicity, gender, nationality, social class, or anything else that somebody somewhere chooses to dislike. Usually, intolerance toward the less powerful by the more powerful includes discrimination, in order to perpetuate the latter's power.

Even religious convictions can be an arena for prejudice. Ironically, although religion is meant to uplift our spirits, religious intolerance is one of the most common kinds. Sri Ramakrishna observes that "common man in ignorance says, 'My religion is the only one, my religion is the best.'" He advises: "As you rest firmly on your own faith and opinion, allow others also the equal liberty to stand by their own faiths and opinions. . . . So long as a man quarrels and disputes about doctrines and dogmas, he has not tasted the nectar of true faith; when he has tasted it, he becomes quiet and full of peace."[1]

In our personal world beyond religion, when we are intolerant toward an individual we usually respond to surface qualities like clothes or hairstyle, with little comprehension of who the other person is inside. When we are intolerant toward a group, such as a political movement or a party, we are not relating to others as real people, but to our mental image of the group and how we think its members differ from what we prefer or believe to be right.

To whatever degree that we are prejudiced, we see only through the lenses of our own biases. Occasionally we get a little peek around the outside of our partialities and preconceptions.

*We?* you might be thinking. *I'm not prejudiced!*

Actually, everyone is at least a little prejudiced in some way. Our unwillingness to perceive our own prejudices is part of the problem. If you form an intention to notice an intolerant attitude or action in yourself when it arises, most likely you will uncover one.

What are the sources of intolerance? Here are several:

**Ignorance.** It's easy to be intolerant toward those about whom we know little or nothing. In turn we tend not to be interested in learning anything about those toward whom we are prejudiced.

**Insecurity.** One response to feeling insecure is to grab on to an ideology (political, religious, economic, or other) and insist that it's the only true reality. Since anyone who believes differently is a potential threat to that fragile feeling of security, we tend to be intolerant toward his views.

**Displacement.** When someone has done something bad to you and you are afraid to express your anger or resentment to her, you're likely to displace (mis-place) your angry feelings onto someone else, who might be an innocent bystander.

**Mistaken generalization.** Someone did something bad to you, and so you assume that all others who resemble that person in some identifiable way will act likewise.

**Past conditioning.** Others have told you that certain people or kinds of people are bad, and you accept their statements uncritically.

Fortunately, as we become better able to perceive our own intolerance, we also become better able to reduce it and to stop ourselves from acting in ways that translate prejudice into discrimination. As John F. Kennedy said so well, "Tolerance implies no lack of commitment to one's own beliefs. Rather it condemns the oppression or persecution of others."

Let's imagine that you'd like to discover and do away with any intolerance that may be lurking in the shadows of your mind. How can you begin? Mahatma Gandhi's reflections offer an excellent starting point: "I claim to have no infallible guidance or inspiration. . . . The claim to infallibility would always be a most dangerous claim to make . . . whenever I see an erring man, I say to myself I have also erred. . . . Differences of opinion should never mean hostility. . . . I have always attempted to regard those who differ from me with the same affection as I have for my nearest and dearest."[2]

Your own intolerance is likely to be less intense and more visible to you when it lacks the engine of self-righteousness to power it.

Swami Vivekananda adds these comments on tolerating qualities or beliefs that you might find bothersome: "Your way is very good for you, but not for me. My way is good for me, but not for you. . . . Do not destroy. . . . Help, if you can; if you cannot, fold your hands, stand by, and see things go on. . . . Take man where he stands, and from thence give him a lift."[3]

Also critical to our inner process is having the wisdom to be accepting and tolerant of our own selves. When we are tolerant toward ourselves, we are more likely to be tolerant toward others. A tolerant person has come to know his or her blind spots and can see around them. At best, we can feel compassion and kindness toward others, and not feel they should be different than they are. But since few of us have reached that point, at least we can notice the times and ways in which we fall back into small-minded attitudes. And we can remind ourselves to be outwardly respectful and courteous with those toward whom we feel inwardly intolerant.

Why should we bother to confront the personal challenge of dealing with our own intolerance? For the excellent reason that intolerance makes it impossible to reconcile the daunting differences that we inevitably meet in life. With peace of mind and mutual respect as the goals, we offer the following practice.

## VIVE LA DIFFÉRENCE!

The essence of big-minded tolerance is not just to endure differences, but to appreciate them. The purpose of this adventure in awareness is to emphasize and practice an attitude of tolerance. It expresses the principles of the Buddha, who said: "The wise welcomes the kindly word, rejects the cruel . . . knows no resentment, does not carp at faults . . . nor crush his rival down."[4]

### The Essence

At your next opportunity, sit down with someone who holds very different views from yours. Or strike up a conversation with someone you don't know who appears to be quite different from you. Your objective is to explore, in the most friendly and cordial manner that you can, some aspects of that person's beliefs, attitudes, or experience that are quite unlike your own.

Listen well, avoid judgmental comments, and say no more than you must to keep the conversation going. If possible, maintain the conversation for at least fifteen minutes. Each time you notice any twinge of thought or feeling that the person "shouldn't be that way," or that there's something bad or wrong in what she is saying, bracket it, that is, mentally set it aside as a distracting thought, and then return your attention to doing your best to hear the other person's subjective reality as it is for her.

In your next contemplative meditation, reflect on what it must be like to be that other person. Try to understand her beliefs, attitudes, and habits as fully as possible without necessarily accepting or sharing them. As you reflect on your reactions, witness how tolerance versus intolerance affects your mind, your emotions, and your body.

## Variations in Technique

Tolerance does not require putting up with another's injurious behavior. If someone makes a prejudiced remark, a useful reply is, "I see it differently." When someone acts in a harmful way, it's appropriate to confront him. The key to mutually respectful interaction is to minimize the degree to which you let your emotions get negatively hooked, and to confront the specific behavior without expressing hostility toward the person.

## Feeling Comfortable

To become more tolerant, it is helpful to adopt an open-minded attitude that accepts differing opinions. Anasuya Devi, an Indian holy woman, recommends focusing not on differences but on recognizing the unity in opposites.[5] In our individual essences, we are all much more alike than different.

## Points in the Process

Shunryu Suzuki-roshi elaborates his perspective on the notion of difference: "Differentiation is equality. . . . Because men and women are different, men are valuable as men and women are valuable as women. To be different is to have value. . . . The usual understanding is that differentiation is the opposite of equality, but our understanding is that they are the same thing."[6]

**CELL 57**

. . . . . . . . . .

# Purpose

## Goals and Meaning

. . . . . . . . . . . . . . . . . . . . . . . . . . . . . . . . . . . .

## THE SACRED WELL

*Possession of a vision is not the same as living it, nor can we
encourage others with it if we do not, ourselves,
understand and follow its truths.*

HIGH EAGLE

**TO LACK A SENSE** of purpose leads to internal confusion. To experience enduring satisfaction, we need to find some meaning in our life.

Some people are content choosing widely accepted goals, like young people who become doctors, lawyers, or executives. Others rebel against traditional definitions of purpose and sculpt their own nonconforming dreams. Pablo Picasso remarked, "My mother said to me, 'If you become a soldier, you'll be a general; if you become a monk, you'll end up as the Pope.' Instead, I became a painter and wound up as Picasso."

For others, such certainty comes less easily. We may find ourselves wondering, *What am I doing with my life?* or *What is the meaning of my life?* as we wander, searching for our higher purpose. We might feel satisfied for the moment, and might even be moving forward, but nonetheless feel a vaguely disturbing emptiness inside.

For some people, their purpose involves simply enjoying life. For others, it concerns finding fame and fortune. Some purposes exist for just a short time, like going to a party to meet someone new, or trying to waste the bad guys in a video game, or trying to synchronize your breathing with your yoga movements. Other purposes can guide us for decades and bring an ongoing sense of meaning to our lives. While some purposes contribute to our peace of mind, others are like junk food—sweet to the taste, but bad in the long term, such as a career that makes you rich but poisons your soul.

Our purpose may be a dream that beckons us onward. It's not unusual to hear an Olympic champion claim that winning a medal has been a goal since childhood.

Still other purposes exist in this very moment, with few links to either past or future—like enjoying a ray of sunlight sparkling through the morning dewdrops on a leaf.

In questions about our own purpose, we are considering what is important enough to put at the center of our lives. "You might at first enjoy a certain freedom by allowing life to take you where it will," write psychologists Lorna Catford and Michael Ray, but then they go on to point out that eventually you might want something more.[1]

"Each and every one [should] have a specific focus, a direction, an aim," says Swami Niranjanananda Saraswati. "One has to strive to attain that aim. . . . The effort should not be half-hearted."[2] Individual fulfillment, he suggests, can be transformed into enduring happiness when the personal qualities one develops are used to further the well-being of others.

Psychiatrist Viktor Frankl faced some complicated questions about purpose when he stepped out of a cattle car at the Auschwitz railway station at the start of an astounding odyssey that led through several Nazi concentration camps. Frankl's parents, his wife, and all his relatives except a sister were exterminated in the death chambers. Frankl survived because he was a doctor with medical skills, because he was befriended by others, and because of some remarkable luck. He saw many men die and saw some survive. In the face of frequent beatings, near starvation, and inhumane treatment of diverse kinds, many lost their will to carry on. Even those who lived sank into a kind of apathy. He wrote, "Reality dimmed, and all efforts and all emotions were centered on one task: preserving one's own life and that of the other fellow."[3]

Frankl observed that those who survived had one quality in common: they all found some purpose for continuing on. Some were committed to staying alive for the family they hoped would still be home when they returned. For others, their purpose was to save their friends. Others wanted to do what they could to ease the suffering of their fellow prisoners. Those who lacked such a guiding star were lost.

Just as some prisoners found sources for meaning in their lives, so did some of their German captors. Unknown to anyone, the commander of the last camp to which Frankl was sent (in which there were no executions), secretly used his own money to buy medicines for the prison clinic. No one ever heard him utter an unkind word, and after the camp was freed, three former prisoners hid him in the woods until the local commander of Allied forces agreed not to harm him.

The source of meaning that offered the greatest sustenance in the camps was love. "I saw . . . that love is the ultimate and the highest goal to which man can aspire," writes Frankl. "A man who has nothing left in this world still may know bliss, be it only for a brief moment, in the contemplation of his beloved."[4]

In your own life, as you seek to find a calling that feels emotionally or spiritually nourishing, you may be tested by circumstances. At that point it's important to find your reserves of inner strength. Kocho Uchiyama-roshi writes that when he faced difficult and demanding circumstances, it "meant I had to meet the reality of my life head-on, whatever it was, without trying to escape. . . . It was essential for me not to look for a way out."[5] It is also useful to find friends or other allies who can help you stay true to your path, or to your search for greater meaning.

## THE SACRED WELL

The following practice can help you contemplate the purposes in your own life. First read through "The Essence," below, in its entirety before you go into this self-guided contemplative meditation.

### The Essence

In Glastonbury, England, the historic site of Avalon, a spiritual sanctuary since King Arthur's time, a lone hill overlooks the town. On it, an ancient tower called the Tor stands as if guarding the small city.

In your mind's eye, imagine that you have made the gentle climb to reach the stone-walled Tor. Sense the potent energy surrounding you as you visit this power spot. Look far into the distance. As you do, see your life spread out before you. Scrutinize it carefully. Notice what feels most important, what gives your life meaning now.

Next, make your way back down the hill to a shady grotto where a spring bubbles into a well. Imagine that you sit down next to it. As you watch the water flow downhill from the well through several pools, recall the view from the hilltop. In the quiet of your mind, see revealed your most enduring purpose with the greatest value to you or to others. You might also realize that some of the ways you have been using your energy have little value, and perhaps some have none at all.

## Feeling Comfortable

During your contemplation, you don't have to do anything special to receive your messages. Insights may reveal themselves through your thoughts, your emotions, your body, or all three. Some may be obvious, while some may require deciphering. As each idea expresses itself, it will tell you what is potentially fulfilling and what's not. You might also receive messages about where to put more of your effort—or less of it. Perhaps you will even receive clues to a new turn in your life that's needed now. And don't forget to give yourself permission to reach for your dreams.

## Points in the Process

Sometimes you may have to do things that don't appear to have much connection with your sense of purpose. What then? You can remind yourself to be as present as you can in what you do or must do. A deep experience of an ordinary moment, whether of acting or observing, can be profoundly moving, as implied here by Zen master Joshu:

"Please teach me," asked a monk.
"Have you had your breakfast?" Master Joshu replied.
"Yes."
"Then wash your bowl."
At these words the monk was enlightened.[6]

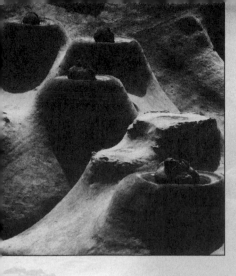

# Creativity

## Inspiration, Exploration, and Evaluation

· · · · · · · · · · · · · · · · · · · · · · · · · · · · · ·

**FOCUSED FANTASY**

*Without the madness of the muses . . . what [one]
creates by means of reason will pale before
the art of inspired beings.*

PLATO

**IT IS USUALLY POSSIBLE** to listen more carefully to our inner creative voices and to use methods that inspire innovative thinking.

When John Daido Loori-roshi, abbot of Zen Mountain Monastery, signed up for his first Zen nature photography course, he had no idea what he'd gotten into. He was sent into the woods with the instruction to photograph his own essence. His teacher's words echoed in his mind: "Venture into the landscape without expectations. Let your subject find you. When you approach it, you will feel resonance, a sense of recognition. . . . Sit with your subject and . . . let your intuition indicate the right moment to release the shutter."[1]

Daido was thoroughly confused: "I had no idea what this resonance was supposed to feel like." At last, he moved away from his normal mode of taking photos: "I realized that there were other ways to photograph . . . that were not so rational or linear."[2]

Daido, like many of us, was not accustomed to shifting from his logical left-brain to using the imaginative, nonlinear right side of his brain. The value of drawing from both sides of our mind was noted even by Einstein when he said: "The intuitive mind is a sacred gift and the rational mind is a faithful servant. . . . We have created a society that honors the servant and has forgotten the gift." Creativity expert Edward de Bono refers to leaps involved in creativity as "lateral" thinking.

Because many of us don't realize that we possess this gift of creative vision, going from linear to lateral thinking can be a big jump. We can also limit our creative potential through the mistaken belief that the word *creativity* means you have the ability to be an artist or musician. But when we break free from this mistaken notion, we can be creative in almost any aspect of our lives. Cooking a meal, fixing a broken item with limited available materials, designing a mortgage that helps someone buy a house, or lifting the spirits of someone who's down in the dumps—all these require creativity. Scholar, psychologist, and teacher Frank Barron, who spent a lifetime studying creativity at the University of California, speaks of being "ready to . . . acknowledge that life, particularly [one's] own unique life, is rich with new possibilities."[3] Psychologist Rollo May defines creativity quite simply as "the process of bringing something new into being."[4]

Realistically there are times when being creative might be difficult because bringing something new into being requires specific technical skills to mold one's vision into tangible form. When that is so, it's sensible to develop the skills you need. Another way to enhance creativity is to modify old ways of encountering the world so that possibilities for using your resourcefulness open up before you. In this sense, most of us possess the capacity to become more creative and original. Actress Bette Davis emphasized that truth with her remark, "Without wonder and insight, acting is just a trade. With it, it becomes creation."

It's easy to see that creativity is enhanced by an ability to be fully in the moment, by flexibility in thinking and by good access to one's imagination. Carl Rogers draws these qualities together in the phrase "openness to experience." This refers to a willingness to step into exploring the puzzling, unknown, and mysterious dimensions of new possibilities.

Luckily, we don't have to be Picasso or Dali to explore creative possibilities and find stimulating ideas. Psychologist Clark Moustakas studied creativity in people's relationships. He found that this involves discovering and creating new feelings and experiences and enlarging both personal and shared realities.[5]

Acknowledging the many sides of creativity opens the door to finding your own forms of creative expression. Your creativity can involve how you approach life itself, how you communicate with those who walk through your life, and how you resolve problems. Living with creative passion can inspire you to find ways of being that open your mind and heart instead of ways that numb your sensitivities and keep you stuck in ruts.

# FOCUSED FANTASY

Many tasks that require creativity have two phases that can be called exploration and evaluation. In the first phase you play with possibilities. In the second, you critique, develop, and improve.

For example, some people suffer from writer's block. That occurs when the creative impulse to "let it all out" and the critical impulse to "make sure it's just right" get jumbled together like a mental omelet. Your creative side starts writing, and then your critical voice jumps in and says, "That's not good."

A solution that often works is to guarantee each of those opposite impulses its own uninterrupted time. Let your initial statement, however ragged, come out freely. Only after that do you invite your critic to revise and rewrite.

In the following activity, we offer a structured approach to enhance your creativity. Because the natural flow of your creative process is what's most important, this process is not engraved in stone—feel free to modify it to fit your needs.

## The Essence

### Step One: Exploration

Consider your problem or creative ideas from different points of view. A process of exploration often includes the following:

*Define the task.* Asking the most thought-provoking questions is a central feature of a good creative process. In regard to what you want to create, what gives you inspiration? Which idea makes your heart smile? What do you want to accomplish? Leave your mental door open to bold solutions.

*Gather data.* First, quickly write out a list of every way you can think of to get useful and relevant information. Tomorrow look at it again. See if other options occur to you. Gather information on resources that look most promising for helping you obtain success. Approach this task from unusual angles.

*Brainstorm the options.* Talking into a voice recorder or writing without stopping to think may take you in creative directions you'd never have anticipated. Or try clustering, in which you write a key word in the center of a page, then circle it, then write related words or phrases around it. Circle each of the related words and draw a line from the first phrase to each. Continue associating in whatever directions the words and page take you, until you've made so many connections that you're full of ideas.

*Elaborate.* Review what you wrote or said. With each possibility that feels like it may hold promise, however wild and crazy it may sound, think of additions, twists, or changes that might make your idea work, or work more effectively.

*Incubate.* Gestalt psychologist Wolfgang Kohler declared that his best ideas came unexpectedly in the "3 B's"—in bed, in the bath, and on the bus. Getting a little distance from your task may be useful.

Most important in brainstorming and elaboration is a taboo on judging and criticizing. Carl Rogers points out that "creative thoughts and actions are just like infants—unprepossessing, weak, easily knocked down." A new idea, he says, usually seems inadequate compared to an established one and is easily trampled by our old mental habits.[6]

## Step Two: Evaluating the Possibilities

Considerations for success include the following:

*Choose intriguing prospects.* Out of all that you have considered, select the ideas that call out to you most strongly, orthodox or unorthodox. Group items that are related together, and consider the value of similar ideas at the same time.

*Critique and respond.* Think carefully about what might possibly work and what might not. But be slow to discard possibilities. Creativity expert George Prince points out that many ideas that are not complete solutions may be good beginnings. We too easily get sucked into "That won't work because . . ." responses and discard possibilities that have potential.[7] Also, if your critiquing is too negative, your creative process may slow to a standstill.

*Face your frustrations.* You'll probably meet unexpected challenges, point out psychologists Lorna Catford and Michael Ray. Welcome them as allies. Often they will push you to a deeper, more detailed understanding than you previously had. It's important to strategize down-to-earth methods for handling those frustrations.[8]

**Try out and improve.** Try your new procedure, or build the new model, and see how it works. Change whatever needs to be changed as many times as needed as you let your creativity flow freely.

**Test your new approach.** Before you put your plans into widespread use, try them out on a small scale, perhaps with friends. Once you feel confident, you can move to a larger arena. In government and business alike, trying and debugging a new approach in one locality before putting it into effect systemwide can avert major mistakes.

## Variations in Technique

Begin with your starting sequence. Once you are centered and comfortable, scan your consciousness for any creative yearning that has not yet been fulfilled. Perhaps you want to write a story or be a dancer. Or find a way to share greater passion with your partner. If you are telling yourself that you're not creative, you need to detach from that thought. In this moment, give yourself permission to believe in your creative vision.

Once you have mentally uncovered a meaningful creative desire, watch your thoughts about it. Are you encouraging yourself or limiting yourself in regard to moving forward with it? Examine your vision from different points of view.

Next, mentally invoke the Divine Spirit, or a god or goddess of creativity, to help you in your quest. You might, for instance, envision Saraswati, beautiful Hindu patroness of poetry, writing, music, and the arts. Or invoke one of the seven Muses from Greek mythology, who were thought to be the source for inspiration and creative genius. Once you have a celestial connection in mind, ask your most important question. Perhaps you might ask what will enable you to fulfill your desire, or how to best use your creativity. Be alert for an answer from any channel through which it may come. After you finish your contemplation, get pen and paper or an electronic equivalent to record any ideas, insights, and reflections that came to you.

## Points in the Process

Some people are afraid to be creative because they fear other people's criticisms. Put your passion into expressing your creativity, and don't worry about what others say. Much of the value of creativity is in the aliveness it brings you. Besides, external authorities aren't always in agreement. An item one person sells at the flea market for ten dollars may be something a collector puts in his shop and sells for $5,000.

# Gratitude

## Resentment versus Appreciation

·····················

### THE DIRECT PATH AND THE
### MERRY-GO-ROUND

*Our inner soul is like a garden. Gratitude is the healthy soil
from which the tree of paradise will grow, and the birds of
heaven will come to roost.*

ROSE CRESCENT SUFIS

MEETING THE WORLD WITH gratitude usually feels better than meeting it
with resentment. Some people live with this understanding, while others
take the steep path toward finding it.

Late one afternoon, as Zen master Bankei was walking, a wolf trotted
into the road, looked his way, and opened its jaws. Bankei peered into its
mouth, saw a large bone stuck in its throat, and reached in and removed it.
Overjoyed, the wolf wagged its tail and ran off. From then on, whenever
Bankei came down that road, the wolf appeared and walked with him to his
destination. As this true story shows, gratitude can be expressed in the most
unexpected ways.[1]

Gratitude for life's events usually feels better than resentment. Both attitudes tend to perpetuate themselves. When you feel grateful, your good feelings tend to evoke friendly words and acts from others in response. When
you feel resentful and express it, sometimes others close up, leaving you alone
in your alienation.

That doesn't mean that you shouldn't express your pain, or that you have
to be grateful for everything. You don't have to thank people who act in
small-minded or small-hearted ways that cause you pain or trouble. In such

cases, your gratitude can take the form of appreciating your ability to perceive unjust or hurtful acts. Perhaps you can find a way to transcend what's negative, or feel glad that you're not the one who's causing misery.

There are two different ways to move from a bitter or indifferent attitude toward a more grateful one. One often recommended by spiritual teachers is a direct route, in which you count your blessings. Another, often recommended by psychologists, is an indirect route, in which you work through your resentments to the point where you're willing to let go of them.

Stoic philosopher Epictetus described the direct path long ago: "He is a wise man who does not grieve for the things which he has not, but rejoices for those which he has." Oprah Winfrey elaborates: "Be thankful for what you have; you'll end up having more. If you concentrate on what you don't have, you will never, ever have enough."

Feeling grateful isn't always easy. You have probably been through times that felt more like hiking through a field of sharp, jagged rocks on a moonless night than like dancing barefoot through green meadows on a sunny day. When there are troubles it's normal to wish events had gone a different way. If you have ever lost your job unexpectedly, or if someone you dearly love leaves you, it can be hard to see the positive, let alone give thanks. At such times, if someone offers a helping hand, a kind word, or a hug to inspire you to get through, you can be grateful for that. If no one extends a helping hand, be grateful for your reserve of inner strength and resilience that carries you through tough times.

When in emotional uncertainty, sometimes deeper appreciation for what you've taken for granted can prevent a descent into negativity. One day on her TV program, Oprah was talking with a woman whose marriage had been on the rocks: "I didn't have his heart and soul anymore," the woman said. "A year went by with no intimacy. Then I saw a video that suggested that I start looking at what I was grateful for with my husband rather than what I resented, which was what I'd been doing. I started to appreciate him again. I focused on little things. I surprised him with a rose and his favorite cookies." Her husband loved the changes, and passion returned to their relationship.

Commenting, Oprah observed that "gratitude was crucial. The woman started to be grateful for all the things he did for her that she'd been overlooking." That shift changed everything.

The wish to be appreciated has deep roots in human nature. If a person does something you appreciate, let her know. It nurtures the soul. But if someone has gone out of his way to do something nice for us and we ignore it, ah, how cruel! "Blow, blow, thou winter wind," said Shakespeare. "Thou are not so unkind as man's ingratitude."

If you are grateful to be who you are and to have what you have, you are on your way to peace of mind. But if you've been troubled by resentment or hate, and revenge looks sweet, gratitude may feel far away. Working through bitterness and antagonism is the slow road to gratitude. Nonetheless, if that's where you are, it's probably where you have to start. It's seldom helpful to tell yourself that you feel differently than you really do, such as thinking that you're "supposed to" feel grateful when actually you don't. Morita therapy in Japan and Gestalt therapy in the West share the principle that effective change to improve our well-being begins by becoming deeply aware of how we truly feel and what we are doing now. Gestalt therapy calls this the "paradoxical theory of change."[2] In many cases, difficult feelings need to be worked through.

The following methods allow two quite different ways of making contact with that place within yourself where you can feel gratitude.

## THE DIRECT PATH
## AND THE MERRY-GO-ROUND

Proverbs from around the world say that if you are not grateful for what you have now, then regardless of what you get in the future, you probably won't be happy with your lot then, either. Perhaps you can test this theory while doing the following contemplative meditations.

### The Essence

The direct path moves easily into gratitude. Mind-body instructor Monique Danielle suggests a technique called "gratitude yoga."[3] When you wake up, you make a mental note of five things you're grateful for. As you go through each day, pay attention to the small miracles all around you and be grateful for each small blessing the day bestows on you. Then end each day by recalling five things that occurred during the day that you're thankful for. "In every moment of your life you will find gratitude," says Danielle.

You can also do this as a formal meditative practice. Focus on your breath. On each inhalation, contemplate a grateful thought. Then on each exhalation, breathe out a self-conscious, judgmental, or stressful thought. Breathe in positive energy, breathe out negative energy.

## Variations in Technique

The Merry-Go-Round (or slow road) involves going around and around and in and out of difficulties or states of mind that make it hard for you to feel grateful. In relation to one person or emotion, mentally return to an incident in which you felt mistreated. In your mind, tell the offender your issues, and perhaps your demands as well.

After you have reflected deeply on the situation, you might write a letter to the person involved, in which you pour out your resentments. (You don't have to send it—such written statements are often better left discarded.) Or imagine that the person is sitting in a chair in front of you and tell him all the unsaid resentments that you've been carrying.

Do this technique as many times as necessary in order to feel finished with your negative feelings about the event. One day you will probably find that your energy for holding on to the anguish of your resentment is almost gone. When you feel ready, you can either move on to another situation that interferes with feeling grateful, or try the direct path process to see if it will work for you at that point.

## Feeling Comfortable

If you don't want to extend yourself beyond your usual mental and emotional zone, just be real with what you are feeling. Christian mystic Meister Eckhart said, "If the only prayer you said in your whole life was, 'Thank you,' that would suffice." But say it only when you feel it.

## Points in the Process

Some spiritual teachers suggest being grateful for our difficulties and our enemies. Since it is harder to stay composed in such circumstances, that is an advanced course in the practice of appreciating life. In such a context, an opponent is considered one of the best gurus, for he or she is like an arrow pointing to the lessons we need to learn to keep our heart from falling into a pit of negativity. "The twisted pine clinging to its rock above the sea, buffeted and bent by the wind, has a more enduring strength than the beautiful rose grown in a sheltered garden," writes mythographer J. L. Walker.[4]

# Apology

## Repentance, Atonement, and Restitution

· · · · · · · · · · · · · · · · · · · · · · · · · · · · ·

**PERSONAL ACCOUNTING**

*Blindly I have brought forth wickedness . . . tricked and overmastered by my ignorance. . . . I'll go beyond the evils of my past, and ever after turn my face from them.*

SHANTIDEVA

**WHEN WE HAVE HURT** another person in some way, the best course is to find a way to make amends.

Three little words, *I am sorry,* can be hard to say. Our feelings of self-righteousness often get in the way, even when we are in the wrong. Ordinary thinking is frequently driven by unconscious motives and by our wish to see ourselves as virtuous. Most of us prefer to avoid assuming that we are at fault if we can get away with it. Mostly we prefer to blame others. When we do acknowledge our wrongdoing, we may struggle with how to apologize.

When your heart rules, if you have offended someone, you can always say, "I didn't mean to hurt you. Please accept my sincere apology." Such words can help. In an intriguing study, three social psychologists asked people to imagine that their partners had either flirted or had sex with someone else, and then asked how they felt about different explanations from their partner. The possible responses included excuses, justifications, and apologies. Apologies, paired with respect, were most preferred.[1] An apology is a simple statement that says: "I did wrong. I recognize that my act was harmful to you. I accept responsibility for it, and I hope for your forgiveness." An excuse or justification, by contrast, is a kind of denial of responsibility and wrongdoing.

Long ago the I Ching recognized this. A person "should not take shelter in trivial excuses, but should look within and examine himself. And if he has done something wrong, he should make a noble-hearted resolve to confess his fault."[2]

Of course, sensitivity to the circumstances is paramount. If what you confess is comparable to a one-ton brick falling from the sky, a different approach may be better.

We have all sometimes hurt others or their interests. Everyone makes mistakes. With actions or distasteful remarks that warrant more than an apology, there are several steps one can take. These are recognition, remorse, repentance, restitution, atonement, and reformation. Although each doesn't fit every situation, we will explore their value one by one.

Recognition is a willingness to perceive how you have wronged another. In Japanese Naikan therapy, a question used for self-examination and extended contemplation is, "What troubles and difficulties have I caused?" In the Naikan process, you go through your relationships one by one, answering this question in relation to each person.[3] Similarly, Alcoholics Anonymous's Twelve-Step Program includes taking a "fearless moral inventory." It also recommends, "Make a list of all persons we have harmed, and become willing to make amends to them."[4]

To clean the slate of our consciousness, we can't escape knowing our shadow side as well as our sunny side. Understandably, if a thought about how we have been unkind comes up, often we conveniently distract ourselves. "The moment we ponder a twisted or broken relationship with another person," AA points out, "our emotions go on the defensive. To escape looking at the wrongs we have done another, we resentfully focus on the wrong he has done us."[5]

Knowing ourselves includes accepting ourselves as no more or less than we are—fallible human beings who sometimes act selfishly or incorrectly. Once we admit this universal truth we are less likely to feel compelled to stop ourselves from perceiving our wrong actions. When we let ourselves see our faults, we can change them.

Remorse involves feeling bad about your hurtful or harmful actions in the past or present. Sometimes this occurs automatically as you reach a deeper level of understanding. Other times it happens only after you feel the anger, pain, or retaliation of someone you've wronged. Feeling regretful about an old behavior might not require any present action. But recognizing remorseful feelings may motivate you to go on to the next step: repentance.

Repentance is widely misunderstood. In some circles it is thought that if someone has been acting badly, all he or she needs to do is change incorrect thinking. In that view, saying, "I repent!" turns past wrongs into rights, or at least makes it okay. Too many people go on doing the same old thing—and then come back and repent again. The musical jingle in the collection boxes of churches grows louder when people want to repent, but that's bogus repentance. To repent is to resolve to act differently, and then change your behavior. If someone has been causing some kind of real suffering, saying "I repent" or "I am sorry" is not enough. Acting differently is what is needed.

Remorse and repentance apply to acts carried out with an intent to harm others, and also to acts that harmed others with no conscious intent to do so. With greater awareness in the moment, we are less likely to act thoughtlessly or carelessly. The Hebrew word for repentance, *teshuvah,* implies our return back to our truest nature.

Restitution is setting right past mistakes with those we have wronged. "You can [counteract] the effects of past wrong actions with good effects set in motion by present right actions," says Paramahansa Yogananda.[6] The simplest example is when a thief returns a stolen item to its rightful owner.

By making restitution, you have paid off the debt, or sincerely tried to—or you would if you could. But often we can't, because the people have vanished from our lives. Even so, the willingness to recognize that we harmed them, and how, removes our blinders and makes us better able to perceive how we affect others now.

There are also times when we could make restitution but it is wiser to avoid it. Where it would cause bad feelings and warring words, often it is better not to reopen old wounds. Going moralistically from sinner to saint often will create still more trouble. The important thing is to treat those you have offended with respect and kindness in the present.

Atonement means making up for harm you have caused, by performing altruistic actions, even though you can't fix things with the one you hurt. Restitution and atonement are sometimes confused. People in trouble with the law may be sentenced to community service as restitution. That is restitution only in the sense that they are paying the community back for its expenses and trouble in dealing with their situation. For the most part it is actually atonement, since their action doesn't directly help the one who was harmed. Atonement can also be a personal and private vow that you make to yourself: *I'm taking these active steps to be helpful to others to compensate for what I did wrong.*

It may be the case that some people are so annoyed by past abuses that no form of apology you could offer would affect their feelings. If you are motivated to apologize, do it for the sake of doing it, and don't expect anything in return. People forgive when and if they want to, not when you wish they would.

Since many people sometimes do unto others as they've been done to, it can take more than apology for some negative matters to be settled. But when your heart and mind are in the right place, something good should come from your positive efforts.

## PERSONAL ACCOUNTING

This practice applies the spirit of the Naikan and Twelve-Step procedures on a small, self-reflective scale. If you repeat this contemplation, you may gain new insights. You can also use this technique outside the realm of apology.

### The Essence

Take a pen and some paper. For the next several moments, look within. Scan your memory and select one of your past actions that was hurtful to another person. As you hold it in mind, finish each sentence below. Do this quickly, in no more than ten minutes. Then use the answers you have written as the basis for a brief self-reflective meditation.

- What I did was . . .
- I feel sorry that . . .
- I realize that I . . .
- From now on I intend to . . .
- If possible, I'll try to make it right by . . .
- Now and henceforth I'll avoid causing such hurt by . . .

### Variations in Technique

If your heart is heavy from wishing you could right your wrongs, but the person you wish to apologize to can't be reached, you might do a meditation on releasing the past. After relaxing and becoming comfortable, visualize a lighted candle in front of your third eye (the middle of your forehead). Imagine the person you have wronged before you, and let yourself say everything you'd like to say in your apology if you could. Then using your in-breath like a broom, sweep together your emotions related to that incident or person. On your out-breath, see those bad feelings and sensations burn up in the candle flame and vanish into smoke.

## Feeling Comfortable

During meditation, thoughts of how you have hurt another may come up from time to time. When they do, focus on seeing clearly how you caused that person pain or harm, and also notice your internal responses to those memories. Watch your thoughts and other reactions with detachment. That may be enough. If you have lingering emotional attachments, imagine blowing those feelings out of your mind with your outgoing breath as in the "Variations in Technique" just above. Finally, be grateful for your increasing wholeness and happy about the good things that you have done.

# Beauty

## Grace and Charm

· · · · · · · · · · · · · · · · · · · · · · · · · · · ·

**AS IF NEVER BEFORE**

*The best and most beautiful things in the world cannot be
seen, nor touched . . . but are felt in the heart.*

HELEN KELLER

A HEIGHTENED SENSITIVITY TO beauty brightens life.

We all like beauty in our lives. When we think about beauty, we tend
to first consider things that take our breath away: a spectacular landscape,
a captivating painting or sculpture, or an actress with a one-in-a-thousand
face and figure. Whether great or small, our experiences of beauty can be
mesmerizing moments that make our souls smile.

As Helen Keller points out, if our hearts are open, we can sense beauty
in whatever form it takes. We can see it in a mountain ringed with billowing
clouds or we can find it in tiny leaves and flowers. We can feel it in the way
a person acts toward us.

What is beauty? The dictionary calls it "a combination of qualities that
make something pleasing and impressive." Aristotle suggested that it exists
when everything fits in harmony with the rest of the whole. Psychotherapist
Rollo May speaks of it as evoking a sense of joy and wonder, of timelessness
and serenity. He says, "When Plato considered the great trilogy of Beauty,
Truth and Goodness, he placed Beauty at the top because Beauty is harmony, and whether Truth or Goodness are harmonious is the test of their
integrity."[1]

Where can we find beauty? Almost everywhere, if we are sensitive enough
to appreciate it. Ralph Waldo Emerson said, "Though we travel the world
over to find the beautiful, we must carry it with us or we find it not." Two

people can be standing next to something very lovely, but one sees it and the other does not. This ability to uncover beauty lies in our attitude and our presence. We can easily miss attractive qualities hidden beneath deceptively mundane reality.

Outer beauty consists of things seen, heard, or touched. Inner beauty includes kindness, warmth, generosity and caring. All these, in ourselves or others, can enrich our lives. When we say someone is a beautiful person, often we don't mean physical appearance. Voltaire says, "Beauty pleases the eye only; sweetness of disposition charms the soul." Actress Audrey Hepburn adds, "For beautiful eyes, look for the good in others; for beautiful lips, speak only words of kindness."

Physical beauty of the face and body is a lovely gift if you can avoid defining yourself by it so completely that its loss is too poignant as it fades with the years. The inner beauty that Kahlil Gibran called "a light in the heart" can be watered and tended like a rose so that it grows with time. The Jewish concept of Tifereth is a term for Beauty that includes "awe and honor for people of wisdom and experience, and our respect for inherent worth regardless of outward appearance."[2]

Throughout history, the beauty found in various forms of creative expression such as poetry, music, and dance has been revered. These arts and their gifts of enjoyment beyond measure have been linked with divinity. In ancient Greek mythology, Aphrodite, who was known as Venus in Roman times, was the goddess of love and the humanities. In India, lovely Lakshmi presides over prosperity, and Saraswati is regarded as the goddess of beauty in the form of wisdom, music, and creativity. "Whatever is beautiful here in this world is so because of the spark of this divine beauty in it," says the Bhagavad Gita.[3]

In a sense, a good painting or sculpture, song or sonata, invites us to share the artist's consciousness, to perceive and imagine as the artist did. It is a window on alternative realities, or alternative ways of perceiving our familiar reality. Rollo May observes that sometimes the artist creates new order, whereas when society has grown too rigid, the artist creates chaos. Both can be beautiful.

Great art lies outside the realm of progress. Today's paintings are no finer than the masterpieces of the past. Today's architecture has no claim to greater beauty than ancient temples, cathedrals, castles, palaces, and villas around the world. And beauty in the natural environment can soothe and heal the spirit. John Muir said, "Everybody needs beauty as well as bread, places to play in and pray in, where nature may heal and give strength to body and soul."

Hindu spiritual teacher Anandamayi Ma adds, "Gaze to your heart's content at the lofty mountains or the wide ocean. . . . If you cannot do anything else, at least peer at the open sky whenever you have the chance. Little by little the rigid knots that make up your shackles will be loosened and you will find yourself becoming freer."[4]

There is also beauty, or lack of it, in the environments we human beings create. In traditional Japanese culture, sensitivity to beauty has long been regarded as essential to life. An old and well-used object is sometimes regarded as lovelier than the shiniest new item, and pots and bowls with small imperfections are highly prized. In that spirit, a Japanese potter may carefully avoid making a piece too perfect. Anyone who has seen a Japanese garden has some sense of this aesthetic sensibility. It draws one into a miniature world that embodies all the elements of the larger world of nature, arranged in a way that has a sense of perfect harmony, and often is a kind of living artistic masterpiece.

Another kind of beauty that we may not usually think of as such lies in functional problem solving that works out especially well. "When I am working on a problem," says inventor Buckminster Fuller, "I never think about beauty. I only think about how to solve the problem. But when I have finished, if the solution is not beautiful, I know it is wrong."

## AS IF NEVER BEFORE

Here you reexperience and look for loveliness in that which has become so familiar that you barely notice it.

### The Essence

Walk down a block, or several, of a street you have been down many times before. Clear your mind, summon your attention, and as you walk, look around as if you had never previously been on that street. Be especially attuned to sensing small and subtle points of beauty. You will probably discover things that you had no idea were there. (If your mind drifts away from present awareness, practice Walking and Breathing, cell 18, as you do this.)

Next, visit a friend you have visited many times before. While there, take a few minutes to look around just as you did on your familiar street, as if it were your first visit. Look with precise attention, with a special focus on finding beauty in that environment.

Finally, return to your own home, choose a room, and spend some time examining it. Look for beauty that you may be taking for granted because it has become so familiar. Can you look without seeing through the lens of previous perception? Try to conjure up a first-time sensitivity to your surroundings.

## Variations in Technique

Contemplate any place, subject, or problem that you can affect. This might range from objects on a tabletop to the way you organize a project. In your mind's eye imagine that you are an artistic production manager who is capable of creating beauty. Look at the whole and at the parts of your chosen object, place, or situation. What is the artistic focal point? What changes might make your subject or situation more beautiful or pleasing to you? Find your sensitivity to beauty within yourself, breathe it throughout your being, and express it in your actions.

## Points in the Process

Some kinds of beauty become more obvious while meditating. Indeed, a meditation can itself have its own beauty. Think of your consciousness as a gentle stream. Follow its meandering course in your meditation, suggests Venerable Master Sheng-yen, a Zen Buddhist teacher, and it's likely to take you where you need to go.[5]

# Celebration

## Small Miracles and Rejoicing

· · · · · · · · · · · · · · · · · · · · · · · · · · · · · ·

**MOMENTS OF APPRECIATION**

*Life is filled with . . . many wonders, like the blue sky, the
sunshine, the eyes of a baby. . . . They are within us and all
around us, everywhere, any time.*

THICH NHAT HANH

**EACH DAY WE CAN** take at least a moment to rejoice and celebrate the gift
of life.

Hearing the word *celebration,* many people think of parties and festivals.
We celebrate birthdays, holidays, holy days, weddings, births, retirements,
and many other happy occasions. Amid everyday reality, such events are like
fireworks lighting up the sky.

Celebrations don't, however, have to be big and showy. "Every day brings
a chance for you to draw in a breath, kick off your shoes, and dance," says
Oprah Winfrey. Whether small or large, there's a great festival of life going
on around us at every moment if we have the acumen to appreciate it. As
we learn to see what's special in small, everyday events, we can celebrate
every moment that presents us with the priceless opportunity to enjoy life.
We can't avoid some moments that are inherently unpleasant, and we usually hope these will end quickly. But much of our existence consists of
moments in which we seek chances to be happy. When possible, it's only
sensible to celebrate life's revolving and evolving cycles and enjoy what
they bring.

This truth has been recognized throughout the ages. "Carpe diem!
Rejoice while you are alive; enjoy the day; live life to the fullest; make the
most of what you have," said Roman poet Horace long ago. In a sense, a cel-

ebration is a step beyond gratitude: we can be grateful for what the moment offers and rejoice in it.

On the other hand, we can all too easily forget our sense of wonder, like the edge on a knife blade that has been well used and seldom sharpened. "Isn't a little bird flying through the vast sky a miracle?" asks Amma. "Isn't a tiny fish swimming in the depths of the ocean a miracle? Unfortunately, people think that only a fish flying through the sky can be called a miracle."[1]

When we take the time to look around us, we can find many reasons to be joyful. In an intriguing turn of thought, St. Theresa of Avila points out that we can even find something to celebrate in our mistakes and wrongdoings: "To reach something good it is very useful to have gone astray, and thus acquire experience."

We can rejoice in the good company of others who enrich our lives, whether by friendship through the years or by a one-time pleasant conversation with someone we may never see again. We can even appreciate relationships that have ended although we wish they hadn't. In its time, each such relationship brought a special light into our life. Our connection may have helped us learn to love or see more deeply into who we really are, which can be very useful for our future. It's normal to regret the end of a relationship that we wish had continued. Even so, we need to move through our disappointment and be open to new beginnings and unexpected possibilities when they occur.

With greater wakefulness, we can avoid the judging and blaming that dim our inner light in our relationships and deflate joyful moments. Anandamayi Ma observed that "to find fault with others creates obstacles for everyone all around; for him who criticizes, for him who is blamed, as well as for those who listen to the criticism. Whereas what is said in a spirit of appreciation is fruitful to everybody."[2]

Achievements and play are also worth celebrating. Celebration creates positive energy that can multiply itself. Former General Electric CEO Jack Welch says, "Imagine a team winning the World Series without champagne spraying everywhere. And yet companies win all the time and let it go without so much as a high five. Work is too much a part of life not to recognize moments of achievement. Make a big deal out of them. If you don't, no one will."[3] Celebration is a stepping-stone to inspiration. When someone's work or achievements are recognized and celebrated, they and probably others too will be more inspired to think optimistically and do well in the future.

Music, dance, and ritual are a kind of celebration of life's beauty and surging vitality. Both religious and popular music can make our hearts want to sing. Gregorian chants in the West, kirtans and shabads in India, and other forms of sacred chanting are known to carry us into states of bliss. So are ecstatic rhythmic movements, like Sufi dancing, Native American dancing, or dancing around the Maypole, which awakens our spirit of aliveness and connection with the soul.

## MOMENTS OF APPRECIATION

Many of us are so busy worrying about being on time and moving on to our next commitment that we let the present moment slip away without ever noticing it. Most moments offer something. Here we can use the widespread preoccupation with time as a reminder to celebrate the present before the opportunity is gone.

### The Essence

Throughout the day, each time you look at your watch or a clock, once you have noted the time, no matter what else you are doing, let it remind you to step into a tiny instant of enjoyment of the moment. Notice something—anything—about your environment, or someone you're with, or even something related to yourself that can add beauty or value to this instant in your life. It might be noticing a worn chair in your study that serves you well, or a bird flying high, or an action by a person who deserves appreciation. It might even be something you've just done especially well for which you can commend yourself.

Let your inner mind silently say the phrase *No words, no concepts, just appreciation*. Let those six words clear away all other words, ideas, and imagery from your mind for at least thirty seconds. Perceive clearly whatever you have chosen to celebrate with 100 percent of your attention. Momentarily suspend any other thoughts that are in your mind except for your appreciation of this moment.

The watch or clock is not a requirement for doing this practice. Of course, you are free to celebrate anything that seems to deserve it at any time. A single day can include many moments of rejoicing.

### Variations in Technique

Without having any special occasion, plan an amazing event, small or large, that gives you an opportunity to celebrate your life. Your celebration can be experienced solely in your mind in a self-guided visualization, or you can decide to host your event in reality. The point is to take some time to think about how you would like to honor and celebrate yourself.

Perhaps this might include a minute, or a few, to celebrate each of the four elements—earth, air, fire, and water, that sustain our lives. Walking in a meditative manner allows you to notice the air as you look up at the sky or feel a breeze on your cheek. You can rejoice in the waters of life as you sip from a glass or as your gaze falls on a stream or pond. As you think about what you want to eat at your celebration, you can rejoice in the earth and appreciate your life's harvest. Feeling the fire in the sun's warmth is almost always a reason to celebrate.

## Points in the Process

Celebration can be a part of each moment. Instead of being uninterested in people or events that differ from what we are accustomed to, we can strive to actively enjoy the differences. That which is outside our usual frame of reference is often more interesting than more of the same old thing. In many cases, rather than just tolerating differences, we can recognize that they enlarge our perspective, and can rejoice in them. This attitude literally feels better than its opposite. Newspaper columnist Art Hoppe writes, "If we all celebrated life, who could oppress or kill or hate his fellow man?" After all, the love living inside you is one of the best reasons of all to celebrate.

# Generosity

## Giving and Receiving

**EVERYDAY SEVA**

*Let us focus on what we can give to others and not what
we can take for ourselves. This will bring great
transformation in our life.*

AMMA (SRI MĀTĀ AMRITANANDAMAYĪ DEVI)

**GIVING OF OURSELVES IS** an important thread in the fabric of our lives.

In the American colonies, settlers from Europe were puzzled when a
Native American gave them a gift and later asked for it back, or asked them
to pass it on to someone else. They coined the derogatory term *Indian giver*
for such behavior. What they failed to comprehend was that whereas they
expected to keep their possessions, Native Americans viewed ownership as a
transitory state. Someone would keep and enjoy an item for a time, then give
it to another. In many tribes, when one family became wealthy in possessions, they would hold a giveaway and distribute almost everything to others.
As a result, no one became extremely rich or poor.

Although modern society has a different approach, gift giving is still an
honored tradition. Giving can be of a material nature or an intangible offering of the heart. One prototype is of a mother who gives up her career in
order to give her infant nurturing. Another is the good old dad who works
late hours to make sure he can give his children privileges he never had.

A different example is giving help, such as one person assisting another
who has been hurt. Offering a shoulder to cry on can mean a lot to someone
who is grieving. Or a person might give his or her time and work to benefit
a worthy cause. We might even give someone the gift of an adventure or an
entertaining time.

When we don't know what to give, we can give of ourselves.

What else do we give? When possible we can give hugs and kisses! In all societies, affection and love rank high among the currencies of giving and receiving. A man giving his sweetheart love captures almost everyone's smile (or envy). Appreciation may seem like a minor item, but it's also highly valued. Even if you're busy, when you pause for a moment to find something to appreciate in another, your comment may give that person the gift of a better day.

Knowledge is yet another gift. It can take the form of sharing useful information or of asking questions that draw out another's thoughtfulness to help him clarify a problem. But advice, when requested, is often best framed in the form of several options, which leaves a person free to find her own solution.

From his spiritual point of view, Paramahansa Yogananda offers this summary: "You can be helpful materially by giving to the needy; and mentally by giving comfort to the sorrowful, courage to the fearful, divine friendship and moral support to the weak. . . . Every day do some good to help others, even if it is only a pittance."[1] Often the most important thing is that you are responding from your heart.

Receiving is the other side of giving. The Stoic philosopher Seneca said, "There is as much greatness of mind in receiving a good turn as in doing it." We can be gracious in our acceptance of another person's gift, although sometimes that's not so easy. We may feel undeserving. We might be afraid that today's gift of affection will be gone tomorrow, and as a result we withdraw to avoid feeling hurt. When we close the shutters on today's sunshine because tomorrow might bring rain, we also shut out some of the joyful moments life can offer. It can be a hard call.

There is also the complication that a gift may imply an obligation, if it has subtle, manipulative strings attached. In politics or business, declining such gifts may be basic ethical behavior, and may even avoid legal entanglements. In daily life, usually your heart knows which gifts carry unwanted obligations. Handling such delicate situations requires both tact and presence.

A different problem exists when one person in a relationship consistently gives more and receives less than the other. If one feels deprived, it is not unusual to take resentment out on the other in hidden ways. A spouse who feels slighted and controlled by an overbearing partner, for example, may unconsciously respond by withdrawing love. Whether an issue is between spouses, co-workers, or friends, chronic feelings of unfairness need to be addressed. One approach is for whoever receives less to more fully appreciate what he or she is receiving and let go of feeling deprived. A different approach is to use direct communication and address the problem in a conflict-resolution mode: "Something important is not working for me here. Can we talk about it?"

A further stage in giving and receiving involves putting the interests of others whose needs are greater than yours ahead of your own. That requires a generosity of spirit in which you look past your own needs and respond to those of others. Fortunately, that generosity can be cultivated. Winston Churchill comments, "We make a living by what we get. We make a life by what we give."

By some strange alchemy, becoming more generous toward others often helps us feel better about ourselves. "Go out and serve the suffering," says Amma. "In this way you will discover your own inner harmony."[2]

Eknath Easwaran describes giving as a chance to reduce self-centeredness, and adds a useful insight:

> This does not mean making yourself a doormat, saying yes to anything people say or do. . . . If someone close to you wants something that is in no one's best interests, or something which you feel is wrong, it is necessary to say no, respectfully but firmly. The point . . . is not to weaken good judgment but to . . . become more sensitive to others' needs and less insistent about our own.[3]

The Eastern word for selfless service to benefit others is *seva*. The first step is finding out what needs to be done. The next step is doing it. Since for many, seva is part of their spiritual journey and is seen as an opportunity to work on the inner self, a subsequent step is examining motives and working on letting of ego attachments connected to your activity. Self-congratulation, such as "See how great I am for doing this," attitudes of false charity or self-righteousness, and feeling worthier than others who are doing less, don't fit with the soul-expanding ideal of seva. When you freely give of yourself and try to reduce or release your attachment to self-centered motives, you are carrying out a kind of housecleaning of your mind, heart, and spirit.

# EVERYDAY SEVA

Service to benefit others, other living beings, or the environment can be carried out at any level, from the very small to the very large. In the following practice, you will experiment with your ability to give selflessly. Think about stretching your ability to give of yourself beyond your normal community of family and friends. If you feel awkward, don't feel pressure to do more than what feels right.

## The Essence

Begin this sitting meditation with your starting sequence and take several minutes to focus your mind with a concentrative or mindfulness meditation. Next, invoke the feeling of compassion. Where does this feeling live within your mind and body?

In your mind's eye, look at activities you are hoping to do tomorrow. Let acts of generosity or service that might be possible float through your mind. You might see yourself responding to requests others have made of you. You might think of people or organizations in need that could benefit from your involvement. Most of the possibilities you consider will drop away, but one may move to the forefront. If not, then consciously choose an act of giving or service that appeals most to you. After your meditation, when the appropriate time arrives, carry out the action(s) if you can.

## Variations in Technique

Structure your meditation as you did just above. Now envision a gift that you want to give yourself. Contemplate how you can be more compassionate and giving to yourself. Is there something you can give yourself that will help you feel inspired? Pay attention to what you experience, and what you want to do with insights that come.

## Feeling Comfortable

If thoughts arise that reveal ways in which you have a hard time giving of yourself or to yourself, witness them. Then for the moment, replace them with a mantra or a mantra passage (cell 25). Or just be present with your feelings in wordlessness. Let go of any tendency to evaluate your inner process. What part of yourself do you see reflected through this practice?

## Points in the Process

You might think you have little to give. An Arabian proverb says: "If you have much, give of your wealth. If you have little, give of your heart." Most of us can offer at least our hands and heart. Whether your gift is painting the walls in your church, playing cards with lonely seniors, or giving food donations to homeless shelters, there is almost always greater need than there are hands to help. When you give to others you're likely to find that in unexpected ways you are also giving to yourself.

# Unity

## Every Person, Every Being

·  ·  ·  ·  ·  ·  ·  ·  ·  ·  ·  ·  ·  ·  ·  ·  ·  ·  ·  ·  ·  ·  ·  ·

**ILLUMINATING YOUR OWN PATH**

> *We must learn to live together as brothers or*
> *perish together as fools.*
>
> MARTIN LUTHER KING

**WE ARE ALL FAR** more like one another than we are different, with similar needs, hopes, fears, and feelings.

Long ago the Mundaka Upanishad declared: "The soul shines equally in people on the farthest island, and in people close at hand. . . . The soul shines in the hearts of all living beings."[1] To emphasize that an underlying unity runs through all beings Martin Luther King said, "The good neighbor looks beyond the external accidents and discerns those inner qualities that make [us] all human, and therefore, brothers [and sisters]."[2]

Recognizing that we are all deeply connected does not mean that most of us will reach a utopian state in which we dive into a sea of cosmic consciousness and achieve an actual experience of feeling our oneness with all beings. Historically it has been easier for us to be in touch with our individuality and separation from others. We are, after all, hardwired for self-preservation as well as for relating.

To extend ourselves from the limiting, self-serving *I* to the heart-awakening unity of the *we*, philosopher Martin Buber emphasized treating the other person as *Thou* rather than as *It*. His *Thou* implies a unity of mutual respect and altruistic caring about the other's needs and interests.[3] The great spiritual teachers have said that enlightenment includes feeling ourselves to be part of a unitary field of existence in which at least for a fleeting moment boundaries disappear. Amma says, "Let us

365

strive to reach a state in which we are able to see all beings on Earth as part of our own self."[4]

When we have such moments of realization, says Yamada Koun-roshi, "we feel as though the heavy burdens we have been carrying in our heart or on our shoulders, indeed all over our body and soul, suddenly disappear as if thrown away. The joy and happiness at that time is beyond all words. And there are no philosophies or theologies attached to it."[5]

How can we give such inspiring words a practical turn? How can we feel more deeply connected to our family, partner, friends, and those who nourish our soul? Is it possible to stop drawing rigid boundary lines between us and others who appear to be quite different from ourselves, even though their minds and dreams are almost like our own? Is it even possible for us to truly comprehend that our bodies, a hummingbird, and the nucleus of a star in a distant galaxy are all made of molecules, atoms, and subatomic particles that are more alike than different?

Such questions are essential for those who hold power. The I Ching declares that a true leader "organizes human society so that . . . its parts cooperate for the benefit for the whole." It adds that such a person, "by means of good government, sets a lofty example for the masses."[6] Pilot Baba suggests a guiding principle that has broad application: "Any leader who brings people together is good. Any leader who divides is not good." When we notice that we have fallen into the latter pattern, we can step out of it and act more consciously to expand our understanding of those who live outside our personal world. Jesus echoed this attitude. Recognized as a teacher of universal love, he told us to act from our inner wisdom of the heart, to love our neighbors as ourselves, and to give up the greedy grasping that separates us from others.

Perceiving the unity of our world is crucial for living in the ecosphere. Swami Prajnanpad points out that in nature, "everything is connected to everything else. . . . Nothing is isolated. Everything is linked, and interdependent."[7]

Former Norwegian prime minister Gro Harlem Brundtland says simply, "Human health and the health of ecosystems are inseparable."

No spiritual tradition grasps the relationship between humans and the rest of nature more deeply than that of Native Americans. Oglala Sioux chief Luther Standing Bear says, "We are of the soil and the soil is of us. We love the birds and beasts that grew with us on this soil. They drink the same water and breathe the same air. We are all one."[8]

Sioux medicine man Black Elk recognized that all people are linked both with one another and with the earth:

> I was standing on the highest mountain of them all, and round about beneath me was the whole hoop of the world. . . . I was seeing the shapes of all things in the spirit, and the shape of all shapes as they must live together like one being. . . . And I saw that the sacred hoop of my people was one of many hoops that made one circle, wide as daylight and as star-light, and in the center grew one mighty flowering tree to shelter all. . . . We are of Earth, and belong to You. Every step that we take upon You should be done in a sacred manner; each step should be as a prayer.[9]

Black Elk and Luther Standing Bear were extraordinary thinkers whose visions can guide all who choose to listen. But don't read their words with just your intellect. You can most fully experience their wisdom if you also open your heart.

## ILLUMINATING YOUR OWN PATH

If you have done the meditation or awareness practice in each cell, at this point you are probably a skilled meditator. From within the Matrix you have accessed a spectrum of different tools to develop your mental strength. More than ever before, it is time to take some of the skills you've gained into your daily life.

### The Essence

Now you have reached the last guidepost on this road to learning diverse med-itative and awareness skills. Consider which practices work best for you, under what circumstances. Use your best judgment about what you find most help-ful at a given moment. If modifications in some of these methods make them work more effectively for you, change them in those ways. Find the right bal-ance between your mind, body, emotions, and actions. Listen to the integrity of your inner voice, and follow your wisdom to know and perform the kind or kinds of meditation that are most valuable for you at any given moment. Trust your own insight to further your progress at each point of your journey.

### Feeling Comfortable

You can do a contemplative meditation with almost any question, problem, or creative endeavor. This usually works best when you first go through your starting sequence and a few minutes of a concentrative meditation to quiet your mind. Then contemplate your question as if it were a candle flame, returning your attention to it when you notice that your mind has wandered.

Sometimes you will probably find that your attention keeps drifting off and you have a hard time maintaining focus as you contemplate. At those times, you can tell yourself, *Listen, mind, here's my concern. I'd appreciate it if you come up with some insight.* Then go into an attentive meditation—a concentration or mindfulness practice—that helps you maintain focus. There's a good chance that ideas or solutions to your question will percolate through and around the edges of your attentive practice.

Avoid conventional problem solving during contemplative meditation. When you are using linear, logical reasoning, your conceptualizing mind may block the kind of creative mental open space from which deeper insights often emerge. You have plenty of time for logical problem solving when you're not meditating.

## Points in the Process

Unity is a concept that holds out a promise of widespread peace and harmony. Within our personal attempts to strengthen our minds lies the potential for transforming our collective consciousness in ways that could bring a worldwide renaissance of creative thought and action, and a widespread reduction of selfishness and negativity. For instance, says Eknath Easwaran, "through many years of [meditative] practice, you can gain such command over your thinking process that if there is a spurt of hostility toward someone you have only to look at your mind and say, 'No.' The hostility will wither."[10]

It appears possible that our planetary culture has begun a historic transition toward recognizing that inner development, cooperative relationships, and the health of the life-sustaining ecosphere are our most priceless treasures. To be fully healed and whole within ourselves, we must help one another and the natural environment become healed and whole as well. If we do so, in tomorrow's world we will fight less and dance more. We will be able to focus on enriching our relationships, freeing our creativity, and helping those in need become genuinely self-supporting. With the greater awareness that comes through meditation we can unlock the potential to spread beauty throughout the world to a degree that only the great prophets and poets have imagined. Personally and collectively, the future is ours to shape. Let us do our best to awaken our sense of unity, and collectively make wise choices.

# Notes

## INTRODUCTION. INNER AWAKENING

1. Alfred Huang, *The Complete I Ching,* xvii, 500–502.

## CHAPTER 1. STARTING POINTS

1. Ram Dass, *Still Here: Embracing Aging, Changing, and Dying,* 16.
2. Robert Langan, *Minding What Matters: Psychotherapy and the Buddha Within,* 5.
3. The Dalai Lama's Introduction to Mark Epstein, *Thoughts Without a Thinker: Psychotherapy from the Buddhist Perspective,* xiii.
4. Richard Wilhelm and Cary F. Baynes, *The I Ching, or Book of Changes,* 177–78.

## CHAPTER 2. YOUR PERSONAL RENAISSANCE

1. Richard Tarnas, *The Passion of the Western Mind,* 224.

## CHAPTER 4. AN INCREDIBLE LENS

1. Wolf-Dieter Storl, *Shiva: The Wild God of Power and Ecstasy,* 215.
2. Meher Baba, *Discourses,* vol. 2, 123, 137.

## CHAPTER 5. ATTENTION

1. William James, *The Principles of Psychology.*
2. Sharon Salzberg and Joseph Goldstein, *Insight Meditation,* 15.
3. Swami Vivekananda, *Raja-Yoga,* rev. ed., 132–35, 183.
4. Swami Rama, *Meditation and Its Practice,* 37.
5. Rhonda Byrne, *The Secret,* 4, 13–14, 19.

## CHAPTER 6. MESSAGES OF THE HEART

1. Bhagavan Sri Ramana Maharshi, *The Teachings of Bhagavan Sri Ramana Maharshi . . . ,* 33.
2. Robert W. Funk, Bernard Brandon Scott, and James R. Butts, *The Parables of Jesus,* 30.
3. Ibid., 31.
4. Amma, *Embracing the World,* 22, 66.
5. In Frederick S. Perls, *Gestalt Therapy Verbatim,* 80.
6. Carl Rogers, *On Becoming a Person,* 25.

## CHAPTER 7. YOUR INNER GUIDE

1. Ernest Becker, *The Denial of Death,* 71–90.
2. Simone de Beauvoir, *The Second Sex.*
3. Ibid.
4. Carlos Castaneda, *The Teachings of Don Juan: A Yaqui Way of Knowledge.*
5. Swami Vivekananda, quoted in Folmi, *Wisdom: 365 Thoughts from Indian Masters.*

## CHAPTER 8. PREPARING FOR YOUR JOURNEY

1. Sharon Salzberg and Joseph Goldstein, *Insight Meditation,* 15.
2. Swami Rama, *Meditation and Its Practice,* 15.
3. Ibid., 35.
4. Tarthang Tulku, *Gesture of Balance,* 70.
5. Sri Ramana Maharshi, *The Teachings of Bhagavan Sri Ramana Maharshi . . . ,* 140.
6. Swami Vivekananda, *Raja-Yoga,* 127.
7. Meher Baba, *Discourses,* vol. 2, 135.
8. Eknath Easwaran, *Meditation,* 12.

## CELL 0. BREATH

1. John C. H. Wu, tr., Lao-tzu, *Tao Te Ching,* 93.
2. Daniel Odier, *Tantric Quest: An Encounter with Absolute Love,* 108.

## CELL 1. BALANCE

1. Swami Vivekananda, *Raja-Yoga,* 23.

## CELL 2. RELAXATION

1. Harish Johari, *Ayurvedic Massage,* 4.
2. Edmund Jacobson, *Progressive Relaxation.*

## CELL 3. INNER PEACE

1. Shunryu Suzuki, *Zen Mind, Beginner's Mind,* 39.
2. Ibid., 50–51.

## CELL 5. FLEXIBILITY

1. Buddha, *The Kalama Sutra.*
2. Alfred Korzybski, *Science and Sanity.*
3. Maurice Merleau-Ponty, *The Primacy of Perception.*
4. Laura Archera Huxley, *You Are Not the Target,* 204.
5. Matthew 9:17; Mark 2:22; Luke 5:37–39.

## CELL 6. RENEWAL

1. Omar Khayyám, *Rubaiyat,* verses VII, VIII, LXXVI.
2. Rachel Carson, *Silent Spring.*

## CELL 7. CONTENTMENT

1. Dōgen Zenji, *Shobogenzo,* 112.
2. Albert Ellis and R. Grieger, *Handbook of Rational Emotive Therapy,* 10.

## CELL 8. FOCUS

1. Lee Hixon, *Living Buddha Zen,* 154–59.
2. Lawrence LeShan, *How to Meditate,* 8.

## CELL 9. CONTACT

1. Kirk Schneider and Rollo May, *Existence: An Integrative, Clinical Perspective.*
2. Wilhelm Reich, *Character Analysis.*

## CELL 10. STRESS

1. Kenneth R. Pelletier, *Mind as Healer, Mind as Slayer.*
2. Wilhelm Reich, *Character Analysis.*

## CELL 11. VISUALIZATION

1. Carl Hodges, "Metaphor as Field."
2. Carl Jung, *Psyche and Symbol;* and *Man and His Symbols.*

## CELL 12. CHOICE

1. José Ortega y Gassett, *Man and People.*
2. Jean-Paul Sartre, *Essays in Existentialism,* 134–35, and *Existentialism and Humanism,* 43–44.
3. Walt Anderson (a.k.a. Walter Truett Anderson), *Open Secrets.*

## CELL 13. FAITH

1. Emmanuel Yeboa, *Emmanuel's Gift* (a film), 2005.
2. William Cantwell Smith, *Patterns of Faith around the World.*

## CELL 14. SECURITY

1. Albert Bandura, "Self-efficacy Mechanisms in Human Agency," *American Psychologist;* also Victor Daniels and Laurence J. Horowitz, *Being and Caring,* 268. *Self-efficacy* and *sense of effectiveness* are synonomous.

## CELL 15. INTEGRITY

1. Carl Rogers, *On Becoming a Person,* 16.
2. A. R. Orage, *Psychological Exercises and Essays,* 106.

## CELL 16. KARMA

1. Judith Tyberg, *The Language of the Gods.*
2. Swami Rama, *Living with the Himalayan Masters,* 132.
3. Dainin Katagiri, *Each Moment Is the Universe: Zen and the Way of Being Time,* 174, 199, 206.
4. Peter Marchand, *The Yoga of the Nine Emotions,* 112.
5. Joseph Goldstein, *One Dharma,* 29.

## CELL 18. HEALTH

1. Victor Daniels, lecture, "Psychology in Greek Philosophy."

2. Harish Johari, *Aryuvedic Massage,* 7.
3. Deepak Chopra, *Ageless Body, Timeless Mind: The Quantum Alternative to Growing Old,* 128.
4. Sivananda Yoga Vedanta Center, *Yoga Mind and Body,* 13.

## CELL 19. ENVY

1. Heather Smith, in Tyler, Boeckmann, Smith, and Huo, *Social Justice in a Diverse Society.*
2. Richard Lazarus, *Emotion and Adaptation,* 259.
3. Amma, in a question-and-answer session, San Ramon, Calif., November 2007.
4. Laura Archera Huxley, *You Are Not the Target,* 30.

## CELL 20. COURAGE

1. Eknath Easwaran, *Gandhi the Man,* 114–16.
2. Ibid., 117.
3. Stanley J. Rachman, *Fear and Courage,* 246.
4. S. Stouffer, A. Lumsdaine, R. Williams, M. Smith, I. Janis, S. Star, and L. Cottrell, *The American Soldier: Combat and Its Aftermath.*
5. Rollo May, *The Courage to Create,* 3–16.
6. Albert Bandura, *Social Learning Theory,* 139–40, 264–65.

## CELL 21. SOUND AND SILENCE

1. Derek Biermann, *Samadhi,* 84.
2. Harish Johari, *Chakras,* 13.
3. Deepak Chopra, *Ageless Body, Timeless Mind,* 163.
4. Eknath Easwaran, *Gandhi the Man,* 117.
5. Swami Rama, *Living with the Himalayan Masters,* 417.
6. Sanskrit Dictionary for Spoken Sanskrit.
7. Swami Rama, *Meditation and Its Practice,* 40–43.
8. Maharishi Mahesh Yogi, *Transcendental Meditation.*

## CELL 22. SENSATION

1. Swami Rama, *Living with the Himalayan Masters,* 249.
2. Daniel Odier, *Tantric Quest.*
3. Victor Daniels, lecture, "Psychology in Greek Philosophy."
4. Richard Wilhelm, *The Secret of the Golden Flower.*

## CELL 23. SELF-ACCEPTANCE

1. David Feinstein and Stanley Krippner, *The Mythic Path,* 4–9.
2. Ibid.
3. Aaron Beck, *Cognitive Therapy and the Emotional Disorders,* 32–37.
4. Ibid.
5. Erving Polster, *Every Person's Life Is Worth a Novel,* 1–4.
6. Joseph Melnick and Sonia March Nevis, "Gestalt Therapy Methodology," 106.
7. Shunryu Suzuki, *Zen Mind, Beginner's Mind: Informal Talks on Zen Meditation and Practice,* 38.

## CELL 24. SHADOW

1. Carl Jung, *Psyche and Symbol; Two Essays on Analytical Psychology.*
2. Roberto Assagioli, *Psychosynthesis,* 19–20.
3. Fritz Perls, *The Gestalt Approach / Eyewitnesss to Therapy.*
4. Sally J. Nelson, *Night Wings.*

## CELL 25. DESIRE

1. Patanjali, *Yoga Sutras.*
2. Nikos Kazantzakis, *Zorba the Greek.*
3. Shankara, *Crest Jewel of Discrimination.*
4. Harish Johari, *Tools for Tantra,* 2.
5. Archie Bahm, *Philosophy of the Buddha,* 49.
6. The Dalai Lama, *How to Practice,* 71.
7. Sri Aurobindo, *Integral Yoga: Sri Aurobindo's Teaching & Method of Practice,* 143.
8. See also Eknath Easwaran, *Meditation: A Simple 8-Point Program for Transforming Spiritual Ideals Into Daily Life,* 70–71.

## CELL 26. LISTENING

1. Carl Rogers, *A Way of Being,* 7.

## CELL 27. LOSS

1. Betty Kelen, *Gautama Buddha in Life and Legend,* 133.
2. Jakusho Kwong, *No Beginning, No End: The Intimate Heart of Zen,* 128–30.
3. David Brazier, *Zen Therapy: Transcending the Sorrows of the Human Mind,* 242–43.
4. Sylvia Boorstein, *Pay Attention, For Goodness' Sake.*
5. *The I Ching,* Wilhelm/Baynes translation, 199.

## CELL 28. JUDGMENT

1. John 7:53, *The New English Bible.*
2. Luke 6:37–38, *The New English Bible.*
3. Chogyam Trungpa, *Training the Mind and Cultivating Loving-Kindness,* 96–97.
4. Ken Wilber, *No Boundary: Eastern and Western Approaches to Personal Growth,* 9–10.
5. Lao-tzu, *Tao Teh Ching,* translated by John C. H. Wu.
6. Carl Rogers and H. Jerome Freiburg, *Freedom to Learn,* 3rd ed.

## CELL 29. PRESENCE

1. Pilot Baba, untitled talk, Occidental, Calif., 2000.
2. Ram Dass, *Be Here Now,* 22–23.
3. Erving Polster, *Every Person's Life Is Worth a Novel.*
4. Dainin Katagiri, *Each Moment Is the Universe: Zen and the Way of Being Time,* 3, 9, 20.
5. Philip Zimbardo, "'Putting Time in Perspective': Minds, Individuals, and Contexts."
6. Philip Zimbardo and John Boyd, *The Time Paradox,* 90–93.
7. Ibid., 106–10.

## CELL 30. RESPECT

1. Johannes Fabian, *Time and the Other.*
2. Meher Baba, *Discourses,* vol. 1, 27, 30, 52.
3. *The I Ching,* Wilhelm-Baynes translation, 160, 224.

## CELL 31. LIMITS

1. *The I Ching,* Wilhelm-Baynes translation, 231–32.
2. Frederick Perls, Ralph Hefferline, and Paul Goodman, *Gestalt Therapy.*

## CELL 32. COMMUNICATION

1. Virginia Satir, quoted in Lynn Namka, "A Tribute to the Most Marvelous Virginia Satir."
2. Virginia Satir, *The New Peoplemaking,* 93–95.
3. *Chinese Proverbs from Olden Times.*
4. Virginia Satir, *The New Peoplemaking,* 80–93.
5. Shunryu Suzuki, *Zen Mind, Beginner's Mind,* 87–91.
6. Hazrat Inayat Khan, *The Inner Life,* 16.

## CELL 33. WHOLENESS

1. Jakusho Kwong, *No Beginning, No End,* 134.
2. J. L. Walker, "The Perilous Garden," *Parabola.*
3. C. G. Jung, *Two Essays on Analytical Psychology.*
4. J. Krishnamurti, *Freedom from the Known.*

## CELL 34. FREEDOM

1. Paolo Freire, *Pedagogy of the Oppressed,* 45, 46, 108.
2. Erich Fromm, *Escape from Freedom,* 17.
3. Shunryu Suzuki, *Not Always So,* 50–51.
4. Pilot Baba, untitled talk, Occidental, Calif., 1999.
5. Amma, *Awaken Children,* vol. 8, 67.

## CELL 35. WORRY

1. Fritz Perls, *Gestalt Therapy Verbatim,* 3, 30.
2. Amma, *Awaken Children,* vol. 8, 128–29.
3. Fritz Perls, *Gestalt Therapy Verbatim,* 31.
4. Chogyam Trungpa, *Cutting Through Spiritual Materialism,* 108.
5. Peter Marchand, *The Yoga of the Nine Emotions,* 100–101.
6. Bertrand Russell, *The Conquest of Happiness.*
7. Joseph Wolpe, *The Practice of Behavior Therapy.*
8. Maxwell Maltz, *Psycho-Cybernetics,* ch. 14.

## CELL 36. ANGER

1. Daniel Goleman, *Emotional Intelligence,* 170–71.
2. Peter Marchand, *The Yoga of the Nine Emotions,* 78.
3. Swami Dayananda Saraswati, "Prevent inappropriate expression of anger."
4. Daniel Goleman, *Emotional Intelligence,* 62.

## CELL 37. ATTACHMENT

1. Will Durant, *The Story of Philosophy*, Part I, 366, 506.
2. Ram Dass, *Be Here Now*, 35.
3. Sita Wiener, *Swami Satchidananda*, 18.
4. Tarthang Tulku, *Gesture of Balance*, 9.
5. Thich Nhat Hanh, "Twenty Exercises from the Satipatthana Sutra."

## CELL 38. ATTITUDE

1. Martin Seligman, *Authentic Happiness*, 28.
2. Willie Nelson, quoted in Alanna Nash, *Behind Closed Doors*, 369–70.
3. Shunryu Suzuki, *Zen Mind, Beginner's Mind*, 35.
4. Shunryu Suzuki, *Not Always So*, 53.
5. Swami Sivananda Saraswati, "High on Waves," *Yoga*.

## CELL 39. TRUST

1. Jack Gibb, *Trust: A New View of Personal and Organizational Development*, 16, 19.
2. Karen Horney, *Feminine Psychology*, 108–9.
3. Erik Erikson, *Childhood and Society*.

## CELL 40. DIFFICULTIES

1. *The I Ching*, Wilhelm-Baynes translation, 120–21.
2. Chogyam Trungpa, *Training the Mind and Cultivating Loving-Kindness*, 47–51.
3. Dōgen, *Shobogenzo: Zen Essays by Dōgen*, trans. by Thomas Cleary. Also Reiho Masunaga, *A Primer of Soto Zen: A Translation of Dōgen's Shobogenzo Zuimonki*.
4. Joseph Goldstein and Jack Kornfield, *Seeking the Heart of Wisdom: The Path of Insight Meditation*, 45.
5. Sita Wiener, *Swami Satchidananda*, 47.

## CELL 41. EGO

1. Walter Truett Anderson, *Open Secrets*, 58, 86, 118.
2. Swami Niranjanananda Saraswati, "Towards Freedom," *Yoga* (March–April 2003), 15.
3. Sri Aurobindo, *An Introduction to the Psychological Thought of Sri Aurobindo*, ed. by A. S. Dalal, 2–6. *The Life Divine*, 532–34.
4. Meher Baba, *Discourses*, 67.
5. Chogyam Trungpa, *Cutting Through Spiritual Materialism*, 7.

## CELL 42. HEALING

1. Andrew Weil, *8 Weeks to Optimum Health*, 18.
2. Deepak Chopra, *Ageless Body, Timeless Mind*, 162–65.
3. B. K. S. Iyengar, *Light on the Yoga Sutras of Patanjali*.
4. Wilhelm Reich, *Character Analysis*.
5. Amma, *Being with Amma*.

## CELL 43. JOY

1. Swami Ramakrishnananda Puri, *Eye of Wisdom*, 75.

2. Amma, *Being with Amma.*
3. Thich Nhat Hanh, *The Path of Emancipation,* 98.
4. Stella Resnick, *The Pleasure Zone,* 9–10.
5. Sharon Salzberg, *Loving-Kindness.*
6. Abraham Maslow, *The Farther Reaches of Human Nature.*

## CELL 44. SUCCESS

1. Paramahansa Yogananda, *Where There Is Light,* 64.
2. Norman Vincent Peale, *The Power of Positive Thinking,* 57.
3. Dale Carnegie, *How to Win Friends and Influence People.* Also Stephen R. Covey, *The 7 Habits of Highly Effective People.* Also Deepak Chopra, *The Seven Spiritual Laws of Success.*
4. Paramahansa Yogananda, *Where There Is Light,* 66.

## CELL 45. TRANSFORMATION

1. David Brazier, *Zen Therapy,* 126.
2. Pilot Baba, untitled talk, Occidental, Calif., 2000.
3. Amma, *Being with Amma.*

## CELL 46. HANG-UPS

1. Carl Jung, "The Structure and Dynamics of the Psyche," *Collected Works,* vol. 8, par. 210, 628. See also Mary Ann Mattoon, *Jungian Psychology in Perspective,* 115–25.
2. Sigmund Freud, "Repression," in *Collected Papers,* vol. 4, 84–97.
3. Meher Baba, *Discourses,* vol. 1, 26, 54, 113.

## CELL 47. LOVE

1. Jalalu'ddin Rumi, *Sun of Tabriz,* 10–11.
2. Meher Baba, *Discourses,* vol. 1, 129.
3. Pilot Baba, untitled talk, Occidental, Calif., 2000.
4. Amma, *Embracing the World,* 35, 36, 68; *Being with Amma.*
5. Meher Baba, *Discourses,* vol. 1, 24.

## CELL 48. DEFENSIVENESS

1. Abraham Maslow, *Motivation and Personality.*
2. Excerpts from Deepak Chopra, *The Seven Spiritual Laws of Success.* www.spiritsite.com/writing/deecho/part16. shtml. Accessed on January 26, 2009.
3. Pema Chödrön, *The Places that Scare You.*
4. Judge Jim Tamm, "Relationship Advice: Defensiveness: The Poison Pill to Relationships."

## CELL 49. CONFLICT

1. Lao-tzu, *Tao Teh Ching,* verses 8 and 10.
2. Sam Keen, *Faces of the Enemy: Reflections of the Hostile Imagination.*
3. Martin Luther King, from multiple speeches.
4. Krishna Kripalani, ed., *Gandhi.*
5. Dwight D. Eisenhower, inaugural address, January 20, 1953.

## CELL 50. STRENGTH

1. Harish Johari, *Chakras,* 110–11.
2. Jean Shinoda Bolen, *The Ring of Power,* 4, 24, 30, 37.
3. Ibid.
4. Pema Chödrön, *The Places that Scare You,* 83.
5. Laura Archera Huxley, *You Are Not the Target,* 201–3.

## CELL 51. CONFUSION

1. Kurt Lewin, *A Dynamic Theory of Personality.*

## CELL 52. KINDNESS

1. The Prophet Muhammad, Comments at Tirmidhi, Hadith, 1315 CE, Turn to Islam.
2. The Dalai Lama, *The Meaning of Life,* 88.
3. Sylvia Boorstein, *It's Easier Than You Think,* 128.
4. Joseph Goldstein, *One Dharma,* 108.
5. The Dalai Lama, *How to Practice,* 37.
6. Ibid., 81.

## CELL 53. MODERATION

1. Ram Dass, *Be Here Now,* 42.
2. Betty Kelen, *Gautama Buddha in Life and Legend,* 64–67.
3. Jakusho Kwong, *No Beginning, No End,* 46.

## CELL 54. INTUITION

1. Paramahansa Yogananda, *Where There Is Light,* 64.
2. Harish Johari, *Dhanwantari,* 66.

## CELL 55. FORGIVENESS

1. John Stevens, *Zen Masters,* 130.
2. Paramahansa Yogananda, *Where There Is Light,* 129.
3. Robert D. Enright and Richard P. Fitzgibbons, *Helping Clients Forgive,* 18–19.
4. Amma, "A Great Lesson in Forgiveness," *From Amma's Heart,* 257–61.
5. Luke 6:28, *The New English Bible.*
6. Geshe Langritanpa, cited in Geshe Sonam Rinchen, *Eight Verses for Training the Mind,* 53.
7. Geshe Sonam Rinchen, Ibid., 55.

## CELL 56. TOLERANCE

1. "The Works of Sri Ramakrishna," in *The Bible of the World,* 166.
2. Krishna Kripalani, ed., *Gandhi,* 20, 22, 61, 74.
3. Swami Vivekananda, quoted for the dates Nov. 16, Aug. 21, and Sept. 28, in Föllmi, *Wisdom: 365 Thoughts from Indian Masters.*
4. *Anguttara Nikaya* (a book of sutras translated as "*Gradual Collection*" or "*Numerical discourses*"), in Laurence-Khantipalo Mills, *Tolerance: A Study from Buddhist Sources,* 51.
5. Anasuya Devi, quoted in Timothy Conway, *Women of Power and Grace,* 220.
6. Shunryu Suzuki, *Branching Streams Flow in the Darkness,* 42.

## CELL 57. PURPOSE

1. Lorna Catford and Michael Ray, *The Path of the Everyday Hero*, 51, 52.
2. Swami Niranjanananda Saraswati, "Satsang at Ganga Darshan," Aug. 8, 2002.
3. Viktor E. Frankl, *Man's Search for Meaning*, 47.
4. Ibid., 56–57.
5. Kosho Uchiyama, *Opening the Hand of Thought*, 119.
6. Paul Reps, *Zen Flesh, Zen Bones*. Also Miriam Levering, *Zen: Images, Texts, and Teachings*, 81.

## CELL 58. CREATIVITY

1. John Daido Loori, *The Zen of Creativity*.
2. Ibid.
3. Frank Barron, *Creativity and Psychological Health*.
4. Rollo May, *The Courage to Create*, 37.
5. Clark Moustakas, *Creativity and Conformity*, 1, 131–33.
6. Carl Rogers, *Freedom to Learn for the 80s*, 142.
7. George Prince, *The Practice of Creativity*, 39.
8. Lorna Catford and Michael Ray, *The Path of the Everyday Hero*.

## CELL 59. GRATITUDE

1. Peter Haskel, *Bankei Zen*, 147.
2. Arnold Beisser, "The paradoxical theory of change," in Joan Fagan and Irma Lee Shepherd, eds., *Gestalt Therapy Now*, 77–80.
3. Monique Danielle, "Yoga Concept: Benefits of Gratitude Yoga.
4. J. L. Walker, "The Perilous Garden," *Parabola*, February 2001, 52, 57.

## CELL 60. APOLOGY

1. Hupka et al., "Strategies for Impression Management . . ."
2. *The I Ching*, Wilhelm/Baynes translation, 99–100.
3. "Naikan: A Method of Self-Reflection."
4. Alcoholics Anonymous World Services, *Twelve Steps and Twelve Traditions*, 42, 77, 78, 80.
5. Ibid.
6. Paramahansa Yogananda, *Where There Is Light*, 15.

## CELL 61. BEAUTY

1. Rollo May, *My Quest for Beauty*, 20, 27.
2. Rabbi Wayne Dosick, *Soul Judaism: Dancing with God into a New Era*, 80.
3. William Theodore de Bary, *Sources of Indian Tradition*, vol. 1, 257.
4. Anandamayi Ma quoted in Timothy Conway, *Women of Power and Grace*, 155.
5. Sheng-yen quoted in Miriam Levering, *Zen: Images, Texts, and Teachings*, 69.

## CELL 62. CELEBRATION

1. Amma, *Being with Amma*.
2. Anandamayi Ma quoted in Timothy Conway, *Women of Power and Grace*, 160.
3. *Passionate About Life: "Becoming a Good Leader—Winning, Jack Welch."*

## CELL 63. GENEROSITY

1. Paramahansa Yogananda, *Where There Is Light,* 71.
2. Amma, *Embracing the World,* 94.
3. Eknath Easwaran, *Conquest of Mind,* 37.

## CELL 64. UNITY

1. Mundaka Upanishad quoted in Föllmi, *Wisdom: 365 Thoughts from Indian Masters,* Feb. 17.
2. Martin Luther King Jr., *Strength to Love.*
3. Martin Buber, *I and Thou.*
4. Amma, *Being with Amma.*
5. Yamada Koun, "Zazen and Christianity."
6. *The I Ching,* Wilhelm/Baynes translation.
7. Swami Prajnanpad, in Föllmi, *Wisdom.*
8. Luther Standing Bear quoted in T. C. McCluhan, *Touch the Earth,* 45.
9. Black Elk, quoted at www.odysseyroad.com/weblog/?p=53 and from www.moderjord.org/artiklar/MJ_indian_ecology.html. Accessed August 6, 2008.
10. Eknath Easwaran, *Conquest of Mind,* 31.

# Bibliography

Alcoholics Anonymous World Services. *Twelve Steps and Twelve Traditions*. New York: Alcoholics Anonymous World Services, 1981.

Amma (Sri Mata Amritanandamayi Devi). *Awaken Children: Dialogues with Sri Mata Amritanandamayi*. Vol. 8. San Ramon, Calif.: Mata Amritanandamayi Mission Center, 1996.

———. *Being with Amma: A Collection of Photos and Saying*. San Ramon, Calif.: Mata Amritanandamayi Mission Center, 2005.

———. *Embracing the World: Images and Sayings of Sri Mata Amritanandamayi Devi*. Kollam, Kerala, India: Mata Amritanandamayi Mission Trust, 2003.

———. *From Amma's Heart: Conversations with Sri Mata Amritanandamayi Devi*. Translated and edited by Swami Amritaswarupananda. Kollam, Kerala, India: Mata Amritanandamayi Mission Trust, 2003.

———. *May Peace and Happiness Prevail*. Keynote Address by Sri Mata Amritanandamayi Devi at the Parliament of World Religions, Barcelona, Spain, 2004.

Anderson, Walter Truett. *Open Secrets: A Western Guide to Tibetan Buddhism*. New York: Viking, 1979.

*Anguttara Nikaya*. *See* Thera, Nyanaponika.

Ansbacher, Hans, and Rowena Ansbacher, eds. *The Individual Psychology of Alfred Adler*. New York: Harper/Basic Books, 1956.

Assagioli, Roberto. *Psychosynthesis*. New York: Viking, 1965.

Aurobindo, Sri. *A Greater Psychology: An Introduction to Sri Aurobindo's Psychological Thought*. Ed. A. S. Dalal. New York: Tarcher Penguin/Putnam, 2001.

———. *Integral Yoga: Sri Aurobindo's Teaching & Method of Practice*. Hollywood, Calif., Vendanta Press, 1970.

———. *The Life Divine*. Sri Aurobindo Birth Centenary Library, vol. 19. Pondicherry, India: Sri Aurobindo Ashram, 1970–75.

———. *The Mind of Light*. New York: Dutton, 1953.

Bahm, Archie J. *The Heart of Confucius*. Berkeley: Asian Humanities Press, 1992.

———. *Philosophy of the Buddha*. New York: Capricorn, 1958.

Ballou, Robert O., ed. *The Bible of the World*. New York: Viking, 1939.

Bandura, Albert. "Self-efficacy Mechanisms in Human Agency." *America Psychologist* 37, no. 2 (1982): 122–47.

———. *Social Learning Theory.* Englewood Cliffs, N.J.: Prentice Hall, 1977.

Barron, Frank. *Creativity and Psychological Health: Origins of Personal Vitality and Creative Freedom.* New York: Van Nostrand, 1963.

Bary, William Theodore de. *Sources of Indian Tradition.* Vol. 1. New York: Columbia University Press, 1958.

Beauvoir, Simone de. *The Second Sex.* New York: Bantam, 1953.

Beck, Aaron. *Cognitive Therapy and the Emotional Disorders.* New York and London: Penguin Meridian, 1979.

Becker, Ernest. *The Birth and Death of Meaning.* New York: Free Press, 1962.

———. *The Denial of Death.* New York: Free Press, 1973.

Beisser, Arnold. "The Paradoxical Theory of Change." In *Gestalt Therapy Now: Theory, Techniques, Applications.* Edited by J. Faga and I. L. Shepherd. New York: Harper Colophon, 1970.

Bhagavad Gita. See Prabhavananda, Swami, and Christopher Isherwood.

Biermann, Derek. *Samadhi: Personal Journeys to Spiritual Truth.* Boston: Shambhala Publications, 2000.

Black Elk, quoted in *American Indian Ecology,* J. Donald Hughes, "The Unspoiled Continent." www.moderjord.org/artiklar/MJ_indian_ecology.html.

Bolen, Jean Shinoda. *The Ring of Power: Symbols and Themes in Wagner's Ring Cycle and in Us.* San Francisco: Harper San Francisco, 1992.

Boorstein, Sylvia. *It's Easier Than You Think: The Buddhist Way to Happiness.* San Francisco: Harper San Francisco, 1997.

———. *Pay Attention, For Goodness' Sake: Practicing the Perfections of the Heart—The Buddhist Path of Kindness.* New York: Ballantine, 2002.

Brazier, David. *Zen Therapy: Transcending the Sorrows of the Human Mind.* New York: Wiley, 1995.

Brihadarayaka Upanishad. See Easwaran, Eknath.

Buber, Martin. *I and Thou.* New York: Scribner's, 1970.

Buddha. See Byles, Marie Beuzeville; Byron, Thomas; Kalama Sutra; Mills, Laurence-Khantipalo; Rahula, Walpola; Rama, Swami (*Living with the Himalayan Masters*); Saddhatissa, H.

Byles, Marie Beuzeville. *Footprints of Gautama the Buddha.* Wheaton, Ill.: Quest, 1957.

Byrne, Rhonda. *The Secret.* New York: Atria, 2006.

Byron, Thomas. *The Dhammapada: The Sayings of the Buddha, a New Rendering.* New York: Random House Vintage, 1976.

Carnegie, Dale. *How to Win Friends and Influence People.* New York: Pocket Books, 1940.

Carson, Rachel. *Silent Spring.* New York: Houghton Mifflin, 1962.

Castaneda, Carlos. *The Teachings of Don Juan: A Yaqui Way of Knowledge.* New York: Ballantine Books, 1969.

Catford, Lorna, and Michael Ray. *The Path of the Everyday Hero: Drawing on the Power of Myth to Meet Life's Most Important Challenges.* Los Angeles: Tarcher, 1991.

*Chinese Proverbs from Olden Times.* Mt. Vernon, N.Y.: Peter Pauper Press, 1956.

Chödrön, Pema. *The Places that Scare You: A Guide to Fearlessness in Difficult Times.* Boston: Shambhala, 2007.

Chopra, Deepak. *Ageless Body, Timeless Mind: The Quantum Alternative to Growing Old.* New York: Harmony Books, 1993.

———. *The Seven Spiritual Laws of Success: A Practical Guide to the Fulfillment of Your Dreams.* New York: New World Library, 1994.

Cleary, Thomas, trans. *Shobogenzo: Zen Essays by Dōgen.* Honolulu: University of Hawaii Press, 1986.

Conway, Timothy. *Women of Power and Grace: Nine Astonishing, Inspiring Luminaries of Our Time.* Santa Barbara, Calif.: The Wake-Up Press, 1994.

Covey, Stephen R. *The 7 Habits of Highly Effective People: Restoring the Character Ethic.* New York: Simon and Schuster/Free Press, 1989.

Criswell, Eleanor. *How Yoga Works: An Introduction to Somatic Yoga.* Novato, Calif.: Freeperson Press, 1989.

Crossley, Hastings, trans. *The Golden Sayings of Epictetus.* New York: Collier Harvard Classics, 1937.

Daido. See Loori, John Daido.

Dalai Lama. See Gyatso, Tenzin.

Dalal, A. S., ed. *A Greater Psychology: An Introduction to the Psychological Thought of Sri Aurobindo.* New York: Tarcher, 2001.

Danielle, Monique. "Yoga Concept: Benefits of Gratitude Yoga." In *Naples Yoga News,* www.naplesyoganews.com/october–2007.html. Accessed on January 26, 2009.

Daniels, Kooch N., and Victor Daniels. *Tarot d'Amour: Find Love, Sex, and Romance in the Cards.* Boston: Redwheel Weiser, 2003.

Daniels, Victor, and Laurence J. Horowitz. *Being and Caring: A Psychology for Living,* 2d ed. Palo Alto, Calif.: Mayfield Press, 1984.

Daniels, Victor. "Psychology in Greek Philosophy." Presentation at Western Psychological Association Conference, Seattle, Wash., 1997. www.sonoma.edu/users/d/daniels. Accessed on January 27, 2009.

Dayananda Saraswati, Swami. "Prevent inappropriate expression of anger." In *The Hindu Business Line,* interviewed by D. Murali on December 18, 2006. www.thehindubusinessline.com/mentor/2006/12/18/stories/2006121800151300.htm. Accessed on January 27, 2009.

Dōgen Zenji. *See* Cleary, Thomas.

Dosick, Rabbi Wayne. *Soul Judaism: Dancing with God into a New Era.* Woodstock, Vt.: Jewish Lights Publishing, 1999.

Durant, Will. *The Story of Civilization, Part I: Our Oriental Heritage.* New York: Simon and Schuster, 1954.

Easwaran, Eknath. *Conquest of Mind.* Tomales, Calif.: Nilgiri Press, 1988.

———. *Gandhi the Man.* Petaluma, Calif.: Nilgiri Press, 1978.

———, trans. *The Upanishads.* Tomales, Calif.: Nilgiri Pres, 1987.

———. *Meditation: A Simple 8-Point Program for Transforming Spiritual Ideals into Daily Life.* Tomales, Calif.: Nilgiri Press, 2001.

———. *Take Your Time: Finding Balance in a Troubled World.* Tomales, Calif.: Nilgiri Press, 1994.

Eisenhower, Dwight D. Inaugural address, January 20, 1953.

Ellis, Albert, and Russell Grieger. *Handbook of Rational Emotive Therapy.* Berlin: Springer-Verlag, 1977.

Enright, Robert D. and Richard P. Fitzgibbons. *Helping Clients Forgive: An Empirical Guide for Resolving Anger and Restoring Hope.* Washington, D.C.: American Psychological Association, 2000.

Epictetus. See Crossley, Hastings.

Epstein, Mark. *Thoughts Without a Thinker: Psychotherapy from the Buddhist Perspective*. New York: Basic Books, 1995.

Erikson, Erik H. *Childhood and Society*. New York: Norton, 1950.

Fabian, Johannes. *Time and the Other: How Anthropology Makes Its Object*. New York: Columbia University Press, 1983.

Fagan, Joan, and Irma Lee Shepherd, eds. *Gestalt Therapy Now: Theory, Techniques, Applications*. New York: Harper Colophon, 1970.

Feinstein, David, and Stanley Krippner. *The Mythic Path: Discovering the Guiding Stories of Your Past—Creating a Vision for Your Future*, 3rd ed. Santa Rosa, Calif.: Energy Psychology Press/Elite Books, 2006.

Fitzgerald, Edward. *The Rubaiyat of Omar Khayyám, Rendered into English Verse*. New York: Weathervane, 1985.

Föllmi, Danielle, and Oliver Föllmi. *Wisdom: 365 Thoughts from Indian Masters*. New York: Harry N. Abrams, 2004.

Frankl, Viktor E. *Man's Search for Meaning*. New York: Pocket Books, 1984.

Freire, Paolo. *Pedagogy of the Oppressed*. Hamondsworth, England: Penguin, 1972.

Freud, Sigmund. *Collected Papers*. Vol. 4. New York: Basic Books, 1959.

Fromm, Erich. *Escape from Freedom*. New York: Avon, 1941.

———. *To Have or to Be*. New York: Harper and Row, 1976.

Funk, Robert W., Roy W. Hoover, and the Jesus Seminar. *The Five Gospels: The Search for the Authentic Words of Jesus*. New York: Scribner/Polebridge, 1993.

———, Bernard Brandon Scott, and James R. Butts. *The Parables of Jesus: Red Letter Edition*. Sonoma, Calif.: Polebridge Press, 1988.

Gibb, Jack. *Trust: A New View of Personal and Organizational Development*. Los Angeles: Guild of Tutors Press, 1978.

Gibran, Kahlil. *The Garden of the Prophet*. New York: Knopf, 1968.

———. *The Prophet*. New York: Knopf, 1962.

Goldstein, Joseph. *One Dharma: The Emerging Western Buddhism*. San Francisco: HarperCollins, 2003.

Goldstein, Joseph, and Jack Kornfield. *Seeking the Heart of Wisdom: The Path of Insight Meditation*. Boston and London: Shambhala, 1987.

Goleman Daniel. *Emotional Intelligence: Why It Can Matter More than I.Q.* New York: Bantam, 1995.

Gyatso, Tenzin, the Fourteenth Dalai Lama. *How to Practice: The Way to a Meaningful Life*. Translated by Jeffrey Hopkins. New York: Atria Books, 2002.

———. *The Meaning of Life: Buddhist Perspectives on Cause and Effect*. Translated by Jeffrey Hopkins. Boston: Wisdom Publications, 1992.

———. *A Policy of Kindness: An Anthology of Writings by and about the Dalai Lama*. Ithaca, N.Y.: Snow Lion Publications, 1990.

Hanh, Thich Nhat. *Cultivating the Mind of Love: The Practice of Looking Deeply in the Mahayana Buddhist Tradition*. Berkeley: Parallax Press, 1996.

———. "Twenty Exercises from the Satipatthana Sutra." From lectures given in June 1990. www.abuddhistlibrary.com/Buddhism/J%20-%20Navigation%20Pages%20and%20A%20 List%20of%20Books/Navigation%20Pages/Lists%20of%20Files/Thich%20Nhat%20 Hahn.htm#45. Accessed on January 27, 2009. Also at www.plumvillage.org.

——. *The Path of Emancipation*. Berkeley: Parallax Press, 2000.

Haskel, Peter. *Bankei Zen: Translations from the Record of Bankei*. New York: Grove Weidenfield, 1984.

Hertzberg, Arthur. *Great Religions of Modern Man*. Vol. 6: *Judaism*. New York: G. Braziller, 1961.

Hixon, Lee. *Living Buddha Zen*. Burdett, N.Y.: Larson Publications, 1995.

Hodges, Carl. "Metaphor as Field." Presentation at the Association for the Advancement of Gestalt Therapy Conference, Vancouver, Canada. August 9–13, 2006.

Hoover, Thomas. *Zen Culture*. New York: Random House Vintage, 1978.

Horney, Karen. *Feminine Psychology*. New York: Norton, 1967.

Huang, Alfred. *The Complete I Ching*. Rochester, Vt.: Inner Traditions, 1998.

Hupka, Ralph B., John Jung, and Robert Porteus. "Strategies for Impression Management in Romantic Jealousy Situations." Exploring Sexual Jealousy symposium. A presentation at the American Psychological Association Convention, Eliot Aronson (chairman). Los Angeles: August 1981.

Huxley, Laura Archera. *You Are Not the Target*. North Hollywood, Calif.: Wilshire Book Company, 1963.

I Ching. See Huang, Alfred; Murphy, Joseph; Wilhelm, Richard and Cary F. Baynes.

Iyengar, B. K. S. *Light on Yoga*. New York: Schocken, 1977.

——. *Light on the Yoga Sutras of Patanjali*. New York: HarperCollins, 1993.

——. *The Tree of Yoga*. Boston: Shambhala, 2002.

Jacobson, Edmund. *Progressive Relaxation*. Chicago: University of Chicago Press, 1938.

James, William. *The Principles of Psychology*. New York: Holt, 1890.

Johari, Harish. *Ayurvedic Massage: Traditional Indian Techniques for Balancing Body and Mind*. Rochester, Vt.: Healing Arts Press/Inner Traditions, 1996.

——. *Breath, Mind, and Consciousness*. Rochester, Vt.: Destiny Books, 1989.

——. *Chakras: Energy Centers of Transformation*. Rochester, Vt.: Destiny Books, 2000.

——. *Dhanwantari: A Complete Guide to the Ayurvedic Life*. San Francisco: Ram's Head, 1996.

——. *Leela: The Game of Self-Knowledge*. Rochester, Vt.: Destiny Books, 1993.

——. *Tools for Tantra*. Rochester, Vt.: Destiny Books, 1986.

Jung, C. G. *Man and His Symbols*. New York: Dell, 1968.

——. *Psyche and Symbol: A Selection from the Writings of C. G. Jung*. Edited by Violet de Laszlo. Garden City, N.Y.: Doubleday Anchor, 1958.

——. "The Structure and Dynamics of the Psyche." *Collected Works*. Vol. 8. Translated by R. F. C. Hull. New York: Princeton University Press, 1968.

——. *Two Essays on Analytical Psychology,* 2d ed. Translated by R. F. C. Hull. New York: Princeton University Press, 1972. Also in *Collected Works*. Vol. 7. Princeton University Press, 1966.

Kabat-Zinn, Jon. *Wherever You Go, There You Are: Mindfulness Meditation in Everyday Life*. New York: Hyperion, 2005.

Kalama Sutra. www.abuddhistlibrary.com/.../Miscellaneous%20Buddhism/An%20 Introduction%20to%20Buddhism%20I/The%20Buddha.rtf. Accessed on June 1, 2008, site now discontinued. Another translation is by Thich Nhat Hanh at Deer Park Monastery. www .deerparkmonastery.org/teachings/dharma-talks-by-thich-nhat-hanh/buddhism-and-science.

Katagiri, Dainin. *Each Moment Is the Universe: Zen and the Way of Being Time*. Boston: Shambhala, 2007.

Katantzakis, Nikos. *Zorba the Greek*. New York: Simon and Schuster, 1952.

Keen, Sam. *Faces of the Enemy: Reflections of the Hostile Imagination*. San Francisco: Harper & Row, 1988.

Kelen, Betty. *Confucius in Life and Legend*. Camden, N.J.: Thomas Nelson, 1971.

———. *Gautama Buddha in Life and Legend*. New York: Avon Camelot, 1967.

Khan, Hazrat Inayat. *The Inner Life*. Boston and London: Shambhala, 1997.

Khayyám, Omar. See Fitzgerald, Edward.

King, Martin Luther, Jr. *Strength to Love,* 1963. MLK Online: Your One-Stop Source for MLK on the Net. www.mlkonline.net. Accessed on January 17, 2009.

King, Martin Luther, Jr. and James M. Washington. *A Testament of Hope: The Essential Writings and Speeches of Martin Luther King, Jr.* New York: HarperCollins, 1991.

Korzybski, Alfred. *Science and Sanity: An Introduction to Non-Aristotelian Systems and General Semantics,* 4th ed. New York: Institute of General Semantics, 1958.

Kripalani, Krishna, ed. *Gandhi*. Ahmedabad, India: Navijivan Publishing House, n.d.

Krishnamurti, Jiddu. *Freedom from the Known*. London: Victor Gollancz Ltd., 1969.

Kwong, Jakusho. *No Beginning, No End: The Intimate Heart of Zen*. New York: Harmony, 2003.

Langan, Robert. *Minding What Matters: Psychotherapy and the Buddha Within*. Boston: Wisdom Publications, 2006.

Langritampa, Kadampa Geshe. See Rinchen, Geshe Sonam.

Lao-tzu. See Sih, Paul K. T.

Lazarus, Richard. *Emotion and Adaptation*. Oxford, England: Oxford University Press, 1991.

LeShan, Lawrence. *How to Meditate: A Guide to Self-Discovery*. New York: Bantam, 1975.

Levering, Miriam. *Zen: Images, Texts, and Teachings*. London: Duncan Baird, 2000.

Lewin, Kurt. *A Dynamic Theory of Personality*. New York: McGraw Hill, 1935.

Long, George, trans. *The Meditations of Marcus Aurelius*. New York: Collier Harvard Classics, 1937.

Loori, John Daido. *The Zen of Creativity: Cultivating Your Artistic Life*. New York: Ballantine, 2005.

Lowe, Janet. *Oprah Winfrey Speaks: Insights from the World's Most Influential Voice*. New York: Wiley, 1998.

Mahabharata. See Yogananda, Paramahansa.

Maharishi Mahesh Yogi. *Transcendental Meditation*. New York: New American Library, 1975.

Maharshi, Sri Ramana. See Osborne, Arthur.

Maltz, Maxwell. *Psycho-Cybernetics*. New York: Pocket Books, 1966.

Marchand, Peter. *The Yoga of the Nine Emotions*. Rochester, Vt.: Destiny Books, 2006.

Marcus Aurelius. See Long, George.

Maslow, Abraham H. *The Farther Reaches of Human Nature*. New York: Viking, 1971.

———. *Motivation and Personality*. 3rd ed. New York: HarperCollins, 1987.

Masunaga, Reiho. *A Primer of Soto Zen: A Translation of Dōgen's Shobogenzo Zuimonki*. Honolulu: East-West Center Press, 1971.

Mattoon, Mary Ann. *Jungian Psychology in Perspective*. New York: Free Press, 1985.

May, Rollo. *The Courage to Create*. New York: Bantam, 1985.

———. *My Quest for Beauty*. Dallas, Tex.: Saybrook Publishing Company, 1985.

McCluhan, T. C. *Touch the Earth*. New York: Promontory Press, 1973.

———. *The Way of the Earth: Encounters with Nature in Ancient and Contemporary Thought*. New York: Simon and Schuster/Touchstone, 1995.

Meher Baba. *Discourses*. Vols. 1, 2, and 3. San Francisco: Sufism Reoriented, 1973.

Melnick, Joseph, and Sonia March Nevis. "Gestalt Therapy Methodology." In *Gestalt Therapy*. Edited by Ansel L. Woldt and Sarah M. Toman. Thousand Oaks, Calif.: Sage Publications, 2005.

Merleau-Ponty, Maurice. *The Primacy of Perception*. Evanston, Ill.: Northwestern University Press, 1967.

Mills, Laurence-Khantipalo. *Tolerance: A Study from Buddhist Sources*. London: Rider, 1964.

Mipham, Lama. *See* Tulku Tarthang.

Mohammed; also Mohammad. See Muhammad.

Miura, Isshū and Ruth Fuller Sasaki. *The Zen Koan*. New York: Harcourt Brace, 1965.

Moustakas, Clark. *Creativity and Conformity*. Princeton, N.J.: Van Nostrand, 1967.

Muhammad. Comments at Tirmidhi, Hadith, 1315, and other occasions. In www .TurnToIslam.com. "Words of Wisdom from the Prophet Mohammad." www.TurnToIslam .com/forum/showthread.php?t=36681.

Murphy, Joseph. *Secrets of the I Ching*. West Nyack, N.Y.: Parker Publishing, 1970.

"Naikan: A Method of Self-Reflection." From www.todoinstitute.org/naikan.html. Accessed on January 26, 2009.

Namka, Lynn. "A Tribute to the Most Marvelous Virginia Satir." www.angriesout.com/satir .htm. Accessed on January 20, 2009.

Nash, Alanna. "Willie Nelson" interview in *Behind Closed Doors: Talking With the Legends of Country Music*. New York: Knopf, 1988.

Nelson, Sally J. *Night Wings: A Soulful Dreaming and Writing Practice*. Berwick, Maine: Nicolas-Hays, 2004.

*The New English Bible*. Cambridge, England: Cambridge University Press, 1961.

Niranjanananda Saraswati, Swami. "Towards Freedom." *Yoga,* March–April 2003: 9–15.

———. "Satsang at Ganga Darshan." In *Yoga,* Sivananda Math, Munger, India. May–June 2003.

———. "Satsang at Ganga Darshan." In *Yoga,* Sivananda Math, Munger, India. July–August 2004.

Odier, Daniel. *Tantric Quest: An Encounter with Absolute Love*. Translated by Jody Gladding. Rochester, Vt.: Inner Traditions, 1997.

Orage, Alfred Richard. *Psychological Exercises and Essays*. London: Janus Press, 1930.

Ortega y Gasset, José. *Man and People*. New York: Norton, 1957.

Osborne, Arthur, ed. *The Teachings of Bhagavan Sri Ramana Maharshi in His Own Words*. New York: Samuel Weiser, 1971.

Patanjali. See Iyengar, B. K. S.; Prabhavananda, Swami, and Christopher Isherwood.

Peale, Norman Vincent. *The Power of Positive Thinking*. New York: Prentice-Hall/Fawcett, 1952.

Pelletier, Kenneth R. *Mind as Healer, Mind as Slayer: A Holistic Approach to Preventing Stress Disorders*. New York: Dell, 1977.

Perls, Frederick S. (Fritz). *The Gestalt Approach* and *Eyewitness to Therapy*. Palo Alto, Calif.: Science and Behavior Books, 1973.

———. *Gestalt Therapy Verbatim*. Moab, Utah: Real People Press, 1969.

———. *In and Out of the Garbage Pail.* Moab, Utah: Real People Press, 1969.

———, Ralph Hefferline, and Paul Goodman. *Gestalt Therapy: Excitement and Growth in the Human Personality.* New York: Delta, 1951.

Pilot Baba, Mahayogi (a.k.a. Kapil Adwait). Untitled talks in Occidental, Calif., 1999, 2000.

———. *Himalaya Unveils Mystery.* New Delhi: Mahayog Foundation. Undated.

Polster, Erving. *Every Person's Life Is Worth a Novel.* New York and London: Norton, 1987.

Prabhavananda, Swami, and Christopher Isherwood, trans. *The Bhagavad Gita.* New York: Mentor, 1951.

———, trans. *How to Know God: The Yoga Sutras (Aphorisms) of Patanjali.* New York: New American Library, 1969.

———, trans. *Shankara's Crest Jewel of Discrimination.* New York: New American Library, 1970.

Prince, George M. *The Practice of Creativity: A Manual for Dynamic Group Problem Solving.* New York: Harper and Row, 1970.

Progoff, Ira. *At a Journal Workshop: Writing to Access the Power of the Unconscious and Evoke Creative Ability.* New York: Dialogue House, 1975.

Rachman, Stanley J. *Fear and Courage.* San Francisco: W. H. Freeman, 1978.

Rahula, Walpola. *What the Buddha Taught.* New York: Grove Press, 1959.

Ram Dass. *Be Here Now.* New York: Crown Publishing, 1971.

———. *Journey of Awakening: A Meditator's Guidebook.* Toronto, New York, London, Sydney, and Auckland: Bantam Books, 1978.

———. *Miracle of Love: Stories about Neem Karoli Baba.* New York: Dutton, 1979.

———. *Still Here: Embracing Aging, Changing, and Dying.* New York: Penguin Riverhead, 2000.

Rama, Swami. *Living with the Himalayan Masters.* Honesdale, Pa.: Himalayan Institute Press, 1978.

———. *Meditation and Its Practice.* Honesdale, Pa.: Himalayan Institute Press, 1998.

———. *The Royal Path: Practical Lessons on Yoga.* Honesdale, Pa.: Himalayan Institute Press, 1996.

Ramakrishna, Sri. See Ballou, Robert O. (*The Bible of the World*)

Ramakrishnananda Puri, Swami. *Eye of Wisdom.* San Ramon, Calif.: Mata Amritanandamayi Center, 2007.

Ramana Maharshi, Sri. See Osborne, Arthur.

Reich, Wilhelm. *Character Analysis.* New York: Noonday Press, 1949.

Reps, Paul. *Zen Flesh, Zen Bones: A Collection of Zen and Pre-Zen Writings.* Garden City, N.Y.: Doubleday, 1989

Resnick, Stella. *The Pleasure Zone: Why We Resist Good Feelings and How to Let Go and Be Happy.* San Francisco: Conari Press, 1997.

Rinchen, Geshe Sonam. *Eight Verses for Training the Mind.* Translated and Edited by Ruth Sonam. Ithaca, N.Y., and Boulder, Colo.: Snow Lion Publications, 2001.

Rogers, Carl. *Carl Rogers on Personal Power.* New York: Delacorte, 1977.

———. "The Core of Guidance." *Harvard Educational Review* 32, no. 4 (1962).

———. *Freedom to Learn for the 80s.* New York: Macmillan, 1983.

———. *On Becoming a Person.* New York: Houghton Mifflin, 1961.

———. *A Way of Being.* New York: Houghton Mifflin, 1980.

———, and H. Jerome Freiberg. *Freedom to Learn.* 3rd ed. New York: Macmillan, 1994.

Rose Sufi Crescent, The. "Sufism and Gratitude, Monday, May 29, 2006. http://rose-sufi-crescent.blogspot.com/search?q=sufism-and-gratitude. Accessed on January 27, 2009.

Rumi, Jalalu'ddin. *Sun of Tabriz: A Lyrical Introduction to Higher Metaphysics*. Cape Town: Johnston and Neville, 1969.

Russell, Bertrand. *The Conquest of Happiness*. New York and London: Norton/Liveright, 1971.

Saddhatissa, H. *The Buddha's Way*. New York: George Braziller, 1971.

Salzberg, Sharon. *Loving-Kindness: The Revolutionary Art of Happiness*. Boston: Shambhala, 1995.

Salzberg, Sharon, and Joseph Goldstein. *Insight Meditation: Workbook*. Boulder: Sounds True, 2001.

Saraswati, Swami. See Niranjanananda Saraswati, Swami; See also Sivananda Saraswati, Swami.

Sartre, Jean-Paul. *Essays in Existentialism*. New York: Citadel, 1967.

———. *Existentialism and Humanism*. London: Eyre Methuen, 1973.

Satchidananda. *See* Wiener, Sita.

Satir, Virginia. *The New Peoplemaking*. Mountain View, Calif.: Science and Behavior Books, 1988. *See also* Namka, Lynn.

Schneider, Kirk, and Rollo May. *Existence: An Integrative, Clinical Perspective*. New York: McGraw Hill, 1995.

Seligman, Martin E. P. *Authentic Happiness: Using the New Positive Psychology to Realise Your Potential for Lasting Fulfillment*. New York: Simon and Schuster/Free Press, 2002.

Shah, Idries. *The Sufis*. Garden City, N.Y.: Doubleday, 1964.

Shantideva. *The Way of the Bodhisattva*. Translated by Padmakara Translation Group. Boston: Shambhala, 2003.

Shree Purohit, Swami, and W. B. Yeats, translators. *The Ten Principal Upanishads*. London: Faber and Faber, 1937, 1971.

Sih, Paul K. T., ed., and John C. H. Wu, trans. *Tao Teh Ching*. New York: St. John's University Press, 1961.

Sivananda Saraswati, Swami. "High on Waves." In *Yoga,* Sivananda Math, Munger, India, May–June 2003.

Sivananda Yoga Vedanta Centre. *Yoga Mind and Body*. London, New York, Stuttgart, and Moscow: Doris Kindersley, 1996.

Smith, Heather. See Tyler, T., et al.

Smith, William Cantwell. *Patterns of Faith around the World*. Oxford, England: OneWorld Publications, 1998.

Sonam Rinchen, Geshe. *Eight Verses for Training the Mind*. Ithaca, N.Y., and Boulder: Snow Lion Publications, 2001.

Sanskrit dictionary for Spoken Sanskrit. http://spokensanskrit.de. Accessed on January 28, 2008.

Stevens, John. *Zen Masters: A Maverick, a Master of Masters, and a Wandering Poet*. Tokyo: Kodansha International, 1999.

Storl, Wolf-Dieter. *Shiva: The Wild God of Power and Ecstasy*. Rochester, Vt.: Inner Traditions, 2004.

Stouffer, S., A. Lumsdaine, R. Williams, M. Smith, I. Janis, S. Star, and L. Cottrell. *The American Soldier: Combat and Its Aftermath*. Princeton, N.J.: Princeton University Press, 1949.

Suzuki, Shunryu. *Branching Streams Flow in the Darkness: Zen Talks on the Sandokai*. Berkeley, Calif.: University of California Press, 1999.

———. *Not Always So: Practicing the True Spirit of Zen*. New York: HarperCollins, 2002.

——. *Zen Mind, Beginner's Mind: Informal Talks on Zen Meditation and Practice.* New York and Tokyo: Weatherhill, 1970.

Tamm, Jim. "Relationship Advice: Defensiveness: The Poison Pill to Relationships." www.self growth.com/artman2/publish/relationship_advice_articles/Defensiveness_The_Poison_ Pill_to_Relationships_printer.html. Accessed on January 26, 2009.

Tarnas, Richard. *The Passion of the Western Mind: Understanding the Ideas that Have Shaped Our World View.* New York: Ballantine, 1993.

——, trans. *Calm and Clear: Lama Mipham.* Emeryville, Calif.: Dharma Publishing, 1973.

Thera, Nyanaponika. *Anguttara Nikaya.* London: Pali Text Society, 2000.

Trungpa, Chogyam. *Cutting Through Spiritual Materialism.* London: Watkins, 1973.

——. *Training the Mind and Cultivating Loving-Kindness.* Edited by Judith L. Lief. Boston: Shambhala Classics, 2003.

Tulku, Tarthang. *Gesture of Balance: A Guide to Awareness, Self-Healing, and Meditation.* Emeryville, Calif.: Dharma Publishing, 1977.

Tyberg, Judith. *The Language of the Gods.* Los Angeles: East-West Cultural Center, 1970.

——. *Sanskrit Keys to the Wisdom-Religion.* San Diego, Calif.: Point Loma Publications. 1984.

Tyler, Tom R., Robert J. Boeckmann, Heather J. Smith, and Yuen J. Huo. *Social Justice in a Diverse Society.* Boulder: HarperCollins Westview, 1997.

Uchiyama, Kosho. *Opening the Hand of Thought: Foundations of Zen Buddhist Practice.* Boston: Wisdom Publications, 2004.

Upanishads. See Shree Purohit, Swami, and W. B. Yeats.

Vivekananda, Swami. *Raja-Yoga,* rev. ed. New York: Ramakrishna-Vivekananda Center, 1955.

——. In Föllmi, Danielle & Oliver's *Wisdom: 365 Thoughts from Indian Masters.* New York: Harry N. Abrams, 2004.

Walker, J. L. "The Perilous Garden: Death and Decay in Buddhist Practice." *Parabola* 26, no. 1 (February 2001).

Weil, Andrew. *8 Weeks to Optimum Health: A Proven Program for Taking Full Advantage of Your Body's Natural Healing Power.* New York: Knopf, 1997.

Welch, Jack. From *Passionate About Life: "Becoming a Good Leader—Winning, Jack Welch."* http://susan-passionateaboutlife.blogspot.com/2007/05/becoming-good-leader-winning-jack-welch.html. Accessed on January 26, 2009.

Westen, Robin. *Oprah Winfrey: "I Don't Believe in Failure."* Berkeley Heights, N.J.: African American Biography Library, Enslow Publications, 2005.

Wiener, Sita. *Swami Satchidananda: His Biography.* San Francisco and New York: Straight Arrow Books, 1970.

Wilber, Ken. *No Boundary: Eastern and Western Approaches to Personal Growth.* Boston: Shambhala, 1985.

Wilhelm, Richard, trans. *The Secret of the Golden Flower: A Chinese Book of Life.* London: Routledge and Kegan Paul.

Wilhelm, Richard, and Cary F. Baynes, trans. *The I Ching, or Book of Changes.* Princeton, N.J.: Princeton University Press, 1967.

Wolpe, Joseph. *The Practice of Behavior Therapy.* 3rd ed. New York: Pergamon, 1982.

Wu, John C. H., trans. *Tao Te Ching* by Lao-Tzu. Boston: Shambhala, 1989.

Yamada Koun. "Zazen and Christianity." Talk given on May 9, 1975, at San-un Zendo, in Kamakura, Japan.

Yeboa, Emmanuel. *Emmanuel's Gift*. N.l., Triumph Marketing, 2006.

Yogananda, Paramahansa. *Autobiography of a Yogi*. Los Angeles: Self-Realization Fellowship, 1998.

——. *The Essence of Self-Realization: The Wisdom of Paramahansa Yogananda*. Recorded and compiled by Kriyananda (J. Donald Walters). Nevada City, Calif.: Crystal Clarity Publishers, 1990.

——. *Where There Is Light: Insight and Inspiration for Meeting Life's Challenges*. Los Angeles: Self-Realization Fellowship, 1988.

Zimbardo, Philip. "'Putting Time in Perspective': Minds, Individuals, and Contexts." Presidential address, Western Psychological Association Convention, Maui Marriott Resort, Hawaii, May 3, 2001.

Zimbardo, Philip and John Boyd. *The Time Paradox: The New Psychology of Time That Will Change Your Life*. New York: The Free Press, 2008.

# Index

# About the Authors

BOTH VICTOR AND KOOCH have traveled extensively in India, Japan, and other Asian countries, deepening their knowledge of the meditative traditions drawn on here.

**Victor Daniels** has taught a spectrum of courses in psychology for forty years and has taught meditation in workshops and courses for several decades. He received his Ph.D. from UCLA, where he worked with both scientifically and clinically oriented faculty, with concentrations in social psychology, personality, motivation, and the history of psychology. Along the way, he studied both Western and Eastern philosophies and spiritual traditions, including the original teachings of Jesus. When he joined the faculty at Sonoma State University in 1968, it was a regular stop on the Northern California "swami circuit" for traveling yogic and Buddhist teachers. Victor's colleague Nirmal Singh-Dhesi asked him to serve as the first director of then newly created India Studies Program, which diversified his exposure to Asian spiritual teachers and meditation practices. At the same time, he undertook extensive training in Gestalt therapy. He has served as chair of the psychology department at Sonoma State University and is the coauthor, with Laurence J. Horowitz, of *Being and Caring: A Psychology for Living,* and coauthor, with Kooch Daniels, of *Tarot d'Amour*. His most influential personal meditation teachers have been Jakusho Kwong-roshi and Harish Johari.

**Kooch N. Daniels** graduated from Ohio University, and obtained her M.A. from Sonoma State University, with concentrations in Jungian psychology and parapsychological disciplines. Krishnamurti and a sojourn to India inspired her early quest to learn more about esoteric traditions and meditative practices. A mother of two children, she learned to balance her love for family with her inner quest. In her professional world, she has been working as an intuitive throughout her life, guiding people to improve their lives through meditation, visualization, and positive affirmations. For two decades, Kooch studied with Harish Johari, a tantric scholar who motivated her to do meditative practices that can be carried out amid the activities of daily life. Kooch if the coauthor, with Victor Daniels, of *Tarot d'Amour*.

Kooch comments: "My quest to find answers led me on a series of journeys from Indiana to India to seek out teachers, healers, shamans, masters and saints. Amma, or Sri Mātā Amritanandamayī Devi—the Hugging Saint of India—has been an ongoing source of love and inspiration for me." Above all, Kooch says, Amma is a *bhakti* (devotional), *karma* (selfless service), and *jnana* (wisdom) yogi. In Amma's words: "Meditation is like a health tonic. It strengthens one's relation to the essential essence of one's self. It is a powerful tool that enables you to experience direct communication with your inner self and the force of life surging within your being."

...............................

**To contact the authors visit**
**www.matrixmeditations.com**